DB2 for the COBOL programmer

Part 1: An Introductory Course

DB2

for the
COBOL
programmer

Part 1: An Introductory Course

Steve Eckols

Mike Murach & Associates, Inc.

4697 West Jacquelyn Avenue, Fresno, California 93722, (209) 275-3335

Editorial team:	Doug Lowe
	Sheila Lynch
Production/Design:	Steve Ehlers

Related books

DB2 for the COBOL Programmer, Part 2: An Advanced Course,
    Steve Eckols
Structured ANS COBOL, Part 1: A Course for Novices,
    Mike Murach & Paul Noll
Structured ANS COBOL, Part 2: An Advanced Course,
    Mike Murach & Paul Noll
VS COBOL II: A Guide for Programmers and Managers, Anne Prince
MVS TSO, Part 1: Concepts and ISPF, Doug Lowe
MVS TSO, Part 2: Commands and Procedures, Doug Lowe
IMS for the COBOL Programmer, Part 1: Data Base Processing,
    Steve Eckols
*IMS for the COBOL Programmer, Part 2: DC and Message Format
    Service ,* Steve Eckols
How to Design and Develop Business Systems, Steve Eckols

ISBN: 0-911625-59-3

Library of Congress Cataloging-in-Publication Data

Eckols, Steve.
  DB2 for the COBOL Programmer / Steve Eckols.
    p. cm.
  Includes index.
  Contents: Pt. 1. An introductory course
  ISBN 0-911625-59-3 (pbk. : v. 1 : alk. paper)
  1. Data base management. 2. IBM Database 2. 3. COBOL (Computer
program language) 4. SQL (Computer program language)
QA76.9.D3E32 1991
005.75'65--dc20   91-30359
                                                                 CIP

Contents

Preface

If you design and develop application programs, it's likely that you work with a data base management system now, or that you will soon. DB2, developed for IBM's MVS operating system, has become the foremost DBMS in the IBM mainframe world, and it sets the DBMS standard for other computers.

To access DB2 data, you issue statements in SQL, the Structured Query Language. Originally developed by IBM, SQL has become the industry-wide standard for relational data base languages. That means you can use SQL in programs written in a variety of different languages. And you can use it on computers from PCs to mainframes, developed by many different computer manufacturers.

As a result, knowing DB2 is a plus for any application programmer, and it's essential for MVS programmers. *DB2 for the COBOL Programmer* is a two-part series that's designed to teach you all you need to know. This book, *Part 1: An Introductory Course*, covers all of the basic features and functions you need to write programs that process DB2 data. *Part 2: An Advanced Course* expands the material in *Part 1* and presents advanced topics, like using DB2 with CICS and using IBM's QMF (Query Management Facility).

If you're not working on an MVS system, you can easily apply what you learn in this book to other SQL-based products. You simply have to learn how the product you'll be using is different from DB2. Usually, the differences are slight.

For example, for IBM mainframe computers that run under the VM or VSE operating system, the SQL-based product is SQL/DS. DB2 and SQL/DS are highly compatible, so you can easily apply what you learn from this book in those environments. The same is true for SQL/400 for computers in IBM's AS/400 line.

What's more, the SQL statements you use in your programs are the same whether you're working in COBOL, PL/I, C, or some other language.

So even though this book focuses on COBOL, if you're an experienced programmer in another language, you can use this book to learn how to handle DB2 data in your programs.

Why this book is effective

I've been an application programmer, so I know the challenges you'll face in designing and developing programs that process DB2 data. This book is effective because I kept your needs in mind constantly as I planned, illustrated, and wrote it. My overall goal is to help you build on what you already know so you can quickly become an effective, productive, and professional DB2 programmer. As a result, the book has the following characteristics that you won't find in any other DB2 book on the market.

Emphasis on the practical rather than the theoretical   Several successful DB2 books have been written by computer scientists who are interested in theoretical topics. For example, you can find pages and pages on topics like how thoroughly DB2 and SQL implement all possible operations from mathematical set theory. If you're a theoretician, these are important issues.

If you're an application programmer, they're not. Although they can help you gain insight into why DB2 works the way it does, more often than not, they get in the way of what you *really* need to know. So I've covered only a few theoretical issues in this book (there are a few you *do* need to know about), and I've put them in their proper perspective for an application programmer.

Emphasis on programming rather than data base administration   Many of the DB2 books on the market have been written by people who have lots of experience as data base administrators (DBAs). And their books reflect that. DBAs have to deal with issues like the detailed internal structure of stored DB2 data and technical options that optimize system performance. If you're a DBA, these are critical points.

If you're an application programmer, they're not. The whole point of having DBAs is so users like programmers won't have to deal with technicalities. So, as with theoretical issues, I've put technical DBA topics in their proper perspective. I've covered them when they relate directly to application programming, but not as mainline content in and of themselves.

Emphasis on COBOL programs rather than ad hoc processing   One argument in favor of relational data base systems like DB2 is that they put greater computing power in the hands of end users. Most other DB2 books make this a central point and present SQL as it can be used interactively by an end user to access and process DB2 data on demand. This is called "ad-hoc" processing.

However, the fact is that performance considerations cause many shops to restrict the amount of ad hoc work users can do. Moreover, it's not as easy for end users to work with SQL as its planners might have hoped. And finally, letting end users change stored data in an uncontrolled way can quickly lead to corrupted data bases.

So, although DB2 supports online, user-directed processing, most DB2 work is still done the old-fashioned way: through application programs. When changes are made to stored data by properly designed and tested programs, everyone can be confident that the data is consistent and correct. That's true whether the programs are online transaction processing programs or whether they're batch edit and update programs. As for data retrieval tasks, they execute more efficiently when they're done by application programs than when they're requested on an ad hoc basis. And application programs operate in predictable ways; the same certainly isn't true when different users are issuing queries from scratch. These benefits apply both to online inquiry programs and to batch report-preparation programs.

Unfortunately, when other DB2 books address application programming, it's often as an aside or as a topic that appears three-quarters of the way through the book. In this book, though, I'm assuming from the start that you're a programmer and you want to develop application programs. By far, COBOL is the most commonly used programming language for application development, so that's what I've used for the examples in this book. You'll learn enough about SQL to issue ad hoc requests, but my emphasis is on how to use SQL through COBOL.

If you're an experienced programmer, you'll discover that this emphasis on using DB2 through COBOL has an added advantage. You'll find DB2 surprisingly easy to learn because you won't be flooded with strange examples in a strange context. Instead, you'll see familiar application program examples that you can relate to. These examples use DB2 in ways that often parallel other file processing techniques you already use.

Required background

Although you can use DB2 in application programs written in other programming languages, you'll get the most from this book if you have a basic understanding of COBOL. If you work as a COBOL programmer or have taken a COBOL course, you probably have all the background you need. If you don't have any COBOL training, though, you can learn what you need to know from *Structured ANS COBOL, Part 1* and *Part 2*, by Mike Murach and Paul Noll. (You can order these books by using the order form at the back of this book.)

To use DB2 in a production environment, you also need to know TSO. TSO is the MVS telecommunications monitor that lets you work at a terminal. If TSO is new to you, you can learn what you need from Doug Lowe's book, *MVS TSO, Part 1: Concepts and ISPF*. (Again, you can find ordering information at the back of this book.)

How to use this book

I've arranged the content of this book in the most logical sequence for a "typical" programmer with "typical" tasks to do. So my general recommendation is that you read the book straight through. However, you're probably not "typical," nor are the things you need to do. As a result, you can also skip around in the book to learn just what you need to know, once you've mastered the fundamentals.

Sections 1 and 2 present those fundamentals. Section 1 consists of one chapter that gives you an overview of DB2 and orients you to the rest of the book. Section 2 consists of three chapters that together make up the basic subset of your DB2 training. Here, then, you'll learn how to design and code application programs that retrieve and update DB2 data.

After you've finished section 2, you can read the material in the other two sections in any order you like. Section 3 contains five chapters that expand on the basic subset you learned in section 2. Although I recommend you read these chapters in order, you can also move back and forth between them to learn about features that sound especially interesting or that you need to use right away.

You can also go directly to section 4 after you've finished section 2. The first chapter in that section shows you how to use TSO facilities for developing DB2 programs. The second chapter shows you how to create job streams to run batch DB2 programs.

After you've developed your DB2 skills, you'll find this book will make a handy reference for you to use on the job. To add to its reference value, I've included appendixes that give you the syntax of all the SQL commands in the book, the SQL error code values you may need to look up, and a summary of the data types DB2 supports with their equivalent COBOL descriptions. Perhaps most important for reference, though, are the program examples you'll find throughout the book. So let me tell you about those in a little more detail.

A note on the sample programs

One of the strengths of this book is the set of sample programs it includes. Each chapter in sections 2 and 3 gives you at least one complete program: source code, structure chart, and sample input and output. Altogether, there are 11 different programs in this book. They perform tasks as diverse as online inquiries, report preparation, and data base updates. One is even a subprogram.

Although the programs do different things, they all operate on the same set of realistic DB2 data. As a result, although the programs are independent, they do have some features in common. Those shared features will make it easier for you to understand the programs themselves and the DB2 concepts and features they illustrate.

After you've used the program examples for training, they'll become handy references for you to use on the job every day. In fact, if you use them as models for your own programs, you'll save yourself hours of coding, testing, and debugging.

I developed and tested all of the sample programs with DB2 version 2.2, under VS COBOL II version 2.0. As I write this preface, IBM is two months from releasing the next version of DB2, version 2.3. The changes that will come with version 2.3 are almost all in areas that don't affect application programs (they involve performance issues that are behind the scenes for programmers). So the program examples in this book will all continue to work and be useful models for you under DB2 version 2.3.

Conclusion

I'm enthusiastic about DB2. It's a powerful, comprehensive, and sophisticated program that lets you handle complicated tasks with relative ease. But I'm just as enthusiastic about the prospect of helping you learn DB2. So please let me know how this book works for you by sending me any comments you have on it (feel free to use the postage-paid comment form at the back of this book). Good luck!

Steve Eckols
Fresno, California
August, 1991

Introduction

The one chapter in this section presents the background information you need before you can learn how to develop COBOL programs that use DB2. If you're already familiar with DB2, this information may be review for you. But even if it is, I recommend that you skim this chapter to make sure you're familiar with its terms and concepts. Because they're used throughout this book, you should make sure you understand them before you continue.

Chapter 1

An introduction to DB2

DB2, or *Database 2*, is a relational data base management system that runs on IBM mainframe computers under the MVS operating system. Although you can use DB2 with a variety of end-user tools to access its data bases directly, you can also develop application programs that access its data bases. In this book, I'll show you how to develop these application programs using the COBOL programming language.

Whether you're an experienced COBOL programmer or a novice, learning DB2 can be a challenge. As a COBOL programmer, your first inclination may be to start by studying the syntax of the new commands that DB2 requires you to use. Unfortunately, that approach can quickly lead to frustration. You'll soon discover that although DB2's commands seem simple, the functions they provide are often anything but simple. In addition, these commands are often different from what your experience in COBOL may lead you to expect. So, before I get into the details of DB2 command syntax in sections 2 and 3, I want to show you some of the basic principles of what DB2 is and how it works.

To teach you these basic principles, I'll present five basic questions about DB2. I'm convinced that a COBOL programmer who can answer these questions is ready to learn the details of coding application programs. The questions are:

- What is a data base management system?
- How does DB2 fit into the MVS environment?
- How does DB2 organize and access information?
- How does a COBOL program use DB2 services?
- What steps are required to develop a DB2 COBOL program?

I'll answer each of these questions in this chapter. Then, you should have no trouble learning the more detailed information that follows.

If you're already familiar with relational data base management systems, IBM mainframe computing, and Structured Query Language (SQL), you may want to skim my discussion of the first three questions. However, you should read the discussions of the fourth and fifth questions carefully.

What is a data base management system?

A *data base management system* (*DBMS*) is a software package that manages data stored in *data bases*. You use a DBMS to control and use the information stored on your computer system more effectively and efficiently than you can with standard file processing.

Programs that use standard file processing facilities to access and store data issue COBOL statements like READ and WRITE to do file input and output functions. Such statements invoke the services of operating system components called *access methods*. An access method handles details such as the disk location of each record, the physical block size, and so on. As a result, the COBOL programmer can concentrate on the logical processing required by the application. Although several access methods are available under MVS, most application programs use *VSAM*, the *Virtual Storage Access Method*. As you can see in the left side of figure 1-1, the access method stands between the application program and the data sets that program accesses.

Although the access method insulates a program from the stored data's physical format, the program is still closely tied to it. For example, the program needs to keep track of the complete structure of the data in each record, even if it needs to use only a small part of that data. That's because the access method isn't aware of the logical content of a record. So, if the structure of the stored data changes, the program needs to be modified, even if the change to the data has nothing to do with the program's function.

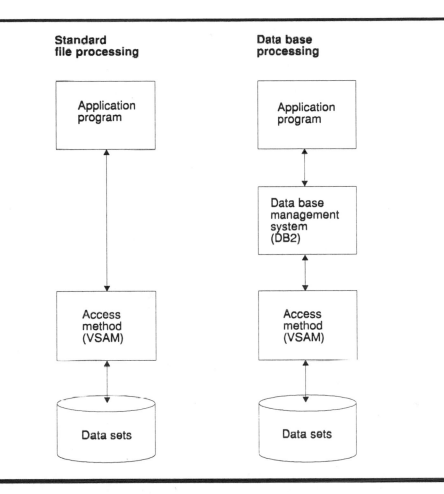

**Standard
file processing**

**Data base
processing**

Figure 1-1   Layers of software involved to process stored data with and without a data base management system

When a program uses DB2 or another data base management system, however, that's not the case. The DBMS is an additional layer of software between the program and the stored data, as the right side of figure 1-1 shows. Here, it's the DBMS rather than the application program that has a complete picture of the physical and logical structure of the stored data.

As a result, the application program can deal with stored data on a logical level and leave the physical data management concerns to the DBMS. In other words, the program doesn't need descriptions of the physical data sets that contain data base data. Moreover, it doesn't need a description of any data element it doesn't use to perform its tasks. These characteristics make application programs that use a DBMS *data independent*. So if the physical structure of the stored data changes, no programs are affected.

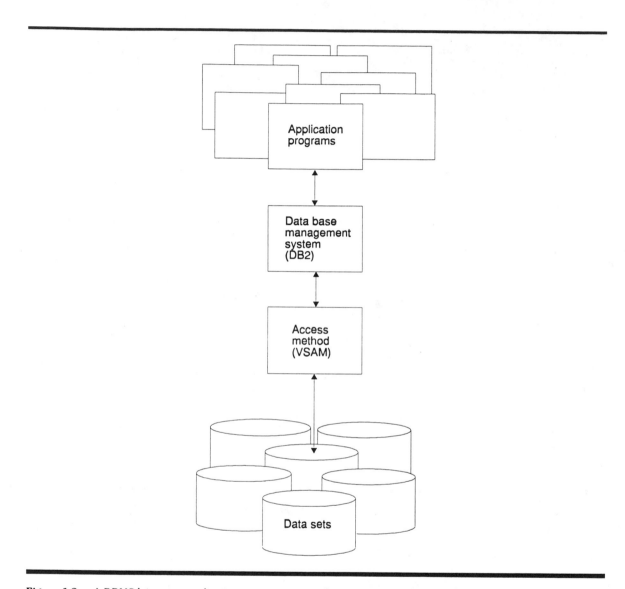

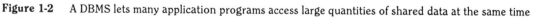

Figure 1-2   A DBMS lets many application programs access large quantities of shared data at the same time

And if the logical contents of the stored data changes, only the programs that use the changed elements are affected.

Because a DBMS centralizes control over a large collection of data, it lets many programs access the data at the same time, as shown in figure 1-2. As you can see, the DBMS can serve many programs and access much stored data. It also coordinates access to the data and controls what happens when.

When a shop uses a DBMS, its staff usually includes specialized technical personnel called *data base administrators* (*DBAs*). Data base administrators are responsible for defining, keeping current, and protecting the information the DBMS stores. Because they usually have a broad perspective on the information needs of an entire enterprise, DBAs are in the best position to make high-level decisions about data organization. In addition, DBAs usually know the most about how the DBMS operates. As a result, when you develop programs that use DB2 data, you're likely to work with a DBA in some way.

How does DB2 fit into the MVS environment?

MVS mainframe users work with DB2 in several ways. Here, I'll describe the differences between two broad ways to look at DB2's uses: application program processing and ad hoc processing.

Application programs and DB2   Most business uses of DB2 involve doing the same inquiry, data capture, and update tasks in the same ways many times, perhaps thousands of times a day. That's where *application programs* come in. Application programs for processing DB2 data make it possible to standardize the data that is entered into the system. They also make it easier for users to process this data.

Application programs that process DB2 data can run in both interactive and batch environments. *Interactive programs* let terminal operators access and update DB2 data directly. Terminal operators use these programs to do *inquiries* that extract information from the data base and to enter *transactions* that update the data base.

DB2 can work with three different IBM products to let users run interactive applications: *CICS* (*Customer Information Control System*), *IMS* (*Information Management System*), and *TSO* (*Time Sharing Option*). The program examples in this book run in the TSO environment. Even so, the DB2 techniques you'll learn from them apply directly to using DB2 in CICS and IMS programs. In *Part 2: An Advanced Course*, I'll introduce DB2 under CICS.

Interactive transaction processing is typical in today's shops. Often, though, the resource demands for updating online data bases from interactive programs may be too taxing for a system. For example, DB2 protects large chunks of information when it does updates, and that can prevent other programs from using that information. Therefore, many shops use interactive programs to capture their transaction information. Then, during off-hours, they use *batch programs* to post that transaction information to the DB2 data bases. Many shops also use batch programs to produce reports that contain information extracted from DB2 data bases.

Ad hoc processing and DB2   Although developing an application program that processes DB2 data is appropriate in many circumstances, it's not always the best way to get information from a data base. For a one-time task, like an inquiry with unusual search criteria to answer a unique question, developing an application program is simply too much trouble. Instead, it makes more sense to use one of the software packages that let you use DB2 for this sort of *ad hoc processing*. Probably the most popular package for this type of processing is IBM's *Query Management Facility* (*QMF*).

With QMF, when an end-user formulates a data base request at a terminal, DB2 responds to it on the spot. For example, a marketing manager may have questions about the geographic distribution of a firm's customers. She may wonder, for instance, if an unusually large proportion of customers is from just a few cities. With QMF, she can use her terminal to key in directions to tell DB2 to show the number of customers who live in New York, Chicago, Los Angeles, Philadelphia, and San Francisco. QMF then issues the instructions DB2 needs to extract this information from the data base. After DB2 retrieves and processes the appropriate data, QMF displays it on her terminal screen.

Although this is an easy way to work with DB2, ad hoc processing does have its drawbacks. First, users need to have a thorough understanding of both the logical structure of the stored data and the proper techniques to process that data. Second, the resources some ad hoc processing requires can be substantial enough to slow down the performance of an entire online system.

But despite its drawbacks, ad hoc processing is sure to remain a significant feature of the DB2 world. It's especially useful for programmers during program development and testing. I'll describe QMF and show you how to use it in *Part 2: An Advanced Course*.

How does DB2 organize and access information?

I told you earlier that DB2 is a data base management system. A more complete description is that DB2 is a relational data base management system that uses the industry-standard Structured Query Language (SQL) as a central component. Once you understand what these are, you'll have a clear picture of how DB2 organizes and accesses information.

The relational data model   A *relational data base* system presents all information in the form of tables. A *table* is just a two-dimensional array

Customer number	First name	Last name	Street	City	State	Zip
400001	KEITH	MCDONALD	4501 W MOCKINGBIRD	DALLAS	TX	75209
400002	ARREN	ANELLI	40 FORD RD	DENVILLE	NJ	07834
400003	SUSAN	HOWARD	1107 SECOND AVE #312	REDWOOD CITY	CA	94063
400004	CAROL ANN	EVANS	74 SUTTON CT	GREAT LAKES	IL	60088
400005	ELAINE	ROBERTS	12914 BRACKNELL	CERRITOS	CA	90701
400006	**PAT**	**HONG**	**73 HIGH ST**	**SAN FRANCISCO**	**CA**	**94114**
400007	PHIL	ROACH	25680 ORCHARD	DEARBORN HTS	MI	48125
400008	TIM	JOHNSON	145 W 27TH ST	SO CHICAGO HTS	IL	60411
400009	MARIANNE	BUSBEE	3920 BERWYN DR S #199	MOBILE	AL	36608
400010	ENRIQUE	OTHON	BOX 26729	RICHMOND	VA	23261
400011	WILLIAM C	FERGUSON	BOX 1283	MIAMI	FL	34002-1283
400012	S D	HOEHN	PO BOX 27	RIDDLE	OR	97469
400013	DAVID R	KEITH	BOX 1266	MAGNOLIA	AR	71757-1266
400014	R	BINDER	3425 WALDEN AVE	DEPEW	NY	14043
400015	VIVIAN	GEORGE	229 S 18TH ST	PHILADELPHIA	PA	19103
400016	J	NOETHLICH	11 KINGSTON CT	MERRIMACK	NH	03054

Row ⟶ (points to row 400006)

Value (points to SAN FRANCISCO)   **Column** ↑

Figure 1-3 A customer table that contains name and address information

with horizontal *rows* and vertical *columns*. The intersection of a row and a column is a *value*. The term *value* can be a little confusing, though, since the content of a value may be a text string, a number, or nothing (the *null* value).

Figure 1-3 shows a table that contains customer name and address information. In this example, the table contains 16 rows and 7 columns. As you can see, one column and one row are bold. Their intersection is a value. In this case, the content of that value is San Francisco.

The *relational model* came from mathematical theory. As a result, if you read other books or articles about DB2, you're likely to come across more technical terms. For example, the name *relational* data base comes from the technical term for a table, a *relation*. In addition, the formal names for the elements of a relation are *tuple* (for a row) and *attribute* (for a column).

But these aren't the only terms you'll see applied to a table's rows and columns. For instance, some people call a row a *record* and a column a *field*. And that makes sense when you realize that if you were working with a VSAM data set that contains the same information listed in figure 1-3, you would probably think about it the same way. Then, each row in the table would correspond to one record in the file, and each column would correspond to a field in the record description of the file.

This isn't the only similarity between a file and a DB2 table. In a file, each field has a specific data type and length. For example, if figure 1-3 represented a file, the last name field would be defined as alphanumeric and might have a length of 30 characters. In the same way, each column in a table has a particular data type and length.

Although files and tables have similar structures, they're processed differently. In standard file processing, the unit of processing is the individual record. As a result, you might expect the unit of processing in DB2 to be the row. Instead, it is the entire table, which may have one, many, or no rows. That might sound confusing to you, so let me illustrate.

Suppose you had to write a program to process a standard file that contains the data in figure 1-3 to find the names of people who live in California. Your program must first open the file and then read the records, one by one. For each record, your program must evaluate the contents of the state field. If it contains the state code CA, the program either writes the contents of the name fields to another data set or prints them. So, to process a file that contains the data in figure 1-3, your program has to issue 17 separate READ statements: one for each record, plus one more to detect the end-of-file condition.

In contrast, if the same data is a DB2 table, you can direct DB2 to select only the rows and columns that you want in a single operation. Specifically, you request just the first and last name columns from rows where the state column contains CA. The result is a temporary *results table* that contains what you asked for. Figure 1-4 shows the selection criteria, the DB2 source (or "base") table, and the results table for this operation.

When table rows uniquely represent entities, like customers, invoices, or parts, it makes sense to identify each with a unique value in a particular column. (This is the same idea that system designers use when they create VSAM data sets with unique keys that allow programs to retrieve specific records directly.) When a DB2 table includes a column whose contents serve as *key* values, you can do single-row operations that closely simulate standard file processing.

For example, figure 1-5 shows how a single row can be retrieved from the customer table based on the key value in the customer number column. For applications that must retrieve specific single rows, you and your DBA are likely to use this approach. However, I want you to realize that this technique represents a special case. DB2 is able to handle results tables with many rows as well as those with just one.

DB2's ability to produce a results table that may contain many rows as a result of just one statement isn't limited to operations that access a single base table. In fact, one of DB2's great strengths is that it can combine, or *join*, data from two or more tables in a single operation. I'll describe joins in detail in chapter 7. For now, though, I want to present an example to help you understand the concept.

Selection criteria	Access the customer table.
	Return the first and last names of customers who live in California.

Customer table

Customer number	First name	Last name	Street	City	State	Zip
400001	KEITH	MCDONALD	4501 W MOCKINGBIRD	DALLAS	TX	75209
400002	ARREN	ANELLI	40 FORD RD	DENVILLE	NJ	07834
400003	**SUSAN**	**HOWARD**	**1107 SECOND AVE #312**	**REDWOOD CITY**	**CA**	**94063**
400004	CAROL ANN	EVANS	74 SUTTON CT	GREAT LAKES	IL	60088
400005	**ELAINE**	**ROBERTS**	**12914 BRACKNELL**	**CERRITOS**	**CA**	**90701**
400006	**PAT**	**HONG**	**73 HIGH ST**	**SAN FRANCISCO**	**CA**	**94114**
400007	PHIL	ROACH	25680 ORCHARD	DEARBORN HTS	MI	48125
400008	TIM	JOHNSON	145 W 27TH ST	SO CHICAGO HTS	IL	60411
400009	MARIANNE	BUSBEE	3920 BERWYN DR S #199	MOBILE	AL	36608
400010	ENRIQUE	OTHON	BOX 26729	RICHMOND	VA	23261
400011	WILLIAM C	FERGUSON	BOX 1283	MIAMI	FL	34002-1283
400012	S D	HOEHN	PO BOX 27	RIDDLE	OR	97469
400013	DAVID R	KEITH	BOX 1266	MAGNOLIA	AR	71757-1266
400014	R	BINDER	3425 WALDEN AVE	DEPEW	NY	14043
400015	VIVIAN	GEORGE	229 S 18TH ST	PHILADELPHIA	PA	19103
400016	J	NOETHLICH	11 KINGSTON CT	MERRIMACK	NH	03054

Results table

First name	Last name
SUSAN	HOWARD
ELAINE	ROBERTS
PAT	HONG

Figure 1-4   DB2 can create a results table that contains a subset of the columns and a subset of the rows in a base table

The customer table you've already seen contains name and address information, but no sales transaction information. That information exists in an invoice table. A single row in the invoice table corresponds to one sale transaction and includes the invoice number, date, product total, shipping charges, tax, and total amount billed. The invoice number column is a key for this table because its contents uniquely identify each row.

In addition to financial information, each row in the invoice table contains the number of the customer involved in the sale transaction. This value is called a *foreign key*. A foreign key identifies a related row in another table and establishes a logical relationship between rows in the two tables. In this application, the invoice table may contain zero, one, or many rows for any given customer in the customer table.

Selection criteria

> Access the customer table.
>
> Return all the information for the customer whose number is 400011.

Customer table

Customer number	First name	Last name	Street	City	State	Zip
400001	KEITH	MCDONALD	4□□ W MOCKINGBIRD	DALLAS	TX	75209
400002	ARREN	ANELLI	40 FORD RD	DENVILLE	NJ	07834
400003	SUSAN	HOWARD	1107 SECOND AVE #312	REDWOOD CITY	CA	94063
400004	CAROL ANN	EVANS	74 SUTTON CT	GREAT LAKES	IL	60088
400005	ELAINE	ROBERTS	12914 BRACKNELL	CERRITOS	CA	90701
400006	PAT	HONG	73 HIGH ST	SAN FRANCISCO	CA	94114
400007	PHIL	ROACH	25680 ORCHARD	DEARBORN HTS	MI	48125
400008	TIM	JOHNSON	145 W 27TH ST	SO CHICAGO HTS	IL	60411
400009	MARIANNE	BUSBEE	3920 BERWYN DR S #199	MOBILE	AL	36608
400010	ENRIQUE	OTHON	BOX 26729	RICHMOND	VA	23261
400011	**WILLIAM C**	**FERGUSON**	**BOX 1283**	**MIAMI**	**FL**	**34002-1283**
400012	S D	HOEHN	PO BOX 27	RIDDLE	OR	97469
400013	DAVID R	KEITH	BOX 1266	MAGNOLIA	AR	71757-1266
400014	R	BINDER	3425 WALDEN AVE	DEPEW	NY	14043
400015	VIVIAN	GEORGE	229 S 18TH ST	PHILADELPHIA	PA	19103
400016	J	NOETHLICH	11 KINGSTON CT	MERRIMACK	NH	03054

Results table

Customer number	First name	Last name	Street	City	State	Zip
400011	WILLIAM C	FERGUSON	BOX 1283	MIAMI	FL	34002-1283

Figure 1-5   DB2 can simulate standard record-oriented data processing by returning all of the columns from a single row of a base table

Now, consider this application problem: List the numbers, dates, and amounts billed for all invoices issued to customers who live in California. In addition, for each invoice, list the first and last names and city for the customer associated with it. Figure 1-6 shows that DB2 retrieves the requested columns from both the invoice and customer tables and combines them in a single results table. In chapter 7, I'll show you how to code a statement that creates a results table like this one. But for now, I just want you to realize that if you had to solve this application problem with standard file processing techniques, you'd need to use more complicated logic and your program would have to issue many READ statements.

Structured Query Language   To work on the data in DB2 tables, your programs issue statements in *SQL,* the *Structured Query Language.*

Selection criteria

Access the customer table and the invoice table.

For each invoice issued to a customer who lives in California, return the invoice's number, date, and total billed, plus the customer's number, first name, last name, and city.

Customer table

Customer number	First name	Last name	Street	City	State	Zip
400001	KEITH	MCDONALD	4501 W MOCKINGBIRD	DALLAS	TX	75209
400002	ARREN	ANELLI	40 FORD RD	DENVILLE	NJ	07834
400003	**SUSAN**	**HOWARD**	**1107 SECOND AVE #312**	**REDWOOD CITY**	**CA**	**94063**
400004	CAROL ANN	EVANS	74 SUTTON CT	GREAT LAKES	IL	60088
400005	**ELAINE**	**ROBERTS**	**12914 BRACKNELL**	**CERRITOS**	**CA**	**90701**
400006	**PAT**	**HONG**	**73 HIGH ST**	**SAN FRANCISCO**	**CA**	**94114**
400007	PHIL	ROACH	25680 ORCHARD	DEARBORN HTS	MI	48125
400008	TIM	JOHNSON	145 W 27TH ST	SO CHICAGO HTS	IL	60411
400009	MARIANNE	BUSBEE	3920 BERWYN DR S #199	MOBILE	AL	36608
400010	ENRIQUE	OTHON	BOX 26729	RICHMOND	VA	23261
400011	WILLIAM C	FERGUSON	BOX 1283	MIAMI	FL	34002-1283
400012	S D	HOEHN	PO BOX 27	RIDDLE	OR	97469
400013	DAVID R	KEITH	BOX 1266	MAGNOLIA	AR	71757-1266
400014	R	BINDER	3425 WALDEN AVE	DEPEW	NY	14043
400015	VIVIAN	GEORGE	229 S 18TH ST	PHILADELPHIA	PA	19103
400016	J	NOETHLICH	11 KINGSTON CT	MERRIMACK	NH	03054

Results table

Customer number	Invoice number	Invoice date	First name	Last name	City	Invoice total
400003	003585	1991-07-23	SUSAN	HOWARD	REDWOOD CITY	292.83
400005	003587	1991-07-23	ELAINE	ROBERTS	CERRITOS	22.09
400003	003590	1991-07-23	SUSAN	HOWARD	REDWOOD CITY	110.49

Invoice table

Customer number	Invoice number	Invoice date	Invoice subtotal	Shipping charges	Sales tax	Invoice total	Promo code
400015	003584	1991-07-23	50.00	1.75	0.00	51.75	PROM1
400003	**003585**	**1991-07-23**	**265.00**	**9.28**	**18.55**	**292.83**	**PROM1**
400007	003586	1991-07-23	66.54	2.33	0.00	68.87	PROM1
400005	**003587**	**1991-07-23**	**19.99**	**0.70**	**1.40**	**22.09**	**PROM1**
400004	003588	1991-07-23	55.68	1.95	0.00	57.63	PROM1
400016	003589	1991-07-23	687.00	24.05	0.00	711.05	PROM1
400003	**003590**	**1991-07-23**	**99.99**	**3.50**	**7.00**	**110.49**	**PROM1**

Figure 1-6   DB2 can combine information from rows in two different tables into one row in the results table

```
CREATE TABLE MMADBV.CUST
    (CUSTNO      CHAR(6)   NOT NULL,
     FNAME       CHAR(20)  NOT NULL,
     LNAME       CHAR(30)  NOT NULL,
     ADDR        CHAR(30)  NOT NULL,
     CITY        CHAR(20)  NOT NULL,
     STATE       CHAR(2)   NOT NULL,
     ZIPCODE     CHAR(10)  NOT NULL)
IN DATABASE MMADB
```

Figure 1-7   A data definition language statement that defines the customer table in figure 1-3

Depending on who you talk to, you may hear SQL pronounced like the word *sequel* or spelled out as *S-Q-L*.

The complete set of SQL statements provides facilities not just for application programming, but also for data base management. DBAs use SQL's *data definition language (DDL)* statements to do tasks like defining tables. For example, the DDL statement in figure 1-7 defines the customer table shown in figures 1-3 through 1-6. DDL statements also let data base administrators change and delete tables, control who can access them, and manage the disk space where they reside.

In contrast, application programmers typically work with SQL's *data manipulation language (DML)*. DML statements retrieve data from tables and change tables by inserting, deleting, and updating data. For example, to select a results table like the one in figure 1-4, you use a statement like the one in figure 1-8. (By the way, a complete DML statement that you'd code in an application program is a little more complicated than the one in figure 1-8. I'm showing you this example just to give you a taste of what SQL's DML is like.)

How does a COBOL program use DB2 services?

When you use DB2 through COBOL, you invoke DB2 services by including SQL statements in your program. These statements often appear in the same places you'd use standard file processing statements like READ and WRITE, and they often perform the same tasks. In the next chapters, you'll learn how to code the elements a COBOL program needs to access DB2 data. For now, though, I just want to introduce three things you must include in your COBOL source code to process DB2 data: host variables, the SQL communication area, and SQL statements.

```
SELECT FNAME, LNAME
       FROM MMADBV.CUST
       WHERE STATE = 'CA'
```

Figure 1-8   A data manipulation language statement that creates a results table like the one in figure 1-4

Host variables   When you create your COBOL source code, you include definitions for fields that can be used both to receive the data DB2 returns to your program and from which DB2 can get the data it will use to update tables. These are called *host variables* because they reside in storage owned by the host program. In the examples in this book, the host variables are COBOL Working-Storage fields.

Communication area   When you request a DB2 service, you need to be able to find out if it worked. DB2 provides feedback about the success of each operation by storing information in the *SQL communication area*, or *SQLCA*. You have to put a definition of the SQLCA in your COBOL program, so I'll show you how to do that in chapter 2. I'll also describe the structure of the SQLCA and show you how to deal with results that you discover through it.

SQL statements   SQL statements accomplish the data base work your program does. You code them to retrieve or change table data. You need to learn only a few SQL statements, and most of them are simple to use. As you can see in figure 1-9, they fall into six groups.

The first group contains the statement I've already introduced, SELECT. You use SELECT and the other statements in the first group to retrieve data from a table. To use an SQL statement in a COBOL program, you have to add some elements to it that you don't need when you use it through a product like QMF. In the chapters that follow, you'll learn all the details for coding SQL statements, but I want to show you one example now.

Figure 1-10 presents a SELECT statement you could code in an application program to retrieve each column from a single row in the customer table, as figure 1-5 illustrated. While this SELECT statement creates a results table with just one row, the SELECT statement can also create a results table with none, or many rows. You'll learn how to use SELECT's features throughout this book.

Notice that this statement specifies not only the seven columns whose values it will retrieve but also the seven corresponding COBOL host variables in which it will store those values. The line with the SELECT

Data retrieval	SELECT
	DECLARE CURSOR
	OPEN
	FETCH
	CLOSE
Data modification	INSERT
	UPDATE
	DELETE
Program development	INCLUDE
	DECLARE TABLE
Recovery and restart	COMMIT
	ROLLBACK
Error handling	WHENEVER
Dynamic SQL	PREPARE
	EXECUTE

Figure 1-9   SQL statements you'll use in COBOL programs

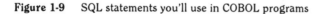

```
EXEC SQL
    SELECT     CUSTNO,   FNAME,   LNAME,    ADDR,
               CITY,     STATE,   ZIPCODE
        INTO :CUSTNO, :FNAME, :LNAME,  :ADDR,
             :CITY,    :STATE, :ZIPCODE
        FROM   MMADBV.CUST
        WHERE CUSTNO = '400011'
END-EXEC.
```

Figure 1-10   A sample SQL statement used in a COBOL program

statement name and the one that follows it list the table columns, and the two-line INTO clause names the host variables. When you use a COBOL variable name in a DB2 statement, you need to precede it with a colon. Note also that the names of the columns and of the host variables in this example are the same. Although that's often the case, it isn't a requirement.

The other statements in the first group in figure 1-9 let your application programs work with results tables that contain more than one row. These statements use a DB2 feature called a *cursor*. A cursor is a pointer that identifies one and only one row of a results table that is available to an application program at a given time. I'll describe cursor processing in topic 2 of chapter 3.

When you want to change DB2 table data, you can use the three SQL statements in the second group in figure 1-9. To add a new row to a table, your program first moves the data for the new row into the proper host variables. Then, it directs DB2 to write that data to a new table row by issuing an SQL INSERT statement. To change the data in a row or rows, a program moves the new values into the proper host variables, then issues an SQL UPDATE statement. And finally, to remove a row from a table, the program moves an appropriate identifying value to a host variable, then issues an SQL DELETE statement.

A strength (and danger) of SQL is that a single statement like UPDATE or DELETE can affect many, or all, of the rows in the target table. As a result, it's important that you understand the implications of how you code statements like this. In topic 1 of chapter 4, I'll describe these statements thoroughly.

The next two statements in figure 1-9 let you develop your source language programs more easily. INCLUDE works like the COBOL COPY statement. You use it to combine source code library members with your program code. DECLARE TABLE defines the contents of a table in an application program. You'll learn about both the INCLUDE and DECLARE TABLE statements in chapter 2.

You use the COMMIT and ROLLBACK statements to insure the integrity of the DB2 tables rather than to perform operations on them. I'll describe these two statements in topic 2 of chapter 4.

The last two groups of statements in figure 1-9 are for special purposes. You use the WHENEVER statement to specify the actions a program should take when certain errors occur during DB2 processing. Finally, the PREPARE and EXECUTE statements let you use an advanced DB2 feature called dynamic SQL. I'll cover WHENEVER, PREPARE,and EXECUTE in *Part 2: An Advanced Course.*

```
                        DBZI PRIMARY OPTION MENU
===>

Select one of the following DB2 functions and press ENTER.

    1   SPUFI                   (Process SQL statements)
    2   DCLGEN                  (Generate SQL and source language declarations)
    3   PROGRAM PREPARATION     (Prepare a DB2 application program to run)
    4   PRECOMPILE              (Invoke DB2 precompiler)
    5   BIND/REBIND/FREE        (BIND, REBIND, or FREE application plans)
    6   RUN                     (RUN an SQL program)
    7   DB2 COMMANDS            (Issue DB2 commands)
    8   UTILITIES               (Invoke DB2 utilities)
    D   DB2I DEFAULTS           (Set global parameters)
    X   EXIT                    (Leave DB2I)




  F1=HELP      F2=SPLIT      F3=END      F4=RETURN    F5=RFIND      F6=RCHANGE
  F7=UP        F8=DOWN       F9=SWAP     F10=LEFT     F11=RIGHT     F12=RETRIEVE
```

Figure 1-11   The DB2I Primary Option Menu

What steps are required to develop a DB2 COBOL program?

If you're an experienced COBOL programmer, you're already familiar with the basic steps you must follow to develop a COBOL program: find out exactly what the program is supposed to do, design the program, code it, compile it, and test it. The sequence of steps you must follow to develop a DB2 COBOL program is similar. However, there are important variations you should be aware of, and I'll introduce them here.

The easiest way to prepare a DB2 program is to use *DB2I*, which stands for *DB2 Interactive*. You access DB2I through TSO/ISPF. When you enter DB2I, it displays the Primary Option Menu shown in figure 1-11. If you're familiar with ISPF, you should have no trouble learning how to use DB2I.

Here, I'll briefly describe the three DB2I options you'll use most: SPUFI, DCLGEN, and Program Preparation. When you're ready to learn the details of using DB2I, you can find that information in chapter 10.

SPUFI   *SPUFI*, which stands for *SQL Processor Using File Input* and is pronounced *spoofy*, lets you compose SQL statements interactively, submit them for execution, and get immediate feedback at your terminal. In other words, SPUFI lets you execute SQL statements without coding and compiling a COBOL program.

As you develop DB2 programs, you'll use SPUFI for many different purposes. For example, you might use SPUFI to enter the SQL statements required to create a test table or to load data into a test table. Or, you might use SPUFI to display the contents of a table after a test run. Still another common use of SPUFI is to test your SQL statements before you code them in a program, so you can be certain that they work the way you expect them to.

DCLGEN   When you develop a COBOL program that processes standard files, you generally use a COPY statement to include a record description for each file the program will process. The DB2 equivalent to a record description is called a *host structure*. A host structure is simply a COBOL group item that contains the host variables that will be used to store data for the table's columns.

Although you can create a host structure yourself, it's much easier to let DB2 do it for you. DB2 provides a utility called *DCLGEN*, which stands for *Declarations Generator*, for this purpose.

You invoke DCLGEN by selecting option 2 from the DB2I Primary Option Menu. Then, you simply tell DCLGEN which table you want to process and where you want the resulting host structure stored. Normally, the DCLGEN output is stored as a member of a partitioned data set that can be included in your COBOL program.

Besides the host structure, the DCLGEN output also includes an SQL DECLARE TABLE statement that names the columns the table contains. Like the host structure, this DECLARE TABLE statement is created automatically by DCLGEN. So you don't have to code it yourself.

Program preparation   The DB2I program preparation option prepares an executable program from a DB2 COBOL source program and, optionally, runs it. Like any COBOL program, this involves compiling the source program to produce an object module, then link-editing the object module to produce an executable load module. However, two additional steps are required for DB2 programs. Figure 1-12 shows the complete program preparation process for DB2 COBOL programs.

As you can see, before the COBOL program can be compiled, it must be processed by the DB2 *precompiler*. The precompiler produces two output files. The first is an intermediate source program, in which each of the SQL statements has been translated into COBOL that invokes the appropriate DB2 interface function. The precompiler leaves the original SQL statements in the source program, but converts them to comment lines so they will be

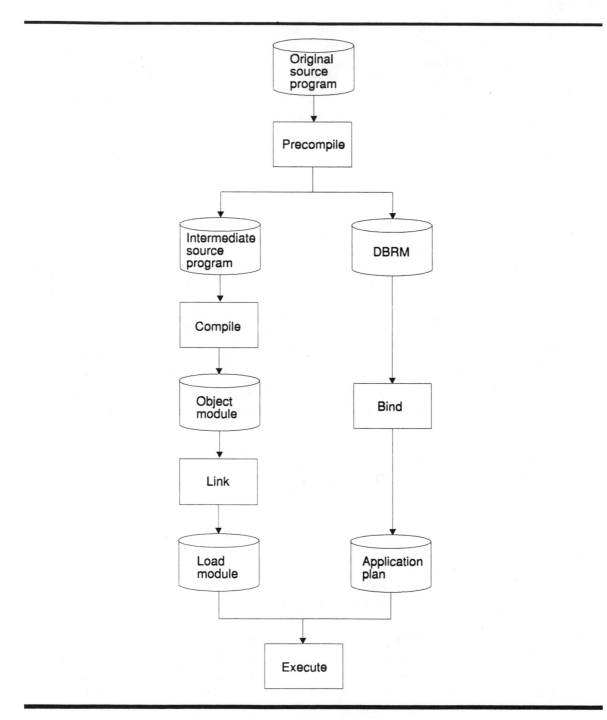

Figure 1-12   The steps required to prepare a DB2 COBOL program for execution

ignored by the COBOL compiler. The second file produced by the precompiler is called a *data base request module*, or *DBRM*. It contains information about how your program will use DB2 and will be used as input in a later step of the program preparation process.

After the precompiler is finished, the standard COBOL compiler is invoked to compile the intermediate source program to produce an object module. Then, the linkage-editor is invoked to produce a load module from the object module. The linkage-editor includes not only the COBOL modules your program needs, but DB2 interface modules as well.

Before the load module can be executed, however, DB2 must *bind* the program. The bind procedure uses the DBRM to double-check all of the DB2 functions in the program to make sure they are valid and that you are authorized to perform them. In addition, the bind procedure selects the most efficient way for DB2 to implement the functions your program requests. The output of the bind process is an *application plan*. It contains information about how DB2 will complete each data base request made by your program. As you can see in figure 1-12, both the load module and the application plan are required to execute a DB2 program.

All of the steps I've just described can be carried out automatically when you select the program preparation option from the DB2I Primary Option Menu. Once you get the DB2I panels set up properly so that DB2I knows where your program libraries reside and what options you want to use, preparing a program is as simple as selecting the program preparation option from the DB2I Primary Option Menu and typing the member name for the source program.

Discussion

Now that you have a broad picture of what DB2 is and how it works, you're ready to learn the details of using DB2. If you're feeling a little overwhelmed right now, don't worry. As long as you understand this chapter's terms and objectives, you're ready to move on to section 2. And as you build on what you've just learned, you'll begin to feel more comfortable working with DB2.

Terms

DB2
Database 2
data base management system
DBMS
data base

access method
VSAM
Virtual Storage Access Method
data independent
data base administrator
DBA
application program
interactive program
inquiry
transaction
CICS
Customer Information Control System
IMS
Information Management System
TSO
Time Sharing Option
batch program
ad hoc processing
Query Management Facility
QMF
relational data base
table
row
column
value
null
relational model
relation
tuple
attribute
record
field
results table
key
join
foreign key
SQL
Structured Query Language
data definition language
DDL
data manipulation language
DML

host variable
SQL communication area
SQLCA
cursor
DB2I
DB2 Interactive
SPUFI
SQL Processor Using File Input
host structure
DCLGEN
Declarations Generator
precompiler
data base request module
DBRM
bind
application plan

Objectives

1. Describe the difference between a data base management system and an access method.

2. Describe the difference between ad hoc processing and application program processing.

3. Describe the difference between interactive and batch processing.

4. Describe how information is organized according to the relational data model.

5. Describe how processing a DB2 table can differ from standard record-oriented file processing.

6. List the major elements you must include in a COBOL program that will process DB2 data.

7. List, in the right order, the steps you must follow to create and run a COBOL program that will process DB2 data.

8. Answer the five questions I asked at the start of this chapter.

Section

2

A basic subset of embedded SQL

The three chapters in this section teach you how to code COBOL programs that process DB2 data. This material is essential to your DB2 training, so I encourage you to spend the time you need to learn it. And since these three chapters build upon each other, I recommend that you read them in sequence.

Chapter 2 presents the COBOL elements that let you use DB2 services and introduces the SQL SELECT statement. This is the statement you'll code in your programs to retrieve data from DB2 tables. Chapter 3 expands your knowledge of SQL data retrieval. In it, you'll learn more details of the SELECT statement and how your application programs can use DB2's cursor feature to process multiple-row tables. Chapter 4 rounds out your knowledge of basic SQL by showing you how to use the INSERT, UPDATE, and DELETE statements to change the data in a table, and how to use basic error handling and data integrity techniques.

Chapter 2

An introduction to embedded SQL

To process DB2 table data in a COBOL program, you must use embedded SQL statements. The term *embedded SQL* refers simply to SQL statements that are included in an application program. This chapter is an introduction to embedded SQL. Here, you'll learn the coding requirements for embedded SQL statements. You'll also learn how to include definitions of host variables and the SQL communication area in your COBOL program. And you'll learn how to code a simple SQL SELECT statement that retrieves a single row from a table.

A simple inquiry program

To help you put the details in this chapter into context, I want to show you a complete COBOL program. This program, called CUSTINQ, is an interactive inquiry application. Figure 2-1 presents the TSO screens displayed in the operation of CUSTINQ. The program accepts a customer number from a terminal user, retrieves the corresponding row from the customer table, and displays the contents of the row. The table this program uses is the customer table shown in figure 2-2.

The program begins by prompting the user to enter the number for the customer whose data he wants to see. In part 1 of figure 2-1, the user keys in the customer number 400001 and presses enter. The program retrieves the corresponding row from the customer table, formats its contents, and displays the results, as you can see in part 2 of figure 2-1. Then the user keys in another customer number, 400017, and presses enter. This time, the number the user entered doesn't identify a row in the customer table, so in part 3 of figure 2-1, the program displays an error message and prompts the user to enter another number. The user doesn't want to do any more inquiries, so he keys in 999999. The program recognizes that value as a signal to end, and it does.

Nearly all DB2 shops have programs that do tasks like this. In a production environment, however, these programs are more likely to run under CICS, IMS, or ISPF than under line-mode TSO. Unfortunately, both CICS, IMS, and ISPF add their own complexities to program development, so any example from those environments would be unnecessarily difficult for you to understand. As a result, although it's not typical for a "real-world" application, I chose TSO as the execution environment for CUSTINQ. The program under TSO is so simple that you can focus directly on the critical DB2 elements it illustrates. Then, you can apply the DB2 concepts you learn from this simple TSO program in more complicated environments.

Figure 2-3 presents the COBOL source code for the CUSTINQ program. Throughout this chapter, I'll point out what you need to notice in this program.

Rules for coding SQL statements

To request any DB2 function in a COBOL program, you issue an SQL statement. The CUSTINQ program in figure 2-3 contains three SQL statements. I've shaded them so you can locate them easily. Two of them are in the Data Division, and one is in the Procedure Division. Before I talk about what SQL statements do and where they belong, I want to give you an overview of the syntax rules you have to follow for every SQL statement you code. Figure 2-4 lists the SQL syntax rules you need to keep in mind all the time, plus some special case rules that may affect you.

General rules for coding SQL statements

The first general rule for coding SQL statements is that each statement must begin with EXEC SQL and end with END-EXEC as in

```
EXEC SQL
    INCLUDE CUST
END-EXEC.
```

Part 1

For the first inquiry, the user keys in the customer number 400001 and presses enter.

```
-------------------------------------------------
KEY IN THE NEXT CUSTOMER NUMBER AND PRESS ENTER,
OR KEY IN 999999 AND PRESS ENTER TO QUIT.
400001
```

Part 2

The program responds to the user's first inquiry by displaying the data it retrieved from the customer table. For the second inquiry, the user keys in the customer number 400017 and presses enter.

```
-------------------------------------------------
KEY IN THE NEXT CUSTOMER NUMBER AND PRESS ENTER,
OR KEY IN 999999 AND PRESS ENTER TO QUIT.
400001
-------------------------------------------------
    CUSTOMER 400001
    NAME     KEITH            MCDONALD
    ADDRESS  4501 W MOCKINGBIRD
             DALLAS           TX 75209
-------------------------------------------------
KEY IN THE NEXT CUSTOMER NUMBER AND PRESS ENTER,
OR KEY IN 999999 AND PRESS ENTER TO QUIT.
400017
```

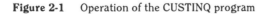

Figure 2-1 Operation of the CUSTINQ program

Part 3

The second customer
number the user entered
doesn't have a
corresponding row in the
customer table. The user
keys in 999999 to end
the program.

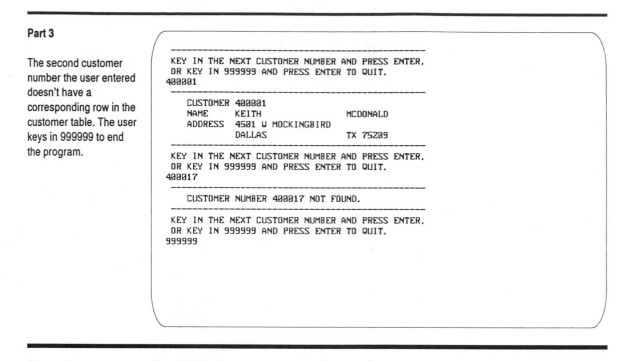

```
-------------------------------------------------------
KEY IN THE NEXT CUSTOMER NUMBER AND PRESS ENTER,
OR KEY IN 999999 AND PRESS ENTER TO QUIT.
400001
-------------------------------------------------------
     CUSTOMER 400001
     NAME     KEITH              MCDONALD
     ADDRESS  4501 W MOCKINGBIRD
              DALLAS                TX 75209
-------------------------------------------------------
KEY IN THE NEXT CUSTOMER NUMBER AND PRESS ENTER,
OR KEY IN 999999 AND PRESS ENTER TO QUIT.
400017
-------------------------------------------------------
     CUSTOMER NUMBER 400017 NOT FOUND.
-------------------------------------------------------
KEY IN THE NEXT CUSTOMER NUMBER AND PRESS ENTER,
OR KEY IN 999999 AND PRESS ENTER TO QUIT.
999999
```

Figure 2-1   Operation of the CUSTINQ program (continued)

Notice that a space separates EXEC and SQL in the opening delimiter, but a
hyphen separates END and EXEC in the closing delimiter. (If you're a CICS
programmer, you're sure to recognize this coding technique since CICS
uses an EXEC interface for its statements too.)

The second general rule is to code your SQL statements in columns 12
through 72. This is true whether the SQL statement is in your program's
Procedure Division or in the Data Division.

SQL gives you lots of coding flexibility, so you can use as many lines as
you need for each statement. For example, if you look at the SELECT statement in the Procedure Division of the CUSTINQ program, you'll see that I
used 10 lines to code it. Here, I used spaces within the lines to separate the
different elements. You can do this as long as your code stays in columns
12 through 72, and you use commas properly to mark the ends of items.
(When I introduce each SQL statement, I'll show you when you need to use
commas.)

The last general rule listed in figure 2-4 is to use spacing and alignment
to make the statement readable. If you don't follow this rule, your statement will still work correctly. But it won't be as easy to read. To illustrate,
figure 2-5 shows three ways to code the SELECT statement from the

Customer number	First name	Last name	Street	City	State	Zip
400001	KEITH	MCDONALD	4501 W MOCKINGBIRD	DALLAS	TX	75209
400002	ARREN	ANELLI	40 FORD RD	DENVILLE	NJ	07834
400003	SUSAN	HOWARD	1107 SECOND AVE #312	REDWOOD CITY	CA	94063
400004	CAROL ANN	EVANS	74 SUTTON CT	GREAT LAKES	IL	60088
400005	ELAINE	ROBERTS	12914 BRACKNELL	CERRITOS	CA	90701
400006	PAT	HONG	73 HIGH ST	SAN FRANCISCO	CA	94114
400007	PHIL	ROACH	25680 ORCHARD	DEARBORN HTS	MI	48125
400008	TIM	JOHNSON	145 W 27TH ST	SO CHICAGO HTS	IL	60411
400009	MARIANNE	BUSBEE	3920 BERWYN DR S #199	MOBILE	AL	36608
400010	ENRIQUE	OTHON	BOX 26729	RICHMOND	VA	23261
400011	WILLIAM C	FERGUSON	BOX 1283	MIAMI	FL	34002-1283
400012	S D	HOEHN	PO BOX 27	RIDDLE	OR	97469
400013	DAVID R	KEITH	BOX 1266	MAGNOLIA	AR	71757-1266
400014	R	BINDER	3425 WALDEN AVE	DEPEW	NY	14043
400015	VIVIAN	GEORGE	229 S 18TH ST	PHILADELPHIA	PA	19103
400016	J	NOETHLICH	11 KINGSTON CT	MERRIMACK	NH	03054

Figure 2-2   The customer table used in figure 2-1

CUSTINQ program. Although all three examples in figure 2-5 are acceptable to SQL, I think you'll agree that the first two are harder to read than the third one. In the first example, I coded the elements too closely together. In the second, I coded the elements of the statement on too many lines. But in the third example, the version of the statement I coded in the program, I used a few spaces to separate elements on the same line (such as CUSTNO, FNAME, and LNAME), and I aligned elements on the SELECT and INTO clauses that are related to each other (such as CITY and :CITY).

Although SQL doesn't require that you adopt any particular coding technique, many shops do. As a result, you should find out what your shop's standards for coding SQL statements are and stick to them. And if your shop doesn't have any standards, just try to make your code as readable as possible.

Special case rules for coding SQL statements

The simple SQL rules in the top half of figure 2-4 are worth memorizing because you should follow them for every SQL statement you code. In addition to these basic rules, you might need to know what I call special case rules that apply under less common circumstances. The bottom half of figure 2-4 lists them.

Because you have such flexibility when you code SQL, you usually don't need to take special action to continue a statement to another line.

```
000100 IDENTIFICATION DIVISION.
000200*
000300 PROGRAM-ID          CUSTINQ.
000400*
000500 ENVIRONMENT DIVISION.
000600*
000700 INPUT-OUTPUT SECTION.
000800*
000900 FILE-CONTROL.
001000*
001100 DATA DIVISION.
001200*
001300 FILE SECTION.
001400*
001500 WORKING-STORAGE SECTION.
001600*
001700 01  SWITCHES.
001800*
001900     05  END-OF-INQUIRIES-SW      PIC X   VALUE "N".
002000         88  END-OF-INQUIRIES              VALUE "Y".
002100     05  CUSTOMER-FOUND-SW        PIC X   VALUE "Y".
002200         88  CUSTOMER-FOUND               VALUE "Y".
002300*
002400     EXEC SQL
002500         INCLUDE CUST
002600     END-EXEC.
002700*
002800     EXEC SQL
002900         INCLUDE SQLCA
003000     END-EXEC.
003100*
003200 PROCEDURE DIVISION.
003300*
003400 000-DISPLAY-CUSTOMER-ROWS.
003500*
003600     PERFORM 100-DISPLAY-CUSTOMER-ROW
003700         UNTIL END-OF-INQUIRIES.
003800     STOP RUN.
003900*
004000 100-DISPLAY-CUSTOMER-ROW.
004100*
004200     PERFORM 110-ACCEPT-CUSTOMER-NUMBER.
004300     IF NOT END-OF-INQUIRIES
004400         MOVE "Y" TO CUSTOMER-FOUND-SW
004500         PERFORM 120-GET-CUSTOMER-ROW
004600         IF CUSTOMER-FOUND
004700             PERFORM 130-DISPLAY-CUSTOMER-LINES
004800         ELSE
004900             PERFORM 140-DISPLAY-ERROR-LINES.
005000*
```

Figure 2-3   COBOL source code for the CUSTINQ program (part 1 of 2)

```
005100 110-ACCEPT-CUSTOMER-NUMBER.
005200*
005300     DISPLAY "-------------------------------------------------".
005400     DISPLAY "KEY IN THE NEXT CUSTOMER NUMBER AND PRESS ENTER,".
005500     DISPLAY "OR KEY IN 999999 AND PRESS ENTER TO QUIT.".
005600     ACCEPT CUSTNO.
005700     IF CUSTNO = "999999"
005800         MOVE "Y" TO END-OF-INQUIRIES-SW.
005900*
006000 120-GET-CUSTOMER-ROW.
006100*
006200     EXEC SQL
006300         SELECT CUSTNO,          FNAME,              LNAME,
006400                ADDR,            CITY,               STATE,
006500                ZIPCODE
006600         INTO   :CUSTNO,         :FNAME,             :LNAME,
006700                :ADDR,           :CITY,              :STATE,
006800                :ZIPCODE
006900         FROM   MMADBV.CUST
007000         WHERE  CUSTNO = :CUSTNO
007100     END-EXEC.
007200*
007300     IF SQLCODE NOT = 0
007400         MOVE "N" TO CUSTOMER-FOUND-SW.
007500*
007600 130-DISPLAY-CUSTOMER-LINES.
007700*
007800     DISPLAY "-------------------------------------------------".
007900     DISPLAY "   CUSTOMER " CUSTNO.
008000     DISPLAY "   NAME     " FNAME " " LNAME.
008100     DISPLAY "   ADDRESS  " ADDR.
008200     DISPLAY "            " CITY " " STATE " " ZIPCODE.
008300*
008400 140-DISPLAY-ERROR-LINE.
008500*
008600     DISPLAY "-------------------------------------------------".
008700     DISPLAY "   CUSTOMER NUMBER " CUSTNO " NOT FOUND.".
008800*
```

Figure 2-3   COBOL source code for the CUSTINQ program (part 2 of 2)

The only time you may is when you want to code a text string that's too long to fit on a single line. Then, you follow similar rules you follow to continue a line of standard COBOL. First, you code as much of the string as will fit in columns 12 through 72 of the first line. Then, on subsequent lines, the first non-blank character needs to be a quotation mark. (Whether you use a single quote or a double quote depends on the options you use for the DB2 precompiler.) Immediately after the quotation mark, continue with the string's characters. Then, when you reach the end of the string, code a closing quotation mark.

General rules	Start the SQL statement with EXEC SQL, and end it with END-EXEC.
	Code the lines of the SQL statement in columns 12 through 72.
	Use spacing and alignment that make the statement readable.
Special case rules	Individual lines of SQL statements may be continued. If you continue a string constant from one line to another, the first non-blank character in the continued line must be a quotation mark.
	Don't code an SQL statement in a COBOL COPY member.
	When one SQL statement immediately follows another, always code a period after the first's END-EXEC.

Figure 2-4   Rules for coding SQL statements in COBOL programs

Although you may need to use this continuation technique from time to time, you won't need it often. That's because when you work with long character strings in an application program, you're likely to store and process them not as literals, but through host variables. Long text strings you code explicitly are more common in the ad hoc DB2 environment than in application programs.

The next rule is that you can't code an SQL statement in a COBOL COPY member. When you prepare a program for execution, the DB2 precompiler translates each SQL statement into COBOL source code. However, since the precompiler doesn't recognize COBOL COPY statements, it can't process an SQL statement that is in a COPY member. Fortunately, this isn't a problem because you can use SQL's INCLUDE statement to direct the precompiler to combine source members with your program. The effect is the same as if you had been able to use COBOL's COPY statement. I'll show you how to use the INCLUDE statement later in this chapter.

The last rule in figure 2-4 has to do with whether you must code a period after an SQL statement's END-EXEC. The only time you have to is when one DB2 statement immediately follows another in your program. Then, the first one must end with a period. (If you're a CICS programmer, this will surprise you because CICS doesn't require a period in the same situation.)

Frankly, it's unlikely that this requirement will be a problem for you. The only time it can cause trouble is when the two adjacent SQL statements are part of an IF structure. Then, the period that ends the first statement also ends the IF. You can get around this by coding the SQL statements in separate paragraphs, and invoking those paragraphs from within the condition with PERFORM statements.

Coding SQL elements too closely together makes statements less readable

```
EXEC SQL
    SELECT CUSTNO,FNAME,LNAME,ADDR,CITY,STATE,ZIPCODE
    INTO :CUSTNO,:FNAME,:LNAME,:ADDR,:CITY,:STATE,:ZIPCODE
    FROM MMADBV.CUST WHERE CUSTNO = :CUSTNO
END-EXEC.
```

Coding SQL elements on too many lines makes statements less readable

```
EXEC SQL
    SELECT CUSTNO,
           FNAME,
           LNAME,
           ADDR,
           CITY,
           STATE,
           ZIPCODE
    INTO   :CUSTNO,
           :FNAME,
           :LNAME,
           :ADDR,
           :CITY,
           :STATE,
           :ZIPCODE
    FROM   MMADBV.CUST
    WHERE  CUSTNO - :CUSTNO
END-EXEC.
```

Thoughtful spacing and alignment of SQL elements makes statements more readable

```
EXEC SQL
    SELECT CUSTNO,         FNAME,         LNAME,
           ADDR,           CITY,          STATE,
           ZIPCODE
    INTO   :CUSTNO,        :FNAME,        :LNAME,
           :ADDR,          :CITY,         :STATE,
           :ZIPCODE
    FROM   MMADBV.CUST
    WHERE  CUSTNO = :CUSTNO
END-EXEC.
```

Figure 2-5   Different ways to code the SELECT statement from the CUSTINQ program

How to get and use definitions for DB2 data areas

As you can tell from the program in figure 2-3, it's easy to define the Data Division fields a program needs to work with DB2 data. My source code for CUSTINQ has only two SQL INCLUDE statements in the Data Division, and each is only three lines long. Here, I'll describe the data area definitions that result from these two INCLUDE statements. But first, I want to point out what you *don't* code for a DB2 table that you do for a standard file.

What you don't have to code when you work with a DB2 table

Much of the COBOL coding that you have to provide when you process a standard file isn't necessary when you process a DB2 table. The result is that the source code for a COBOL program that works with DB2 data may seem like it's missing some important elements.

To see what I mean, look back to the Environment Division and the Data Division's File Section in the CUSTINQ program in figure 2-3. When you work with a standard file in a COBOL program, you have to code two entries to identify each file. First, you have to code a COBOL SELECT statement in your program's Environment Division. This is not the same as a DB2 SELECT statement. The COBOL SELECT statement is a declaration that specifies an external name for a data set, while the DB2 SELECT is an action statement with a function similar to a COBOL READ statement.

In addition to coding a COBOL SELECT statement for a standard file, you have to code a file description (FD) entry and a record description in the File Section of the Data Division. The access method uses the record description to move data to and from your program.

A DB2 table does not need a COBOL SELECT or an FD statement. It's enough just to name the table you want to access when you code an SQL statement like SELECT. Then, DB2 keeps track of the tables your program needs and what their structures are. (Of course, if your program processes both standard files and DB2 tables, you must include the usual COBOL elements for the standard files.)

How to use DCLGEN output for table declarations and host variables

Although you don't code a record description in a program's File Section for a DB2 table, you do need to provide host variables in the Working-Storage Section that serve the same function. These host variables are the fields DB2 uses when it moves data between your program and a table.

If you know exactly how a table is structured, you can code host variable descriptions yourself from scratch. However, it's easier to let DB2 generate the host variable definitions through DCLGEN. In some shops, programmers do DCLGENs themselves, while in others, DBAs or systems designers do them. (I'll show you how to use DCLGEN in chapter 10.)

In either case, DCLGEN creates source code output that it stores as a member of a partitioned data set. Figure 2-6 shows the library member

```
*************************************************************************
* DCLGEN TABLE(MMADBV.CUST)                                             *
*        LIBRARY(MMA002.DCLGENS.COBOL(CUST))                            *
*        ACTION(REPLACE)                                                *
*        STRUCTURE(CUSTOMER-ROW)                                        *
*        APOST                                                          *
* ... IS THE DCLGEN COMMAND THAT MADE THE FOLLOWING STATEMENTS          *
*************************************************************************
      EXEC SQL DECLARE MMADBV.CUST TABLE
      ( CUSTNO                      CHAR(6) NOT NULL,
        FNAME                       CHAR(20) NOT NULL,
        LNAME                       CHAR(30) NOT NULL,
        ADDR                        CHAR(30) NOT NULL,
        CITY                        CHAR(20) NOT NULL,
        STATE                       CHAR(2) NOT NULL,
        ZIPCODE                     CHAR(10) NOT NULL
      ) END-EXEC.
*************************************************************************
* COBOL DECLARATION FOR TABLE MMADBV.CUST                               *
*************************************************************************
 01   CUSTOMER-ROW.
      10 CUSTNO             PIC X(6).
      10 FNAME              PIC X(20).
      10 LNAME              PIC X(30).
      10 ADDR               PIC X(30).
      10 CITY               PIC X(20).
      10 STATE              PIC X(2).
      10 ZIPCODE            PIC X(10).
*************************************************************************
* THE NUMBER OF COLUMNS DESCRIBED BY THIS DECLARATION IS 7              *
*************************************************************************
```

Figure 2-6   DCLGEN output for the customer table

DCLGEN created for the customer table shown in figure 2-2. As you can see in the comments at the start of this member, it describes the table named MMADBV.CUST, and it resides in a member named CUST in the library MMA002.DCLGENS.COBOL. The blocks of code I've shaded in figure 2-6 are the two main components DCLGEN creates. The first block is a table declaration, and the second is a set of COBOL field definitions for host variables.

DCLGEN's table declaration   The first shaded block in figure 2-6 is an SQL DECLARE TABLE statement. A DECLARE TABLE statement is a *table declaration* that names the table and each of its columns. This information (column names, data types, lengths, and characteristics) is similar to the information a DBA supplies to define a table.

It might surprise you to learn that you don't have to code a table declaration to use a table; it's optional. So, if you had to code a table declaration like the one in figure 2-6 yourself, you'd probably skip it. However, DCLGEN creates it for you automatically, and it's good documentation. You can refer to the DECLARE TABLE statement if you need to check the exact name of a column. And because DCLGEN extracts the information for the table declaration right out of the DB2 catalog, you can be sure it's right.

A DECLARE TABLE statement does more than provide reference documentation for you. When it's present, the DB2 precompiler uses it to verify your other SQL statements. As a result, the precompiler may catch some errors that otherwise might slip through.

DCLGEN's host variable definitions   The second shaded block of code in figure 2-6 contains what you really want in the DCLGEN output: the COBOL definitions of the host variables you can use for a table. It should be easy for you to see the relationship between these host variables and the column descriptions in the table declaration. For example, the customer number column

```
    CUSTNO                              CHAR(6) NOT NULL
```

corresponds to the host variable

```
    10   CUSTNO              PIC X(6).
```

Note that DCLGEN used the column's name from the DB2 catalog for the host variable name. It also derives the COBOL PICTURE clause for the host variable from the column's length and data type.

In the host variable definitions in figure 2-6, all of the fields contain character data. That's because each corresponding table column also contains character (CHAR) data. However, DB2 supports ten other data types. I've listed them in figure 2-7 in two groups: basic data types and advanced data types. The seven basic data types are easy to understand, and you'll use them often.

Three of the seven basic data types are for numeric data: SMALLINT, INTEGER, and DECIMAL. The first two specify columns that contain binary numeric data. COBOL host variables for SMALLINT and INTEGER columns specify COMP usage, but have pictures that allow different size values (PIC S9(4) for SMALLINT and PIC S9(9) for INTEGER). The DECIMAL data type specifies packed-decimal data. A host variable for a column with this type has COMP-3 usage and a picture clause with an implied decimal point.

The last three basic data types in figure 2-7 are DATE, TIME, and TIMESTAMP. Host variables for these types are defined as alphanumeric strings. However, those strings have a meaningful internal structure that isn't reflected in the host variables DCLGEN produces. For example, as you

Basic data types	Typical COBOL definition	
CHAR Character (EBCDIC) data	10 CITY	PIC X(20).
SMALLINT Halfword integer data	10 SMALL-COUNT-FIELD	PIC S9(4) COMP.
INTEGER Fullword integer data	10 LARGE-COUNT-FIELD	PIC S9(9) COMP.
DECIMAL Packed-decimal data	10 INVOICE-TOTAL	PIC S9(7)V99 COMP-3.

DATE
    Date data
    (yyyy-mm-dd)
	10 INVOICE-DATE	PIC X(10).

TIME
    Time data
    (hh.mm.ss)
	10 INVOICE-TIME	PIC X(8).

TIMESTAMP
    Date and time data, with microseconds
    (yyyy-mm-dd-hh.mm.ss.mmmmmm)
	10 INVOICE-TIMESTAMP	PIC X(26).

Advanced data types	For more information see
VARCHAR Variable-length character (EBCDIC) data	Chapter 9
GRAPHIC Double-byte character set (DBCS) data	Appendix C
VARGRAPHIC Variable-length DBCS data	Appendix C
FLOAT Floating point data	Appendix C

Figure 2-7   DB2 data types

can see in the figure, the character string for the DATE data type is ten bytes long; bytes 1-4 contain the year, bytes 6-7 contain the month, and bytes 9-10 contain the day. The values for TIME and TIMESTAMP have similar structures. DB2 provides a rich set of features for processing data with these types. I'll cover them in *Part 2: An Advanced Course*.

The four data types I classified as advanced in figure 2-7 are for specialized applications or require particular programming techniques. So, I'm not going to describe them in this chapter. If you need to use any of these data types, you can refer to the text section the figure lists.

You can depend on DCLGEN to produce correct field definitions for host variables, but you're responsible for defining any Working-Storage work fields correctly. Just be sure that the work fields have sizes and usages that agree with their related host variable fields. Otherwise, you might find data truncations or conversions you don't expect or want.

Notice in figure 2-6 that the fields are level-10 items, all subordinate to a level-01 item called CUSTOMER-ROW. The higher level item, CUSTOMER-ROW, is a *host structure*. A host structure is a named set of elementary items. (I entered the name CUSTOMER-ROW when I performed the DCLGEN procedure; I could have used any valid COBOL name.)

Although standard COBOL lets you create complex data structures with many levels, DB2 lets you use only host structures with two levels, like this one. That makes sense, because a characteristic of relational tables is that they're two-dimensional, with no structures nested inside other structures. (The only exception to this two-level structure limit is for variable-length columns, and it's not a violation of the principle. You'll learn more about variable-length columns in chapter 9.)

Also, DB2 doesn't support groups of repeating items. So you're not going to find host variable definitions that use the COBOL OCCURS clause in DCLGEN output. Applications that require repeating data structures are implemented instead with separate, but related, tables. Although you can get around this restriction by "tricking" DB2 and redefining a row in your program with an OCCURS structure you code yourself, it defeats the design intention of DB2.

Including DCLGEN output in your program   DCLGEN output like that in figure 2-6 has to be combined with your source code. The simplest way to do that is to direct the precompiler to do it for you. All you have to do is code an SQL INCLUDE statement in your program's Data Division where you want the declaration to be inserted. The statement

```
EXEC SQL
    INCLUDE CUST
END-EXEC.
```

The SQL INCLUDE statement

```
EXEC SQL
      INCLUDE  {member-name}
END-EXEC.        {SQLCA      }
```

Explanation

member-name   The name of a library member to be inserted in your source code. May appear in the Data Division or the Procedure Division.

SQLCA   Specifies that the SQL communication area definition should be inserted in your source code. May appear only in the Working-Storage Section of the Data Division.

Figure 2-8   The SQL INCLUDE statement

directs the precompiler to retrieve the member CUST and insert it in place of the SQL statement.

Figure 2-8 presents the syntax of the INCLUDE statement. If you did the DCLGEN yourself, you know the name of the member to specify on the INCLUDE statement because you created it. If you didn't, be sure to get the name from your DBA or systems analyst.

In effect, SQL's INCLUDE statement does the same thing as a COBOL COPY statement. You might be tempted to use COPY instead, but since the precompiler doesn't recognize the COPY statement, you must use the SQL INCLUDE statement.

How to define and use the SQL communication area fields in your program

Each time a program executes an SQL statement, DB2 passes information about its success back to the program. It does that through a set of fields called the *SQL communication area* (*SQLCA*). You must define the SQLCA's fields in each DB2 COBOL program.

As you can see in figure 2-8, an option of the INCLUDE statement is SQLCA. To have the precompiler include the communication area fields in your program, just code

```
EXEC SQL
      INCLUDE SQLCA
END-EXEC.
```

When you use the INCLUDE statement for this purpose, it must be in your program's Working-Storage Section. Then, DB2 replaces these lines with the field definitions in figure 2-9.

Although you don't need to worry about most of the fields in the SQLCA, you will need to check one of them, SQLCODE, after almost every SQL statement. *SQLCODE* is DB2's return code field. DB2 can put any one of many of different numeric values into SQLCODE to report the success or failure of a statement. IBM's manual *Database 2 Messages and Codes* documents all of those values, and you'll probably need to refer to it from time to time. For your convenience, I've listed a subset of error code values you may encounter during normal program development in appendix B.

If you had to check for every possible value of SQLCODE individually, error processing would be overwhelming. Fortunately, you can simplify what you need to check when you examine SQLCODE. As figure 2-10 shows, if the value of SQLCODE is zero, your statement executed normally. If, on the other hand, the value of SQLCODE is positive, your statement executed successfully, but some exceptional condition occurred. You'll often check for one particular positive code, +100. It means a row couldn't be found or, as you'll learn in the next chapter, that you reached the end of a cursor-controlled results table.

If SQLCODE's value is negative, one of many possible errors occurred, but its implication is simply that the statement failed. What your program should do when a statement fails depends on the application. In some cases, it might be reasonable to ignore the error and continue processing. In other cases, you may be able to continue processing, but in a different way. And in still others, you may need to reverse work the program has already done and end the program immediately.

In this book, you'll see examples of return code checking for specific SQL statements and techniques for handling various error conditions. And, where it's appropriate, I'll mention cases where you may need to check the contents of SQLCA fields other than SQLCODE.

A closer look at the logic of the CUSTINQ program

Now that you've seen how to provide the Data Division elements you need in a DB2 program, I'd like to discuss the Procedure Division of the CUSTINQ program. The program isn't hard to understand, but it's even easier to follow if you use the program's structure chart in figure 2-11 as a guide.

The top-level module, 000-DISPLAY-CUSTOMER-ROWS, represents the operation of the entire program. The program responds to a customer

```
01 SQLCA.
   05 SQLCAID      PIC X(8).
   05 SQLCABC      PIC S9(9) COMP-4.
   05 SQLCODE      PIC S9(9) COMP-4.
   05 SQLERRM.
      49 SQLERRML PIC S9(4) COMP-4.
      49 SQLERRMC PIC X(70).
   05 SQLERRP      PIC X(8).
   05 SQLERRD      OCCURS 6 TIMES
                   PIC S9(9) COMP-4.
   05 SQLWARN.
      10 SQLWARN0 PIC X.
      10 SQLWARN1 PIC X.
      10 SQLWARN2 PIC X.
      10 SQLWARN3 PIC X.
      10 SQLWARN4 PIC X.
      10 SQLWARN5 PIC X.
      10 SQLWARN6 PIC X.
      10 SQLWARN7 PIC X.
   05 SQLEXT       PIC X(8).
```

Figure 2-9   The SQL communication area (SQLCA) fields

SQLCODE value	Meaning
Zero	Statement successful
Positive	Statement successful, but with some exceptional condition
+100	Row not found or end of data
Negative	Serious error detected

Figure 2-10   SQLCODE values you should know

inquiry by displaying data from a row in the customer table. The program does this until there aren't any more inquiries, then it ends. If this program required COBOL OPEN and CLOSE statements, you'd expect to find them in module 000. However, just as you don't need to code COBOL SELECTs and FDs for DB2 tables, you don't need to code COBOL OPEN and CLOSE statements for them.

Module 100 is the program's main processing module. Each time it runs, it performs 110-ACCEPT-CUSTOMER-NUMBER to prompt the user to key in the next customer number. If the user keys in 999999 to end the

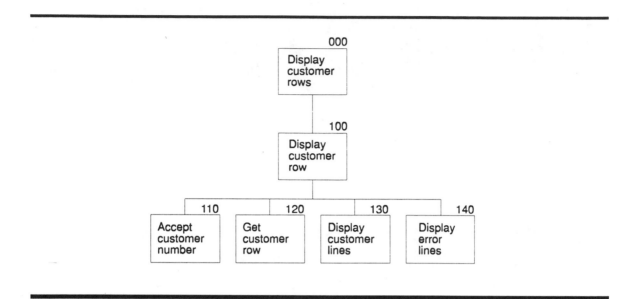

Figure 2-11   Structure chart for the CUSTINQ program

program, module 110 sets the value of a switch, END-OF-INQUIRIES-SW, to Y. If that happens, module 100 doesn't do anything else, and module 000 doesn't invoke 100 again. The program ends.

If the user enters any value other than 999999 in response to module 110's prompt, module 100 proceeds. It invokes 120-GET-CUSTOMER-ROW to retrieve the desired row from the customer table. As you'll see in a moment, module 120 uses an SQL SELECT statement. If the SELECT statement in module 120 is successful, module 100 performs 130-DISPLAY-CUSTOMER-LINES to show the user the data from that row. If module 120 isn't able to find the desired row, module 100 performs 140-DISPLAY-ERROR-LINES. Modules 130 and 140 use COBOL DISPLAY statements to produce the output you saw in figure 2-1.

I want you to look closely at module 120 in CUSTINQ's source code. I've printed it again in figure 2-12. As you can see, this module has two parts. The first is the SELECT statement. The second is a simple error-checking condition that evaluates the SQLCODE field. This module's organization is similar to what you'd expect in a module that uses a standard COBOL READ statement to retrieve a record from a VSAM data set.

Even though the SELECT statement in this program contains several lines of code, I'm sure you'll find it easy to understand. The SELECT has

```
*
 120-GET-CUSTOMER-ROW.
*
     EXEC SQL
         SELECT CUSTNO,          FNAME,          LNAME,
                ADDR,            CITY,           STATE,
                ZIPCODE
         INTO   :CUSTNO,         :FNAME,         :LNAME,
                :ADDR,           :CITY,          :STATE,
                :ZIPCODE
         FROM   MMADBV.CUST
         WHERE  CUSTNO = :CUSTNO
     END-EXEC.
*
     IF SQLCODE NOT = 0
         MOVE "N" TO CUSTOMER-FOUND-SW.
*
```

Figure 2-12   Module 120 from the CUSTINQ program

four clauses. The first, called the SELECT clause, consists of these three lines:

```
SELECT CUSTNO,          FNAME,          LNAME,
       ADDR,            CITY,           STATE,
       ZIPCODE
```

This clause tells SQL to create a results table that contains the seven columns from the table it accesses. (Remember, these column names appear in the table declaration component of the DCLGEN output you saw in figure 2-6.)

The second clause in the SELECT statement,

```
INTO   :CUSTNO,         :FNAME,         :LNAME,
       :ADDR,           :CITY,          :STATE,
       :ZIPCODE
```

names the COBOL host variables where SQL will return the values it retrieves from the table. Notice that a colon precedes the name of each host variable in the INTO clause. When SQL encounters a name that's preceded with a colon, it interprets it as the name of a host variable.

As you can see, the columns in the SELECT clause and the host variables in the INTO clause have a one-to-one correspondence. DB2 moves the value for the first column in the SELECT clause into the first host variable in the INTO clause, the second into the second host variable, and so on. Although the names of these COBOL host variables and their corresponding columns are the same in this example, that doesn't have to be the case. You can use host variables that have any valid COBOL names in an SQL statement. But, to avoid confusion, it's best to use identical names. And if you use DCLGEN to create your host data structure, the names will be identical.

The third clause in this SELECT statement,

```
FROM   MMADBV.CUST
```

tells DB2 to take this information from the table named MMADBV.CUST. And the last clause,

```
WHERE CUSTNO = :CUSTNO
```

is the selection criterion for this statement. It directs DB2 to extract data from rows where the value of the CUSTNO column is the same as the current value of the COBOL host variable CUSTNO. (Notice that the host variable name is preceded by a colon.)

After the program does the SELECT, it executes the second block of code in module 120 to evaluate the results of the statement. The last two lines in module 120,

```
IF SQLCODE NOT = 0
    MOVE "N" TO CUSTOMER-FOUND-SW.
```

handle any exceptional condition that might occur related to the SELECT statement. This program isn't too particular about how it handles an unsuccessful SELECT. If anything unusual happens, the program simply sets the value of CUSTOMER-FOUND-SW to N. Then, module 100 displays an error message by performing 140-DISPLAY-ERROR-LINES.

If a program like this issues a SELECT statement that produces a results table with more than one row, the statement fails. DB2 doesn't return any data from the table to your program, and it reports the failure by setting the value of the SQLCODE field to -811.

If the SELECT is successful, module 100 invokes module 130 to format and present the data it retrieved. Module 130 displays the data in each host variable with a label that identifies it. Notice in module 130 that I didn't code colons before the host variable names. Colons are necessary only in SQL statements. You don't code them in standard COBOL statements.

Discussion

Now that you've finished this chapter, you have the background you need to develop a simple DB2 program. Specifically, you should be able to code the DB2 elements a COBOL program needs to retrieve a single row from a table. That's the case whether the application is interactive, like the example you've just seen, or batch.

It may seem surprising to you that an interactive COBOL program that extracts data from a DB2 table can be as short as the one in figure 2-3. However, you need to remember that the DB2 precompiler adds a substantial amount of code to your original program. Not only does it include any DCLGEN members you request and the SQLCA fields, but it also adds a number of other fields it needs. Moreover, it replaces action SQL statements like SELECT with COBOL that uses those fields.

Terms

embedded SQL
table declaration
host structure
SQL communication area
SQLCA
SQLCODE

Objectives

1. Code SQL statements so they follow all the necessary syntax rules.

2. Code SQL statements so they're readable.

3. List the COBOL elements you must use to work with standard files that you don't use to work with a DB2 table.

4. Describe the two main blocks of code in DCLGEN output.

5. Explain why DB2 host structures in COBOL programs can be no more than two levels deep.

6. Given the name of the library member that contains the DCLGEN output for a table a program needs to use, include that member in your program.

7. Explain why you can't use the COBOL COPY statement to include DCLGEN output in a DB2 COBOL program.

8. List and explain the meanings of the values you need to keep in mind when you evaluate the SQLCODE field after your program executes an SQL statement.

9. Given application and table specifications, code a simple SQL SELECT statement to retrieve a row from the table.

10. Given the specifications for a simple inquiry program that will retrieve a single row from a DB2 table, design and code the program.

Chapter 3

How to retrieve DB2 data

In the last chapter, you saw an example of SELECT, the DB2 statement that lets you retrieve data from a table. With just what you learned in chapter 2, you can code SELECT statements that meet many application programming needs. The limitation is that your SELECT statements can produce results tables that contain no more than one row.

Restricting your DB2 skills to applications that use single-row results tables is too limiting. In fact, much of the value of DB2 is that it can easily generate multi-row results tables that meet complicated application requirements. To be able to take advantage of this strength of DB2, you need to know how to do two things.

First, you need to know how to code more sophisticated SELECT statements. So in the first topic in this chapter, I'll show you more details of the syntax of the SELECT statement. Many of the features you'll learn in topic 1 are likely to produce multi-row tables, or are appropriate for use only with multi-row results tables.

Second, after you've learned how to code SELECT statements that may create multi-row results tables, you need to know how to use DB2's cursor feature so you can process multi-row results tables in your programs. Cursors bridge the gap between the set-at-a-time approach DB2 takes to data processing and the record-at-a-time approach you have to take in COBOL. I'll show you how to use cursors in topic 2.

Although you'll learn how to use a number of new features in this chapter, it doesn't present all of SELECT's capabilities. In later chapters, you'll learn about other SELECT features, such as column functions, joins, unions, and subqueries. However, those chapters assume that you've learned the information this chapter presents. So be prepared to spend as much time as it takes to master the material in this chapter.

Topic 1   The basic form of the SELECT statement

In the program example in chapter 2, you saw a SELECT statement that retrieved data from one table row. That statement illustrated the basic clauses of SELECT, and it's a good model for the kinds of SELECT statements you'll need to code in many programs.

This topic extends what you know about the SELECT statement's four basic clauses. Many of the features of SELECT this topic presents work in the kinds of stand-alone SELECT statements you can code directly in the Procedure Division of your programs. (I call those kinds of statements *embedded SELECT statements*.) Always remember that stand-alone, or "embedded," SELECT statements must generate single-row results tables. However, some of the features you'll learn in this topic tend to yield multi-row results tables. To use a SELECT statement that generates a multi-row results table in an application program, you must use DB2's cursor feature. I'll describe it in the next topic.

Figure 3-1 presents the syntax elements of SELECT that I'll cover in this topic. I'll describe in detail the SELECT statement's SELECT, FROM, INTO, and WHERE clauses. For the examples I'll present, I've used the same CUST table you saw in chapters 1 and 2. Because I'll refer to this table throughout this chapter, you may want to refer to it from time to time. For your convenience, figure 3-2 presents the host structure from the DCLGEN output for this table.

The SELECT clause of the SELECT statement

If you refer to the syntax of the embedded SELECT statement in figure 3-1, you'll see that the SELECT clause consists of one or more *column specifications*. Each column specification indicates what DB2 should store in the corresponding column of the results table it creates. The first column specification in the SELECT clause is for the first column in the results table, the second column specification is for the second column, and so on.

DB2 provides four ways to code a column specification. Figure 3-3 lists each and points you to the part of this book that covers each option. Here, I'll introduce each of the four ways and present examples that illustrate them.

Specifying base table columns for results table columns   By far the most common way to code a column specification is to name a column in a

---

The SQL embedded SELECT statement

```
EXEC SQL
        SELECT          column-specification[,column-specification...]
                INTO  {:host-var[,:host-var...]}
                      {:host-structure          }
                FROM    table-name[ synonym][,table-name[ synonym] ...]
                [WHERE  selection-condition]
    END-EXEC.
```

Explanation

column-specification	A description of what the SELECT statement should put in the corresponding column of the results table. Most often this is simply the name of a column you want DB2 to retrieve from the base table. However, DB2 provides a range of options. See figure 3-3 for details. You may code no more than 300 column-specifications.
host-var	The COBOL name of the host variable into which DB2 will place the data for the corresponding column-specification in the SELECT clause. You must precede each COBOL host variable name with a colon.
host-structure	The COBOL name of the group item into which DB2 will place the data it retrieves from the table.
table-name	The DB2 name of the table or view from which you want to retrieve data.
synonym	An alternate table name, also called a correlation name. Synonyms are described in chapter 7.
selection-condition	Specifies a test that SQL will apply to each row in the base table to determine whether to include it in the results table. A simple selection condition has the format

```
expression-1 operator expression-2
```

where the value of *expression-1*, usually a column-name, is compared using *operator* to the value of *expression-2*, usually a host variable or a literal.

Figure 3-1   The SQL embedded SELECT statement

base table that you want DB2 to include in your results table. For example, the SELECT statement in figure 3-4 will create a results table with contents drawn from the seven columns in the CUST table: CUSTNO, FNAME, LNAME, ADDR, CITY, STATE, and ZIPCODE.

You don't have to retrieve all the columns that make up a base table. This is a big difference between how DB2 and standard file processing work. When a program reads a record from a standard file, it gets all the record's fields. In contrast, when a program gets data from a DB2 table, it gets only the columns it requests in the SELECT statement.

```
01    CUSTOMER-ROW.
      10   CUSTNO                 PIC  X(6).
      10   FNAME                  PIC  X(20).
      10   LNAME                  PIC  X(30).
      10   ADDR                   PIC  X(30).
      10   CITY                   PIC  X(20).
      10   STATE                  PIC  X(2).
      10   ZIPCODE                PIC  X(10).
```

Figure 3-2   The host structure from the DCLGEN output for the customer table

Not only does DB2 let you retrieve a subset of the columns that make up a table, but it also lets you change their order. To do that, you just code the column names in the sequence you want DB2 to return them to your program. Their order in the base table doesn't matter. (From the point of view of an application programmer, this is a limited benefit; it's more significant in ad hoc processing.)

Yet another difference between DB2 and standard file processing is that a single SELECT statement can retrieve and combine data from two or more base tables. This is a called a *join* operation. I'll show you what you need to know to code SELECT statements that do joins in chapter 7. For now, though, I just want you to realize that a SELECT statement's column specifications can name columns from more than one base table.

The first group of options in figure 3-3 shows four ways you can specify columns from base tables for a results table. The first option, an *unqualified column name*, is the one I used for all seven column specifications in the statement in figure 3-4. *Unqualified* simply means that you don't explicitly name the table that contains the column you want. In this example, I didn't have to because all the columns came from the same base table. As a result, there was no chance for ambiguity.

If you want to retrieve all of the columns from a base table in the order they're defined to DB2, you can use a shortcut. Instead of naming each column individually, you can just code an asterisk, as the second option in figure 3-3 shows. For the sample SELECT I showed you in figure 3-4, I could have used this technique to simplify the statement. Unfortunately, using SELECT * has its drawbacks. I'll describe these drawbacks when I tell you about the INTO clause.

When you want to extract data from more than one table with a single SELECT statement, it's possible that the same column name may be used in two or more tables. If that's the case, you have to resolve the ambiguity that an unqualified name presents. You do that by prefixing it with a qualifier. The *qualifier* in a *qualified column name* can be the name of a base table or a synonym you create. You can use the qualifier either with a specific

Results table column data source

	Option	Syntax	Covered in
Base table column value	Unqualified column name	`column-name`	This topic
	All columns	`*`	This topic
	Qualified column name	${table-name \brace synonym}$`.column-name`	Chapter 7
	All columns from a qualified source	${table-name \brace synonym}$`.*`	Chapter 7
Program-supplied value	Host variable name	`:host-var`	This topic
	Constant value	`literal`	This topic
DB2 user id	Authorization id of user	`USER`	This topic
Computed value	Result of a calculation	`expression`	This topic
	Result of a function	`function`	Chapter 6

Figure 3-3   Column specification options for the SQL SELECT statement

column name or an asterisk, as the third and fourth options in figure 3-3 show. I'll illustrate qualification and synonyms in chapter 7 when I cover joins.

Specifying program-supplied values for results table columns   The next group of options in figure 3-3 shows you how to supply values from your program for DB2 to include in a results table. As you can see, SELECT statements can specify both variable and literal data.

Figure 3-5 shows two SELECT clauses that both produce a results table that contains a customer's name. In addition, the results table includes the customer's state. The clauses differ because the first retrieves the state for a customer from the CUST table, while the second draws it from the host variable in the application program. If you ever need to generate a results table like this, it is slightly more efficient to use the second technique because

```
EXEC SQL
    SELECT     CUSTNO,           FNAME,           LNAME,
               ADDR,             CITY,            STATE,
               ZIPCODE
        INTO   :CUSTNO,          :FNAME,          :LNAME,
               :ADDR,            :CITY,           :STATE,
               :ZIPCODE
        FROM   MMADBV.CUST
        WHERE  CUSTNO = :CUSTNO
END-EXEC.
```

Figure 3-4   A typical embedded SELECT statement

A SELECT clause that uses three column names

```
SELECT FNAME,LNAME,STATE
```

A SELECT clause that uses two column names and one host variable

```
SELECT FNAME,LNAME,:STATE
```

Figure 3-5   How you can use a host variable in the SELECT clause

each column of data DB2 retrieves from a table imposes additional overhead.

Frankly, the use of host variables and literals in simple SELECT clauses such as the ones in figure 3-5 may not seem particularly useful. You're more likely to use these techniques in more complex SELECT statements.

From time to time, you may want to add a literal value to a results table in an application program. Figure 3-6 shows a SELECT statement that retrieves the names of all the customers who live in California and includes a literal value in the third column of each row of the results table. Admittedly, this technique is of limited value in application programs. However, you may be able to apply it when you use DB2's union feature. I'll describe unions in chapter 7.

```
SELECT FNAME,LNAME, 'IS A CALIFORNIA RESIDENT'
```

Figure 3-6   How you can use a literal in the SELECT clause

In the example in figure 3-6, the literal is a text string. As a result, I coded it between quotation marks. If you want to use a numeric value as a column specification, you must code the number without quotation marks.

Specifying DB2 user-ids for results table columns   A third way to specify a value for a column in a results table is to direct DB2 to extract the id of the current user from its catalog and add it to the results table. If you need to use this technique, code the keyword

    USER

as one of the column specs on the SELECT clause. Although this option works, it's unlikely that you'll have many uses for it.

Specifying calculated values for results table columns   You can also direct DB2 to do some basic manipulations of the data it returns in a results table. For example, you can code an arithmetic expression as a column specification. An expression can include a combination of host variables, column values, and literals connected to each other with operators. DB2 uses the current values of these variables and columns to evaluate the expression for each row it includes in the results table. It stores the result in the corresponding column of the results table.

All of the items you use in an arithmetic expression must be numeric. As a result, you can't use columns with character type data, host variables with non-numeric pictures, or alphanumeric literals. You code an arithmetic expression much as you would an algebraic equation. You use the operators +, -, *, and / to specify addition, subtraction, multiplication, and division. You can precede an operand with a minus sign to indicate that the inverse of its value should be used in the calculation. (You can also precede an operand with a plus sign, but it's not necessary)

You can use parentheses to control the sequence DB2 uses as it evaluates the expression and to improve readability. Unless you specify otherwise with parentheses, DB2 performs multiplication and division before addition and subtraction, and it performs operations at the same level as it works from left to right through an expression.

To understand how to code an arithmetic expression, think back to the INV table I introduced in chapter 1. It has four numeric columns that contain financial information: INVSUBT, INVSHIP, INVTAX, and INVTOTAL. The value stored in the total column is the sum of the values in the other three (that is, the invoice subtotal, shipping charges, and sales tax). In many situations, a table like this wouldn't contain a column like INVTOTAL because it's redundant. You can easily derive the total like this:

```
SELECT INVNO
       INVSUBT + INVSHIP + INVTAX
```

Here, DB2 will add the subtotal, shipping, and sales tax values and will return the sum in a single column in the results table.

You're more restricted with what you can do with character data in an expression. The only operator you can use with character data, ||, lets you combine, or *concatenate* two items. For example, the SELECT clause

```
SELECT FNAME || ' ' || LNAME,
       ADDR,
       CITY || ' ' || STATE || ' ' || ZIPCODE
```

combines columns from the CUST table into a results table formatted for printing mailing labels. The first column of the results table contains the value from the FNAME column followed by one space, then by the value from the LNAME column. The second column of the results table contains only the value from the ADDR column. Finally, the third column of the results table contains the values from the CITY, STATE, and ZIPCODE columns separated by single spaces.

When you concatenate two or more base table columns, the length of the column in the results table is the sum of the lengths of the elements that make it up. For example, the length of the third column in the example I just showed you would be 34 characters: 20 for CITY, 2 for STATE, 10 for ZIPCODE, and 1 for each separator space.

Also, instead of coding an expression that produces a calculated value, you can use one of DB2's built-in functions to perform an operation like totaling or averaging a column's contents. You'll learn how to use these features in chapter 6.

The INTO clause of the SELECT statement

The second clause of the SELECT statement, INTO, names the COBOL host variables where DB2 will place results table data. These host variables correspond directly to the columns you list on the SELECT clause. In other words, DB2 moves the value in the first results table column in the SELECT clause into the first host variable in the INTO clause, the value from the second column into the second host variable, and so on.

In figure 3-4, I used the same alignment pattern for the host variables I coded on the INTO clause as I did for the column specifications on the SELECT clause. As a result, it's easy to see how they correspond.

You need to be sure that your host variables and their corresponding results table columns have matching data types. Also, the host variables you use need to be long enough to contain the information DB2 tries to store in them. If fields are the wrong size, truncation errors can occur. Or worse, a DB2 assignment error might occur, and the SELECT statement won't retrieve all the data you expect. Naturally, if you use DCLGEN host variable definitions and you match the right host variables with the SELECT clause column specifications you code, this won't be a difficulty.

If you want to retrieve data from each column in a table when you use the embedded SELECT statement, DB2 provides a short cut for both the SELECT and INTO clauses. As I mentioned a moment ago, you can code an asterisk in place of a list of column names on the SELECT clause. Then, for the INTO clause, you can code the name of a host structure rather than a series of host variable names. For example, the SELECT statement in figure 3-7 achieves the same result as the more complex SELECT statement in figure 3-4. The data name CUSTOMER-ROW on the INTO clause is a host structure whose elementary items are the host variables for all the columns of the CUST table.

Although this form of the SELECT statement works, if your DBA changes the structure of a table you refer to with SELECT *, the statement may return values to your program that don't have matching host variables. So, although coding SELECT * may save you some time, I suggest you avoid it. Instead, code the column names explicitly on the INTO clause. Your program will be easier to read and less error-prone.

The FROM clause of the SELECT statement

The third clause of the SELECT statement, FROM, identifies the table that contains the columns you want to retrieve. The typical table name has two parts, separated by a period. The first part is an identifier for the person who created the table. The second part describes the contents of the table. In the example in figure 3-7, the table name is MMADBV.CUST. MMADBV is my identifier, and CUST describes the contents of the table.

Instead of specifying a table name on the FROM clause, you can specify a view name. A *view* is an alternative representation of DB2 table data. A

```
EXEC SQL
    SELECT     *
        INTO   CUSTOMER-ROW
        FROM   MMADBV.CUST
        WHERE  CUSTNO = :CUSTNO
END-EXEC.
```

Figure 3-7   A SELECT statement that names a host structure in the INTO clause

table and a view are different entities as far as the DBA is concerned. However, as a programmer, you can usually think of them as the same thing.

For either a table or a view, you can specify an alternate name, or *synonym*, for the table name that you can use elsewhere in the SELECT statement instead. The DB2 literature also uses the technical term *correlation name* for this alternate name. You're likely to use a synonym for a table or view only when you have to create qualified names, so I'll wait until I present advanced DB2 features in section 3 to say more about it.

The WHERE clause of the SELECT statement

The last clause you code on the embedded SELECT statement is WHERE. You use it to specify a *selection condition* that identifies what rows DB2 should retrieve. For example,

```
WHERE CUSTNO = :CUSTNO
```

specifies that DB2 should select a row for the results table if the value in its CUSTNO column is the same as the value of the host variable CUSTNO. Of course, before the COBOL program issues this SELECT statement, it must move the appropriate customer number to the host variable CUSTNO.

In this case, the CUST table's design insures that no two rows have the same value in the CUSTNO column. Therefore, a SELECT that uses this selection condition will never return more than one row.

Using the WHERE clause is like specifying a key when you read a record from a standard file like a VSAM data set. However, DB2 lets you use any column in a WHERE clause. In contrast, standard file processing lets you use only fields that are primary or alternate keys.

Actually, DB2 *does* use keys in some circumstances, but their purpose is to improve performance or to insure that relationships between rows in different tables are maintained. Moreover, they're behind the scenes, so as a programmer, you often don't even need to know they exist. You can generate a results table based on any column's contents, whether the DBA

defined it as a key or not. (However, when you develop programs that
change the data in a table, keys that relate rows to one another can affect
how your SQL statements operate. I'll describe how in chapter 4.)

As the brackets around the WHERE clause in figure 3-1 suggest, it's
optional. But if you omit the WHERE clause, you'll retrieve every row in
the table. That's almost sure to be unacceptable in an embedded SELECT
statement.

The selection condition in the basic form of the WHERE clause figure
3-1 presents has three parts, two expressions and a comparison operator,
like this:

```
WHERE expression-1 operator expression-2
```

Usually, the first expression is a column name, and the second is either a
host variable or a literal value. The operator (such as =) specifies the relation that needs to exist between the two expressions for the condition to be
met and for DB2 to include the corresponding base table information in the
results table.

When you code a selection condition, you need to be sure that you compare like items. You can compare character data to character data and
numeric data to numeric data. However, you can't compare character data
to numeric data, even if the character data contains nothing other than
numbers. Columns that contain date and time data can be compared only to
other columns of the same kind or to properly formatted character strings.
(You can refer to figure 2-7 to see the correct formats of date and time character strings.)

If you're sure you won't create a results table with more than one row,
you can use other operators in a stand-alone SELECT. Figure 3-8 lists
them. The *greater than* and *less than* operators (> and <) are straightforward. The two-character combinations may seem confusing because they
give you two options for coding each condition. One option uses the logical
not character (¬), and the other doesn't. The operators for *not equal to* and
less than or greater than (¬= and <>) mean the same thing. Similarly, less
than or equal to and not greater than (<= and ¬>) are equivalent. So are
greater than or equal to and not less than (>= and ¬<).

When you code a SELECT statement, you can specify a constant value
instead of a variable name in the selection condition of the WHERE clause.
For example,

```
EXEC SQL
    SELECT     FNAME,   LNAME
         INTO :FNAME,   :LNAME
         FROM  MMADBV.CUST
         WHERE CUSTNO = '445354'
END-EXEC.
```

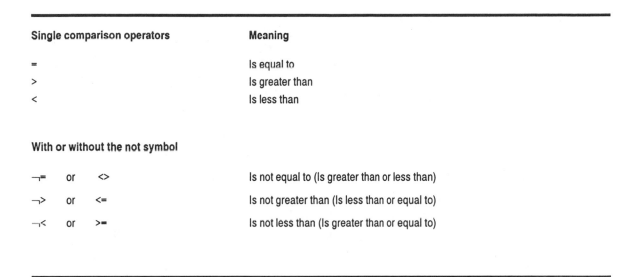

Single comparison operators	Meaning
=	Is equal to
>	Is greater than
<	Is less than

With or without the not symbol

			Meaning
¬=	or	<>	Is not equal to (Is greater than or less than)
¬>	or	<=	Is not greater than (Is less than or equal to)
¬<	or	>=	Is not less than (Is greater than or equal to)

Figure 3-8   Comparison operators you can use in the WHERE clause of the SQL SELECT statement

is a perfectly acceptable SQL statement. Although you can code an embedded SELECT statement with a literal condition, it's something that you're more likely to do if you're working with SQL to do ad hoc inquiries. In an application program, you're almost certain to use a host variable, so your program can change the value of the variable. Otherwise, your SELECT statement will retrieve the same row each time it is executed.

Although you're unlikely to code a SELECT statement with a literal in the WHERE clause in an application program, I do want you to notice something about this literal. You must enclose a literal in the WHERE clause in quotation marks if it's character data, and you must *not* if it's numeric data. Here, the customer number 445354 is called a number and looks like a number, but the column that contains it has the CHAR data type. Therefore, I coded the literal value 445354 between quotation marks.

Also, I'd like you to notice in this example that the column I used in the WHERE clause isn't one I listed for retrieval in the SELECT clause. DB2 lets you specify a selection criterion that's based on data you don't retrieve.

You may be interested to know that the WHERE clause provides many other options for coding selection criteria. For example, you can create compound conditions that link multiple selection conditions and control the sequence DB2 uses to evaluate multiple selection conditions. I'll cover these and other advanced features of the WHERE clause in chapter 5.

Discussion

Now that you know the syntax of the embedded SELECT statement, you can use it to simulate standard file processing. However, if you limit yourself to the SELECT features I've presented in this topic, you're ignoring one of the chief advantages DB2 has over standard file processing: its ability to retrieve multiple rows in one operation. I'll show you how to do that in the next topic.

Terms

embedded SELECT statement
column specification
join
unqualified column name
qualifier
qualified column name
concatenate
view
synonym
correlation name
selection condition

Objectives

1. Given application and table specifications, code an SQL SELECT statement to generate an appropriate results table.

2. Explain why you're most likely to use WHERE clauses that specify equality conditions on key fields when you code stand-alone SELECT statements.

3. Explain why it's wise to avoid SELECT *.

In the last topic, you learned how to code SELECT statements that can produce multi-row results tables. It's easy to do this. However, it's not so easy to process these tables in a COBOL program. That's because the set-at-a-time approach DB2 takes to data processing is incompatible with the record-at-a-time approach you have to take in COBOL.

To be able to process a results table that contains more than one row in a COBOL program, you have to learn to use another technique: cursors. This topic introduces you to cursors. First, it presents the SQL statements that let you use cursors to retrieve DB2 data. Next, it illustrates those statements with a sample inquiry program. Then, it shows you how to create a results table that's sorted by the values in any column. Finally, it describes how you can use more than one cursor at the same time.

How to work with a cursor-controlled results table

A cursor is a pointer that identifies the *current row* in a results table. No matter how many rows there are in a results table, a cursor identifies just one as the current row. You use a cursor to work through a results table one row at a time, much as you read through a standard sequential file.

Figure 3-9 shows the four SQL statements you use for cursor processing and their COBOL equivalents. Only one, DECLARE CURSOR, doesn't have a direct parallel in standard COBOL. If you keep the relationships in figure 3-9 in mind as you read on, I think you'll find cursor processing easy to understand.

To show you how to use the four SQL statements figure 3-9 lists, I'll describe how to create and process the results table shown in figure 3-10. Here, DB2 retrieves the first and last name columns from rows in the base table where the value of the state column is *CA*. The results table, as the figure shows, consists of three rows. Because it has more than one row, you have to use a cursor to process this table in an application program.

Figure 3-11 shows the four steps you need to create and use this table. First, you use a DECLARE CURSOR statement to specify the results table and establish a cursor for it. Second, you issue an OPEN statement to begin the cursor processing. Third, you issue one FETCH statement for each row in the results table. And fourth, you conclude the cursor processing by issuing a CLOSE statement.

SQL statement	Standard COBOL
DECLARE CURSOR	no equivalent
OPEN cursor-name	OPEN file-name
FETCH column-name...	READ file-name
CLOSE cursor-name	CLOSE file-name

Figure 3-9   SQL statements for cursor processing and their parallels in standard COBOL

Customer table

CUSTNO	FNAME	LNAME	ADDR	CITY	STATE	ZIPCODE
400001	KEITH	MCDONALD	4501 W MOCKINGBIRD	DALLAS	TX	75209
400002	ARREN	ANELLI	40 FORD RD	DENVILLE	NJ	07834
400003	SUSAN	HOWARD	1107 SECOND AVE #312	REDWOOD CITY	CA	94063
400004	CAROL ANN	EVANS	74 SUTTON CT	GREAT LAKES	IL	60088
400005	ELAINE	ROBERTS	12914 BRACKNELL	CERRITOS	CA	90701
400006	PAT	HONG	73 HIGH ST	SAN FRANCISCO	CA	94114
400007	PHIL	ROACH	25680 ORCHARD	DEARBORN HTS	MI	48125
400008	TIM	JOHNSON	145 W 27TH ST	SO CHICAGO HTS	IL	60411
400009	MARIANNE	BUSBEE	3920 BERWYN DR S #199	MOBILE	AL	36608
400010	ENRIQUE	OTHON	BOX 26729	RICHMOND	VA	23261
400011	WILLIAM C	FERGUSON	BOX 1283	MIAMI	FL	34002-1283
400012	S D	HOEHN	PO BOX 27	RIDDLE	OR	97469
400013	DAVID R	KEITH	BOX 1266	MAGNOLIA	AR	71757-1266
400014	R	BINDER	3425 WALDEN AVE	DEPEW	NY	14043
400015	VIVIAN	GEORGE	229 S 18TH ST	PHILADELPHIA	PA	19103
400016	J	NOETHLICH	11 KINGSTON CT	MERRIMACK	NH	03054

Results table

FNAME	LNAME
SUSAN	HOWARD
ELAINE	ROBERTS
PAT	HONG

Figure 3-10   A results table that contains only the first and last name columns from rows in the base table whose state column contains CA

Step 1:   Use a DECLARE CURSOR statement to specify an appropriate results table and name a cursor for it

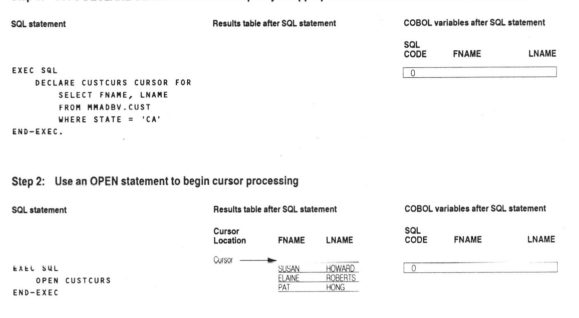

SQL statement	Results table after SQL statement	COBOL variables after SQL statement		
		SQL CODE	FNAME	LNAME

```
EXEC SQL
    DECLARE CUSTCURS CURSOR FOR
        SELECT FNAME, LNAME
        FROM MMADBV.CUST
        WHERE STATE = 'CA'
END-EXEC.
```
SQL CODE: 0

Step 2:   Use an OPEN statement to begin cursor processing

SQL statement	Results table after SQL statement			COBOL variables after SQL statement		
	Cursor Location	FNAME	LNAME	SQL CODE	FNAME	LNAME

```
EXEC SQL
    OPEN CUSTCURS
END-EXEC
```

Cursor →

Cursor Location	FNAME	LNAME
	SUSAN	HOWARD
	ELAINE	ROBERTS
	PAT	HONG

SQL CODE: 0

Figure 3-11   How the SQL statements for cursor processing work (part 1 of 2)

Declaring a cursor   The first step in using a cursor is to specify what the results table should contain. For that, you use the SQL DECLARE CURSOR statement. Figure 3-12 presents its syntax. As you can see, DECLARE CURSOR contains a SELECT. In it, you name the columns you want to retrieve, the table that contains them, and the selection conditions for them. You can use the full range of options available for the SELECT and WHERE clauses of the stand-alone SELECT statement that you learned in the last topic.

In addition, you can code the DISTINCT keyword in the SELECT component of a DECLARE CURSOR statement. DISTINCT directs DB2 to exclude duplicate rows (that is, rows that are identical to another) from the results table. If you don't code DISTINCT, DB2 includes duplicate rows in the results table.

You can see an example of the DECLARE CURSOR statement in step 1 in figure 3-11. Here, the statement defines a results table with a cursor named CUSTCURS. This table will contain the FNAME and LNAME columns from rows in the MMADBV.CUST table where the state column contains the value *CA*.

Step 3:   Use the FETCH statement to fetch one row after another from the results table until none remain

SQL statement	Results table after SQL statement			COBOL variables after SQL statement		
	Cursor Location	FNAME	LNAME	SQL CODE	FNAME	LNAME

```
EXEC SQL
    FETCH CUSTCURS
        INTO :FNAME, :LNAME
END-EXEC.
```
Cursor ➝ SUSAN / HOWARD, ELAINE / ROBERTS, PAT / HONG

COBOL: 0   SUSAN   HOWARD

	Cursor Location	FNAME	LNAME	SQL CODE	FNAME	LNAME

```
EXEC SQL
    FETCH CUSTCURS
        INTO :FNAME, :LNAME
END-EXEC.
```
Rows: SUSAN / HOWARD, Cursor ➝ ELAINE / ROBERTS, PAT / HONG

COBOL: 0   ELAINE   ROBERTS

	Cursor Location	FNAME	LNAME	SQL CODE	FNAME	LNAME

```
EXEC SQL
    FETCH CUSTCURS
        INTO :FNAME, :LNAME
END-EXEC.
```
Rows: SUSAN / HOWARD, ELAINE / ROBERTS, Cursor ➝ PAT / HONG

COBOL: 0   PAT   HONG

	Cursor Location	FNAME	LNAME	SQL CODE	FNAME	LNAME

```
EXEC SQL
    FETCH CUSTCURS
        INTO :FNAME, :LNAME,
END-EXEC.
```
Rows: SUSAN / HOWARD, ELAINE / ROBERTS, PAT / HONG, Cursor ➝

COBOL: 100   PAT   HONG

Step 4:   Use a CLOSE statement to end cursor processing

SQL statement	Results table after SQL statement	COBOL variables after SQL statement		
		SQL CODE	FNAME	LNAME

```
EXEC SQL
    CLOSE CUSTCURS
END-EXEC.
```
COBOL: 0   PAT   HONG

Figure 3-11   How the SQL statements for cursor processing work (part 2 of 2)

The SELECT that's a part of this DECLARE CURSOR statement is similar to the embedded SELECT statements you've already seen, but it's not exactly the same. First, notice that it doesn't have an INTO clause. The FETCH statements that retrieve individual rows from the table specify host variables.

The SQL DECLARE CURSOR statement

```
EXEC SQL
    DECLARE cursor-name CURSOR FOR
        SELECT [DISTINCT] column-specification[,column-specification...]
                  FROM  table-name[ synonym][,table-name[ synonym] ...]
                  [WHERE selection-condition]
               [ { FOR UPDATE OF update-column[,update-column...]    } ]
                 { ORDER BY sort-column[ DESC][,sort-column[ DESC]...] }
END-EXEC.
```

Explanation

cursor-name	The name to be used for the new cursor.
DISTINCT	Specifies that duplicate (identical) rows should not be included in the results table.
column-specification	Describes what the SELECT statement should put in the corresponding column of the results table. Most often, simply the name of a column you want DB2 to retrieve from the base table. However, DB2 provides a range of options. Look back to figure 3-3 for details. You may code no more than 300 column-specifications.
table-name	The DB2 name of the table or view from which you want to retrieve data.
synonym	An alternate name you want to use within this statement instead of the table-name that immediately precedes it. Use one space to separate synonym from table-name.
selection-condition	Specifies a test that DB2 will apply to each row in the table to determine whether to include it in the results table. A simple selection condition has the format
	`expression-1 operator expression-2`
	where the value of *expression-1*, usually a column-name, is compared using *operator* to the value of *expression-2*, which, in its simple form, may be a host variable or a literal. See figure 3-8 for valid operators and chapter 5 for more WHERE clause options.
update-column	The DB2 name of a column for which you want to enable updates.
sort-column	The name or number of the column in the results table by which DB2 should sort the results table. The first sort-column you specify is the primary sort column, the second is the secondary sort column, and so on.
DESC	Specifies that the values in the associated sort-column should be presented in descending sequence. If you omit DESC, the values will be presented in ascending sequence.

Figure 3-12   The SQL DECLARE CURSOR statement

Another difference has to do with timing. When you code a stand-alone SELECT statement, DB2 creates the table immediately. But DB2 doesn't create the results table based on the SELECT in a DECLARE CURSOR statement immediately. Instead, DB2 builds the results table when you issue the SQL OPEN statement for the cursor you name in the DECLARE CURSOR statement.

The SELECT in the DECLARE CURSOR statement simply specifies the characteristics of the results table that will be associated with the cursor. So, no matter how many times a program needs to generate a cursor-controlled results table, the DECLARE CURSOR statement that describes it needs to be present only once. You can code it in the Working-Storage Section or in the Procedure Division, as long as it appears before any other statements that refer to the cursor. I recommend that you code it in the Working-Storage Section because the statement is just a declaration, not an action statement.

Figure 3-12 shows two other elements that I won't illustrate here: the FOR UPDATE OF and ORDER BY clauses. FOR UPDATE OF lets you name columns in the results table that you intend to modify. Chapter 4 deals with changing DB2 tables, so I'll describe the FOR UPDATE OF clause there. The ORDER BY clause lets you direct DB2 to sort the rows in a cursor-controlled results table. I'll describe that clause later in this chapter.

Opening a cursor   The OPEN statement generates the results table a DECLARE CURSOR statement specifies. As you can see in figure 3-13, all you code on the OPEN statement is the cursor name you supplied on the DECLARE CURSOR statement. For the example in figure 3-11,

```
EXEC SQL
    OPEN CUSTCURS
END-EXEC.
```

is all that's necessary.

When DB2 processes the OPEN statement, it positions the cursor just before the first row of the new results table, as you can see in step 2 in figure 3-11. At this point in time, DB2 hasn't moved any values into FNAME and LNAME, the host variables the program uses. The only feedback the program gets about the success of this statement is the value in the SQLCODE field.

Retrieving a row from a cursor-controlled results table   The third step in working with a cursor-controlled results table is to retrieve its rows, one by one, with the FETCH statement. As you can see in figure 3-14, the

The SQL OPEN statement

```
EXEC SQL
    OPEN cursor-name
END-EXEC.
```

Explanation

cursor-name   The name of a cursor that has already been specified in a DECLARE CURSOR statement.

Figure 3-13   The SQL OPEN statement

FETCH statement contains an INTO clause. (Remember that the INTO clause is not part of the SELECT component of the DECLARE CURSOR statement.)

The FETCH statement that appears four times in the third step in figure 3-11,

```
EXEC SQL
    FETCH CUSTCURS
        INTO :FNAME, :LNAME
END-EXEC.
```

does two things. First, it advances the cursor one row in the results table. Then, it causes DB2 to move the column data from the new current row into FNAME and LNAME, the COBOL host variables.

A typical application program will fetch rows one after another, processing the data it retrieves from each. This directly parallels how you'd use the READ statement to work through each record in a sequential file. Because you can fetch just one row at a time, step 3 in figure 3-11 shows one FETCH statement for each row in the table.

When you process a sequential file, you have to take care to detect the end-of-file condition so you can end your processing loop at the right time. You need to do the same thing when you work with a cursor-controlled results table. When you try to retrieve a row after you've already fetched the last one in the table, DB2 stores the value +100 in the SQLCODE field, as you can see in step 3 in figure 3-11. If you evaluate SQLCODE after each FETCH statement, you'll know when you've reached the end of the results table.

The SQL FETCH statement

```
EXEC SQL
    FETCH cursor-name
          INTO {:host-var[,:host-var...]}
               {:host-structure         }
END-EXEC.
```

Explanation

cursor-name	The name of an open cursor.
host-var	The COBOL name of the host variable into which DB2 will place the data it fetches from the corresponding column in the results table. Be sure to precede each COBOL host variable name with a colon.
host-structure	The COBOL name of the group item into which DB2 will place the data it fetches from the table. Be sure to precede the COBOL host structure name with a colon.

Figure 3-14   The SQL FETCH statement

Closing a cursor   When you finish using a cursor-controlled results table, you should issue the SQL CLOSE statement. Just as with the OPEN statement, the syntax for CLOSE, shown in figure 3-15, is simple. As step 4 in figure 3-11 shows, the statement

```
EXEC SQL
    CLOSE CUSTCURS
END-EXEC.
```

releases the results table associated with the cursor CUSTCURS.

Strictly speaking, you don't have to issue the CLOSE statement here because DB2 closes the table automatically when your program ends. However, if your program will do any significant processing after you've finished with a cursor-controlled results table, you should code a CLOSE statement for it. That's because DB2 won't release resources it used for the table until you do. Sometimes, those resources can be substantial. Also, you must close the cursor if you plan to open it again without ending your program.

The SQL CLOSE statement

```
EXEC SQL
    CLOSE cursor-name
END-EXEC.
```

Explanation

cursor-name   The name of an open cursor.

Figure 3-15   The SQL CLOSE statement

Putting the DB2 cursor statements to work in a sales inquiry program

To help you understand how to use SQL's cursor processing statements, I want to show you an expansion of CUSTINQ, the inquiry program I presented in chapter 2. This program is called SALESINQ because in addition to customer information, it displays sales information. Here, I'll describe how the expanded program works, show its design, and explain the code in its Working-Storage Section and its Procedure Division.

The operation of the SALESINQ program   Just like the simple inquiry program in chapter 2, SALESINQ runs at a TSO terminal and accepts a series of customer numbers from the user. However, in addition to accessing the CUST table, this program also accesses INV, the table that contains invoice information. The DCLGEN output for both the CUST and INV tables is shown in figure 3-16. The program finds the invoices for each customer, and displays each invoice number, invoice date, and invoice amount. Because the INV table may contain more than one row for a given customer, the SALESINQ program must use a cursor to process it.

Figure 3-17 shows output from two typical sessions with the SALESINQ program. The first example shows an inquiry for a customer who has made four purchases. To produce the first line of the display,

```
CUSTOMER 400001 -- KEITH          MCDONALD
```

the SALESINQ program accessed the CUST table much as the CUSTINQ program in chapter 2 did. However, this program retrieves only the FNAME and LNAME columns.

```
*****************************************************************
* DCLGEN TABLE(MMADBV.CUST)                                     *
*        LIBRARY(MMA002.DCLGENS.COBOL(CUST))                    *
*        ACTION(REPLACE)                                        *
*        STRUCTURE(CUSTOMER-ROW)                                *
*        APOST                                                  *
* ... IS THE DCLGEN COMMAND THAT MADE THE FOLLOWING STATEMENTS  *
*****************************************************************
      EXEC SQL DECLARE MMADBV.CUST TABLE
      ( CUSTNO                          CHAR(6) NOT NULL,
        FNAME                           CHAR(20) NOT NULL,
        LNAME                           CHAR(30) NOT NULL,
        ADDR                            CHAR(30) NOT NULL,
        CITY                            CHAR(20) NOT NULL,
        STATE                           CHAR(2) NOT NULL,
        ZIPCODE                         CHAR(10) NOT NULL
      ) END-EXEC.
*****************************************************************
* COBOL DECLARATION FOR TABLE MMADBV.CUST                       *
*****************************************************************
  01  CUSTOMER-ROW.
      10  CUSTNO                PIC X(6).
      10  FNAME                 PIC X(20).
      10  LNAME                 PIC X(30).
      10  ADDR                  PIC X(30).
      10  CITY                  PIC X(20).
      10  STATE                 PIC X(2).
      10  ZIPCODE               PIC X(10).
*****************************************************************
* THE NUMBER OF COLUMNS DESCRIBED BY THIS DECLARATION IS 7      *
*****************************************************************
```

Figure 3-16   The DCLGEN output for the tables used by the CUSTINQ program (part 1 of 2)

Besides showing the name of the customer associated with a specific customer number, the program also displays information from each row in the INV table for that customer. In example 1 in figure 3-17, there were four related INV table rows for the customer number the user entered. After it retrieved and displayed information from the related INV table rows, the program displayed the total dollar amount billed and the total number of invoices issued.

As with the CUSTINQ program you saw in the last chapter, SALESINQ lets the user inquire about more than one customer during a single execution of the program. But, in example 1 of figure 3-17, the user ended the program after reviewing the information for customer 400001.

Example 2 in figure 3-17 shows two other situations the program handles. In the first inquiry in example 2, the customer number the user entered wasn't associated with any rows in the INV table. As a result, the program displayed no invoice lines and showed zero as the total for both

```
*****************************************************************
* DCLGEN TABLE(MMADBV.INV)                                      *
*        LIBRARY(MMA002.DCLGENS.COBOL(INV))                     *
*        ACTION(REPLACE)                                        *
*        STRUCTURE(INVOICE-ROW)                                 *
*        APOST                                                  *
* ... IS THE DCLGEN COMMAND THAT MADE THE FOLLOWING STATEMENTS  *
*****************************************************************
     EXEC SQL DECLARE MMADBV.INV TABLE
     ( INVCUST                         CHAR(6) NOT NULL,
       INVNO                           CHAR(6) NOT NULL,
       INVDATE                         DATE NOT NULL,
       INVSUBT                         DECIMAL(9, 2) NOT NULL,
       INVSHIP                         DECIMAL(7, 2) NOT NULL,
       INVTAX                          DECIMAL(7, 2) NOT NULL,
       INVTOTAL                        DECIMAL(9, 2) NOT NULL,
       INVPROM                         CHAR(10) NOT NULL
     ) END-EXEC.
*****************************************************************
* COBOL DECLARATION FOR TABLE MMADBV.INV                        *
*****************************************************************
 01  INVOICE-ROW.
     10   INVCUST            PIC X(6).
     10   INVNO              PIC X(6).
     10   INVDATE            PIC X(10).
     10   INVSUBT            PIC S9999999V99 USAGE COMP-3.
     10   INVSHIP            PIC S99999V99 USAGE COMP-3.
     10   INVTAX             PIC S99999V99 USAGE COMP-3.
     10   INVTOTAL           PIC S9999999V99 USAGE COMP-3.
     10   INVPROM            PIC X(10).
*****************************************************************
* THE NUMBER OF COLUMNS DESCRIBED BY THIS DECLARATION IS 8      *
*****************************************************************
```

Figure 3-16   The DCLGEN output for the tables used by the CUSTINQ program (part 2 of 2)

the amount billed and invoices issued. This inquiry session wasn't very productive because the second customer number the user entered didn't even
result in a matching row in the CUST table. Here, the SALESINQ program
displayed an error message for the user.

To be able to retrieve invoice information, this program needed to
include DCLGEN output that describes the INV table. This DCLGEN output
is shown in part 2 of figure 3-16. As you can see, this table isn't more complex than the CUST table, but it does use a wider variety of data types for
its columns.

The first column in the table, INVCUST, contains the number for the
customer in the CUST table that is associated with a specific invoice. In
other words, INVCUST is used as a foreign key. Because a single customer
may have made many sales transactions, many invoice rows may contain
the same customer number. So although the customer number uniquely

Example 1

During the first inquiry session, the program displays information from four invoice rows for the customer number the user enters.

```
--------------------------------------------------------
KEY IN THE NEXT CUSTOMER NUMBER AND PRESS ENTER,
OR KEY IN 999999 AND PRESS ENTER TO QUIT.
400001
--------------------------------------------------------
   CUSTOMER 400001 -- KEITH                 MCDONALD

   INVOICE 062308 1991-03-03     204.45
   INVOICE 061937 1991-02-22      15.00
   INVOICE 061936 1991-02-22     147.50
   INVOICE 059437 1990-09-14     181.42
                               ----------
   TOTAL BILLED                  548.37
   INVOICES ISSUED                    4

--------------------------------------------------------
KEY IN THE NEXT CUSTOMER NUMBER AND PRESS ENTER,
OR KEY IN 999999 AND PRESS ENTER TO QUIT.
999999
```

Example 2

During the second inquiry session, the user requests sales information for two customers. The first customer has no sales on file. The second customer's number wasn't found.

```
--------------------------------------------------------
KEY IN THE NEXT CUSTOMER NUMBER AND PRESS ENTER,
OR KEY IN 999999 AND PRESS ENTER TO QUIT.
400008
--------------------------------------------------------
   CUSTOMER 400008 -- TIM                   JOHNSON

   TOTAL BILLED                   0.00
   INVOICES ISSUED                   0

--------------------------------------------------------
KEY IN THE NEXT CUSTOMER NUMBER AND PRESS ENTER,
OR KEY IN 999999 AND PRESS ENTER TO QUIT.
400020
--------------------------------------------------------
   CUSTOMER NUMBER 400020 NOT FOUND.
--------------------------------------------------------
KEY IN THE NEXT CUSTOMER NUMBER AND PRESS ENTER,
OR KEY IN 999999 AND PRESS ENTER_TO_QUIT.
999999
```

Figure 3-17   Operation of the SALESINQ program

identifies a row in the CUST table, it doesn't uniquely identify a row in the INV table. The next column, INVNO, contains invoice numbers that serve that purpose.

Another column in the INV table, INVDATE, has the data type DATE. A column with this data type uses 10 bytes and has the default format

```
yyyy-mm-dd
```

The host variable definition that corresponds to this column contains the simple PICTURE clause

```
PIC X(10)
```

As you can see, this host variable description doesn't reflect the structure of the data in the column. But for the display the SALESINQ program produces, that's fine. In other programming situations, you may need to move the contents of a host variable like INVDATE to a work field where you can manipulate its components separately. Or, it may be appropriate to use DB2 special features for processing date and time data. I'll cover those features in *Part 2: An Advanced Course.*

This table also has four numeric columns that contain financial information. The one the SALESINQ program needs is INVTOTAL, the total amount billed for an invoice.

The design for the SALESINQ program   Now that you have a picture of what this program does and of the tables it accesses, I'd like to describe its structure. Figure 3-18 presents its structure chart. At the highest level of control, this program works like the CUSTINQ program you saw in chapter 2. The top-level module, 000-PROCESS-SALES-INQUIRIES, performs the main-processing module, 100-PROCESS-SALES-INQUIRY, repeatedly until the user signals the end of the program by entering 999999 as a customer number.

The structure of this program is different than the CUSTINQ program where it deals with the INV table. Module 140-GET-INVOICES-INFORMATION manages the functions necessary to retrieve all the rows from the INV table for the current customer. It opens the cursor-controlled results table in module 150-OPEN-INVOICE-CURSOR. If that module is successful, module 140 then performs module 160-GET-INVOICE-INFORMATION repeatedly until it has processed each row in the results table. Module 160 has two subordinates: 170-FETCH-INVOICE-ROW and 180-DISPLAY-INVOICE-INFORMATION.

When the FETCH statement in module 170 has passed the last row in the results table, module 140 stops invoking module 160 and instead closes

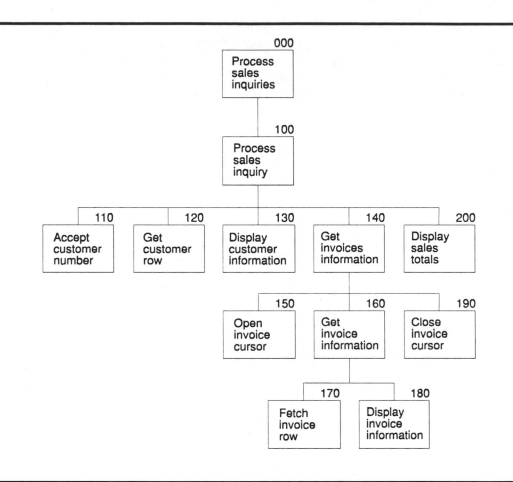

Figure 3-18   Structure chart for the SALESINQ program

the cursor by performing module 190. Then, module 100 performs module 200-DISPLAY-SALES-TOTALS to show the totals on the screen.

The Working-Storage Section of the SALESINQ program   Figure 3-19 presents the source code for the SALESINQ program. This program's Working-Storage Section contains a few more elements than the CUSTINQ program in chapter 2 did. Note, for example, that this program requires more switch fields. That's because the logic of this program is more complicated than the logic of the CUSTINQ program.

Also, I coded two sets of fields for the totals the program accumulates as it processes the invoice rows for a customer. One group contains the INVOICES-COUNT and INVOICES-TOTAL fields. The program increments

```
000100 IDENTIFICATION DIVISION.
000200*
000300 PROGRAM-ID.        SALESINQ.
000400*
000500 ENVIRONMENT DIVISION.
000600*
000700 INPUT-OUTPUT SECTION.
000800*
000900 FILE-CONTROL.
001000*
001100 DATA DIVISION.
001200*
001300 FILE SECTION.
001400*
001500 WORKING-STORAGE SECTION.
001600*
001700 01  SWITCHES.
001800*
001900     05  END-OF-INQUIRIES-SW     PIC X    VALUE "N".
002000         88  END-OF-INQUIRIES             VALUE "Y".
002100     05  CUSTOMER-FOUND-SW       PIC X    VALUE "Y".
002200         88  CUSTOMER-FOUND               VALUE "Y".
002300     05  VALID-CURSOR-SW         PIC X    VALUE "Y".
002400         88  VALID-CURSOR                 VALUE "Y".
002500     05  END-OF-INVOICES-SW      PIC X    VALUE "N".
002600         88  END-OF-INVOICES              VALUE "Y".
002700*
002800 01  INVOICE-TOTAL-FIELDS        COMP-3.
002900*
003000     05  INVOICES-COUNT       PIC S9(5)    VALUE ZERO.
003100     05  INVOICES-TOTAL       PIC S9(7)V99 VALUE ZERO.
003200*
003300 01  EDITED-TOTAL-FIELDS.
003400*
003500     05  EDITED-COUNT        PIC Z(4)9.
003600     05  EDITED-TOTAL        PIC Z(6)9.99.
003700*
003800     EXEC SQL
003900         INCLUDE CUST
004000     END-EXEC.
004100*
004200     EXEC SQL
004300         INCLUDE INV
004400     END-EXEC.
004500*
004600     EXEC SQL
004700         INCLUDE SQLCA
004800     END-EXEC.
004900*
005000     EXEC SQL
005100         DECLARE INVCURS CURSOR FOR
005200             SELECT   INVNO, INVDATE, INVTOTAL
005300                 FROM MMADBV.INV
005400                 WHERE INVCUST = :CUSTNO
005500     END-EXEC.
005600*
```

Figure 3-19   COBOL source code for the SALESINQ program (part 1 of 3)

```
005700 PROCEDURE DIVISION.
005800*
005900 000-PROCESS-SALES-INQUIRIES.
006000*
006100     PERFORM 100-PROCESS-SALES-INQUIRY
006200          UNTIL END-OF-INQUIRIES.
006300     STOP RUN.
006400*
006500 100-PROCESS-SALES-INQUIRY.
006600*
006700     MOVE "Y" TO CUSTOMER-FOUND-SW.
006800     PERFORM 110-ACCEPT-CUSTOMER-NUMBER.
006900     IF NOT END-OF-INQUIRIES
007000         PERFORM 120-GET-CUSTOMER-ROW
007100         PERFORM 130-DISPLAY-CUSTOMER-INFO
007200         IF CUSTOMER-FOUND
007300             PERFORM 140-GET-INVOICES-INFORMATION
007400             PERFORM 200-DISPLAY-SALES-TOTALS.
007500*
007600 110-ACCEPT-CUSTOMER-NUMBER.
007700*
007800     DISPLAY "---------------------------------------------".
007900     DISPLAY "KEY IN THE NEXT CUSTOMER NUMBER AND PRESS ENTER,".
008000     DISPLAY "OR KEY IN 999999 AND PRESS ENTER TO QUIT.".
008100     ACCEPT CUSTNO.
008200     IF CUSTNO = "999999"
008300         MOVE "Y" TO END-OF-INQUIRIES-SW.
008400*
008500 120-GET-CUSTOMER-ROW.
008600*
008700     EXEC SQL
008800         SELECT    FNAME,  LNAME
008900             INTO :FNAME, :LNAME
009000             FROM MMADBV.CUST
009100             WHERE CUSTNO = :CUSTNO
009200     END-EXEC.
009300     IF SQLCODE NOT = 0
009400         MOVE "N" TO CUSTOMER-FOUND-SW.
009500*
009600 130-DISPLAY-CUSTOMER-INFO.
009700*
009800     DISPLAY "---------------------------------------------".
009900     IF CUSTOMER-FOUND
010000         DISPLAY "  CUSTOMER " CUSTNO " -- " FNAME " " LNAME
010100         DISPLAY " "
010200     ELSE
010300         DISPLAY "  CUSTOMER NUMBER " CUSTNO " NOT FOUND.".
010400*
010500 140-GET-INVOICES-INFORMATION.
010600*
010700     MOVE "Y" TO VALID-CURSOR-SW.
010800     PERFORM 150-OPEN-INVOICE-CURSOR.
010900     IF VALID-CURSOR
011000         MOVE "N" TO END-OF-INVOICES-SW
011100         MOVE ZERO TO INVOICES-COUNT
011200         MOVE ZERO TO INVOICES-TOTAL
011300         PERFORM 160-GET-INVOICE-INFORMATION
011400             UNTIL END-OF-INVOICES
011500         PERFORM 190-CLOSE-INVOICE-CURSOR.
011600*
```

Figure 3-19   COBOL source code for the SALESINQ program (part 2 of 3)

```
011700 150-OPEN-INVOICE-CURSOR.
011800*
011900     EXEC SQL
012000         OPEN INVCURS
012100     END-EXEC.
012200     IF SQLCODE NOT = 0
012300         MOVE "N" TO VALID-CURSOR-SW.
012400*
012500 160-GET-INVOICE-INFORMATION.
012600*
012700     PERFORM 170-FETCH-INVOICE-ROW.
012800     IF NOT END-OF-INVOICES
012900         IF VALID-CURSOR
013000             ADD 1         TO INVOICES-COUNT
013100             ADD INVTOTAL TO INVOICES-TOTAL
013200             PERFORM 180-DISPLAY-INVOICE-INFO.
013300*
013400 170-FETCH-INVOICE-ROW.
013500*
013600     EXEC SQL
013700         FETCH INVCURS
013800             INTO :INVNO, :INVDATE, :INVTOTAL
013900     END-EXEC.
014000     IF SQLCODE NOT = 0
014100         MOVE "Y" TO END-OF-INVOICES-SW
014200         IF SQLCODE NOT = 100
014300             MOVE "N" TO VALID-CURSOR-SW.
014400*
014500 180-DISPLAY-INVOICE-INFO.
014600*
014700     MOVE INVTOTAL TO EDITED-TOTAL.
014800     DISPLAY "  INVOICE " INVNO " " INVDATE " " EDITED-TOTAL.
014900*
015000 190-CLOSE-INVOICE-CURSOR.
015100*
015200     EXEC SQL
015300         CLOSE INVCURS
015400     END-EXEC.
015500     IF SQLCODE NOT = 0
015600         MOVE "N" TO VALID-CURSOR-SW.
015700*
015800 200-DISPLAY-SALES-TOTALS.
015900*
016000     IF VALID-CURSOR
016100         MOVE INVOICES-TOTAL              TO EDITED-TOTAL
016200         MOVE INVOICES-COUNT              TO EDITED-COUNT
016300         IF INVOICES-TOTAL > 0
016400             DISPLAY "                          ------------"
016500         END-IF
016600         DISPLAY "  TOTAL BILLED              "    EDITED TOTAL
016700         DISPLAY "  INVOICES ISSUED          " EDITED-COUNT
016800         DISPLAY " "
016900     ELSE
017000         DISPLAY " "
017100         DISPLAY "     *** INVOICE RETRIEVAL ERROR   ***"
017200         DISPLAY " ".
017300*
```

Figure 3-19   COBOL source code for the SALESINQ program (part 3 of 3)

these fields for each invoice row it processes. If you refer back to the
DCLGEN output for the INV table, shown in part 2 of figure 3-16, you'll see
that I gave the INVOICES-TOTAL field the same size and usage as the
INVTOTAL host variable. The other group contains the numeric-edited
items EDITED-COUNT and EDITED-TOTAL. These are the fields the program actually displays.

Next, the program contains four SQL statements. The first two are
INCLUDE statements that direct the precompiler to add the library members that contain the DCLGEN output for the CUST and INV tables to the
program. The third statement, another INCLUDE, adds the SQL communication area field definitions to the program.

The last SQL statement in the Working-Storage Section,

```
EXEC SQL
    DECLARE INVCURS CURSOR FOR
        SELECT    INVNO, INVDATE, INVTOTAL
            FROM   MMADBV.INV
            WHERE INVCUST = :CUSTNO
END-EXEC.
```

names a cursor and specifies the selection condition for the invoice results
table the program will use. The name of the cursor, INVCURS, will show up
in the OPEN, FETCH, and CLOSE statements that use it. The SELECT component specifies that the results table should contain three columns
(INVNO, INVDATE, and INVTOTAL) from the MMADBV.INV table. As you
can tell from the WHERE clause, when the OPEN statement generates the
table, DB2 compares the current value of the host variable CUSTNO with
the contents of the INVCUST column in the INV table to determine which
rows to select.

The Procedure Division of the SALESINQ program   The logic of the
program's Procedure Division code is straightforward, so I won't describe
the function of each module. Even so, I would like to call your attention to
several points.

The SELECT statement in module 120,

```
EXEC SQL
    SELECT    FNAME,        LNAME
        INTO :FNAME,        :LNAME
        FROM   MMADBV.CUST
        WHERE CUSTNO = :CUSTNO
END-EXEC.
```

retrieves a single row from the CUST table. This statement retrieves data
from only two of the CUST table's seven columns. This statement also uses

a column in the WHERE clause (CUSTNO) that it doesn't include in the results table.

If the SELECT statement for the customer row is successful, module 100 invokes module 140 to retrieve and display invoice rows for the current customer. Module 140 starts by setting the value of VALID-CURSOR-SW to Y. Then, it invokes the first of its three subordinates, module 150.

Module 150 actually creates the results table that contains invoice information for the current customer by issuing this SQL statement:

```
EXEC SQL
    OPEN INVCURS
END-EXEC.
```

When the program executes this module, DB2 processes the SELECT statement in the DECLARE CURSOR statement. At that time, the current value of the host variable CUSTNO (the value the user entered and that the program just used successfully to retrieve the customer row) is compared to the values in the INVCUST column in the INV table. When DB2 finds a row for which the comparison is equal, it adds that row to the results table.

If the OPEN statement is successful, DB2 sets the value of the SQLCODE field to 0. If SQLCODE contains a value other then zero, there was some problem establishing the results table. Then, module 150 moves N to VALID-CURSOR-SW.

If VALID-CURSOR-SW is equal to Y, module 140 first initializes three fields with proper starting values, and then performs module 160 repeatedly to work through the results table. Module 160, in turn, has two subordinates. The first, module 170, retrieves the next row from the results table with this FETCH statement:

```
EXEC SQL
    FETCH INVCURS
        INTO :INVNO, :INVDATE, :INVTOTAL
END-EXEC.
```

This statement advances the cursor to identify the new current row. Then it retrieves the values from the columns named in the DECLARE CURSOR's SELECT component into INVNO, INVDATE, and INVTOTAL, the host variables the FETCH statement specifies in its INTO clause.

After it fetches data from the current row of the results table, module 170 evaluates the SQLCODE field with a two-level nested IF. If the value of SQLCODE is anything other than zero, the program shouldn't try to retrieve any more rows using the cursor. So, the first IF sets the value of END-OF-INVOICES-SW to Y. (Both modules 140 and 160 evaluate this switch.)

The program also needs to check SQLCODE for one specific non-zero value: +100. This value means that the program has already retrieved the last row in the table. (It parallels the end-of-file condition for a standard sequential data set.) If the value of SQLCODE is any non-zero value other than +100, then some processing error has occurred, and the program sets the value of VALID-CURSOR-SW to N. If no processing error occurs, the value of VALID-CURSOR-SW remains Y.

When module 170 ends, control passes back to module 160. If module 170 didn't reach the end of the results table (that is, if the value of END-OF-INVOICES-SW is N) and it didn't detect some other processing error (if the value of VALID-CURSOR-SW is Y), module 160 increments INVOICES-COUNT and INVOICES-TOTAL. Then, it performs its other subordinate, module 180, to display the data from the invoice row it just processed.

When module 140 detects that module 170 has reached the end of the results table, it stops invoking module 160 and instead performs module 190. The code in module 190,

```
EXEC SQL
    CLOSE INVCURS
END-EXEC.
```

closes the cursor. Although DB2 automatically closes any open cursors when a program ends, an explicit CLOSE statement is necessary in this program because it needs to use the cursor to create a new results table for each valid customer number the user enters. To be able to open a new results table for a cursor, that cursor must be closed. If it isn't, the OPEN statement fails.

Sorting the rows in a results table

Often, you'll want to work with the data in a cursor-controlled results table in a particular order. That's especially true when you need to develop a report-preparation program. To do this, you direct DB2 to sort the rows in a results table by coding the ORDER BY clause on the SELECT component of the DECLARE CURSOR statement.

As you can see in the syntax of the DECLARE CURSOR statement in figure 3-12, ORDER BY is the last clause of the SELECT. Note that you can't code this clause if you need to use the FOR UPDATE OF clause. On the ORDER BY clause, you name the column (or columns) by which you want DB2 to sort the results table. DB2's default is to order rows in ascending sequence. As a result, if you want to produce a results table that's ordered in descending sequence, you need to code the DESC keyword.

For example, suppose you want to be sure the invoice rows the SALESINQ program displays are presented in sequence by amount billed, from most to least. All you need to do is add the ORDER BY clause to the SELECT component of the DECLARE CURSOR statement, like this:

```
EXEC SQL
    DECLARE INVCURS CURSOR FOR
        SELECT    INVNO, INVDATE, INVTOTAL
            FROM  MMADBV.INV
            WHERE INVCUST = :CUSTNO
            ORDER BY INVTOTAL DESC
END-EXEC.
```

Notice that I coded the DESC keyword on the ORDER BY clause to tell DB2 to use descending rather than ascending sequence.

If you need secondary sort sequences, just identify the columns you want DB2 to use in your statement's ORDER BY clause. The first column you name is the primary sort column, the second is the secondary sort column, and so on. You can use DESC keywords with any or all of the columns you name on this clause.

Sometimes, you can't identify a column by name. For instance, if a results table column contains a calculated value, even one derived from a base table column, you can't specify it by name. However, it's still easy to use it in the ORDER BY clause. All you need to do is code the number of the column in the results table as the sort-column operand. In fact, you can use column numbers even if you don't have to. For example,

```
EXEC SQL
    DECLARE INVCURS CURSOR FOR
        SELECT    INVNO, INVDATE, INVTOTAL
            FROM  MMADBV.INV
            WHERE INVCUST = :CUSTNO
            ORDER BY 3 DESC
END-EXEC.
```

is equivalent to the statement I just showed you. The number 3 in the ORDER BY clause identifies the third column in the results table, the one that contains the values from the INV table's INVTOTAL column.

Using more than one cursor at the same time

DB2 lets a program use more than one cursor at the same time. All you have to do is include a DECLARE CURSOR statement for each in your program and code corresponding OPEN, FETCH, and CLOSE statements at the right places in your program's Procedure Division. You might think that you'd seldom, if ever, need to use multiple cursors. However, the relational data structure that's the foundation of DB2 often leads to situations where multiple cursors are necessary.

As an example, let me extend the SALESINQ application you just studied. If you think about the information that the INV table stores, you'll realize that something seems to be missing. A complete picture of a sales transaction would also include details about the products or services that were sold. That information isn't a part of the INV table because a single invoice is likely to have more than one line item. And in the relational data model, a table shouldn't contain repeating elements. Instead, they should be stored in a separate table. So, just as a customer can have many associated invoices, an invoice can have many associated line items.

Suppose the program had to show not just an invoice's number, date, and billing total, but also details about each of its line items. Then, the program would have to use two cursors. The cursor for the INV table would work like it did in the SALESINQ program. But for each invoice row the program fetches, it would open a second cursor, perhaps called LINEITEM, to generate another results table that contains only line item rows for the current invoice.

Figure 3-20 shows the structure of a program that does this. The shaded modules perform the same functions for the line item table that modules 150, 160, 170, 180, and 190 perform for the INV table.

Discussion

You can use cursors to meet a variety of processing needs. In particular, you can use advanced features of the SELECT statement you'll learn in section 3 in the SELECT component of DECLARE CURSOR. For example, you can specify complex selection and grouping criteria in a batch report-preparation program that extracts information from cursor-controlled results tables. Also, you can use more than one cursor on the same table. (In the INVOICE/LINEITEM example I just described, the two cursors were on different tables.)

Term

current row

Objectives

1. Given application and table specifications, code a DECLARE CURSOR statement to define a cursor-controlled results table.

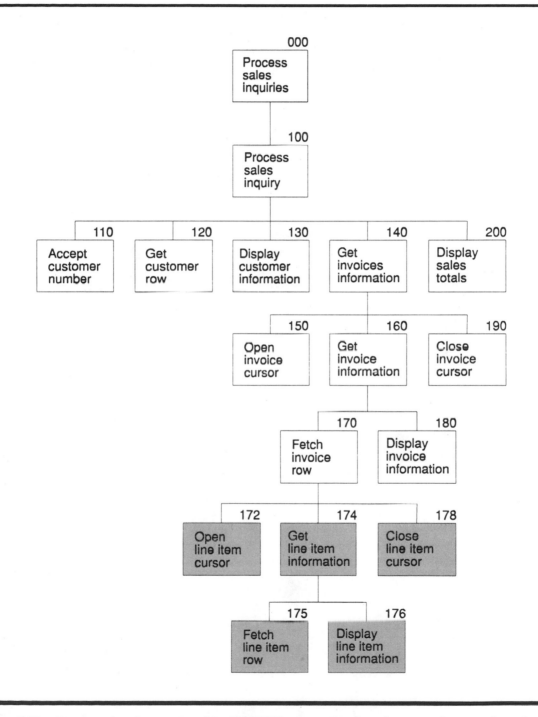

Figure 3-20   Structure chart for a version of the SALESINQ program that shows line item information for each invoice

2. Use the OPEN, FETCH, and CLOSE statements to retrieve rows from a cursor-controlled results table.

3. Given the specifications for a program that will retrieve multiple rows from a cursor-controlled results table, design and code the program.

Chapter 4

How to modify DB2 tables

By now, you should be comfortable using basic forms of the SELECT statement. But to develop a DB2 program that does the sort of data processing you're probably used to doing with standard access methods, you need to be familiar with more than just the SELECT statement. In topic 1 of this chapter, I'll show you how to use the three SQL statements that let you change the data in a table. You'll learn how to use UPDATE to change existing data in a table, how to use DELETE to remove a row or rows from a table, and how to use INSERT to add new rows to a table. In topic 2, I'll introduce DB2's recovery facilities and show you how to use two more SQL statements: COMMIT and ROLLBACK. Each of these topics includes a complete program example that illustrates the features and techniques it presents.

How to use the INSERT, UPDATE, and DELETE statements

In this topic, I'll show you the syntax of the UPDATE, DELETE, and INSERT statements, and I'll present several examples that illustrate how you can use them. Next, I'll discuss a simple application program that uses all three statements to update a DB2 table. And finally, I'll explain how the relationships among tables can affect the ways you use INSERT, UPDATE, and DELETE.

How to use the UPDATE and DELETE statements to modify table data

To modify table data, you use the UPDATE and DELETE statements. Because they work in similar ways, I'm going to describe them together. I'll start by describing how a typical example of each works. Then, I'll show you their formal syntax. Finally, I'll mention some processing restrictions you need to keep in mind when you use UPDATE and DELETE.

How the basic forms of the UPDATE and DELETE statements work

Figure 4-1 presents typical examples of the UPDATE and DELETE statements. Even though these are simple examples, they represent the kind of UPDATE and DELETE statements you're most likely to code in your programs.

The DELETE statement directs DB2 to remove every row that meets the selection condition in the WHERE clause from the table named in the FROM clause. The DELETE statement in figure 4-1, for example, causes DB2 to remove the row from the CUST table where the value of the CUSTNO column is the same as the current value of the program host variable CUSTNO.

An UPDATE statement can contain many more lines than a DELETE statement, but it's not much harder to understand. The UPDATE statement in figure 4-1 directs DB2 to change the values in six columns in a CUST table row. The first line of the statement after EXEC SQL,

```
UPDATE MMADBV.CUST
```

A DELETE statement that removes one row from the customer table

```
EXEC SQL
    DELETE FROM MMADBV.CUST
        WHERE CUSTNO = :CUSTNO
END-EXEC.
```

An UPDATE statement that changes six columns in one row of the customer table

```
EXEC SQL
    UPDATE      MMADBV.CUST
        SET     FNAME   = :FNAME,
                LNAME   = :LNAME,
                ADDR    = :ADDR,
                CITY    = :CITY,
                STATE   = :STATE,
                ZIPCODE = :ZIPCODE
        WHERE   CUSTNO  = :CUSTNO
END-EXEC.
```

Figure 4-1   Typical DELETE and UPDATE statements

names the table the statement will modify. This line is similar in format and purpose to the first line in the DELETE statement, but it doesn't use the FROM keyword.

The last line of the UPDATE statement (before the END-EXEC) is a WHERE clause. In this example, it's the same as the WHERE clause in the DELETE statement in the figure. It specifies that the statement should modify the row where the value of the CUSTNO column is the same as the current value of the program host variable CUSTNO.

The lines in the middle of the UPDATE statement make up the statement's SET clause. These lines identify the table columns the statement will change and provide new values for them. In this example, they direct DB2 to set the value of the table row's FNAME column to what the program host variable FNAME contains, to set the value of the table row's LNAME column to what the host variable LNAME contains, and so on for the ADDR, CITY, STATE, and ZIPCODE columns.

In the UPDATE statement in figure 4-1, the SET clause doesn't include the CUSTNO column. That's because it's the identifying primary key in this table. The primary key in a DB2 table is similar to a primary key in a VSAM key-sequenced data set, because its value must be unique. But, unlike a primary key in a KSDS, a primary key value in a DB2 table can sometimes be changed. In most cases, though, it doesn't make sense to change a primary key value. And, as you'll learn later in this chapter, DB2 doesn't always let you change it.

If you're used to developing programs that process standard files, you might expect that you need to select rows before you issue UPDATE or DELETE statements for them. You don't. With DB2, the basic operations of UPDATE and DELETE are independent. But, as you'll see in a moment, when you want to change or remove a row through a cursor-controlled results table, you do have to retrieve the row first.

Both the UPDATE and DELETE statements may fail under certain circumstances, and both can return several different return codes. I won't list them here, but all the non-zero return codes have the same essential meaning: Your statement wasn't processed and the table is unchanged, regardless of the number of rows the statement might have affected had it worked. So after a program executes an UPDATE or a DELETE statement, it should check the value of SQLCODE to determine whether the statement was successful.

The syntax of the UPDATE and DELETE statements

Figures 4-2 and 4-3 present the complete syntax of the UPDATE and DELETE statements. As you can see, the main difference between the two is that the UPDATE statement contains a SET clause and the DELETE statement doesn't.

How to use the SET clause of the UPDATE statement   The UPDATE statement's SET clause contains one or more assignments that specify a new value for each column you want to change. The basic format of each assignment is

```
column-name = new-value
```

You can specify new-value in four ways, as the syntax for UPDATE in figure 4-2 shows. The most common way is to name a COBOL host variable that contains the value you want to store in the column. That's the approach I took in the example in figure 4-1.

You're less likely to use the other three ways to specify a new value for a column. However, they're all easy to understand. One option is to supply a literal value for a column. If the literal value is a character string, you must code it between quotation marks. If it's a numeric value, don't use quotation marks. Example 1 in figure 4-4 specifies

```
SET ZIPCODE = '00000-0000'
```

The SQL UPDATE statement

```
EXEC SQL
    UPDATE table-name

                                  (:host-var  )                      (:host-var  )
    SET        column-name=       { literal    }  [,column-name=      { literal    }  ...]
                                  { expression }                      { expression }
                                  ( NULL       )                      ( NULL       )

    [WHERE    {selection-condition    }]
              {CURRENT OF cursor-name }

END-EXEC.
```

Explanation

table-name	The DB2 name of the table in which you want to change a row or rows.
column-name	The DB2 name of the column whose value you want to change.
host-var	The COBOL name of the host variable that contains the value to be stored in the specified column in the affected row(s). Be sure to precede each COBOL host variable name with a colon.
literal	A constant value that will be stored in the specified column in the affected row(s). If the value is character data, it must be between quotation marks; if the value is numeric data, it must not be between quotation marks.
expression	An expression whose result will be stored in the specified column in the affected row(s). An expression may include literals and may refer to columns in the table you're updating. Although you can use SQL's arithmetic operators, you can't use the concatenation operator in an expression in the UPDATE statement.
NULL	Indicates that the value of the specified column should be set to null in the affected row(s).
selection-condition	May be any valid selection condition you can code with the SELECT statement. For typical applications, code selection-condition like
	`WHERE column-name = :host-var`
	which specifies that the value in a table column must equal the value you've moved to a COBOL host variable. If the selection condition includes a subquery, the subquery may not refer to the table you're updating. (See chapter 8 for a description of subqueries.) If the condition identifies more than one row, all are updated.
cursor-name	The name of an open cursor. Specifies that the base table row represented by the current row of the cursor-controlled results table should be updated.

Figure 4-2   The SQL UPDATE statement

The SQL DELETE statement

```
EXEC SQL
    DELETE FROM table-name
    [WHERE {selection-condition  }  ]
           {CURRENT OF cursor-name}
END-EXEC.
```

Explanation

table-name   The DB2 name of the table from which you want to delete a row or rows.

selection-condition   May be any valid selection condition you can code with the SELECT statement. For typical
                        applications, code a selection-condition like

                        `WHERE column-name = :host-var`

                        which specifies that the value in a table column must equal the value you've moved to a COBOL host
                        variable. If the selection condition includes a subquery, the subquery may not refer to the table from
                        which rows are to be deleted. (See chapter 8 for a description of subqueries.) If the condition
                        identifies more than one row, all are deleted.

cursor-name   The name of an open cursor. Specifies that the base table row represented by the current row of the
                        cursor-controlled results table should be deleted.

Figure 4-3   The SQL DELETE statement

to supply a default zip code value for customer rows that contain spaces in the ZIPCODE column. Even though this literal looks like numeric data, the ZIPCODE column has the CHAR data type, so I coded the new value in quotation marks.

Another way to supply a value is to code an expression, such as an arithmetic statement. You can apply what you learned in chapter 3 about coding expressions in the SELECT statement to coding expressions in the UPDATE statement. However, you can't use the concatenation operator in an expression in the UPDATE statement's SET clause.

Example 2 in figure 4-4 shows an UPDATE statement with two SET clause elements that illustrate how you can use expressions:

```
SET SALESTOT = SALESTOT + :INVTOTAL,
    SALESCNT = SALESCNT + 1
```

This UPDATE statement is part of a program that processes sales transactions and maintains a customer history table named CUSTHIST. The table

---

Example 1   An UPDATE statement that changes the contents of one column to a literal value in a set of rows

```
EXEC SQL
    UPDATE      MMADBV.CUST
        SET    ZIPCODE = '00000-0000'
        WHERE ZIPCODE = '            '
END-EXEC.
```

Example 2   An UPDATE statement that increments the value of two columns in a specific row

```
EXEC SQL
    UPDATE      MMADBV.CUSTHIST
        SET    SALESTOT = SALESTOT + :INVTOTAL,
               SALESCNT = SALESCNT + 1
        WHERE CUSTNO = :CUSTNO
END-EXEC.
```

Figure 4-4   UPDATE statements that use different options of the SET clause

contains one row for each customer. Among the columns in this table are SALESTOT and SALESCNT. SALESTOT contains the total dollar value for all sales made to a customer, and SALESCNT is a count of the number of sales made. Whenever a new invoice is issued, its total amount, represented here by the program host variable INVTOTAL, is added to the value in the SALESTOT column. At the same time, the value of the SALESCNT column is incremented by 1.

This UPDATE statement does what would require several steps in a standard COBOL program. It locates the CUSTHIST table row for the customer, gets the SALESTOT and SALESCNT column values from it, increments them properly, and then writes the row back to the table.

The last option you can use in the UPDATE statement's SET clause is NULL. It specifies that a column has no value. You can't specify NULL for a column that the DBA defined with the NOT NULL attribute. If you do, the precompiler will find the error, warn you about it, and end with a return code of 4. If you ignore that and try to bind the program, the bind will fail. In chapter 9, you'll learn how to handle columns that can contain nulls.

How to identify rows for UPDATE or DELETE in a base table   To tell DB2 what rows you want an UPDATE or DELETE statement to affect, you code the WHERE clause. The first form of the WHERE clause lets you use the same kinds of selection conditions you use with the SELECT statement. Usually, you'll code the WHERE clause with an equals condition that identifies a single row in the target table. That's appropriate for most application programming situations, and it's what the examples in figure 4-1 illustrate.

However, you need to realize that unlike a stand-alone SELECT, both UPDATE and DELETE can affect more than one row in a table. If you code a less restrictive WHERE clause than those in figure 4-1, DB2 updates or deletes every row that meets the selection condition. For instance, the UPDATE statement in example 1 in figure 4-4 contains the WHERE clause

```
WHERE ZIPCODE = '                    '
```

Because more than one row in the CUST table may meet this condition, this statement may affect multiple rows. The same principle applies to the DELETE statement. Example 1 in figure 4-5 is a single DELETE statement that will delete all the rows in the CUST table with customer numbers less than 300000.

If you don't code a WHERE clause on an UPDATE or DELETE statement, DB2 changes or removes every row in the table. To illustrate, example 2 in figure 4-5 shows a DELETE statement that would remove every row from the CUST table. Needless to say, there aren't many applications that call for this, for either a DELETE or an UPDATE operation.

Although the UPDATE statement can affect multiple rows, it cannot supply a different set of values for each. Instead, DB2 applies the changes you specify in the SET clause to each row that meets the selection condition.

After it processes either statement, DB2 reports the number of rows that it changed or removed in the SQL communication area. It returns the count of affected rows through an array called SQLERRD that consists of six numeric items. The count field is the third item in that array: SQLERRD(3).

How to identify a row for UPDATE or DELETE in a cursor-controlled results table   The easiest way to update or delete table rows in an application program is to code an UPDATE or DELETE statement that selects just the rows you want, and processes them. But that isn't always possible. When it isn't, you need to update or delete rows through a cursor-controlled results table. Then, you can update or delete rows one at a time.

Before I go on, I want to stress that you're likely to modify a table through a cursor only when you can't write a selection condition for the rows you want. With a cursor, you can go through the rows in the results table one by one, performing any other processing that's necessary for each row to make sure you want to modify or delete it. Or, if the program is interactive, the user can determine whether the row should be processed. And if the row will be updated, the user can also supply the new values.

Example 1   A DELETE statement that removes a set of rows from a table

```
EXEC SQL
    DELETE FROM MMADBV.CUST
        WHERE CUSTNO < '300000'
END-EXEC.
```

Example 2   A DELETE statement that removes every row from a table

```
EXEC SQL
    DELETE FROM MMADBV.CUST
END-EXEC.
```

Figure 4-5   DELETE statement examples

To be able to use the UPDATE and DELETE statements to change a table through a cursor, you have to do the same preparatory work you do to create a cursor-controlled table and to retrieve data from it. First, you need to code a DECLARE CURSOR statement that defines what the results table will contain. (If you plan to use the UPDATE statement, the DECLARE CURSOR statement should include the FOR UPDATE OF clause; I'll describe it in a moment.) Next, you have to issue an OPEN statement to generate the results table. Then, you need to issue the FETCH statement once for each row in the results table to work through it from beginning to end.

When you use UPDATE or DELETE with a cursor, the statement affects only the current row. That is, you can update or delete only the row most recently retrieved from the results table. To do this, you have to name the cursor on the WHERE CURRENT OF clause. So, if you are working with a cursor you named CUSTCURS in the DECLARE TABLE statement, you'd identify it by coding

```
WHERE CURRENT OF CUSTCURS
```

on the UPDATE or DELETE statement. Then, the statement affects only one row: the base table row represented by the current row in the cursor-controlled results table.

Figure 4-6 presents a sample DELETE statement. Notice that it names the base table that will actually be affected by the statement (MMADBV.CUST) in its FROM clause and the cursor the base table is accessed through (CUSTCURS) in its WHERE CURRENT OF clause. You

```
EXEC SQL
    DELETE FROM MMADBV.CUST
        WHERE CURRENT OF CUSTCURS
END-EXEC.
```

Figure 4-6   A DELETE statement that removes a row through a cursor-controlled results table

don't code a selection condition in the WHERE clause of the UPDATE or DELETE statement in this context. That's because the results table has already been defined in the WHERE clause in the DECLARE CURSOR statement's SELECT component.

If there isn't a current row when you issue either a DELETE or an UPDATE statement with the WHERE CURRENT OF clause, the statement won't work. This can happen because the results table isn't open, a row hasn't been retrieved, or the end of the table has been reached. After you issue an UPDATE or a DELETE statement, the cursor position is unchanged. To move ahead to the next row in the results table, just issue another FETCH statement.

To be able to use the UPDATE statement to change the values in a base table through a cursor-controlled results table, you may have to identify the columns that are eligible for modification. To do that, you code the FOR UPDATE OF clause in the DECLARE CURSOR statement. On it, you list all of the base table columns that you may need to change.

For example, the DECLARE CURSOR statement in figure 4-7 enables you to update six columns in the CUST table. When you use UPDATE with DECLARE CURSOR, you need to coordinate what the statements specify. Both statements need to name the base table (MMADBV.CUST in this example) and the cursor (here, CUSTCURS). If the FOR UPDATE OF clause is required, it must list all of the columns that any UPDATE statement in the program will try to change through the cursor.

It's possible that you may not have to supply the FOR UPDATE OF clause. If DB2's NOFOR precompiler option is in effect, you can omit FOR UPDATE OF and still be able to change the contents of a row through a cursor-controlled results table. NOFOR wasn't available until release 2.2 of DB2, so if you're working with an older version of DB2, FOR UPDATE OF isn't optional.

DECLARE CURSOR statement

```
EXEC SQL
    DECLARE CUSTCURS CURSOR FOR
        SELECT CUSTNO,   FNAME,   LNAME,   ADDR,
               CITY,     STATE,   ZIPCODE
        FROM   MMADBV.CUST
        WHERE INVCUST < '300000'
    FOR UPDATE OF    FNAME,   LNAME,   ADDR,
               CITY,     STATE,   ZIPCODE
END-EXEC.
```

UPDATE statement

```
EXEC SQL
    UPDATE MMADBV.CUST
        SET FNAME   = :FNAME,
            LNAME   = :LNAME,
            ADDR    = :ADDR,
            CITY    = :CITY,
            STATE   = :STATE,
            ZIPCODE = :ZIPCODE
        WHERE CURRENT OF CUSTCURS
END-EXEC.
```

Figure 4-7   Statements that let a program change rows in the CUST table through a cursor

Restrictions on the UPDATE and DELETE statements

You can't use the UPDATE or DELETE statement to modify DB2 data in a read-only table. You may have to deal with a read-only table in two situations. One of those situations is when you work with a cursor-controlled results table that was created using certain DB2 features that are incompatible with updates and deletes. The other is when the "table" you want to modify is really a view, and the view was created using similar features.

With what I've presented so far in this book, the only thing you know how to do that makes a cursor-controlled results table read-only is to use the DISTINCT keyword in the SELECT component of a DECLARE CURSOR statement. However, a number of other features produce a read-only results table. If the SELECT in your DECLARE CURSOR statement uses a union, a join, some categories of subqueries, a column function, or any of several keywords (ORDER BY, GROUP BY, or HAVING), the results table will be read-only. You'll learn about these features in section 3.

Similar restrictions apply to views. To create a view, a DBA codes a CREATE VIEW statement that includes a SELECT component, much as in a DECLARE CURSOR statement. If the SELECT component of that

CREATE VIEW statement uses a join, a particular kind of subquery, a column function, GROUP BY, HAVING, or DISTINCT, the view will be read-only. Fortunately, the system designer who prepares specifications for a program that needs to process a view as if it were a table probably won't ask you to do update or delete tasks that DB2 doesn't support.

How to use the INSERT statement to add data to a table

To add a new row to a table, you use the SQL INSERT statement. Its standard file processing equivalent is WRITE. I'll show you how to use the INSERT statement by first presenting a simple example of it. Then, I'll discuss its syntax and illustrate its features with a few more examples.

How simple forms of INSERT work

Figure 4-8 shows a typical INSERT statement. As you can see, this statement contains two clauses. The INTO clause first names the table where DB2 should insert the row. In this case, it's the CUST table. After the table name, the INTO clause specifies the columns that it will supply values for in the new row. The INSERT statement in figure 4-8 lists each of the seven columns in the CUST table. Note that I coded parentheses around the list of column names on the INTO clause. When you code any column names on an INSERT statement's INTO clause, you must code them in parentheses.

The other clause in figure 4-8, VALUES, specifies seven COBOL host variables. The contents of these variables will supply the values for the seven columns the INTO clause lists. The names in the VALUES and INTO clauses correspond to each other. In other words, the contents of the first host variable on the VALUES clause will be moved to the first column on the INTO clause, the contents of the second host variable to the second column, and so on. You need to code the list on the VALUES clause in parentheses, just like the list of column names on the INTO clause.

Several sorts of error conditions can arise as a result of an INSERT statement. One of them, −803, means that you tried to insert a row into a table that has a duplicate value in a column defined by the DBA to have unique values. (In standard file processing terms, this is called a duplicate key situation.) I won't mention any other codes here. Just be aware that when an INSERT statement returns a negative error code value, no data was inserted in the table.

```
EXEC SQL
    INSERT INTO MMADBV.CUST
                ( CUSTNO,         FNAME,         LNAME,
                  ADDR,           CITY,          STATE,
                  ZIPCODE)
        VALUES (:CUSTNO,         :FNAME,         :LNAME,
                  :ADDR,          :CITY,         :STATE,
                  :ZIPCODE)
    END-EXEC.
```

Figure 4-8   A typical INSERT statement

The syntax and operation of the INSERT statement

Figure 4-9 presents the syntax of the SQL INSERT statement. It has three clauses you need to understand: INTO, VALUES, and subselect. INTO is easy to understand, but VALUES and subselect, which are mutually exclusive, can be a little more complicated. You code VALUES when you want to insert one row at a time in the target table and the program supplies the necessary values for all of its columns. In contrast, you code a subselect when you want to insert multiple rows from another table with one statement. Here, I'll describe all three INSERT clauses.

How to use the INTO clause of the INSERT statement   As you saw in the example in figure 4-8, the INTO clause names the table where you want to insert a row and the columns you want to provide values for. You can code the column names in any order you wish, as long as you're careful to code the corresponding VALUES clause items in the same sequence. I recommend that you code the column names in the order they appear in the table's DCLGEN output.

The syntax for the INSERT statement in figure 4-9 shows that the column names are optional on the INTO clause. If you don't specify them, DB2 assumes that the statement's VALUES clause will supply distinct values for each column in the target table in the order they were defined to DB2 when the table was created. The sample INSERT statement in figure 4-10 uses this technique. It accomplishes the same thing as the statement in figure 4-8.

Depending on how your DBA defined the table where you want to insert a row, you may not have to name all of its columns on the INTO clause. If the DBA provided a specific default value for DB2 to use for a column, you don't have to name that column when you add a row. Or if a column's value can be null, you don't have to name it either. In the CUST

The SQL INSERT statement

```
EXEC SQL
    INSERT INTO table-name [(column-name[,column-name...])]
         ⎧        ⎧:host-var⎫ ⎧:host-var⎫    ⎫
         ⎨VALUES ({ literal }[,{ literal }...] )⎬
         ⎪        ⎩NULL     ⎭ ⎩NULL     ⎭    ⎪
         ⎩subselect                          ⎭
END-EXEC.
```

Explanation

table-name	The DB2 name of the table where you want to insert a row or rows.
column-name	The DB2 name of the column where you want to insert a value. If you specify column names, you may code them in any order you wish. If you omit the list of column names, DB2 assumes you're supplying values for each column of the table and that the values are in the order that they were defined to DB2.
host-var	The COBOL name of the host variable that contains the value to be inserted into the corresponding column in the new row. Be sure to precede each COBOL host variable name with a colon.
literal	A constant value to be inserted into the corresponding column in the new row. If the value is character data, it must be between quotation marks; if the value is numeric data, it must not be between quotation marks.
NULL	Specifies that the value of the corresponding column should be set to null.
subselect	A nested SELECT statement that describes a results table that should be inserted into table-name specified on the INSERT's INTO clause. The SELECT statement in a subselect must contain a SELECT and FROM clause, and may contain a WHERE clause; it may not contain an INTO clause. Also, the table you name in the SELECT's FROM clause may not be the one you name in the INSERT's INTO clause. The results table the subselect creates must be type-compatible with the table where its rows will be inserted.

Figure 4-9   The SQL INSERT statement

table, none of the columns has a DB2-supplied default and none may be null. As a result, I had to include all seven of the table's columns, either explicitly as in figure 4-8 or implicitly as in figure 4-10.

How to use the VALUES clause of the INSERT statement   You code the VALUES clause in an INSERT statement when your program needs to add one row at a time to a table, and it can provide all of the required values for each of the row's columns. You must supply one value element for each column you name on the INTO clause.

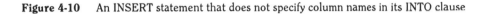

```
EXEC SQL
    INSERT INTO MMADBV.CUST
    VALUES (:CUSTNO,         :FNAME,          :LNAME,
            :ADDR,           :CITY,           :STATE,
            :ZIPCODE)
END-EXEC.
```

Figure 4-10   An INSERT statement that does not specify column names in its INTO clause

Also, you need to make sure the VALUES clause items correspond to the right column names. As I mentioned earlier, DB2 inserts the first VALUES item into the first column you named on the INTO clause, the second VALUES item into the second column, and so on. (Remember, you can list column names in any order you like on the INTO clause; what matters is how you pair them up with their corresponding values in the VALUES clause.)

You can specify values in three ways. The most common way is to use COBOL host variables that your program initializes with proper values before it executes the INSERT statement. That's the technique I used in the examples in figures 4-8 and 4-10. As in any SQL statement, you need to precede each host variable's name with a colon.

The second way you can specify a value for a column is to provide a literal, or constant. If you're coding a literal value for a column with a character data type, surround the value with quotation marks. On the other hand, if the target column has a numeric data type, make sure the value you code is a number and that you don't use quotation marks. You're most likely to insert a literal value into a column to provide a default or starting value for it.

The third way you can specify a value for a column is to code NULL. You should realize that if a column can and should be null, you probably won't even list its name on the INTO clause. Then, you won't need to code the NULL keyword at all. You're more likely to need to be able to code INSERT statements that can specify a particular value *or* null. To do that, you need to use a special programming technique I'll present in chapter 9.

How to use a subselect in an INSERT statement   You can use a subselect instead of the VALUES clause when you want to insert more than one row at a time and the contents of their columns will come from another DB2 table. As its name suggests, a *subselect* is a SELECT statement that's nested inside, or subordinate to, another statement, in this case, INSERT. All of the rows in the results table the subselect generates are added to the table you name in the INSERT statement's INTO clause. In DB2's language, this is a *mass insert*.

(If you've worked much with VSAM space management, the term "mass insert" may sound familiar. However, VSAM's MASSINSERT option and DB2's mass insert operation are different. A DB2 mass insert is a high-level process that adds multiple rows to a table with a single statement. In VSAM, MASSINSERT is a special-purpose option that improves performance when you insert records sequentially into a key-sequenced data set.)

The SELECT statement you code as a subselect is much like a SELECT you'd code in a DECLARE CURSOR statement. It lists the columns you want to retrieve and the table that contains them. The table you specify in the subselect, however, can't be the same table named in the INSERT statement's INTO clause. In other words, you can't insert rows into the table they come from.

A subselect usually includes a WHERE clause that identifies the rows to be selected from the source table and to be inserted into the target table. Just as with a SELECT in a DECLARE CURSOR statement, a subselect in an INSERT doesn't include an INTO clause. That's because a subselect in an INSERT doesn't return data to the program. All of the data transfer takes place within DB2. That's true whether the subselect processes zero, one, ten, or thousands of rows.

When you use a subselect, the column names you list on the SELECT clause must create a results table that matches the target table where you want to insert data. That means they must have the same number of columns, and those columns must have compatible types and lengths.

Figure 4-11 presents an INSERT statement that uses a subselect to do a mass insert. The purpose of this statement is to insert some rows from the CUST table into another table called OLDCUST. The subselect specifies that rows from the CUST table that have customer number column values less than 300000 should be inserted. The two tables in this example, CUST and OLDCUST, have identical structures. As a result, I was able to code abbreviated statements. The INSERT's INTO clause doesn't need a list of column names, and an asterisk was sufficient in the subselect's SELECT clause.

By the way, when you do a mass insert, the rows in the source table are unaffected. So if you want to move rows from one table to another, you need another step. After you use the INSERT statement to copy the rows from the source table to the target table, you use a DELETE statement to remove the copied rows from the source table. For instance, imagine I want to remove the rows from the CUST table that the statement in figure 4-11 copies to the OLDCUST table. All I have to do is follow the INSERT statement with the DELETE statement I showed you in example 1 in figure 4-5.

```
EXEC SQL
    INSERT INTO MMADBV.OLDCUST
        (SELECT      *
            FROM   MMADBV.CUST
            WHERE  CUSTNO < '300000')
END-EXEC.
```

Figure 4-11   An INSERT statement that does a mass insert

When a mass insert is successful, DB2 reports the number of rows it inserted into the target table in the SQL communication area. DB2 uses the same SQLCA field for this information as it does when it processes UPDATE and DELETE statements: SQLERRD(3).

Putting the essential DB2 elements to work in a simple update program

Now that you've learned how to code the INSERT, UPDATE, and DELETE statements, you're ready to see an example of how you can use them together in an application program. Here, I'll give you an overview of how a simple update program works, describe its structure, and step you through its COBOL source code. I'm sure you'll find the program easy to understand.

The operation of the update program

Unlike the inquiry programs I presented in chapters 2 and 3, this program is not interactive. Instead, it works in a batch environment. In many shops, the demands of online systems are so great that it's not feasible to do extensive update processing during peak-use periods. As a result, those shops often use batch programs during off-hours to update their DB2 tables. Such a program can read an input file of transactions that accumulate during the day and post them to the DB2 tables. That's what this program does.

The input to the update program is a standard VSAM entry-sequenced data set that contains transaction records. The record layout for this file is

```
01  CUSTOMER-TRANSACTION-RECORD.
*
    05  CTR-TRANSACTION-CODE        PIC X.
    05  CTR-TRANSACTION-DATA.
        10  CTR-CUSTOMER-NUMBER     PIC X(6).
        10  CTR-CUSTOMER-DETAILS    PIC X(112).
```

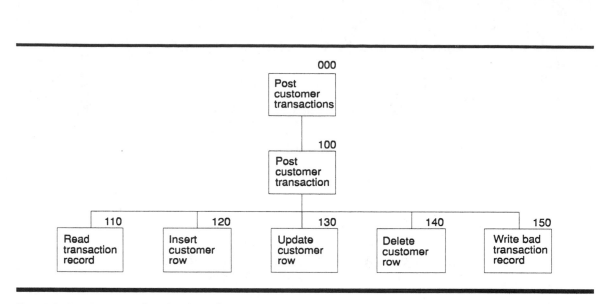

Figure 4-12   Structure chart for the update program

The first field in the record, CTR-TRANSACTION-CODE, can have one of three values: A, R, or D. A means the data that follows should be added to the customer table as a new row. R means the data that follows should replace an existing customer row. And D means the specified customer row should be deleted.

The second item in the transaction record description is a group item (CTR-TRANSACTION-DATA) that mirrors the host structure for the CUST table. The 112-byte field CTR-CUSTOMER-DETAILS contains data for all the columns in the customer table except the customer number column. Because this program assumes that the data elements in the transaction file are valid, it doesn't need to edit them and, as a result, it doesn't need to be able to identify most of them explicitly.

The only exception is the customer number field. Because its value specifies the table row an UPDATE or DELETE operation affects, the program needs to refer to it. As a result, I defined CTR-CUSTOMER-NUMBER separately under the group item CTR-TRANSACTION-DATA.

The design of the update program

Figure 4-12 presents the structure chart for the update program. The top-level module, 000-POST-CUSTOMER-TRANSACTIONS, performs 100-POST-CUSTOMER-TRANSACTION over and over as it works through the transaction file. As you can see, module 100 has five subordinates.

Each time it runs, module 100 performs 110-READ-TRANSACTION-RECORD to get the next record in the transaction file. If module 110 successfully reads a new transaction record, module 100 proceeds. The action it takes depends on the value in the record's transaction code field. It can add a new customer row (module 120), change an existing one (module 130), or delete one (module 140). Each of these modules issues the appropriate SQL statement to perform the action. If the transaction code in the input record is something the program doesn't expect, or if one of the SQL statements fails, module 100 invokes module 150. Module 150 writes a record to a bad transaction file that another program can process later to produce an exception report.

The source code for the update program

Now that you're familiar with the structure of the update program, I think you'll have no problem understanding its source code. Figure 4-13 presents the DCLGEN output for the CUST table the program uses, and figure 4-14 presents the program's source code.

Unlike the other DB2 programs I've shown you, this program includes Environment Division and File Section entries for two standard files. One of those files is the input transaction file, and the other is the bad transaction file where the program stores invalid transaction records. Still, there are no Environment Division or File Section entries for the DB2 table this program uses. Instead, the program's Working-Storage Section contains an SQL INCLUDE statement for the CUST table's DCLGEN output.

The program's Procedure Division is straightforward. In module 100, after it has successfully read a transaction record, the program checks the transaction code field. It uses a COBOL EVALUATE statement to determine whether it should perform the add, replace, or delete module, or flag the transaction as an error.

Because you've already seen examples like the INSERT, UPDATE, and DELETE statements in module 120, 130, and 140, I won't describe them in detail here. However, I would like you to notice the error-checking code in these modules. After the SQL statement in each, I coded a condition that checks the value of SQLCODE. All three modules flag a transaction as invalid if it results in a negative return code. And the modules that do updates and deletes (130 and 140) also flag transactions as invalid if their SQL statements return +100. In this context, +100 means there was nothing to update or delete because a row couldn't be found that meets the selection condition in the statement.

What a program must do in response to invalid conditions depends on the application design and on how the tables are defined. For example, the

```
*********************************************************************
* DCLGEN TABLE(MMADBV.CUST)                                         *
*         LIBRARY(MMAOO2.DCLGENS.COBOL(CUST))                       *
*         ACTION(REPLACE)                                           *
*         STRUCTURE(CUSTOMER-ROW)                                   *
*         APOST                                                     *
* ... IS THE DCLGEN COMMAND THAT MADE THE FOLLOWING STATEMENTS      *
*********************************************************************
      EXEC SQL DECLARE MMADBV.CUST TABLE
      ( CUSTNO                          CHAR(6) NOT NULL,
        FNAME                           CHAR(20) NOT NULL,
        LNAME                           CHAR(30) NOT NULL,
        ADDR                            CHAR(30) NOT NULL,
        CITY                            CHAR(20) NOT NULL,
        STATE                           CHAR(2) NOT NULL,
        ZIPCODE                         CHAR(10) NOT NULL
      ) END-EXEC.
*********************************************************************
* COBOL DECLARATION FOR TABLE MMADBV.CUST                           *
*********************************************************************
  01  CUSTOMER-ROW.
      10 CUSTNO            PIC X(6).
      10 FNAME             PIC X(20).
      10 LNAME             PIC X(30).
      10 ADDR              PIC X(30).
      10 CITY              PIC X(20).
      10 STATE             PIC X(2).
      10 ZIPCODE           PIC X(10).
*********************************************************************
* THE NUMBER OF COLUMNS DESCRIBED BY THIS DECLARATION IS 7          *
*********************************************************************
```

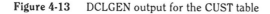

Figure 4-13   DCLGEN output for the CUST table

INSERT statement in this program shouldn't add a row to the customer table if a row already exists that contains the same customer number. However, the program doesn't have to do any explicit checking to see if that's the case. That's because an index exists for the table that makes the customer number column a unique key.

An *index* is a DB2 object that a DBA can use for performance and control reasons. Whether an index is associated with a table is completely transparent to application programs. Because a unique index exists in this situation, DB2 doesn't let programs add rows to the table that would contain duplicate key values. (An attempt to insert a row with a duplicate key value results in SQLCODE value −803.)

If the DBA doesn't define the table in a way that insures that there would be no duplicate customer numbers in the CUST table, the programmer must. To do that, you have to issue a SELECT statement in the program to find out if the customer number in the transaction is already in use

```
000100 IDENTIFICATION DIVISION.
000200*
000300 PROGRAM-ID.        UPDTCUST.
000400*
000500 ENVIRONMENT DIVISION.
000600*
000700 INPUT-OUTPUT SECTION.
000800*
000900 FILE-CONTROL.
001000*
001100     SELECT CUSTTRAN ASSIGN TO AS-CUSTTRAN.
001200     SELECT BADTRAN  ASSIGN TO AS-BADTRAN.
001300*
001400 DATA DIVISION.
001500*
001600 FILE SECTION.
001700*
001800 FD  CUSTTRAN
001900     LABEL RECORDS ARE STANDARD
002000     RECORD CONTAINS 119 CHARACTERS.
002100*
002200 01  CUSTOMER-TRANSACTION-RECORD.
002300*
002400     05  CTR-TRANSACTION-CODE      PIC X.
002500     05  CTR-TRANSACTION-DATA.
002600         10  CTR-CUSTOMER-NUMBER   PIC X(6).
002700         10  CTR-CUSTOMER-DETAILS  PIC X(112).
002800*
002900 FD  BADTRAN
003000     LABEL RECORDS ARE STANDARD
003100     RECORD CONTAINS 119 CHARACTERS.
003200*
003300 01  BAD-TRANSACTION-RECORD.
003400*
003500     05  BTR-TRANSACTION-CODE      PIC X.
003600     05  BTR-TRANSACTION-DATA      PIC X(118).
003700*
003800 WORKING-STORAGE SECTION.
003900*
004000 01  SWITCHES.
004100*
004200     05  END-OF-TRANSACTIONS-SW    PIC X     VALUE "N".
004300         88  END-OF-TRANSACTIONS             VALUE "Y".
004400     05  VALID-TRANSACTION-SW      PIC X     VALUE "Y".
004500         88  VALID-TRANSACTION              VALUE "Y".
004600*
004700     EXEC SQL
004800         INCLUDE CUST
004900     END-EXEC.
005000*
005100     EXEC SQL
005200         INCLUDE SQLCA
005300     END-EXEC.
005400*
```

Figure 4-14   COBOL source code for the update program (part 1 of 3)

```
005500 PROCEDURE DIVISION.
005600*
005700 000-POST-CUST-TRANSACTIONS.
005800*
005900     OPEN INPUT  CUSTTRAN
006000          OUTPUT BADTRAN.
006100     PERFORM 100-POST-CUST-TRANSACTION
006200         UNTIL END-OF-TRANSACTIONS.
006300     CLOSE CUSTTRAN
006400           BADTRAN.
006500     STOP RUN.
006600*
006700 100-POST-CUST-TRANSACTION.
006800*
006900     MOVE "Y" TO VALID-TRANSACTION-SW.
007000     PERFORM 110-READ-TRANSACTION-RECORD.
007100     IF NOT END-OF-TRANSACTIONS
007200         MOVE CTR-TRANSACTION-DATA TO CUSTOMER-ROW
007300         EVALUATE CTR-TRANSACTION-CODE
007400             WHEN "A"   PERFORM 120-INSERT-CUSTOMER-ROW
007500             WHEN "R"   PERFORM 130-UPDATE-CUSTOMER-ROW
007600             WHEN "D"   PERFORM 140-DELETE-CUSTOMER-ROW
007700             WHEN OTHER MOVE "N" TO VALID-TRANSACTION-SW
007800         END-EVALUATE
007900         IF NOT VALID-TRANSACTION
008000             PERFORM 150-WRITE-BAD-TRANS-RECORD.
008100*
008200 110-READ-TRANSACTION-RECORD.
008300*
008400     READ CUSTTRAN
008500         AT END
008600             MOVE "Y" TO END-OF-TRANSACTIONS-SW.
008700*
008800 120-INSERT-CUSTOMER-ROW.
008900*
009000     EXEC SQL
009100         INSERT INTO MMADBV.CUST
009200                 ( CUSTNO,    FNAME,      LNAME,     ADDR,
009300                   CITY,      STATE,      ZIPCODE)
009400         VALUES (:CUSTNO,   :FNAME,    :LNAME,    :ADDR,
009500                 :CITY,     :STATE,    :ZIPCODE)
009600     END-EXEC.
009700     IF SQLCODE < 0
009800         MOVE "N" TO VALID-TRANSACTION-SW.
009900*
```

Figure 4-14   COBOL source code for the update program (part 2 of 3)

before attempting the INSERT. If the SELECT statement is successful, you treat the transaction as invalid. On the other hand, if the SELECT results in an SQLCODE value of +100 to indicate a corresponding row wasn't found, you know it is safe to insert the new row.

```
010000 130-UPDATE-CUSTOMER-ROW.
010100*
010200     EXEC SQL
010300        UPDATE MMADBV.CUST
010400           SET FNAME   = :FNAME,
010500               LNAME   = :LNAME,
010600               ADDR    = :ADDR,
010700               CITY    = :CITY,
010800               STATE   = :STATE,
010900               ZIPCODE = :ZIPCODE
011000        WHERE  CUSTNO  = :CUSTNO
011100     END-EXEC.
011200     IF    SQLCODE < 0
011300        OR SQLCODE = +100
011400           MOVE "N" TO VALID-TRANSACTION-SW.
011500*
011600 140-DELETE-CUSTOMER-ROW.
011700*
011800     EXEC SQL
011900        DELETE FROM MMADBV.CUST
012000           WHERE CUSTNO = :CUSTNO
012100     END-EXEC.
012200     IF    SQLCODE < 0
012300        OR SQLCODE = +100
012400           MOVE "N" TO VALID-TRANSACTION-SW.
012500*
012600 150-WRITE-BAD-TRANS-RECORD.
012700*
012800     WRITE BAD-TRANSACTION-RECORD
012900        FROM CUSTOMER-TRANSACTION-RECORD.
013000*
```

Figure 4-14   COBOL source code for the update program (part 3 of 3)

The issue of unique keys illustrates how DB2 can relieve system designers and programmers of the responsibility of having to attend to trivial, but essential, tasks. You saw an example of this in the INSERT module of the update program. As long as the DBA defines a table with an appropriate index, DB2 can assume part of the burden of maintaining the integrity of the data it manages, at least within the scope of that table. However, data integrity concerns exist not just within individual tables, but between two or more related tables as well.

DB2's referential integrity feature and how it can affect INSERT, DELETE, and UPDATE statements

The current release of DB2 provides a feature that helps you maintain *referential integrity* between two tables. Referential integrity means that all references one table makes to another are valid. DB2 can automatically en-force referential integrity, as long as the DBA defines the related tables properly.

Referential integrity can exist when two tables have a parent/depend-ent relationship. Each row in a *dependent table* is related to (that is, refers to) one and only one row in the *parent table*. Data in a specific column in each row in the dependent table identifies the parent row that it depends on.

The CUST and INV tables I used in the program example in chapter 3 illustrate the parent/dependent relationship well. CUST is the parent table, and INV is the dependent table. A customer in the CUST table may have many invoices in the INV table, but each invoice relates to one and only one customer. To refresh your memory about these tables, figure 4-15 shows the CREATE TABLE statements I coded to define them. (I won't cover the CREATE TABLE statement in this book because it's used more by DBAs than by programmers. If you look carefully at the statements in figure 4-15, though, I'm sure you'll have no problem understanding them.)

Each row in the INV table contains the number of the associated cus-tomer in its INVCUST column. Because I wanted this relationship to make sense, I used unique values for the customer number column (CUSTNO) in the CUST table. That way, there can be no question as to which customer "owns" a particular invoice.

The columns that contain the data that link two tables have special names. The column whose value uniquely identifies a row within a table is called its *primary key*. CUSTNO is the primary key column for the CUST table. The column that contains a value that identifies a related row in another table is called a *foreign key*. The INVCUST column in the INV table is a foreign key because its value in a given row must be the same as the value of the primary key (the CUSTNO column) in the related CUST table row.

Under releases of DB2 before 2.1, it is up to a programmer to make sure any row added to the INV table contains an INVCUST value that identi-fies a row in the CUST table. As I defined the tables in the CREATE TABLE statements in figure 4-15, that's the case. These statements don't take advan-tage of DB2's ability to enforce referential integrity. A program can add a row to the INV table figure 4-15 defines, regardless of what the row's INVCUST column contains. That column's value should identify the parent row in the CUST table, but it's possible to supply a value that doesn't.

In contrast, under later releases of DB2, a DBA can define tables so DB2 enforces the integrity of references between primary and foreign keys. Figure 4-16 shows the CREATE TABLE statements for versions of the CUST and INV tables that do use referential integrity. Look at the elements

```
CREATE TABLE MMADBV.CUST
   (CUSTNO    CHAR(6)    NOT NULL,
    FNAME     CHAR(20)   NOT NULL,
    LNAME     CHAR(30)   NOT NULL,
    ADDR      CHAR(30)   NOT NULL,
    CITY      CHAR(20)   NOT NULL,
    STATE     CHAR(2)    NOT NULL,
    ZIPCODE   CHAR(10)   NOT NULL)
 IN DATABASE MMADB

CREATE TABLE MMADBV.INV
   (INVCUST   CHAR(6)         NOT NULL,
    INVNO     CHAR(6)         NOT NULL,
    INVDATE   DATE            NOT NULL,
    INVSUBT   DECIMAL(9,2)    NOT NULL,
    INVSHIP   DECIMAL(7,2)    NOT NULL,
    INVTAX    DECIMAL(7,2)    NOT NULL,
    INVTOTAL  DECIMAL(9,2)    NOT NULL,
    INVPROM   CHAR(10)        NOT NULL)
 IN DATABASE MMADB
```

Figure 4-15   CREATE TABLE statements that define the CUST and INV tables without support for referential integrity checking

of these statements that I shaded. In the statement that creates the CUST table, I identified CUSTNO as the primary key column.

In the statement that creates the INV table, I identified INVNO as its own primary key. This lets the INV table serve as a parent to other tables, but it's irrelevant in the relationship between INV and CUST. What I want you to notice is the FOREIGN KEY clause. It specifies that the INVCUST column contains values that refer to the CUST table. That means each value in the INVCUST column corresponds to one of the unique values in the primary key of the CUST table, CUSTNO.

These statements specify the relationship between the INV and CUST tables, and DB2 won't process statements that would damage the integrity of that relationship. In particular, it won't process an INSERT statement that tries to add a row to the INV table that doesn't have an INVCUST column value that identifies a row in the CUST table. (By the way, when DB2 rejects a statement because it would violate referential integrity, it returns a value in the -500 range in SQLCODE.)

The last clause I shaded in figure 4-16 specifies a *referential constraint* for the relationship between the INV and CUST tables. A referential constraint specifies what DB2 will and will not let statements that affect these tables do. Actually, the referential constraint in the example in figure 4-16 isn't very constraining. It specifies that if a row in the parent table (CUST)

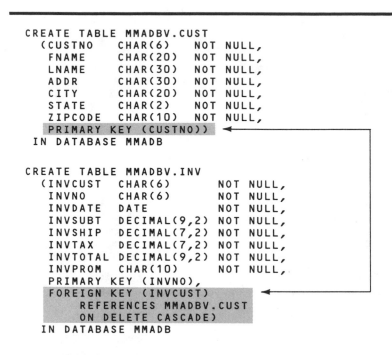

```
CREATE TABLE MMADBV.CUST
  (CUSTNO    CHAR(6)    NOT NULL,
   FNAME     CHAR(20)   NOT NULL,
   LNAME     CHAR(30)   NOT NULL,
   ADDR      CHAR(30)   NOT NULL,
   CITY      CHAR(20)   NOT NULL,
   STATE     CHAR(2)    NOT NULL,
   ZIPCODE   CHAR(10)   NOT NULL,
   PRIMARY KEY (CUSTNO))
 IN DATABASE MMADB

CREATE TABLE MMADBV.INV
  (INVCUST   CHAR(6)        NOT NULL,
   INVNO     CHAR(6)        NOT NULL,
   INVDATE   DATE           NOT NULL,
   INVSUBT   DECIMAL(9,2)   NOT NULL,
   INVSHIP   DECIMAL(7,2)   NOT NULL,
   INVTAX    DECIMAL(7,2)   NOT NULL,
   INVTOTAL  DECIMAL(9,2)   NOT NULL,
   INVPROM   CHAR(10)       NOT NULL,
   PRIMARY KEY (INVNO),
   FOREIGN KEY (INVCUST)
     REFERENCES MMADBV.CUST
       ON DELETE CASCADE)
 IN DATABASE MMADB
```

Figure 4-16   CREATE TABLE statements that define the CUST and INV tables with support for referential integrity checking

is deleted, the effect of the delete should "cascade" downward to delete all related rows in the dependent table (INV).

The chances are that you won't have to code the CREATE TABLE statement that specifies the referential constraints for a new table. However, you will need to code your programs so they don't violate the constraints already in place on the tables they process. So here I'll describe the range of constraints the DBA may impose over INSERT, UPDATE, and DELETE operations for parent and dependent tables. (Because you can only violate a referential constraint when you try to change a table, SELECT isn't subject to referential constraints.)

Referential constraints on INSERT statements

You can add a row at any time to a parent table, because referential integrity doesn't require that a parent table row have a corresponding row in a dependent table. But each row you insert in a parent table must have a unique value in its primary key column.

Before you can insert a row in a dependent table, however, a matching row must already exist in the parent table. That means that the value of the foreign key in the row to be inserted in the dependent table must appear as the primary key in a row in the parent table. I just mentioned an example: You can't add a row to the INV table unless its INVCUST value identifies a row that already exists in the CUST table.

Referential constraints on DELETE statements

Just as you can add a row to a parent table at any time, you can remove a row from a dependent table at any time. Again, that's because referential integrity doesn't require that a parent table row have a corresponding row in a dependent table. However, if you want to delete a parent table row that has dependent table rows, the situation is more complicated. What DB2 does depends on which of three referential constraint options the DBA entered on the CREATE TABLE statement: CASCADE, RESTRICT, or SET TO NULL.

CASCADE is the option I used in figure 4-16. This option can have drastic effects because it causes the deletion of a row in a parent table to be continued through the dependent table. So, with the CUST and INV tables defined as they are in figure 4-16, when I delete a customer row, all of the invoices related to it are deleted as well. That means one DELETE statement has the potential to affect many rows in more than one table.

The effect of a cascading delete can extend into other tables as well. For example, the INV table itself is a parent to a line-item table (LINEITEM) that contains one row for each item sold on any given invoice. If an INV row is deleted, all of its associated LINEITEM table rows are deleted too. So, imagine that a customer has 15 invoice rows, and each of those invoices has 10 line items. A single DELETE statement to remove that customer's row would do that, plus remove 15 rows from the INV table and 150 rows from the LINEITEM table.

The RESTRICT option is probably safer, at least with respect to insuring that changes occur in a controlled, predictable way. RESTRICT specifies that a row in the parent table cannot be deleted if any rows in a dependent table have a foreign key that refers to it. So, if I specified RESTRICT as the delete option for the INVCUST foreign key in the INV table, I couldn't delete a row from the CUST table if it had any dependent INV table rows. If the DBA doesn't specify a referential constraint for a foreign key, DB2 defaults to RESTRICT.

The third option, SET TO NULL, doesn't cause the rows in a dependent table to be removed when their parent rows are deleted. Instead, the foreign key column values in the affected dependent table rows are replaced with nulls. Obviously, for you to be able to use this option, the foreign key column must allow null values. I think this option is less useful than CASCADE and RESTRICT. However, you may encounter situations where it's appropriate.

Referential constraints on UPDATE statements

The only referential constraint a DBA can specify for the UPDATE statement is RESTRICT; CASCADE and SET TO NULL aren't available. Because RESTRICT is the default, you're not likely to find many CREATE TABLE statements that explicitly specify ON UPDATE RESTRICT.

The effect of RESTRICT is to keep you from changing the value in a parent table's primary key if any dependent table rows refer to it. I want you to realize, though, that changing the value of a row's primary key is unlikely. And, if you need to do it, you should also recognize that there are two additional limitations beyond RESTRICT. First, you can't change a primary key value when you're working through a cursor-controlled results table. Second, you can't issue an UPDATE statement to change the value of a primary key column if it will affect more than one row. But this is unlikely too, because primary key values must be unique.

Discussion

At this point, you've learned what you need to know to code COBOL programs that do basic retrieval and update operations. Although this is a useful subset, I've barely scratched the surface of what you can do with SQL in your programs. In particular, you've learned only a fraction of the capabilities of the SELECT statement. In section 3, I'll cover a number of SELECT's features, plus other DB2 topics that you'll find useful.

Terms

subselect
mass insert
index
referential integrity
dependent table
parent table
primary key
foreign key
referential constraint

Objectives

1. Given application and table specifications, code an SQL UPDATE statement to change the contents of a table's columns.

2. Given application and table specifications, code an SQL DELETE statement to remove a row or rows from a table.

3. Given application and table specifications, code an SQL INSERT statement to add a row or rows to a table.

4. Given the specifications for a program that will modify a DB2 table, design and code the program, using INSERT, UPDATE, and DELETE statements as necessary.

5. Describe how referential integrity features may affect what you can do with the INSERT, UPDATE, and DELETE statements.

Topic 2 How to use error handling and data integrity techniques

Whenever a program changes a table, it runs the risk of corrupting the stored data. For example, if a program fails, the changes it makes may not have been written to disk. Or, just as likely, the program may encounter problems in the DB2 environment that prevent it from completing a unit of work. In this topic, I'll describe what DB2 does to prevent problems like these and how you can use basic DB2 facilities to protect stored data.

DB2 spends a large part of its processing time to provide services like recovery, data integrity, and locking. Fortunately, most of these tasks are transparent to you and your programs. And most of what *isn't* transparent has to do with performance options and programming techniques for inter-active programs that process shared data, such as under CICS. In *Part 2: An Advanced Course*, I'll cover these issues in detail.

You don't need a thorough understanding of these features to develop the sorts of programs I've shown you so far. However, you may be expected to use the basic data integrity facilities DB2 provides through its COMMIT and ROLLBACK statements in the first programs you write. So, in this topic, I'll outline the concepts that underlie COMMIT and ROLLBACK, show you how to code the statements, and illustrate how to use them in an application program.

Unit of recovery

It may surprise you to learn that DB2 doesn't write table changes to disk as soon as a program issues an INSERT, UPDATE, or DELETE statement. Instead, it keeps track of the changes a program's SQL statements request in virtual storage buffers and log data sets. Only when a unit of recovery is complete does DB2 actually write those changes to disk.

A *unit of recovery*, also called a *unit of work*, is the amount of process-ing that takes place between the times DB2 writes a program's changes to disk. Those points are called *commit points*. Up to a commit point, DB2 can easily reverse any changes to tables that the program has requested since the last commit point. That's because the changes haven't really been made yet.

Just what constitutes a unit of recovery varies. It can be as small as the update of a single row, or it can be as extensive as the modification, insertion, or deletion of thousands of rows in several tables. Regardless of the scope of a unit of recovery, DB2 maintains the information necessary to reverse all of the changes requested since the last commit point.

Because it commits any remaining changes when a program ends normally, DB2 views the normal termination of a program as an *implicit commit point*. For example, in the simple update program you saw in topic 1, the entire program represents one unit of work. Even if the program issues thousands of SQL statements to insert, update, and delete rows in the customer table, DB2 doesn't commit those changes until the program ends.

If an application program ends abnormally, DB2 automatically reverses all of the table changes requested during its current unit of recovery. Ending "abnormally" means an uncontrolled program failure that would result in a storage dump occurred. It doesn't mean a controlled termination of a program, even if it's premature and in response to an unrecoverable DB2 error. If a COBOL program ends with a normal STOP RUN or GOBACK statement, DB2 considers that the end of a successful unit of recovery and commits the table changes the program requested.

If a program receives an unusual SQLCODE value in response to an UPDATE, DELETE, or INSERT statement, you may be faced with a situation where you will want to reverse the table changes it has requested. For example, imagine a complicated update program that accesses several tables. If one of the tables isn't available, perhaps because the device where it resides is temporarily out of service, statements issued against that table will fail, but they won't cause the program to abend. The program needs to detect errors like this and respond accordingly. To handle conditions like these, you use DB2's COMMIT and ROLLBACK statements.

The syntax and operation of the COMMIT and ROLLBACK statements

As you can see in figures 4-17 and 4-18, the syntax of the COMMIT and ROLLBACK statements is simple. All you do is code the name of the statement between EXEC SQL and END-EXEC. The only keyword you can specify for either is WORK, and it doesn't have any effect. Its only purpose is to make DB2's syntax compatible with that of SQL/DS, IBM's SQL DBMS for mainframes that don't run under MVS. What's challenging about using COMMIT and ROLLBACK isn't mastering their syntax, but deciding when you use them.

A program uses COMMIT to signal to DB2 that all of the table changes it has requested since the last commit point are consistent with one another and should be made permanent, even though the program hasn't ended.

The SQL COMMIT statement (only available under TSO)

```
EXEC SQL
     COMMIT [WORK]
END-EXEC.
```

Explanation

WORK   Optional. This keyword doesn't affect the operation of the COMMIT statement. It's included only for
                              compatibility with SQL/DS.

Figure 4-17   The SQL COMMIT statement

The commit point caused by a COMMIT statement is called an *explicit commit point*.

If you are making several related changes, don't issue a COMMIT statement until all the changes have been made. For example, a program that adds related rows to several tables should not issue a COMMIT statement until it has added the related rows to all of the affected tables.

ROLLBACK causes DB2 to disregard all of the changes made since the last commit point. ROLLBACK is useful if something unexpected makes it impossible to insure the changes to the tables will be consistent. This is the same thing that DB2 does when a program abends, except when a program issues an explicit ROLLBACK statement, it keeps running.

How long a unit of recovery lasts affects system performance. The more data DB2 has to maintain during a unit of recovery, the more system resources the program uses. And at the same time, parts of the tables that are affected during the unit of recovery are protected, or *locked*. That means other users may not be able to change or even access the affected data until the first program's unit of recovery is completed. When multiple tasks compete for access to the same data, it's essential that the data is locked for as short a time as possible.

As a result, it makes sense to keep program tasks simple and short or to issue COMMIT statements frequently to limit the scope of a unit of recovery. However, the COMMIT statement also uses system resources. Issuing it too often can also degrade system performance.

How often is too often? It depends on a number of factors that vary from situation to situation. Some sources recommend that you issue a COMMIT after each statement that changes a table, as long as you maintain consistency among the stored data elements. Other sources recommend

---

The SQL ROLLBACK statement (only available under TSO)

```
EXEC SQL
    ROLLBACK [WORK]
END-EXEC.
```

Explanation

WORK   Optional. This keyword doesn't affect the operation of the ROLLBACK statement. It's included only
                        for compatibility with SQL/DS.

Figure 4-18   The SQL ROLLBACK statement

you use a COMMIT statement after anywhere from 5 to 10 to over 100 changes. This is a situation where you should certainly get the advice of your DBA.

In production environments, standards are usually in place that specify not only how often commits should be performed, but also specific mechanisms for handling rollbacks. These standards usually involve other error processing that your programs should do, such as recording information about processing problems in a system log. You'll learn more about these considerations in *Part 2: An Advanced Course.*

Using the COMMIT and ROLLBACK statements in a sample program

In the last topic, I introduced the INSERT, UPDATE, and DELETE statements in a simple update program. The point of that example was to show you how to use those statements in a COBOL program. As I mentioned earlier in this topic, that program represents a single unit of recovery, regardless of the number of transactions it processes. Although that's fine for a simple example, it's probably not realistic for a production program.

This section presents a more realistic version of the update program. It uses the COMMIT statement to divide its execution into multiple units of work, and it uses the ROLLBACK statement to disregard any changes since the last commit point if an error occurs.

This program commits changes after it processes ten valid transactions. I selected ten to balance opposing resource needs. The number is small enough so DB2 won't have to use excessive resources to maintain interim records of changes and so the program won't have to redo much work in a

```
**********************************************************************
*  DCLGEN TABLE(MMADBV.CUST)                                         *
*         LIBRARY(MMA002.DCLGENS.COBOL(CUST))                        *
*         ACTION(REPLACE)                                            *
*         STRUCTURE(CUSTOMER-ROW)                                    *
*         APOST                                                      *
*  ... IS THE DCLGEN COMMAND THAT MADE THE FOLLOWING STATEMENTS      *
**********************************************************************
      EXEC SQL DECLARE MMADBV.CUST TABLE
      ( CUSTNO                          CHAR(6) NOT NULL,
        FNAME                           CHAR(20) NOT NULL,
        LNAME                           CHAR(30) NOT NULL,
        ADDR                            CHAR(30) NOT NULL,
        CITY                            CHAR(20) NOT NULL,
        STATE                           CHAR(2) NOT NULL,
        ZIPCODE                         CHAR(10) NOT NULL
      ) END-EXEC.
**********************************************************************
*  COBOL DECLARATION FOR TABLE MMADBV.CUST                           *
**********************************************************************
  01   CUSTOMER-ROW.
       10 CUSTNO              PIC X(6).
       10 FNAME               PIC X(20).
       10 LNAME               PIC X(30).
       10 ADDR                PIC X(30).
       10 CITY                PIC X(20).
       10 STATE               PIC X(2).
       10 ZIPCODE             PIC X(10).
**********************************************************************
*  THE NUMBER OF COLUMNS DESCRIBED BY THIS DECLARATION IS 7          *
**********************************************************************
```

Figure 4-19   DCLGEN output for the CUST table

subsequent run if a rollback is necessary. If I wanted to maximize those advantages, I would have issued a COMMIT after each transaction. But because COMMIT uses resources too, I compromised and selected a commit threshold that's neither too large nor too small.

This program uses the same CUST table as the program in topic 1. For your convenience, its DCLGEN output is shown in figure 4-19.

The design of the expanded version of the update program   Figure 4-20 presents the structure chart for UPDTROLL, the expanded update program. Although the design is similar to that of the first version of the program, it includes two new modules. One issues a COMMIT statement, and the other issues a ROLLBACK statement.

I positioned the module that issues the COMMIT statement, 160, subordinate to 100-POST-CUSTOMER-TRANSACTION. That's because COMMIT is part of normal transaction processing. In contrast, I positioned the

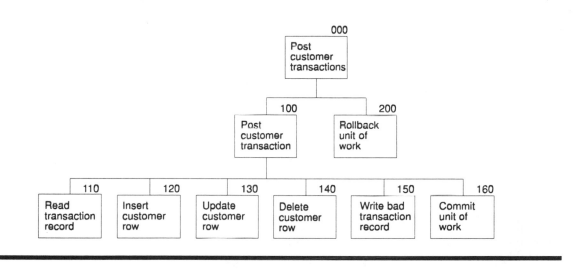

Figure 4-20   Structure chart for the UPDTROLL program

module that issues a ROLLBACK statement, 200, subordinate to the program's top-level module, 000. That's because if a rollback is required, it will be done only once, just before the program ends.

The source code for the expanded version of the update program
Figure 4-21 presents the source code for the expanded update program. Although most of the new code is in the Procedure Division, I did add a few new items to the Working-Storage Section.

First, notice a new switch: ROLLBACK-REQUIRED-SW. After the program issues an INSERT, UPDATE, or DELETE statement, it examines SQLCODE. If the return code is something unexpected, the program sets the value of this switch to Y. Then, the top-level module examines this switch to determine whether or not to invoke module 200 to do a rollback.

I also added three count fields to the Working-Storage Section. The first one keeps track of the number of transactions the program has processed during a unit of recovery. When that number reaches ten, the program issues a COMMIT statement. The other two count fields keep track of the number of valid and invalid transactions processed. When the program ends, it uses these numbers in a status message it displays.

Now, I want to describe the Procedure Division code. Rather than step through the code from beginning to end, I'm going to describe how the program works as it processes one transaction. Just like the first version in

```
000100 IDENTIFICATION DIVISION.
000200*
000300 PROGRAM-ID.          UPDTROLL.
000400*
000500 ENVIRONMENT DIVISION.
000600*
000700 INPUT-OUTPUT SECTION.
000800*
000900 FILE-CONTROL.
001000*
001100      SELECT CUSTTRAN ASSIGN TO AS-CUSTTRAN.
001200      SELECT BADTRAN  ASSIGN TO AS-BADTRAN.
001300*
001400 DATA DIVISION.
001500*
001600 FILE SECTION.
001700*
001800 FD  CUSTTRAN
001900      LABEL RECORDS ARE STANDARD
002000      RECORD CONTAINS 119 CHARACTERS.
002100*
002200 01  CUSTOMER-TRANSACTION-RECORD.
002300*
002400      05  CTR-TRANSACTION-CODE        PIC X.
002500      05  CTR-TRANSACTION-DATA.
002600          10  CTR-CUSTOMER-NUMBER    PIC X(6).
002700          10  CTR-CUSTOMER-DETAILS   PIC X(112).
002800*
002900 FD  BADTRAN
003000      LABEL RECORDS ARE STANDARD
003100      RECORD CONTAINS 119 CHARACTERS.
003200*
003300 01  BAD-TRANSACTION-RECORD.
003400*
003500      05  BTR-TRANSACTION-CODE        PIC X.
003600      05  BTR-TRANSACTION-DATA        PIC X(118).
003700*
003800 WORKING-STORAGE SECTION.
003900*
004000 01  SWITCHES.
004100*
004200      05  END-OF-TRANSACTIONS-SW   PIC X     VALUE "N".
004300          88  END-OF-TRANSACTIONS            VALUE "Y".
004400      05  VALID-TRANSACTION-SW     PIC X     VALUE "Y".
004500          88  VALID-TRANSACTION              VALUE "Y".
004600      05  ROLLBACK-REQUIRED-SW     PIC X     VALUE "N".
004700          88  ROLLBACK-REQUIRED              VALUE "Y".
004800*
004900 01  COUNT-FIELDS               COMP.
005000*
005100      05  VALID-TRANS-COUNT       PIC S9(9)    VALUE 0.
005200      05  INVALID-TRANS-COUNT     PIC S9(9)    VALUE 0.
005300      05  UNIT-OF-WORK-COUNT      PIC S9(9)    VALUE 0.
005400*
```

Figure 4-21   COBOL source code for the UPDTROLL program (part 1 of 4)

```
005500       EXEC SQL
005600           INCLUDE CUST
005700       END-EXEC.
005800*
005900       EXEC SQL
006000           INCLUDE SQLCA
006100       END-EXEC.
006200*
006300 PROCEDURE DIVISION.
006400*
006500 000-POST-CUST-TRANSACTIONS.
006600*
006700       OPEN INPUT  CUSTTRAN
006800            OUTPUT BADTRAN.
006900       PERFORM 100-POST-CUST-TRANSACTION
007000           UNTIL END-OF-TRANSACTIONS.
007100       IF ROLLBACK-REQUIRED
007200           PERFORM 200-ROLLBACK-UNIT-OF-WORK
007300           DISPLAY "****** UPDATE NOT SUCCESSFUL ******"
007400           DISPLAY "        SQLCODE " SQLCODE
007500           DISPLAY "****** ROLLBACK PERFORMED    ******"
007600           SUBTRACT UNIT-OF-WORK-COUNT FROM VALID-TRANS-COUNT
007700       ELSE
007800           DISPLAY "******   UPDATE SUCCESSFUL   ******".
007900       CLOSE CUSTTRAN
008000             BADTRAN.
008100       DISPLAY VALID-TRANS-COUNT
008200             " VALID TRANSACTION RECORDS PROCESSED.".
008300       DISPLAY INVALID-TRANS-COUNT
008400             " INVALID TRANSACTION RECORDS PROCESSED.".
008500       STOP RUN.
008600*
008700 100-POST-CUST-TRANSACTION.
008800*
008900       MOVE "Y" TO VALID-TRANSACTION-SW.
009000       PERFORM 110-READ-TRANSACTION-RECORD.
009100       IF NOT END-OF-TRANSACTIONS
009200           MOVE CTR-TRANSACTION-DATA TO CUSTOMER-ROW
009300           EVALUATE CTR-TRANSACTION-CODE
009400               WHEN "A"   PERFORM 120-INSERT-CUSTOMER-ROW
009500               WHEN "R"   PERFORM 130-UPDATE-CUSTOMER-ROW
009600               WHEN "D"   PERFORM 140-DELETE-CUSTOMER-ROW
009700               WHEN OTHER MOVE "N" TO VALID-TRANSACTION-SW
009800           END-EVALUATE
009900           IF NOT VALID-TRANSACTION
010000               ADD 1 TO INVALID-TRANS-COUNT
010100               PERFORM 150-WRITE-BAD-TRANS-RECORD
010200           ELSE
010300               ADD 1 TO VALID-TRANS-COUNT
010400               ADD 1 TO UNIT-OF-WORK-COUNT
010500               IF UNIT-OF-WORK-COUNT = 10
010600                   PERFORM 160-COMMIT-UNIT-OF-WORK
010700                   MOVE 0 TO UNIT-OF-WORK-COUNT.
010800*
```

Figure 4-21   COBOL source code for the UPDTROLL program (part 2 of 4)

```
010900 110-READ-TRANSACTION-RECORD.
011000*
011100     READ CUSTTRAN
011200         AT END
011300             MOVE "Y" TO END-OF-TRANSACTIONS-SW.
011400*
011500 120-INSERT-CUSTOMER-ROW.
011600*
011700     EXEC SQL
011800         INSERT INTO MMADBV.CUST
011900                 ( CUSTNO,     FNAME,      LNAME,      ADDR,
012000                   CITY,       STATE,      ZIPCODE)
012100         VALUES (:CUSTNO,   :FNAME,     :LNAME,     :ADDR,
012200                 :CITY,     :STATE,     :ZIPCODE)
012300     END-EXEC.
012400     IF SQLCODE = -803
012500         MOVE "N" TO VALID-TRANSACTION-SW
012600     ELSE
012700         IF SQLCODE < 0
012800             MOVE "N" TO VALID-TRANSACTION-SW
012900             MOVE "Y" TO END-OF-TRANSACTIONS-SW
013000             MOVE "Y" TO ROLLBACK-REQUIRED-SW.
013100*
013200 130-UPDATE-CUSTOMER-ROW.
013300*
013400     EXEC SQL
013500         UPDATE MMADBV.CUST
013600             SET FNAME   = :FNAME,
013700                 LNAME   = :LNAME,
013800                 ADDR    = :ADDR,
013900                 CITY    = :CITY,
014000                 STATE   = :STATE,
014100                 ZIPCODE = :ZIPCODE
014200         WHERE   CUSTNO  = :CUSTNO
014300     END-EXEC.
014400     IF SQLCODE = +100
014500         MOVE "N" TO VALID-TRANSACTION-SW
014600     ELSE
014700         IF SQLCODE < 0
014800             MOVE "N" TO VALID-TRANSACTION-SW
014900             MOVE "Y" TO END-OF-TRANSACTIONS-SW
015000             MOVE "Y" TO ROLLBACK-REQUIRED-SW.
015100*
015200 140-DELETE-CUSTOMER-ROW.
015300*
015400     EXEC SQL
015500         DELETE FROM MMADBV.CUST
015600             WHERE CUSTNO = :CUSTNO
015700     END-EXEC.
015800     IF SQLCODE = +100
015900         MOVE "N" TO VALID-TRANSACTION-SW
016000     ELSE
016100         IF SQLCODE < 0
016200             MOVE "N" TO VALID-TRANSACTION-SW
016300             MOVE "Y" TO END-OF-TRANSACTIONS-SW
016400             MOVE "Y" TO ROLLBACK-REQUIRED-SW.
016500*
```

Figure 4-21   COBOL source code for the UPDTROLL program (part 3 of 4)

```
016600 150-WRITE-BAD-TRANS-RECORD.
016700*
016800     WRITE BAD-TRANSACTION-RECORD
016900        FROM CUSTOMER-TRANSACTION-RECORD.
017000*
017100 160-COMMIT-UNIT-OF-WORK.
017200*
017300     EXEC SQL
017400        COMMIT
017500     END-EXEC.
017600*
017700 200-ROLLBACK-UNIT-OF-WORK.
017800*
017900     EXEC SQL
018000        ROLLBACK
018100     END-EXEC.
018200*
```

Figure 4-21   COBOL source code for the UPDTROLL program (part 4 of 4)

topic 1, this program uses an EVALUATE statement in module 100 to determine what module to invoke to post a transaction: 120, 130, or 140.

Look at the code in those modules. As you can see, the program deals with two kinds of errors. The first kind of error is a "normal" error, and the other kind is an "abnormal" error.

For example, think about what would happen if the program tried to insert a row that has a duplicate key value. The INSERT statement in module 120 would return −803 as the SQLCODE value. Although this is an invalid transaction, it's a "normal" error that the program should be able to handle. So, module 120 simply sets VALID-TRANSACTION-SW to N.

However, if DB2 returns any other negative SQLCODE value, that's a signal that an "abnormal" error has occurred. A negative error code other than −803 suggests that there's a serious problem in the DB2 environment, and that other transactions the program tries to process are likely to fail also. So, the module responds to any other negative SQLCODE value from an INSERT by doing more than setting VALID-TRANSACTION-SW to N. It also signals that no more transactions should be processed (by moving Y to END-OF-TRANSACTIONS-SW) and that the current unit of work should be reversed (by moving Y to ROLLBACK-REQUIRED-SW).

The program does similar processing in the UPDATE and DELETE modules (130 and 140). Here, the program treats SQLCODE value +100 as a "normal" error. That's the SQLCODE that results from an attempt to update or delete a row that doesn't exist. However, any negative SQLCODE value represents an "abnormal" error, and the program makes the switch settings necessary to end the program and rollback the current unit of recovery.

After the program has executed module 120, 130, or 140, control passes back to module 100. Execution continues with the condition I've shaded. If the current transaction was flagged as invalid, this condition adds 1 to the count of invalid transactions and invokes module 150 to write the transaction record to the invalid transaction data set. On the other hand, if the transaction was valid, the program adds 1 to the count field for valid transactions and to the field that contains the count of transactions processed since the last commit point (UNIT-OF-WORK-COUNT).

When the value of UNIT-OF-WORK-COUNT reaches ten, the program invokes module 160 and resets the count to zero. As you can see, module 160 contains a COMMIT statement.

After module 100 ends, the PERFORM UNTIL in module 000 evaluates END-OF-TRANSACTIONS-SW. If its value is Y, the main processing the program does is over. The program may have set this switch to Y either because it reached the end of the transaction file in module 110, or because it encountered an exceptional condition in module 120, 130, or 140.

Regardless, after the PERFORM UNTIL is satisfied, the program uses an IF structure that evaluates ROLLBACK-REQUIRED-SW. If its value is Y (set by module 120, 130, or 140 in response to an "abnormal" error), the program invokes module 200 to issue a ROLLBACK statement. Then, the program displays an error message and deducts the number of transactions that the ROLLBACK statement reversed from VALID-TRANS-COUNT.

On the other hand, if a rollback isn't necessary, the program displays a message reporting that the update was successful. Finally, whether a ROLLBACK was necessary or not, the program closes its VSAM data sets and displays counts of valid and invalid transactions.

Discussion

The COMMIT and ROLLBACK statements work only in programs that run in the TSO environment. That means you can use these statements only in programs that will run online directly under TSO or that will run in batch. (As I'll describe in chapter 11, batch DB2 programs run indirectly through TSO.)

DB2 programs that run under CICS or IMS can't issue COMMIT and ROLLBACK statements. That's because CICS and IMS are their own transaction managers. A unit of work for a CICS or IMS program has more implications that just its DB2 dimension. So, both CICS and IMS require that you use their mechanisms to declare commit points. (In CICS, you use the SYNCPOINT command to declare a commit point; in IMS, you use the

CHKP or SYNC call.) In either case, CICS or IMS issues the commit request to DB2 at the right time. Then, DB2 does the same thing it would do if you had issued a COMMIT statement directly to it.

Terms

unit of recovery
unit of work
commit point
implicit commit point
explicit commit point
lock

Objectives

1. Explain why you may need to use COMMIT and ROLLBACK statements in your application programs.

2. Given the specifications for a program that will modify a DB2 table, design and code the program, using COMMIT and ROLLBACK statements as necessary.

Section

3

Expanding the basic subset

This section contains five chapters that expand the basic DB2 information you learned in sections 1 and 2. Chapter 5 shows you how to use the IN, BETWEEN, and LIKE keywords in the SELECT statement's WHERE clause. Chapter 5 also describes how you can combine individual selection conditions with AND, OR, and NOT to create complex conditions. Chapter 6 shows you how to use DB2's column functions to extract summary information from a table. Chapter 7 describes joins and unions, two ways you can combine data from two or more base tables in a single results table. Chapter 8 covers how to nest SELECT statements as subqueries within other SQL statements. And chapter 9 shows you how to work with variable-length data and with nulls.

Each of these chapters stands on its own. As a result, you can read them in any order you like. However, I think it makes most sense to read them in sequence. So unless you have a pressing need to learn about joins, subselects, or variable-length data right away, I suggest you proceed with chapter 5.

Chapter 5

How to use alternative selection conditions

As you know, the SELECT statement's WHERE clause lets you specify a selection condition that determines which rows will be retrieved into the results table. So far, I've only shown you how to code simple selection conditions. In this chapter, I'll show you a variety of alternative ways to code them. First, I'll show you how to code alternative forms of the WHERE clause that use the IN, BETWEEN, and LIKE keywords. Then, I'll show you how to combine single selection conditions with AND, OR, and NOT to create complex selection conditions. Finally, I'll present a simple inquiry program that uses some of the features this chapter introduces.

Because the techniques you'll learn in this chapter tend to produce results tables with more than one row, you'll use them most often in the SELECT component of a DECLARE CURSOR statement. However, you can also use them in a stand-alone SELECT statement, as long as you're sure the statement will return a single-row results table.

How to use alternative forms of the SELECT statement's WHERE clause

You already know how to use basic relational operators (=, >, and so on) in a SELECT statement's WHERE clause. SQL also provides three keywords that let you specify more advanced relationships in a WHERE clause: IN, BETWEEN, and LIKE. Figure 5-1 shows an example of each. With the IN keyword, you supply a list of specific comparison values. In the example of the IN keyword in figure 5-1, the comparison values are the names of three cities. If the CITY column value in a row in the base table is any of these three cities, DB2 will include data from that row in the results table.

With the BETWEEN keyword, you specify a range of comparison values. In figure 5-1, the BETWEEN example uses the values in the ZIPCODE column of the CUST table to select rows for customers who live on the West Coast, or in Alaska or Hawaii. For example, a row whose ZIPCODE column contains 93722-6427 meets this selection condition because that value falls between the lower and upper limits the WHERE clause specifies.

With the LIKE keyword, you specify a comparison string that is similar to the column values in the rows you want to retrieve. DB2 uses this comparison string to evaluate the contents of a column. The LIKE example in figure 5-1 directs DB2 to select rows where the value of the LNAME column begins with the letters ST. (I'll explain what the percent sign in this example means in a moment.)

Before I describe these keywords in more detail, I want you to realize that character comparisons are sensitive to case. For example, two abbreviations for California that we recognize as equivalent, CA and Ca, are not equivalent to DB2. This could cause problems. Fortunately, most shops have rigorous standards for data entry and validation. In addition, many shops use some sort of standard editing subroutine to do data conversions and to insure the validity of the data that's stored in DB2 tables.

How to use the IN keyword in a selection condition   You use the first of the three keywords figure 5-1 illustrates, IN, to specify a set of values when any one of them can satisfy the comparison condition. When you use IN, you have to list all of the different values you want DB2 to check. Figure 5-2 shows the syntax for the WHERE clause with the IN keyword.

For example, if you want to retrieve rows from the CUST table just for customers who live in the three largest cities in the United States, you can code the WHERE clause I showed you in figure 5-1,

```
WHERE CITY IN ('NEW YORK','CHICAGO','LOS ANGELES')
```

in a SELECT.

With IN	Specifies a list of items, such as
	`WHERE CITY IN ('NEW YORK','CHICAGO','LOS ANGELES')`
	The value in the comparison item must match one item in this list for the condition to be met.
With BETWEEN	Specifies beginning and ending values for a range, such as
	`WHERE ZIPCODE BETWEEN '90000-0000' AND '99999-9999'`
	The value of the comparison item must fall within this range for the condition to be met.
With LIKE	Specifies a "fuzzy" value, such as
	`WHERE LNAME LIKE 'ST%'`
	The value of the comparison item must be similar to this value for the condition to be met.

Figure 5-1　Examples of the WHERE clause with the IN, BETWEEN, and LIKE keywords

I want you to notice three things about this sample clause and about the syntax for the IN keyword in figure 5-2. First, commas separate the comparison values. Second, although you can code the items in the list in any order, parentheses must surround the entire list. And third, character literals are enclosed in quotation marks. Numeric comparison values don't require quotation marks.

When you use the IN keyword, you can combine it with NOT. Suppose, for example, you want to create a results table that lists all customers in the CUST table who don't live in California, Oregon, or Washington. You can specify

```
WHERE STATE NOT IN ('CA','OR','WA')
```

to produce the result you want. However, DB2 doesn't use any indexes that may be available when you use NOT with the IN keyword. As a result, the NOT keyword can degrade performance.

As figure 5-2 shows, you can code elements other than literals with the IN keyword. You can use host variables, column names, functions, calculated values, and the USER keyword. Most often, though, you'll use literals or host variables.

Syntax of the WHERE clause with the IN keyword

```
WHERE  ⎧:host-variable ⎫          ⎧:host-variable ⎫  ⎧:host-variable ⎫
       ⎪literal        ⎪          ⎪literal        ⎪  ⎪literal        ⎪
       ⎨column-name     ⎬[NOT] IN (⎨column-name     ⎬[,⎨column-name     ⎬...])
       ⎪function       ⎪          ⎪function       ⎪  ⎪function       ⎪
       ⎪calculated-value⎪          ⎪calculated-value⎪  ⎪calculated-value⎪
       ⎩USER           ⎭          ⎩USER           ⎭  ⎩USER           ⎭
```

Figure 5-2   Syntax of the WHERE clause with the IN keyword

For instance, if you were writing an interactive inquiry application that lets users get the names of customers who live in particular states, you could use a WHERE clause like

```
WHERE STATE IN ('CA',:STATE-CHOICE-1,:STATE-CHOICE-2)
```

in your SELECT. This clause tells DB2 to choose rows where the value of the state column is CA, or either of two other values stored in the host variables STATE-CHOICE-1 and STATE-CHOICE-2. In this case, the program gets the values for those host variables by prompting the user to enter the abbreviations for the appropriate states.

How to use the BETWEEN keyword in a selection condition   If it's not practical for you to specify an entire set of specific values for a condition with the IN keyword, you may be able to use the BETWEEN keyword to specify a *range* of values. Figure 5-3 shows the syntax for the WHERE clause with the BETWEEN keyword. The values you name on this clause specify the range of values that satisfies the condition, and you need to code the lower limit before the upper limit.

To create a results table that contains data from the CUST table for all customers whose last names begin with the letter R, you can code

```
WHERE LNAME BETWEEN 'R' AND 'S'
```

in a SELECT. A value like ROBERTSON, whose first character is R, meets this condition.

The range limits you supply are inclusive. So if a row contains either of the one-character values R or S in its LNAME column, it would meet this condition. Because the value S is almost certain not to be present in the LNAME column, I used it as the upper limit for the BETWEEN clause instead of a slightly more accurate limit like RZZZZZZZZZZ.

Syntax of the WHERE clause with the BETWEEN keyword

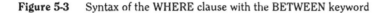

```
        (:host-variable  )                    (:host-variable  )      (:host-variable  )
        | literal        |                    | literal        |      | literal        |
        | column-name    |                    | column-name    |      | column-name    |
WHERE   { function        } [NOT] BETWEEN{ function        } AND{ function        }
        | calculated-value|                    | calculated-value|      | calculated-value|
        ( USER           )                    ( USER           )      ( USER           )
```

Figure 5-3   Syntax of the WHERE clause with the BETWEEN keyword

As with the IN keyword, you can use NOT with BETWEEN. For instance, if you want to create a results table that contains rows with invalid US zip codes, you can code

```
WHERE ZIPCODE NOT BETWEEN '00000-0000' AND '99999-9999'
```

As with the NOT and IN keyword combination, DB2 doesn't use indexes when it processes NOT with BETWEEN, so performance may suffer.

You can also use numeric literals with the BETWEEN keyword. For example, to retrieve rows from the INV table for sales between $1,000 and $10,000, you could code

```
WHERE INVTOTAL BETWEEN 1000 AND 10000
```

on your SELECT statement. Notice that I didn't code quotes around these numeric literals.

As with the IN keyword, you can use host variables, column names, functions, calculated values, and the USER keyword to specify the limits for a range. Most often, though, you'll use literals and host variables.

Host variables are as easy to use as literals. For instance, you may need to develop an interactive program that displays a list of customers whose last names fall within a certain range. Some applications use this technique to let terminal operators browse and choose data when the search values aren't certain. To do this kind of selection, you can code

```
WHERE LNAME BETWEEN :LOW-NAME-VALUE AND :HIGH-NAME-VALUE
```

in your SELECT statement. Of course, the program has to move proper search values to the LOW-NAME-VALUE and HIGH-NAME-VALUE fields before it executes the SELECT.

Syntax of the WHERE clause with the LIKE keyword

```
WHERE column-name [NOT] LIKE {literal
                              :host-variable
                              USER          }
```

Figure 5-4   Syntax of the WHERE clause with the LIKE keyword

How to use the LIKE keyword in a selection condition   Another way to do uncertain searches is to use the LIKE keyword of the WHERE clause. When you code LIKE, you supply a character string that's similar to the column values of the rows you want DB2 to retrieve. Figure 5-4 shows the syntax of the WHERE clause with the LIKE keyword.

As you can see in figure 5-4, the first item you code when you use the LIKE keyword is the name of the table column you want to evaluate. That column must have CHAR as its data type. The second item you code is a character *mask*. A mask is a pattern of characters that DB2 uses to evaluate the contents of the column. Because you're dealing with character data when you use the LIKE keyword, the mask must also contain character data. It can be a literal string, a host variable, or the USER keyword.

The mask can contain two special-purpose characters, the percent sign (%) and the underscore (_). An underscore means that any single character can stand in its position in the column value and still match the mask. The percent sign is even less restrictive. It means that any number of characters, including zero, can stand in its position in the column and still match the mask.

Quite frankly, if you don't need to use a percent sign or an underscore, you don't need to use the LIKE keyword. Instead, you can just code a basic WHERE clause, such as

```
WHERE column-name = literal
```

to find the rows you're looking for.

Figure 5-5 shows several examples that illustrate the effects of different LIKE masks that contain percent signs and underscores. These examples are SELECT statements that retrieve data from a table called CITIES. The CITIES table has only one column, CITY. As in the CUST table, the CITY column is 20 bytes long and contains character type data. You can see the structure of the CITIES table and the contents of its eight rows in the left column of the figure.

CITIES table	SELECT statements	Results tables
| | ```
SELECT CITY
    FROM MMADBV.CITIES
    WHERE CITY LIKE 'LA%'
``` | **CITY**<br><br>LA ROSE<br>LA SALLE<br>LAS VEGAS<br>LAST CHANCE |
| **CITY**<br><br>LA ROSE<br>LA SALLE<br>LAS VEGAS<br>LAST CHANCE<br>LE ROY<br>LEES CREEK<br>LEESVILLE<br>LOS ANGELES | ```
SELECT CITY
    FROM MMADBV.CITIES
    WHERE CITY LIKE 'L%S%'
``` | **CITY**<br><br>LA ROSE<br>LA SALLE<br>LAS VEGAS<br>LAST CHANCE<br>LEES CREEK<br>LEESVILLE<br>LOS ANGELES |
| | ```
SELECT CITY
    FROM MMADBV.CITIES
    WHERE CITY LIKE 'L_S%'
``` | **CITY**<br><br>LAS VEGAS<br>LAST CHANCE<br>LOS ANGELES |
| | ```
SELECT CITY
    FROM MMADBV.CITIES
    WHERE CITY LIKE 'L_S %'
``` | **CITY**<br><br>LAS VEGAS<br>LOS ANGELES |

Figure 5-5   SELECT statements that use the LIKE keyword on the WHERE clause to retrieve city data

To retrieve rows where the values in the CITY column begin with LA, you code a percent sign as the last character of the LIKE mask, as in the first example figure 5-5:

```
WHERE CITY LIKE 'LA%'
```

Four values from the sample table, LA ROSE, LA SALLE, LAS VEGAS, and LAST CHANCE, meet this condition.

When you code a mask with the LIKE keyword, you can use the percent sign in any position. For example,

```
WHERE CITY LIKE 'L%S%'
```

directs DB2 to select rows where the value of the CITY column begins with the letter L and contains the letter S in any other position. As you can see, the results table this statement produces contains all the cities in the base table except LE ROY.

If you want to find the city names that begin with LAS or LOS, you might try coding a clause like the third example in figure 5-5:

```
WHERE CITY LIKE 'L_S%'
```

Here, an underscore in the second position specifies not only that a matching string must begin with L, but that it must contain an S in position three. The results table this statement produces contains only three rows. Two of the values that were selected, LOS ANGELES and LAS VEGAS, are correct. But one, LAST CHANCE, isn't.

The last example in figure 5-6

```
WHERE CITY LIKE 'L_S %'
```

achieves the desired result. This clause specifies that the column value must begin with a three-character word that begins with L and ends with S, followed by a space and any other characters.

Notice in figure 5-5 that each mask ends with a percent sign. That's to handle any extra spaces at the end of the column value. For example, if you code

```
WHERE CITY LIKE 'LOS%S'
```

DB2 won't return any values from the CITIES table in figure 5-5. That's because this mask specifies a value that contains LOS in the first three positions and S in the last position. In this case, that's the 20th position. But if you code this WHERE clause:

```
WHERE CITY LIKE 'LOS%S%'
```

DB2 returns LOS ANGELES.

Notice also, that each example in figure 5-5 uses a literal string for the mask. In application programs, you'll probably use a host variable rather than a literal value for this kind of SELECT.

Suppose you need to develop an interactive program that lets a terminal user find customer information from an incomplete spelling of the customer's last name. You can use a WHERE clause like

```
WHERE LNAME LIKE :SEARCH-STRING
```

in your SELECT. Then, before issuing the statement, you set the value of the host variable SEARCH-STRING so it contains the appropriate mask for the search. If a program prompts the user for the first letter or letters of the last name, you can use COBOL's string-handling statements to concatenate those letters with a percent sign in the SEARCH-STRING field.

For example, if the user enters GR as the first letters of the last name, the program can set the value of SEARCH-STRING to GR% and issue the SELECT. However, you need to be careful if the host variable field you use is longer than the mask you specify, because DB2 will consider the trailing spaces it contains to be part of the mask. I'll show you a way to deal with this problem in the program example at the end of this chapter.

If you also prompt the user for the last letter or letters of the name, you can use that information too. So if the user enters GR as the first letters and R as the last, the value stored in SEARCH-STRING is GR%R. Names like GREER, GRUNER, and GROSVERNOR all match this mask.

When you use the LIKE keyword, you should avoid using the percent sign and underscore characters at the beginning of a mask. If you use them at the beginning of the mask, DB2 may not be able to use an index for the column you're evaluating. The larger the table, the more serious this performance problem is.

Sometimes, you might be able to substitute a WHERE clause that uses the BETWEEN keyword for one that uses LIKE. For example, a SELECT that specifies

```
WHERE LNAME BETWEEN 'GR' and 'GRZZZ'
```

may be more efficient than one that specifies

```
WHERE LNAME LIKE 'GR%'
```

If you need to use these techniques, talk with your DBA about the most efficient approach for your specific situation.

As with both the IN and BETWEEN keywords, you can combine the LIKE keyword with NOT. But also as with IN and BETWEEN, DB2 doesn't use indexes when you combine LIKE and NOT, so performance may suffer.

How to code complex selection conditions

A complex selection condition is one that contains two or more individual selection conditions, also called *predicates*, connected by the operators AND and OR. When you code a complex selection condition, you can also use the NOT operator to specify the opposite of a predicate. Figure 5-6 presents the syntax for complex selection conditions.

```
WHERE [NOT] selection-condition-1 {AND}  [NOT] selection-condition-2 ...
                                  {OR }
```

Figure 5-6   Syntax of complex selection conditions in the WHERE clause

There's no upper limit to the number of predicates you can combine in a single complex condition. However, in practice, you'll seldom need to use more than two or three.

How to combine conditions with the AND and OR operators   When you want to combine two predicates in a complex condition, you code either the AND or the OR operator between them. AND means a row must satisfy both predicates for DB2 to select it, while OR means a row must match at least one of the two.

You can use multiple ANDs and ORs in a single complex condition. When you do, DB2 evaluates all of the AND relationships before it evaluates the ORs. Of course, you can use parentheses to override the default evaluation sequence.

Suppose you want to create a results table that contains rows from the CUST table for customers who live in Virginia or Maryland. You can code this complex selection condition:

```
WHERE STATE = 'VA' OR STATE = 'MD'
```

This achieves the same result as if you code a single predicate with the IN keyword

```
WHERE STATE IN ('VA','MD')
```

In this instance, there's no difference in result or performance between these two approaches, so you can use the one you prefer.

If you want to code a comparison that evaluates the contents of *different* columns, you must use a complex selection condition. For example, if you want to select rows for customers who live in New York City (but not elsewhere in New York) or anywhere in New Jersey, you have to use two conditions connected with OR as in

```
WHERE STATE =  'NJ' OR CITY LIKE 'NEW YORK%'
```

(I used the LIKE keyword for the second predicate in this condition so the values NEW YORK and NEW YORK CITY would both satisfy the condition.)

You should realize that when you use the OR operator to connect predicates that refer to different columns, performance may lag. Again, that's because DB2 can't use an index unless the DBA created one that spans both columns. The severity of the problem depends on the size of the table.

(By the way, an alternative approach may work better: DB2's UNION feature. I'll describe this feature in Chapter 7. If you need to perform a function like this, check with your DBA for advice.)

So far, I've only shown you examples that use the OR operator. AND is no harder to understand. For example, suppose you have to write a program that lets a terminal user enter the first letters of a customer's last name and his state code to see a list of possible matching customer rows. You can code

```
WHERE STATE = :STATE-STRING AND LNAME LIKE :NAME-STRING
```

in your SELECT.

When you want to retrieve a set of records that falls within a specified range, you should use a single-predicate condition with the BETWEEN clause rather than a compound condition. That's because DB2 is likely to process a statement like

```
WHERE INVTOTAL BETWEEN 1000 AND 10000
```

more efficiently than one like

```
WHERE INVTOTAL >= 1000 AND INVTOTAL <= 10000
```

You should note that the AND in the BETWEEN predicate is part of the syntax of BETWEEN; it's not a separate operator that forms a compound condition.

How to use the NOT operator   You can also use NOT in a complex selection condition. The NOT operator applies only to the predicate that follows it.

When you use NOT in this way, it isn't a part of a predicate, as when you use it with the LIKE, BETWEEN, or IN keyword, or in an operator such as ¬=. You need to take care that you don't use the NOT keyword within a predicate unless the predicate's syntax allows it, as BETWEEN, IN, and LIKE do. In particular, you can't code NOT within a simple comparison predicate, although you can use operators that achieve the same results and seem to read the same way. For example, the ¬ operator in

```
WHERE STATE ¬= 'CA'
```

specifies not. However,

```
WHERE STATE NOT = 'CA'
```

doesn't make sense to DB2 because NOT as a keyword isn't a legal part of a simple comparison predicate. On the other hand,

```
WHERE NOT STATE = 'CA'
```

is valid because NOT stands before the predicate, not as a part of it.

As you can imagine, you can create some confusing conditions if you're not reasonable about the operators and keywords you use. When you need to code a complicated condition with the NOT operator, try to choose the most sensible and readable approach.

How to use parentheses to control complex selection conditions   When DB2 interprets a complex selection condition, it follows a predictable order. First, it evaluates the NOT operators that precede individual predicates. Next, it evaluates predicates that are connected by ANDs. Finally, it evaluates predicates that are connected by ORs. If you want, you can use parentheses to change this evaluation sequence. Then, DB2 evaluates the predicates or groups of predicates that are inside parentheses first.

For example, consider how you code a SELECT statement to retrieve data for a list of customers whose last names begin with the letters GR and who live in *either* the state of New Jersey or in New York City. At first thought, you might code a WHERE clause like this:

```
WHERE   STATE   =   'NJ'         OR
        CITY  LIKE  'NEW YORK%'  AND
        LNAME LIKE  'GR%'
```

Unfortunately, although this WHERE clause will produce a results table that contains information for the customers who live in New York City with the right last names, it will include *all* New Jersey customers, regardless of their names. That's because DB2 processes the conditions that are joined by AND before it deals with OR.

To override this evaluation sequence, you can bracket the two predicates connected by OR with parentheses, as in

```
WHERE  (STATE   =   'NJ'         OR
        CITY  LIKE  'NEW YORK%') AND
        LNAME LIKE  'GR%'
```

Then, DB2 checks the LNAME value not only for New York City customers, but also for New Jersey customers.

```
------------------------------------------------------
(ENTER 99 FOR NAME OR STATE TO QUIT.)
ENTER FIRST ONE TO FOUR CHARACTERS OF LAST NAME:
H
 ENTER STATE CODE:

 CUST: 400003--SUSAN            HOWARD              CA
 CUST: 400006--PAT             HONG                CA
 CUST: 400012--S D             HOEHN               OR
       3 CUSTOMER(S) FOUND.
------------------------------------------------------
(ENTER 99 FOR NAME OR STATE TO QUIT.)
ENTER FIRST ONE TO FOUR CHARACTERS OF LAST NAME:
H
 ENTER STATE CODE:
CA
 CUST: 400003--SUSAN            HOWARD              CA
 CUST: 400006--PAT             HONG                CA
       2 CUSTOMER(S) FOUND.
------------------------------------------------------
(ENTER 99 FOR NAME OR STATE TO QUIT.)
ENTER FIRST ONE TO FOUR CHARACTERS OF LAST NAME:
99
```

Figure 5-7   Operation of the NAMEINQ program

Using alternative selection conditions in an inquiry program

To help you understand how to use the WHERE clause options I presented in this chapter, I want to show you another inquiry program. This program, NAMEINQ, displays the customer number, name, and state of each customer whose last name begins with the characters the user enters, or who lives in the state the user enters, or both. In the remainder of this chapter, I'll describe how this program works, show its design, and explain its source code.

The operation of the NAMEINQ program   Figure 5-7 shows a brief terminal session with the NAMEINQ program in which the user did two inquiries. Each inquiry requires the user to reply to two prompts. The first gets the search value for the customer's last name, and the second gets the search value for the state. After the user supplies these search values, the program issues a DECLARE CURSOR statement to produce a results table with just the right information. Then, the program works through the cursor-controlled results table and displays one line for each of its rows.

In the first inquiry in figure 5-7, the user entered the letter H in response to the customer name prompt and entered a blank line in response to the state code prompt. That directed the program to display all customers whose last names begin with the letter H and who live in any state. As you can see, that yielded three rows, two from California and one from Oregon.

I included the second inquiry in the example in figure 5-7 to show you that the user could narrow the selection by also specifying a state code. Here, the user again typed H for the customer last name, but this time entered CA for the state code. The results table for this inquiry contains only the rows for the California customers that showed up in the first inquiry. As you'd expect, the Oregon customer wasn't included.

To end the program, the user can key in 99 in response to either the name or state code prompt. That's what the operator did after the second inquiry in figure 5-7.

The design of the NAMEINQ program   Figure 5-8 shows the structure chart for the NAMEINQ program. The top-level module, 000-PROCESS-CUSTOMER-INQUIRIES, performs the main-processing module, 100-PROCESS-CUSTOMER-INQUIRY, repeatedly until the user keys in 99 to signal the end of the program.

For each inquiry, module 100 performs 110-ACCEPT-SEARCH-VALUES. That module prompts the user to enter the customer last name and state search values, accepts them, and formats them for use as LIKE masks in a WHERE clause. If the user doesn't signal that the program should end by replying with 99 to either the customer or state prompt, module 100 proceeds.

After it accepts the search values, module 100 opens the cursor for the selection by invoking module 120-OPEN-CUSTOMER-CURSOR. Then, module 100 performs module 130 over and over for each row in the results table. Each time it runs, module 130 invokes 140-FETCH-CUSTOMER-ROW to get the next row from the results table and then displays the data it contains. Finally, when a FETCH operation results in the end-of-table condition, module 100 invokes 150-CLOSE-CUSTOMER-CURSOR, so the program can either start a new inquiry or end.

The source code for the NAMEINQ program   Figures 5-9 and 5-10 present the DCLGEN output and COBOL source code for the NAMEINQ program. Because NAMEINQ works much like programs you've already seen, I won't discuss many details of it. However, I would like you to notice two

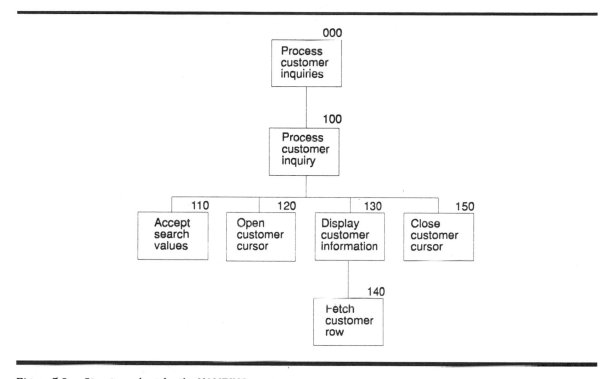

Figure 5-8 Structure chart for the NAMEINQ program

things in its source code in figure 5-10. First, take a look at the program's DECLARE CURSOR statement:

```
EXEC SQL
     DECLARE CUSTCURS CURSOR FOR
          SELECT    CUSTNO, LNAME, FNAME, STATE
             FROM   MMADBV.CUST
             WHERE LNAME LIKE :NAME-STRING
                AND STATE LIKE :STATE-STRING
END-EXEC.
```

The WHERE clause contains a complex condition with two predicates joined by AND. Both of these predicates use the LIKE keyword. One causes DB2 to compare the contents of the CUST table's LNAME column to the host variable NAME-STRING. The other causes DB2 to compare the contents of the STATE column to the host variable STATE-STRING. Before it

```
*********************************************************************
* DCLGEN TABLE(MMADBV.CUST)                                         *
*        LIBRARY(MMA002.DCLGENS.COBOL(CUST))                        *
*        ACTION(REPLACE)                                            *
*        STRUCTURE(CUSTOMER-ROW)                                    *
*        APOST                                                      *
* ... IS THE DCLGEN COMMAND THAT MADE THE FOLLOWING STATEMENTS      *
*********************************************************************
      EXEC SQL DECLARE MMADBV.CUST TABLE
      ( CUSTNO                       CHAR(6) NOT NULL,
        FNAME                        CHAR(20) NOT NULL,
        LNAME                        CHAR(30) NOT NULL,
        ADDR                         CHAR(30) NOT NULL,
        CITY                         CHAR(20) NOT NULL,
        STATE                        CHAR(2) NOT NULL,
        ZIPCODE                      CHAR(10) NOT NULL
      ) END-EXEC.
*********************************************************************
* COBOL DECLARATION FOR TABLE MMADBV.CUST                           *
*********************************************************************
  01   CUSTOMER-ROW.
       10 CUSTNO           PIC X(6).
       10 FNAME            PIC X(20).
       10 LNAME            PIC X(30).
       10 ADDR             PIC X(30).
       10 CITY             PIC X(20).
       10 STATE            PIC X(2).
       10 ZIPCODE          PIC X(10).
*********************************************************************
* THE NUMBER OF COLUMNS DESCRIBED BY THIS DECLARATION IS 7          *
*********************************************************************
```

Figure 5-9   DCLGEN output for the CUST table used by the NAMEINQ program

opens the CUSTCURS cursor for each inquiry, the program must move the
proper LIKE masks to these two host variables.

The block of code I shaded in module 110 of the Procedure Division
does just that. For each inquiry, the program sets the values of the two host
variables to spaces. Then, it prompts the user to enter up to four search
characters for the last name column.

The ACCEPT statement stores the value the user enters in the field
NAME-STRING. If you take a look at the definition of NAME-STRING, you'll
see that it's a five-byte field. That's because it needs to be long enough to
contain the one to four characters the user enters, plus a percent sign to
mark the end of the LIKE mask.

```
000100 IDENTIFICATION DIVISION.
000200*
000300 PROGRAM-ID.          NAMEINQ.
000400*
000500 ENVIRONMENT DIVISION.
000600*
000700 INPUT-OUTPUT SECTION.
000800*
000900 FILE-CONTROL.
001000*
001100 DATA DIVISION.
001200*
001300 FILE SECTION.
001400*
001500 WORKING-STORAGE SECTION.
001600*
001700 01  SWITCHES.
001800*
001900     05  END-OF-INQUIRIES-SW        PIC X     VALUE "N".
002000         88  END-OF-INQUIRIES                 VALUE "Y".
002100     05  END-OF-CUSTOMERS-SW        PIC X     VALUE "N".
002200         88  END-OF-CUSTOMERS                 VALUE "Y".
002300     05  VALID-CURSOR-SW            PIC X     VALUE "Y".
002400         88  VALID-CURSOR                     VALUE "Y".
002500*
002600 01  COUNT-FIELDS.
002700*
002800     05  CUSTOMER-COUNT             PIC S9(7)   COMP-3.
002900     05  EDITED-CUSTOMER-COUNT      PIC Z(6)9.
003000*
003100 01  SEARCH-STRINGS.
003200*
003300     05  NAME-STRING            PIC X(5).
003400     05  STATE-STRING           PIC XX.
003500*
003600     EXEC SQL
003700         INCLUDE CUST
003800     END-EXEC.
003900*
004000     EXEC SQL
004100         INCLUDE SQLCA
004200     END-EXEC.
004300*
004400     EXEC SQL
004500         DECLARE CUSTCURS CURSOR FOR
004600             SELECT    CUSTNO, LNAME, FNAME, STATE
004700                 FROM  MMADBV.CUST
004800                 WHERE LNAME LIKE :NAME-STRING
004900                   AND STATE LIKE :STATE-STRING
005000     END-EXEC.
005100*
```

Figure 5-10   COBOL source code for the NAMEINQ program (part 1 of 3)

```
005200 PROCEDURE DIVISION.
005300*
005400 000-PROCESS-CUST-INQUIRIES.
005500*
005600        PERFORM 100-PROCESS-CUST-INQUIRY
005700            UNTIL END-OF-INQUIRIES.
005800        STOP RUN.
005900*
006000 100-PROCESS-CUST-INQUIRY.
006100*
006200        PERFORM 110-ACCEPT-SEARCH-VALUES.
006300        IF NOT END-OF-INQUIRIES
006400            MOVE "Y" TO VALID-CURSOR-SW
006500            MOVE ZERO TO CUSTOMER-COUNT
006600            PERFORM 120-OPEN-CUSTOMER-CURSOR
006700            IF VALID-CURSOR
006800                MOVE "N" TO END-OF-CUSTOMERS-SW
006900                PERFORM 130-DISPLAY-CUSTOMER-INFO
007000                    UNTIL END-OF-CUSTOMERS
007100                PERFORM 150-CLOSE-CUSTOMER-CURSOR
007200                MOVE CUSTOMER-COUNT TO EDITED-CUSTOMER-COUNT
007300                DISPLAY EDITED-CUSTOMER-COUNT " CUSTOMER(S) FOUND.".
007400*
007500 110-ACCEPT-SEARCH-VALUES.
007600*
007700        MOVE SPACE TO NAME-STRING.
007800        MOVE SPACE TO STATE-STRING.
007900        DISPLAY "-----------------------------------------------".
008000        DISPLAY "(ENTER 99 FOR NAME OR STATE TO QUIT.)".
008100        DISPLAY "ENTER FIRST ONE TO FOUR CHARACTERS OF LAST NAME:".
008200        ACCEPT NAME-STRING.
008300        IF NAME-STRING = "99"
008400            MOVE "Y" TO END-OF-INQUIRIES-SW
008500        ELSE
008600            STRING NAME-STRING "%%%%" DELIMITED BY " "
008700                INTO NAME-STRING
008800            DISPLAY "ENTER STATE CODE:"
008900            ACCEPT STATE-STRING
009000            IF STATE-STRING = "99"
009100                MOVE "Y" TO END-OF-INQUIRIES-SW
009200            ELSE
009300                STRING STATE-STRING "%%" DELIMITED BY " "
009400                    INTO STATE-STRING.
009500*
009600 120-OPEN-CUSTOMER-CURSOR.
009700*
009800        EXEC SQL
009900            OPEN CUSTCURS
010000        END-EXEC.
010100        IF SQLCODE NOT = 0
010200            MOVE "N" TO VALID-CURSOR-SW.
010300*
```

Figure 5-10   COBOL source code for the NAMEINQ program (part 2 of 3)

```
010400 130-DISPLAY-CUSTOMER-INFO.
010500*
010600     PERFORM 140-FETCH-CUSTOMER-ROW.
010700     IF NOT END-OF-CUSTOMERS
010800         IF VALID-CURSOR
010900             DISPLAY "CUST: " CUSTNO "--" FNAME " "
011000                     LNAME " " STATE.
011100*
011200 140-FETCH-CUSTOMER-ROW.
011300*
011400     EXEC SQL
011500         FETCH CUSTCURS
011600         INTO :CUSTNO, :LNAME, :FNAME, :STATE
011700     END-EXEC.
011800     IF SQLCODE = 0
011900         ADD 1 TO CUSTOMER-COUNT
012000     ELSE
012100         MOVE "Y" TO END-OF-CUSTOMERS-SW
012200         IF SQLCODE NOT = 100
012300             MOVE "N" TO VALID-CURSOR-SW.
012400*
012500 150-CLOSE-CUSTOMER-CURSOR.
012600*
012700     EXEC SQL
012800         CLOSE CUSTCURS
012900     END-EXEC.
013000*
```

Figure 5-10   COBOL source code for the NAMEINQ program (part 3 of 3)

To combine the characters the user enters with the percent sign, I used a simple COBOL STRING statement:

```
STRING NAME-STRING "%%%%" DELIMITED BY " "
    INTO NAME-STRING
```

When it executes this statement, the program takes whatever the user entered (which is stored in NAME-STRING) up to the delimiter character (here, a space) and appends five percent signs to it. Then, it stores the result of that operation right back in the NAME-STRING variable.

Suppose the user enters one character in response to the last name prompt, like H in the example in figure 5-7. Just before the program executes the STRING statement, the value in the NAME-STRING field is H followed by four spaces. The STRING statement combines the contents of the field up to the first space with the five percent signs, and the result is stored back in NAME-STRING. Because NAME-STRING is only five characters long, one trailing percent sign is lost in this example. However, the value of NAME-STRING still retains four percent signs, and only one is necessary. So, when the program processes the SQL DECLARE CURSOR statement, this clause

```
WHERE LNAME LIKE :NAME-STRING
```

is effectively replaced by

```
WHERE LNAME LIKE 'H%%%'
```

As a result, each row whose LNAME column value starts with H satisfies this part of the condition.

You may be wondering why the program doesn't append just one percent sign to the NAME-STRING field, like this:

```
STRING NAME-STRING "%" DELIMITED BY " "
       INTO NAME-STRING
```

The reason is simple: to insure that NAME-STRING doesn't include any trailing spaces that might affect the operation of the LIKE keyword.

Module 110 does similar processing for the user's response to the state code prompt. If the user doesn't enter anything for the state code, the program uses %% as the LIKE mask. Any value in the STATE column matches this mask. This could be useful when the user knows the first characters of a customer's last name, but not the customer's state.

Although it's less likely to be useful, the program can also process an inquiry based on just the first letter of the state code. For example, if the user enters just the letter C in response to the state code prompt, the program uses C% as the LIKE mask. This SELECT statement would return rows for customers who live in California, Colorado, or Connecticut.

Terms

range
mask
predicate

Objectives

1. Given specifications for a program that needs to retrieve a set of rows from a table based on any one of a discrete set of comparison values, code an appropriate SELECT statement with the IN keyword of the WHERE clause.

2. Given specifications for a program that needs to retrieve a set of rows from a table based on a value that falls within a specified range, code an appropriate SELECT statement with the BETWEEN keyword of the WHERE clause.

3. Given specifications for a program that needs to retrieve a set of rows from a table based on an imprecise or incomplete value, code an appropriate SELECT statement with the LIKE keyword of the WHERE clause.

4. Given specifications for a program that needs to retrieve a set of rows from a table based on multiple conditions, code an appropriate SELECT statement with predicates connected by ANDs, ORs, and NOTs.

5. Use parentheses within a SELECT statement's WHERE clause to change DB2's default evaluation sequence and to improve readability.

Chapter 6

How to use column functions

In chapter 3, I showed you how to direct DB2 to perform basic arithmetic and concatenation operations on data before returning it to your program. If you found those features useful, you'll probably also be interested in DB2 functions. *Functions* are operations you can specify in a SELECT to have DB2 do things like calculate averages and sums, convert data formats, and manipulate text strings.

This chapter gives an overview of DB2 functions and shows you how to use a category of functions called column functions. Then, it describes how you can use the SELECT statement's GROUP BY and HAVING clauses to apply column functions to specific groups of rows. It ends by presenting a program that illustrates how functions can save coding time and improve program performance.

An overview of DB2 functions

When you code any DB2 function, you first specify a *function name* that tells DB2 what you want it to do. Then, you identify the data elements the function should manipulate. These data elements are called *operands*, or *arguments*. Often, a function requires only one operand.

DB2's functions fall into two categories: column functions and scalar functions. A *column function* yields a single value that results from manipulating or evaluating data in one column through a number of rows. For instance, SUM is a column function. You might use SUM to determine the total amount billed for all invoices issued on a particular date. To do that, DB2 would have to evaluate the contents of the INVTOTAL column from every row in the INV table with the appropriate value in the INVDATE column.

When you use a basic column function in a SELECT statement, DB2 returns a results table that contains only one row. That's because the purpose of a column function is to produce a single aggregate value. In fact, you may see the term *aggregate function* used for a column function.

In contrast to a column function, a *scalar function* doesn't produce an aggregate value. Instead, a scalar function works within the context of a single row. A good example of a scalar function is SUBSTR. The SUBSTR function does basic string manipulation of character data. SUBSTR generates a different value for each row in the results table. As a result, you can use a scalar function in a SELECT that will generate a multi-row results table.

Frankly, DB2's scalar functions do things you're not likely to need often in COBOL programs. Most of them let you convert data from one DB2 format to another. In COBOL, it's easy to do such things just by moving the contents of one field to another. So, I'll cover scalar functions in *Part 2: An Advanced Course*. In this chapter, I'll emphasize just column functions.

How to use column functions

Figure 6-1 presents the syntax for DB2's five column functions and lists the data types for the results they produce. The names of the column functions make it easy for you to understand what they do. AVG computes the average of the values in a numeric column, and SUM computes their total. MIN and MAX return the minimum and maximum values in a column, numeric or otherwise. And COUNT returns the number of rows that meet a selection condition.

To help you understand how the column functions work, I'll show you examples that use the INV table. Since I'll use this table for all the examples in this chapter, you might want to refer to its DCLGEN output. It's shown in figure 6-2. The column function examples are shown in figure 6-3.

Suppose you want to determine the total amount billed based on values in the INVTOTAL column. All you need to code is a SELECT statement like the first example in figure 6-3. This statement produces a one-row results table with one column, and the value of that column is the result of the SUM function. Because a column function creates a one-row results table,

Function syntax	Data type of the result

`AVG(numeric-column-name)`
 	
`SUM(numeric-column-name)`
	If the argument column has the SMALLINT or INTEGER data type, the result will have the INTEGER data type:
	
	`PIC S9(9) COMP`
	
	If the argument column has the DECIMAL data type, the result will have the DECIMAL data type:
	
	`PIC S9(m)V9(n) COMP-3`

`MIN(column-name)`
 	
`MAX(column-name)`
	The same data type as the argument.

`COUNT( { * / DISTINCT column-name } )`	The INTEGER data type: `PIC S9(9) COMP`

Figure 6-1   Syntax of the column functions

you can code a stand-alone SELECT statement like this one and not worry about having to deal with a cursor.

When you code a function in an SQL statement in a COBOL program, you need to be sure that the host variable you use can accept the result the function will produce. If you examine the right-hand column in figure 6-1, you'll see the COBOL descriptions that are appropriate for each function.

Note that I didn't code a WHERE clause on the SELECT statement in example 1 in figure 6-3. As a result, DB2 will include the INVTOTAL column value from each INV table row in the sum it calculates. However, I could have restricted the selection to a subset of the INV table's rows by using a WHERE clause. For example, the second SELECT statement in figure 6-3 uses the value in a host variable to select rows only for a particular customer for the calculation. To do this with standard files, your program would have to initialize a sum-total field, read all the invoice records for the customer, and add the value of each invoice-total field to the total-billed field. As you can see, the task is simpler with DB2.

The AVG function works in a similar way to return the average of the values in the specified column in the selected rows. To determine the

```
**********************************************************************
*  DCLGEN TABLE(MMADBV.INV)                                          *
*          LIBRARY(MMA002.DCLGENS.COBOL(INV))                        *
*          ACTION(REPLACE)                                           *
*          STRUCTURE(INVOICE-ROW)                                    *
*          APOST                                                     *
*  ... IS THE DCLGEN COMMAND THAT MADE THE FOLLOWING STATEMENTS      *
**********************************************************************
      EXEC SQL DECLARE MMADBV.INV TABLE
      ( INVCUST                        CHAR(6) NOT NULL,
        INVNO                          CHAR(6) NOT NULL,
        INVDATE                        DATE NOT NULL,
        INVSUBT                        DECIMAL(9, 2) NOT NULL,
        INVSHIP                        DECIMAL(7, 2) NOT NULL,
        INVTAX                         DECIMAL(7, 2) NOT NULL,
        INVTOTAL                       DECIMAL(9, 2) NOT NULL,
        INVPROM                        CHAR(10) NOT NULL
      ) END-EXEC.
**********************************************************************
*  COBOL DECLARATION FOR TABLE MMADBV.INV                            *
**********************************************************************
  01  INVOICE-ROW.
      10 INVCUST            PIC X(6).
      10 INVNO              PIC X(6).
      10 INVDATE            PIC X(10).
      10 INVSUBT            PIC S9999999V99 USAGE COMP-3.
      10 INVSHIP            PIC S99999V99 USAGE COMP-3.
      10 INVTAX             PIC S99999V99 USAGE COMP-3.
      10 INVTOTAL           PIC S9999999V99 USAGE COMP-3.
      10 INVPROM            PIC X(10).
**********************************************************************
*  THE NUMBER OF COLUMNS DESCRIBED BY THIS DECLARATION IS 8          *
**********************************************************************
```

Figure 6-2   DCLGEN output for the INV table

average amount billed for all invoices issued to a specific customer, for example, your program could issue the statement in example 3 in figure 6-3.

The next two column functions, MIN and MAX, return the minimum and maximum values from the rows that meet the selection condition. To find out the largest and smallest sales made to a specific customer, you could issue the statement in example 4 in figure 6-3.

The last column function, COUNT, returns the number of rows that meet a condition. So, to determine the total number of invoices issued to a particular customer, you could use the statement in example 5 in figure 6-3. The asterisk directs DB2 to use all of the rows that meet the selection condition in its count.

If you take a look at the syntax of the COUNT function in figure 6-1, you'll see that it includes an option that uses the DISTINCT keyword. If you code COUNT with DISTINCT followed by a column name, DB2 doesn't

Example 1   A SELECT statement that uses the SUM function to total the values in the INVTOTAL column for all of the rows
of the invoice table

```
EXEC SQL
    SELECT      SUM(INVTOTAL)
        INTO :TOTAL-BILLED
        FROM  MMADBV.INV
END-EXEC.
```

Example 2   A SELECT statement that uses the SUM function to total the values in the INVTOTAL column for all of the rows
of the invoice table for a specific customer

```
EXEC SQL
    SELECT      SUM(INVTOTAL)
        INTO :TOTAL-BILLED
        FROM  MMADBV.INV
        WHERE INVCUST = :CUSTOMER-NUMBER
END-EXEC.
```

Example 3   A SELECT statement that uses the AVG function to calculate the average INVTOTAL column value for all of the
rows of the invoice table for a specific customer

```
EXEC SQL
    SELECT      AVG(INVTOTAL)
        INTO :AVERAGE-BILLING
        FROM  MMADBV.INV
        WHERE INVCUST = :CUSTOMER-NUMBER
END-EXEC.
```

Example 4   A SELECT statement that uses the MAX and MIN functions to determine the largest and smallest INVTOTAL
column value for a specific customer

```
EXEC SQL
    SELECT      MAX(INVTOTAL), MIN(INVTOTAL)
        INTO :LARGEST-INVOICE, :SMALLEST-INVOICE
        FROM  MMADBV.INV
        WHERE INVCUST = :CUSTOMER-NUMBER
END-EXEC.
```

Example 5   A SELECT statement that uses the COUNT function to count the number of rows in the invoice table for a
specific customer

```
EXEC SQL
    SELECT      COUNT(*)
        INTO :INVOICES-ISSUED
        FROM  MMADBV.INV
        WHERE INVCUST = :CUSTOMER-NUMBER
END-EXEC.
```

Figure 6-3   SELECT statements that use column functions (part 1 of 2)

Example 6   A SELECT statement that uses the COUNT function with the DISTINCT keyword to count the number of
                 customers who have one or more invoices in the invoice table

```
EXEC SQL
    SELECT    COUNT(DISTINCT INVCUST)
         INTO :CUSTOMER-COUNT
         FROM MMADBV.INV
END-EXEC.
```

Figure 6-3   SELECT statements that use column functions (part 2 of 2)

count rows with duplicate values in that column. So, to determine the number of different customers who have been issued invoices, you could issue
the statement in example 6 in figure 6-3. Although the INV table may
contain multiple rows for a given customer, DB2 counts the customer only
once.

If you refer to the complete syntax for the column functions in IBM's
DB2 manuals, you'll find that they all let you code the DISTINCT keyword.
However, the manuals note that for the MIN and MAX functions, the keyword doesn't have any effect, and they don't recommend you use it. After
all, it doesn't matter how many columns contain the minimum or maximum
value.

For AVG and SUM, the situation is different. Although DISTINCT does
make a difference when you use these functions, I can't imagine any time
when you'd want to use it. For example, suppose you're interested in a
column in a five-row table. The value in that column in four of the five rows
is 100. The value in the fifth row is 1. If you used the SUM function without
the DISTINCT keyword for that column, you'd get the result 401, as you'd
expect. However, if you used DISTINCT with the SUM function, you'd get
101 as the result. Because that would be completely misleading, I don't recommend you use the DISTINCT keyword with the SUM and AVG functions.

You should realize that rows that contain nulls in the column you're
processing aren't considered by a function. But remember, spaces and
zeros aren't nulls. Columns that contain zero as their value *are* processed
by column functions.

You should also know that you can specify more than one column function on a single statement, as I did in example 4 in figure 6-3. Figure 6-4
shows a SELECT statement that uses all five column functions. This statement produces a single-row results table with five columns. Each column
contains the result of one of the functions.

```
EXEC SQL
    SELECT      COUNT(*),           SUM(INVTOTAL),  AVG(INVTOTAL),
                MIN(INVTOTAL),      MAX(INVTOTAL)
        INTO :INVOICES-ISSUED,  :TOTAL-BILLED,  :AVERAGE-BILLING,
             :SMALLEST-INVOICE, :LARGEST-INVOICE
        FROM  MMADBV.INV
        WHERE INVCUST = :CUSTOMER-NUMBER
END-EXEC.
```

Figure 6-4   A SELECT statement that uses all five column functions

```
  GROUP BY    column-name[,column-name...]

  [HAVING     selection-condition]
```

Figure 6-5   Syntax of the SELECT statement's GROUP BY and HAVING clauses

How to use the GROUP BY and HAVING clauses

Although SQL's column functions yield single values, you aren't restricted to using them in SELECT statements that return just one row. Instead, you can use the GROUP BY and HAVING clauses to direct DB2 to return multiple rows of summary values. Figure 6-5 shows the syntax of these two clauses.

When you use GROUP BY, DB2 collects the rows that meet the selection condition in the SELECT (that is, what you specify in the WHERE clause) into groups where each row has the same value in the column you specified on the GROUP BY clause. Then, DB2 treats each group like a subordinate table and applies the column function to it. This creates a multi-row results table where each row contains one aggregate value for each subset group.

This can be confusing until you see an example. Suppose you need to determine average sales by customer. You can do that with a single SELECT statement that uses a GROUP BY clause, like example 1 in figure 6-6. Unlike the examples of the column functions I've shown you so far, this statement generates a multi-row results table, one row for each customer represented in the INV table. Each row has two columns. One contains customer numbers, and the other contains the computed average values.

Example 1   A SELECT statement that uses GROUP BY to compute the average invoice total for each customer represented in the INV table

```
SELECT    INVCUST, AVG(INVTOTAL)
     FROM MMADBV.INV
     GROUP BY INVCUST
```

Example 2   A SELECT statement that uses GROUP BY to compute the average invoice total for each customer represented in the INV table and that sorts the results

```
SELECT    INVCUST, AVG(INVTOTAL)
     FROM MMADBV.INV
     GROUP BY INVCUST
     ORDER BY 2
```

Example 3   A SELECT statement that uses GROUP BY to compute the average invoice total by customer for purchases greater than or equal to $1000 and that sorts the results

```
SELECT    INVCUST, AVG(INVTOTAL)
     FROM MMADBV.INV
     WHERE INVTOTAL >= 1000
     GROUP BY INVCUST
     ORDER BY 2
```

Figure 6-6   SELECT statements that use the GROUP BY clause

Because a SELECT that contains a GROUP BY clause can generate a multi-row results table, you shouldn't use GROUP BY in a stand-alone SELECT statement. Instead, you should use it in the SELECT component of the DECLARE CURSOR statement.

The GROUP BY clause doesn't imply any sequencing of the rows in the results table. If you want the rows in the results table to be in a particular sequence, you need to include the ORDER BY clause in your SELECT. The second example in figure 6-6 shows how you might code this. Here, since I wanted to sort the results table by the average value, I specified that column 2 should be the sort key.

Except for the columns you name in the GROUP BY clause, any other columns you specify in the SELECT clause must be named in column functions. That's because the purpose of GROUP BY is to combine data based on grouping criteria.

In the first two examples of GROUP BY in figure 6-6, all of the rows in the base table are evaluated because I didn't code a WHERE clause. But you can also use GROUP BY when you code a WHERE clause. Suppose you need to refine the example I just showed you so it creates a results

Example 1 A SELECT statement that uses GROUP BY with HAVING to produce a results table that contains one row for each customer whose average invoice total is $1000 or more

```
SELECT      INVCUST, AVG(INVTOTAL)
    FROM  MMADBV.INV
    GROUP BY INVCUST
    HAVING AVG(INVTOTAL) >= 1000
    ORDER BY 2
```

Example 2 A SELECT statement that uses GROUP BY with HAVING to produce a results table that contains one row for each customer who has been issued more than five invoices each for $1000 or more

```
SELECT      INVCUST, AVG(INVTOTAL)
    FROM  MMADBV.INV
    WHERE INVTOTAL >= 1000
    GROUP BY INVCUST
    HAVING COUNT(*) > 5
    ORDER BY 2
```

Figure 6-7 Two SELECT statements that use the GROUP BY and HAVING clauses

table to list the average amount of large invoice totals, $1000 or more, by customer. You could use the third SELECT in figure 6-6 to do that.

If you want to SELECT not just specific rows, but also specific groups, you can use the HAVING clause. It tells DB2 that the only rows you want in the results table are those that represent groups that meet a particular condition. You can code the same kinds of conditions in the HAVING clause that you can in the WHERE clause. When you code the HAVING clause, it must follow the GROUP BY clause.

Example 1 in figure 6-7 shows a SELECT that uses both the GROUP BY and HAVING clauses. In this example, the average invoice amount is calculated for each customer. However, the HAVING clause specifies that only customers whose average invoice amount is $1000 or more are to be included in the results table.

The second example in figure 6-7 is a little more complicated. Here, I coded a HAVING clause to direct DB2 that the results table should include only rows for customers where the total number of invoices with an invoice total over $1000 is greater than five. In this example, you can think of DB2 as first generating an interim results table that contains rows from the INV table where the invoice total column's value is 1000 or more. Then, DB2 collects all the rows in the table for each customer together. Finally, it excludes the groups of rows with a count of five or fewer, and it applies the AVG function in the SELECT clause to each group that remains.

Using column functions in an inquiry program

To close this chapter, I'd like to show you a short program that puts
column functions to work. Like the inquiry programs you've already seen,
SUMINQ is designed to work at a TSO terminal. However, its purpose isn't
to reply to specific inquiries, but rather to display a list of summary sales
information for all customers. In fact, this program could be adapted easily
to be a batch report-preparation program. For my purposes, though, I'd
rather present a simple program without the extra code you need for a
report-preparation program, such as the code to print headings and detect
page breaks. That way, you can concentrate on the DB2 elements the program illustrates.

The output of the SUMINQ program   Figure 6-8 shows sample output
from the SUMINQ program. This program displays one line for each customer represented in the INV table. Each line shows the customer number
plus three summary items: the total number of invoices issued to the customer, the total of the billings for those invoices, and the average invoice
amount.

  By the way, I used a small test table to produce the output in figure 6-8.
In a production environment, a program like this would be likely to generate hundreds or thousands of lines of output. Also, the three asterisks after
the last customer line were generated by TSO, not by the SUMINQ program.

The design of the SUMINQ program   The structure of the SUMINQ program is simple, as you can see in figure 6-9. The program first opens a cursor for the task. Then, it fetches each row in the cursor-controlled results
table and, for each, formats its contents and displays them. When the program reaches the end of the results table, it closes the cursor.

The source code for the SUMINQ program   Figure 6-10 presents the
COBOL source code for the SUMINQ program. (If you want to refer to the
DCLGEN output for the INV table, it's shown in figure 6-2.) One of the reasons this program is so simple is that DB2 takes care of calculating averages and totals, counting invoices for customers, determining when control
breaks occur, and sorting the output. You can see how I specified these
operations if you examine the SELECT component from the DECLARE
CURSOR statement in the Working-Storage Section:

```
SELECT     INVCUST,        COUNT(*),
           AVG(INVTOTAL),  SUM(INVTOTAL)
     FROM  MMADBV.INV
     GROUP BY INVCUST
     ORDER BY 2 DESC, 1
```

```
CUSTOMER   COUNT      TOTAL     AVERAGE
400011       7       3922.42     560.34
400012       3        582.67     194.22
400014       3        377.84     125.94
400015       3       3764.65    1254.88
400002       2        320.57     160.28
400003       2        371.30     185.65
400004       2        362.84     181.42
400010       2        295.00     147.50
400001       1        205.60     205.60
400013       1        178.23     178.23
***
```

Figure 6-8 Operation of the SUMINQ program

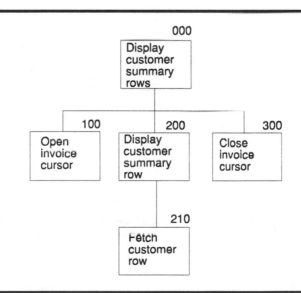

Figure 6-9 Structure chart for the SUMINQ program

```
000100 IDENTIFICATION DIVISION.
000200*
000300 PROGRAM-ID.          SUMINQ.
000400*
000500 ENVIRONMENT DIVISION.
000600*
000700 INPUT-OUTPUT SECTION.
000800*
000900 FILE-CONTROL.
001000*
001100 DATA DIVISION.
001200*
001300 FILE SECTION.
001400*
001500 WORKING-STORAGE SECTION.
001600*
001700 01   SWITCH.
001800*
001900      05   END-OF-CUSTOMERS-SW      PIC X      VALUE "N".
002000           88   END-OF-CUSTOMERS               VALUE "Y".
002100*
002200 01   WORK-FIELDS.
002300*
002400      05   INVOICE-COUNT            PIC S9(9)      COMP.
002500      05   INVOICE-SUM              PIC S9(7)V99   COMP-3.
002600      05   INVOICE-AVG              PIC S9(7)V99   COMP-3.
002700      05   EDITED-INVOICE-COUNT     PIC Z(8)9.
002800      05   EDITED-INVOICE-SUM       PIC Z(6)9.99.
002900      05   EDITED-INVOICE-AVG       PIC Z(6)9.99.
003000*
003100      EXEC SQL
003200           INCLUDE INV
003300      END-EXEC.
003400*
003500      EXEC SQL
003600           INCLUDE SQLCA
003700      END-EXEC.
003800*
003900      EXEC SQL
004000           DECLARE INVCURS CURSOR FOR
004100                SELECT    INVCUST,        COUNT(*),
004200                      AVG(INVTOTAL),   SUM(INVTOTAL)
004300                   FROM   MMADBV.INV
004400                   GROUP BY INVCUST
004500                   ORDER BY 2 DESC, 1
004600      END-EXEC.
004700*
```

Figure 6-10   COBOL source code for the SUMINQ program (part 1 of 2)

The SELECT clause specifies that the results table should contain four
columns: INVCUST and the results of three functions. These functions are
right out of the examples I showed you in this chapter, so you shouldn't
find them confusing.

```
004800 PROCEDURE DIVISION.
004900*
005000 000-DISPLAY-CUSTOMER-SUMMARY-ROWS.
005100*
005200     PERFORM 100-OPEN-INVOICE-CURSOR.
005300     IF NOT END-OF-CUSTOMERS
005400         DISPLAY "CUSTOMER   COUNT      TOTAL      AVERAGE"
005500         PERFORM 200-DISPLAY-CUSTOMER-SUMMARY-ROW
005600             UNTIL END-OF-CUSTOMERS
005700         PERFORM 300-CLOSE-INVOICE-CURSOR.
005800     STOP RUN.
005900*
006000 100-OPEN-INVOICE-CURSOR.
006100*
006200     EXEC SQL
006300         OPEN INVCURS
006400     END-EXEC.
006500     IF SQLCODE NOT = 0
006600         MOVE "Y" TO END-OF-CUSTOMERS-SW.
006700*
006800 200-DISPLAY-CUSTOMER-SUMMARY-ROW.
006900*
007000     PERFORM 210-FETCH-CUSTOMER-ROW.
007100     IF NOT END-OF-CUSTOMERS
007200         MOVE INVOICE-COUNT TO EDITED-INVOICE-COUNT
007300         MOVE INVOICE-AVG   TO EDITED-INVOICE-AVG
007400         MOVE INVOICE-SUM   TO EDITED-INVOICE-SUM
007500         DISPLAY INVCUST "              "
007600             EDITED-INVOICE-COUNT " "
007700             EDITED-INVOICE-SUM   " "
007800             EDITED-INVOICE-AVG.
007900*
008000 210-FETCH-CUSTOMER-ROW.
008100*
008200     EXEC SQL
008300         FETCH  INVCURS
008400         INTO  :INVCUST,        :INVOICE-COUNT,
008500               :INVOICE-AVG,    :INVOICE-SUM
008600     END-EXEC.
008700     IF SQLCODE NOT = 0
008800         MOVE "Y" TO END-OF-CUSTOMERS-SW.
008900*
009000 300-CLOSE-INVOICE-CURSOR.
009100*
009200     EXEC SQL
009300         CLOSE INVCURS
009400     END-EXEC.
009500*
```

Figure 6-10   COBOL source code for the SUMINQ program (part 2 of 2)

I used the GROUP BY clause to direct DB2 to present summary information for each customer represented in the INV table. And, the ORDER BY clause causes DB2 to sort the rows in the results table. In this example, I coded two sort keys on the ORDER BY clause. The first specifies that the results table should be put into descending sequence by the contents of the second column. In other words, the results table rows should be sorted so the customers who have the most invoices appear first. When customers have the same number of invoices, DB2 sorts them into ascending sequence according to the contents of the first column, which contains customer numbers. The value 1 in the ORDER BY clause specifies this secondary key.

For this application, I coded my own host variables for the three columns whose values are generated by functions. For the AVG or SUM function, you need to use a host variable field that has the same size and characteristics as the column the function processes. For the COUNT function, the host variable needs to be a fullword integer field (PIC S9(9) COMP).

If you coded a similar program that accessed a VSAM data set instead of a DB2 table, you'd be responsible for writing substantially more COBOL code. Although it wouldn't be difficult COBOL, it's easier to let DB2 do it for you. Plus, when you use aggregate functions like this, less data has to be passed back and forth between DB2 and the program, and overall performance is better.

This program displays summary invoice information for all customers. If you need to develop an application like this that displays information for particular customers, you can do that easily by adding a HAVING clause to the SELECT component of the DECLARE CURSOR statement. For example, to display summary lines for customers whose average invoice amount is more than a specific amount, you could code

```
EXEC SQL
    DECLARE INVCURS CURSOR FOR
        SELECT     INVCUST,        COUNT(*),
                   AVG(INVTOTAL),  SUM(INVTOTAL)
            FROM   MMADBV.INV
            GROUP BY INVCUST
            HAVING AVG(INVTOTAL) > :MINIMUM-AVERAGE
            ORDER BY 2 DESC, 1
END-EXEC.
```

Here, you'd set the value of the host variable MINIMUM-AVERAGE to whatever amount you were interested in before you open the cursor. Remember, the HAVING clause works for groups much like the WHERE clause works for rows.

Terms

function
function name
operand
argument
column function
aggregate function
scalar function

Objectives

1. Describe the difference between column functions and scalar functions.

2. Given specifications for an application that requires the use of a column function, code an appropriate SELECT statement.

3. Given specifications for an application that requires that column functions be applied to groups of rows from a table, code an appropriate SELECT statement with the GROUP BY clause and, if necessary, the HAVING clause.

Chapter 7

How to use unions and joins

A particular strength of a relational data base management system like DB2 is its ability to combine data from two or more base tables into a single results table. In this chapter, I'll describe two ways DB2 can do this: unions and joins. Unions are straightforward and easy to understand, so I'll describe and illustrate them first. Then, I'll describe joins. As I present both unions and joins, I'll show you several SQL statements for each and the results tables they produce.

Unions

DB2's *union* feature lets you combine the contents of two or more results tables into one. To direct DB2 to do a union, all you need to do is code the individual SELECTs that will generate the results tables and connect them with the UNION keyword. Because this is almost sure to produce a multi-row results table, you should code the SELECTs as part of a DECLARE CURSOR statement.

One way you can use UNION is to combine two results tables that are drawn from the same base table, but that meet different selection

**CUST
table**

CUSTNO	FNAME	LNAME	ADDR	CITY	STATE	ZIPCODE
400001	KEITH	MCDONALD	4501 W MOCKINGBIRD	DALLAS	TX	75209
400002	ARREN	ANELLI	40 FORD RD	DENVILLE	NJ	07834
400003	SUSAN	HOWARD	1107 SECOND AVE #312	REDWOOD CITY	CA	94063
400004	CAROL ANN	EVANS	74 SUTTON CT	GREAT LAKES	IL	60088
400005	ELAINE	ROBERTS	12914 BRACKNELL	CERRITOS	CA	90701
400006	PAT	HONG	73 HIGH ST	SAN FRANCISCO	CA	94114
400007	PHIL	ROACH	25680 ORCHARD	DEARBORN HTS	MI	48125
400008	TIM	JOHNSON	145 W 27TH ST	SO CHICAGO HTS	IL	60411
400009	MARIANNE	BUSBEE	3920 BERWYN DR S #199	MOBILE	AL	36608
400010	ENRIQUE	OTHON	BOX 26729	RICHMOND	VA	23261
400011	WILLIAM C	FERGUSON	BOX 1283	MIAMI	FL	34002-1283
400012	S D	HOEHN	PO BOX 27	RIDDLE	OR	97469
400013	DAVID R	KEITH	BOX 1266	MAGNOLIA	AR	71757-1266
400014	R	BINDER	3425 WALDEN AVE	DEPEW	NY	14043
400015	VIVIAN	GEORGE	229 S 18TH ST	PHILADELPHIA	PA	19103
400016	J	NOETHLICH	11 KINGSTON CT	MERRIMACK	NH	03054

**INACTCST
table**

CUSTNO	FNAME	LNAME	ADDR	CITY	STATE	ZIPCODE
300001	FRED	SHARPE	6134 CHABOT ROAD	OAKLAND	CA	94618
300002	CHRISTINA	SARBER	4366 BROOKFIELD CT	COLUMBIA	SC	29206
300003	GLENN	FIGLIUOLO	777 N. BRYAN ST	ALLENTOWN	PA	18102
300004	SCOTT	GILES	231 MAIN STREET	RAPID CITY	SD	57701
300005	TIM	BARRETTE	5527 SHASTA LANE	LA MESA	CA	92042
300006	LARRY	RITCHEY	1871 REESE ST	SCRANTON	PA	18508
300007	MAUREEN	OBERG	4006 HAYNE BLVD	NEW ORLEANS	LA	70126

Figure 7-1   The base tables for the UNION examples

conditions. This can do the same thing as a single SELECT statement that uses a compound selection condition, and may be able to do it more efficiently. Another way to use UNION is to combine data from two different base tables into one results table. I'll describe and illustrate both of these techniques in this chapter.

To help you understand how unions work, I'll show you several examples that use the two base tables in figure 7-1. One of these tables, CUST, contains information for active customers. The other, INACTCST, contains information for inactive customers. These two tables have the same structures; they even have the same column names. The name of the customer number column in both CUST and INACTCST, for example, is CUSTNO.

Figure 7-2 shows you how to code two SELECT components with the UNION keyword to produce a results table that contains the names and numbers for all the customers in both tables. As you can see, the code is simple. You just code one SELECT component to retrieve the columns and

SQL statement

```
    .
    .
    SELECT CUSTNO,  FNAME,  LNAME
        FROM MMADBV.CUST
UNION ALL
    SELECT CUSTNO,  FNAME,  LNAME
        FROM MMADBV.INACTCST
    .
    .
```

Results table

400001	KEITH	MCDONALD
400002	ARREN	ANELLI
400003	SUSAN	HOWARD
400004	CAROL ANN	EVANS
400005	ELAINE	ROBERTS
400006	PAT	HONG
400007	PHIL	ROACH
400008	TIM	JOHNSON
400009	MARIANNE	BUSBEE
400010	ENRIQUE	OTHON
400011	WILLIAM C	FERGUSON
400012	S D	HOEHN
400013	DAVID R	KFITH
400014	R	BINDER
400015	VIVIAN	GEORGE
400016	J	NOETHLICH
300001	FRED	SHARPE
300002	CHRISTINA	SARBER
300003	GLENN	FIGLIUOLO
300004	SCOTT	GILES
300005	TIM	BARRETTE
300006	LARRY	RITCHEY
300007	MAUREEN	OBERG

Figure 7-2   A union that combines information for active and inactive customers

rows you want from one table, another SELECT for the columns and rows you want from the second, and connect them with UNION.

Note that I aligned the two SELECT components in figure 7-2, and I didn't indent the UNION keyword. This makes the structure more readable. In addition, I didn't use EXEC SQL and END-EXEC because this is part of a DECLARE CURSOR statement. And I used the ALL keyword with UNION. I'll explain the ALL keyword in a moment.

The results table for this statement is also shown in figure 7-2. As you can see, the first group of rows in the results table came from the first SELECT, and the second group came from the second SELECT. This should help you visualize how a union works. Imagine that DB2 performed the two SELECTs separately to create two intermediate results tables. The first contained the customer number and name data for the 16 rows in the CUST table, and the second contained the customer number and name data for the 7 rows in the INACTCST table. After it created these two intermediate tables, it just "stacked" them together to produce the 23-row final results table in figure 7-2.

Although you can always depend on DB2 to return the columns and rows you specify, you can't expect the rows to be in any particular order, unless you sort them using the ORDER BY clause. The example in figure 7-3 shows you how to do this. Here, the union's results table is sorted by customer last name. Notice that I coded the ORDER BY clause only once, after the last SELECT in the union. When you use the ORDER BY clause with a union, it applies to the final results table, not to one of the intermediate results tables. To clearly show this, I aligned the ORDER BY clause with the UNION keyword.

Also, I identified the sort column by number (4) rather than by name, even though LNAME is the name of the column I wanted to use for the sort key in both base tables. I did this because you can't use a column name on an ORDER BY clause in a union.

In the example in figure 7-3, I also used a technique you may find useful when you work with unions: I coded a literal string in the column specifications for each of the SELECT statements. As a result, each row in the final results table that came from the CUST table has the literal value ACTIVE in its first column, and each row that came from the INACTCST table has the literal value INACTIVE in its first column.

The union examples in figures 7-2 and 7-3 use SELECT statements that don't contain WHERE clauses. As a result, all of the rows from both base tables are included in these unions. You can just as easily combine results tables produced by more restrictive SELECT statements. For instance, figure 7-4 shows an example that selects information only for customers who live in Pennsylvania.

Now that you've seen examples of union, figure 7-5 presents its syntax. It's simple enough, and you probably won't need to refer to it after you finish this chapter. However, I do want you to notice two points. First, you can combine more than two results tables with unions. And second, the ALL keyword is optional. ALL just specifies what DB2 should do with duplicate rows. DB2's default action is to exclude them from the final results table. If you want to override that default, you need to specify ALL.

In a union of the CUST and INACTCST tables, it's unlikely there will be duplicates, so the ALL keyword is unnecessary. However, when you code ALL, DB2 doesn't have to do the extra processing required to check for

SQL statement

```
    .
    .
    SELECT 'ACTIVE', CUSTNO, FNAME, LNAME
        FROM MMADBV.CUST
UNION ALL
    SELECT 'INACTIVE', CUSTNO, FNAME, LNAME
        FROM MMADBV.INACTCST
ORDER BY 4
    .
    .
```

Results table

ACTIVE	400002	ARREN	ANELLI
INACTIVE	300005	TIM	BARRETTE
ACTIVE	400014	R	BINDER
ACTIVE	400009	MARIANNE	BUSBEE
ACTIVE	400004	CAROL ANN	EVANS
ACTIVE	400011	WILLIAM C	FERGUSON
INACTIVE	300003	GLENN	FIGLIUOLO
ACTIVE	400015	VIVIAN	GEORGE
INACTIVE	300004	SCOTT	GILES
ACTIVE	400012	S D	HOEHN
ACTIVE	400006	PAT	HONG
ACTIVE	400003	SUSAN	HOWARD
ACTIVE	400008	TIM	JOHNSON
ACTIVE	400013	DAVID R	KEITH
ACTIVE	400001	KEITH	MCDONALD
ACTIVE	400016	J	NOETHLICH
INACTIVE	300007	MAUREEN	OBERG
ACTIVE	400010	ENRIQUE	OTHON
INACTIVE	300006	LARRY	RITCHEY
ACTIVE	400007	PHIL	ROACH
ACTIVE	400005	ELAINE	ROBERTS
INACTIVE	300002	CHRISTINA	SARBER
INACTIVE	300001	FRED	SHARPE

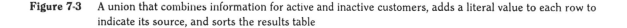

Figure 7-3   A union that combines information for active and inactive customers, adds a literal value to each row to indicate its source, and sorts the results table

duplicates. That can make the operation more efficient. So, as contradictory as it sounds, you should code the ALL keyword to allow duplicates when you're joining tables that you know won't produce any, as I did in figures 7-2, 7-3, and 7-4.

It may seem unlikely that you'd need to worry about duplicates, but they can present a problem when you code a union of two SELECTs that extract data from the same table. To illustrate, the first example in figure 7-6 shows a complex condition I presented in chapter 5. This SELECT

SQL statement

```
    .
    .
    SELECT 'ACTIVE', CUSTNO,  FNAME,  LNAME, CITY
        FROM MMADBV.CUST
        WHERE STATE = PA
UNION ALL
    SELECT 'INACTIVE', CUSTNO,  FNAME,  LNAME, CITY
        FROM MMADBV.INACTCST
        WHERE STATE = PA
ORDER BY 4
    .
    .
```

Results table

INACTIVE	300003	GLENN	FIGLIUOLO	ALLENTOWN
ACTIVE	400015	VIVIAN	GEORGE	PHILADELPHIA
INACTIVE	300006	LARRY	RITCHEY	SCRANTON

Figure 7-4   A union that combines information for customers who live in Pennsylvania

retrieves rows from the CUST table for customers who live in a city named New York or in the state of New Jersey. That's the first example in figure 7-6. The second statement in the figure shows a UNION that accomplishes the same task.

(If you haven't read chapter 5, you need to know that only one of the conditions connected by OR needs to be true for the condition to be met. In addition, the percent sign in

```
WHERE CITY LIKE 'NEW YORK%'
```

can represent any combination of characters, including none. So this statement will return CITY column values such as NEW YORK and NEW YORK CITY.)

If you look closely at the union example in figure 7-6, you'll see that I didn't code the ALL keyword. That's because when you use a union like this, it's possible that a row can satisfy both SELECTs. For example, if a New Jersey city had a name like New York Park, rows for customers who live there would satisfy both SELECTs and appear in both interim results tables. Therefore, if I had coded ALL with UNION, rows for those customers would appear twice in the final results table.

```
    SELECT-statement
 UNION [ALL]
    SELECT-statement
[UNION [ALL]
    SELECT-statement...]

[ORDER BY sort-column[ DESC][,sort-column[ DESC]...]]
```

Figure 7-5 The syntax of the UNION keyword

SQL statement with a complex condition

```
    .
    .
    SELECT CUSTNO,  FNAME,  LNAME,  CITY,  STATE
        FROM MMADBV.CUST
            WHERE STATE - 'NJ' OR CITY LIKE 'NEW YORK%'
    .
    .
```

SQL statement with a union

```
    .
    .
    SELECT CUSTNO,  FNAME,  LNAME,  CITY,  STATE
        FROM MMADBV.CUST
            WHERE STATE = 'NJ'
 UNION
    SELECT CUSTNO,  FNAME,  LNAME,  CITY,  STATE
        FROM MMADBV.CUST
            WHERE CITY LIKE 'NEW YORK%'
    .
    .
```

Figure 7-6 A union can often replace a complex condition that uses the OR operator

UNION can be a practical alternative to coding compound conditions
like the one in figure 7-6. When you use UNION in a situation like this, DB2
is likely to use available indexes, while it won't with an OR construction
that refers to different columns. On the other hand, when it processes a
union, DB2 may have to sort the interim results it uses, and that can be a
resource cost of a different kind. If you have an application problem that
falls into this category, ask your DBA for advice about the most efficient
approach.

Joins

Because the terms join and union have familiar meanings that are similar, it's easy to confuse the two. However, in DB2, joins and unions are quite different. In a union, DB2 combines *rows* from two or more results tables that have identical structures. But in a *join*, DB2 combines specified *columns* from different base tables. The rows in the results table a join produces have a new structure that doesn't exist in the base tables.

Statements that perform joins can be long and complicated, especially when you have to use qualified names. So, after I've presented several examples of joins, I'll show you how to simplify the code in statements that require qualified names. Then, I'll present a batch report program that uses joins to produce an invoice register that combines data from a customer table and an invoice table.

How join operations work

I think you'll find joins easiest to learn if I show you some examples of how they work. To do that, I'll use a set of related inventory tables. After I've introduced these tables, I'll use them to illustrate several ways to use joins.

Three simple inventory tables   Figure 7-7 presents the structures and contents of three simple inventory tables. These tables are part of an inventory data structure for a company that assembles and sells office furniture. The first table contains one row for each completed piece of office furniture. I named this table ASSM, for assemblies. As you can see in figure 7-7, the ASSM table contains three rows. One is for a small table (assembly A1), the second is for a larger table (assembly A2), and the third is a workstation (assembly A3) that consists of assemblies A1 and A2 attached to each other to form one main work surface with a return.

The second DB2 table, CMPT, contains one row for each component required for the assemblies. As you can see, there are four kinds of components. A unique component code identifies each: C1 and C2 are tops for the two sizes of tables, C3 is a table leg that can be used with either top, and C4 is a return connector for the workstation assembly.

The third DB2 table, PARTLIST, contains one row for each component required by each assembly. The rows in this table have three columns. One contains the assembly code (PLACODE), the second contains the component code (PLCCODE), and the third contains the quantity of the component required for the assembly (QTY). The PLACODE and PLCCODE columns are foreign keys because they contain data that identify rows in other tables.

Assembly table (ASSM)

ACODE	ADESC
A1	TABLE 24X36
A2	TABLE 30X60
A3	TABLE & RETURN

Component table (CMPT)

CCODE	CDESC
C1	TABLE TOP 24X36
C2	TABLE TOP 30X60
C3	TABLE LEG
C4	RETURN CONNECTOR

Part list table (PARTLIST)

PLACODE	PLCCODE	QTY
A1	C1	1
A1	C3	4
A2	C2	1
A2	C3	4
A3	C1	1
A3	C2	1
A3	C3	6
A3	C4	1

Figure 7-7   The base tables for the join examples

The PARTLIST table is probably easier to understand through an example. Think about the components you'd need to construct a small table, assembly A1: a top (component C1) and four legs (component C3). Because this assembly requires two kinds of components, it has two rows in the PARTLIST table in figure 7-7. They're the first two rows in the table. The PLACODE column in each contains the code for the assembly (A1). The PLCCODE column contains the code for the small table top (C1) in one row and the code for the table leg (C3) in the other. The QTY column specifies that the small table requires 1 top and 4 table legs.

If you read the other rows in the PARTLIST table, you'll see that the larger table (assembly A2) requires one larger table top (component C2) and four legs (component C3). The workstation assembly (A3) is more complicated. It requires one of each of the table tops (C1 and C2), six table legs (C3), and one return connector (C4).

To get a complete picture of what you need to construct these assemblies, you need information from all three tables: the name of the assembly is in the ASSM table, the name of each part is in the CMPT table, and the relationships between assemblies and components are in the PARTLIST table. As a result, these tables provide a good example to show you how joins work.

An unconstrained join   To join data from more than one table, you need to name the tables in the FROM clause of a SELECT statement. For example, to join all the columns from the ASSM and PARTLIST tables, I could code

```
SELECT *
    FROM MMADBV.ASSM, MMADBV.PARTLIST
```

You can leave it at this, because DB2 can easily process the statement. However, you'd probably be surprised at the result, shown in figure 7-8. As you can see, DB2 combined *every* row in the first table with *every* row in the second. In this case, because the PARTLIST table contains 8 rows and the ASSM table contains 3, the results table contains 24 rows.

This sort of result is called a *Cartesian product* or a *cross product*. The cross product in figure 7-8 contains only 24 rows. But imagine, for example, the impact a cross product would have if you were working with one table with 700 rows and another with 3000 rows. The cross product of these two tables would contain more than two million rows (700 * 3000) and would probably have a notable effect on system performance.

It's bad enough that creating a cross product can take lots of resources. But on top of that, a cross product is almost always useless. If you look down the results table in figure 7-8, you'll see that most of the rows contain matches of ASSM and PARTLIST table information that don't make sense.

For example, the second results table row contains the PARTLIST item that indicates a small table assembly (A1) requires one small table top component (C1). However, that information was matched with the row from the ASSM table for the large table assembly (A2, TABLE 30 X 60). There's no relationship here, so the match is meaningless.

Now, notice the number of columns in this results table. Since the SELECT clause contains an asterisk instead of a list of column specifications, DB2 joins all three columns from the PARTLIST table (PLACODE, PLCCODE, and QTY) with the two columns from the ASSM table (ACODE and ADESC) to produce a five-column results table. I'll show you an example that uses column specifications in a moment.

SQL statement

```
SELECT *
    FROM MMADBV.PARTLIST, MMADBV.ASSM
```

Results table

PLACODE	PLCCODE	QTY	ACODE	ADESC
A1	C1	1	A1	TABLE 24X36
A1	C1	1	A2	TABLE 30X60
A1	C1	1	A3	TABLE & RETURN
A1	C3	4	A1	TABLE 24X36
A1	C3	4	A2	TABLE 30X60
A1	C3	4	A3	TABLE & RETURN
A2	C3	4	A1	TABLE 24X36
A2	C3	4	A2	TABLE 30X60
A2	C3	4	A3	TABLE & RETURN
A2	C2	1	A1	TABLE 24X36
A2	C2	1	A2	TABLE 30X60
A2	C2	1	A3	TABLE & RETURN
A3	C1	1	A1	TABLE 24X36
A3	C1	1	A2	TABLE 30X60
A3	C1	1	A3	TABLE & RETURN
A3	C2	1	A1	TABLE 24X36
A3	C2	1	A2	TABLE 30X60
A3	C2	1	A3	TABLE & RETURN
A3	C3	6	A1	TABLE 24X36
A3	C3	6	A2	TABLE 30X60
A3	C3	6	A3	TABLE & RETURN
A3	C4	1	A1	TABLE 24X36
A3	C4	1	A2	TABLE 30X60
A3	C4	1	A3	TABLE & RETURN

Figure 7-8   An unconstrained join produces a cross product results table

Using a join predicate   To get the benefit of joins, you need to be able to constrain them. Fortunately, it's easy. All you need to do is code one or more appropriate predicates (that is, selection conditions) to specify what relationships exist between the data elements in the base tables. You can constrain the join in figure 7-8, for example, by adding

```
WHERE ACODE = PLACODE
```

as I did in figure 7-9. Notice that this WHERE clause names columns from two different tables. This is called a *join predicate* or a *join condition* because it specifies the condition that must occur for DB2 to join data from the two tables.

SQL statement

```
SELECT *
    FROM  MMADBV.PARTLIST, MMADBV.ASSM
    WHERE ACODE = PLACODE
```

Results table

PLACODE	PLCCODE	QTY	ACODE	DESC
A1	C1	1	A1	TABLE 24X36
A1	C3	4	A1	TABLE 24X36
A2	C3	4	A2	TABLE 30X60
A2	C2	1	A2	TABLE 30X60
A3	C1	1	A3	TABLE & RETURN
A3	C2	1	A3	TABLE & RETURN
A3	C3	6	A3	TABLE & RETURN
A3	C4	1	A3	TABLE & RETURN

Figure 7-9   A join predicate can insure that joins make sense

The example in figure 7-9 specifies that a row from the ASSM table should be joined with a row from the PARTLIST table only when the assembly code values they contain (the ACODE column in ASSM and the PLACODE column in PARTLIST) are equal. If you review the contents of the results table in the example in figure 7-9, you'll see that's what happened. And as a result, all of the rows in the results table make sense.

When you code a join predicate, you need to have a complete understanding of the logic behind the design of the tables you're using. For instance, to be able to code the statement in figure 7-9, I had to know that PLACODE and ACODE contained related data. As far as DB2 is concerned, you can use any columns in a join predicate, whether they make sense or not. For example, DB2 can process

```
WHERE CCODE = PLACODE
```

in a join operation. However, the result would be a results table without any rows because none of the CCODE column values equals any of the PLACODE column values. And if any values in the two columns did match, it would be coincidental and misleading, because CCODE and PLACODE represent different entities.

Although the data in the results table in figure 7-9 is properly joined, the table contains a redundant column. As you can see, the ACODE and

SQL statement

```
SELECT     ACODE, ADESC, PLCCODE, QTY
    FROM   MMADBV.PARTLIST, MMADBV.ASSM
    WHERE  ACODE = PLACODE
```

Results table

ACODE	ADESC	PLCCODE	QTY
A1	TABLE 24X36	C1	1
A1	TABLE 24X36	C3	4
A2	TABLE 30X60	C3	4
A2	TABLE 30X60	C2	1
A3	TABLE & RETURN	C1	1
A3	TABLE & RETURN	C2	1
A3	TABLE & RETURN	C3	6
A3	TABLE & RETURN	C4	1

Figure 7-10   A SELECT clause that names columns to be retrieved to exclude redundant data

PLACODE columns have identical contents. Of course, that's what you'd expect because the join predicate specified it. But you can eliminate one of those columns. When you select data from a single table, you don't have to retrieve a column just because you name it in a WHERE clause, and the same is true in a statement that selects data from more than one table. So you can simplify the results table by excluding one of the two columns.

Figure 7-10 shows a SELECT component that uses column specifications to name all of the columns it retrieves instead of using an asterisk in the SELECT clause. Note that because I'm extracting data from two different tables, I can name columns from both of them on the SELECT clause. I didn't include the PLACODE column in the SELECT clause, however, even though I still named it in the join predicate. If you compare the results table from this statement with the one in figure 7-9, you'll see that they contain the same data, but the columns are in a different order and the redundant column is gone.

Joins that involve more restrictive selection conditions   In the SELECT in figure 7-10, the WHERE clause contains only the join predicate. As a result, DB2 includes all the possible ASSM/PARTLIST combinations in the results table. But suppose you have a requirement for an application that lists the PARTLIST items for a specific assembly. You could use a SELECT statement like the one in figure 7-11. This statement retrieves rows only for

SQL statement

```
SELECT     ACODE, ADESC, PLCCODE, QTY
   FROM  MMADBV.PARTLIST, MMADBV.ASSM
   WHERE ACODE = PLACODE AND ACODE = 'A3'
```

Results table

ACODE	ADESC	PLCCODE	QTY
A3	TABLE & RETURN	C1	1
A3	TABLE & RETURN	C2	1
A3	TABLE & RETURN	C3	6
A3	TABLE & RETURN	C4	1

Figure 7-11   A SELECT statement that uses a second predicate in addition to the join predicate

assembly A3. (This statement uses the AND logical connector to create a compound selection condition. Even if you haven't read about complex conditions in chapter 5, I don't think you'll have any trouble understanding it. It simply means that both of the conditions it connects must be true for a row to be added to the results table.)

When you use a SELECT like this in an application program, you're almost certain to code it in a DECLARE CURSOR statement because it's likely to return a multi-row results table. Also, you're likely to use a variable instead of a literal in the selection condition. For example,

```
SELECT     ACODE, ADESC, PLCCODE, QTY
   FROM  MMADBV.PARTLIST, MMADBV.ASSM
   WHERE ACODE = PLACODE AND ACODE = :ASSEMBLY-CODE
```

uses a host variable called ASSEMBLY-CODE. With this SELECT statement, the program can change the host variable's value to meet differing inquiry requirements.

Joins that combine data from more than two tables   Although most join operations involve two tables, DB2 lets you specify up to 15 different tables in a single SELECT statement. I'm sure you're not going to need to do a join that combines data from that many tables, but you may need to combine data from three tables at some time. So here, I'll show you how.

Because all three tables in the inventory system are related, data from all of them can be joined to produce a results table that contains meaningful data. Imagine you need to prepare a list that names each component,

SQL statement

```
SELECT ACODE, ADESC, PLCCODE, CDESC, QTY
    FROM MMADBV.PARTLIST, MMADBV.ASSM, MMADBV.CMPT
    WHERE ACODE = PLACODE AND CCODE = PLCCODE
```

Results table

ACODE	ADESC	PLCCODE	CDESC	QTY
A1	TABLE 24X36	C1	TABLE TOP 24X36	1
A3	TABLE & RETURN	C1	TABLE TOP 24X36	1
A3	TABLE & RETURN	C2	TABLE TOP 30X60	1
A2	TABLE 30X60	C2	TABLE TOP 30X60	1
A2	TABLE 30X60	C3	TABLE LEG	4
A1	TABLE 24X36	C3	TABLE LEG	4
A3	TABLE & RETURN	C3	TABLE LEG	6
A3	TABLE & RETURN	C4	RETURN CONNECTOR	1

Figure 7-12   A SELECT statement that joins data from three tables

shows all of the assemblies it's a part of, and specifies the quantity of each component required for an assembly. Because this data resides in three different tables, you need to use a three-way join.

The example in figure 7-12 shows a SELECT that produces a results table that meets this requirement. First, notice that the SELECT clause names columns from all three tables: ACODE and ADESC from ASSM; PLCCODE and QTY from PARTLIST; and CDESC from CMPT. The FROM clause names the three base tables.

The WHERE clause has two join predicates connected by AND. The first join predicate,

```
ACODE = PLACODE
```

establishes the relationship between the ASSM and PARTLIST tables that you've already seen in figures 7-9 through 7-11. The second join predicate,

```
CCODE = PLCCODE
```

establishes the relationship between the CMPT and PARTLIST tables. When you combine data from three or more tables, you need to specify an appropriate join predicate for an element in each, or you'll create a cross product.

How to use qualified names

In the join examples I've shown you in this chapter, all of the column names have been unique. I used different names for the assembly code columns in the ASSM and PARTLIST tables (ACODE and PLACODE) and for the component code columns in the CMPT and PARTLIST tables (CCODE and PLCCODE). However, column names aren't always unique.

When you need to join data from two or more tables that use duplicate names for their columns, you have to qualify the duplicate names when you refer to them in your SQL statements. For example, I could have used the name ACODE for the assembly code column in not only the ASSM table, but also in the PARTLIST table. But if I did, whenever I coded a statement that accessed both tables, I could not have used the name ACODE by itself because it would have been ambiguous. Instead, I would have to qualify it.

To form a *qualified name* for a column, you code the name of the table that contains it before the column name and separate them with a period. For example,

```
MMADBV.ASSM.ACODE
```

is the qualified name for the ACODE column in the MMADBV.ASSM table.

As you can imagine, a statement that refers to many columns, some or all with qualified names, will be long and, as a result, hard to code and read. For example, the SELECT statement in figure 7-13 is the same statement I presented in figure 7-12, but with qualified names for each column it accesses. (Qualification isn't necessary in this statement; I'm using it just to give you a taste of how it can affect your code.)

Fortunately, DB2 lets you use the *synonym* feature of the SELECT's FROM clause to specify a shorter name for a table that you can then use in qualified names. (In other contexts, these synonyms may be called *aliases* or *correlation names*.) To specify a synonym, you just code a shorter name that you'd rather use for a table after you name it on the FROM clause.

In the sample SELECT statement in figure 7-14, I've associated PL with the longer table name MMADBV.PARTLIST, A with MMADBV.ASSM, and C with MMADBV.CMPT. Then, in the SELECT clause, I used the shorter qualifiers PL, A, and C. You should realize that when you use a synonym like this, it's in effect only within the statement where you define it. Even within the same program, other statements can't use the synonym unless they declare it in the same way in their own FROM clauses.

```
SELECT    MMADBV.ASSM.ACODE,      MMADBV.ASSM.ADESC,
          MMADBV.PARTLIST.PLCCODE, MMADBV.CMPT.CDESC,
          MMADBV.PARTLIST.QTY

   FROM   MMADBV.PARTLIST, MMADBV.ASSM, MMADBV.CMPT

  WHERE MMADBV.ASSM.ACODE = MMADBV.PARTLIST.PLACODE AND
        MMADBV.CMPT.CCODE = MMADBV.PARTLIST.PLCCODE
```

Figure 7-13   A SELECT statement that uses qualified names

```
SELECT    A.ACODE, A.ADESC, PL.PLCCODE, C.CDESC, PL.QTY

   FROM   MMADBV.PARTLIST PL, MMADBV.ASSM A, MMADBV.CMPT C

  WHERE A.ACODE = PL.PLACODE AND
        C.CCODE = PL.PLCCODE
```

Figure 7-14   A SELECT statement that uses synonyms in qualified names

Using joins in a report program

Now that you've learned how joins work, I'd like to show you how you can use one in an application by presenting a program called INVREG. INVREG produces a printed report, or register, that lists all the invoices in a table, along with the name and number of the customer associated with each.

The input and output for the INVREG program   The INVREG program accesses the two tables, INV and CUST, shown in figure 7-15. You're already familiar with the CUST table. In fact, the CUST table in figure 7-15 contains the same data as the version of the table I showed in figure 7-1 to illustrate unions. You're probably also familiar with the INV table. However, you haven't seen the data in this version of it.

The output the program produces is a printed report like the one in figure 7-16. If you look closely at this report, you'll see that it contains one line for each invoice in the INV table. The first five columns of the report contain data drawn from five of the INV table's columns, INVNO, INVSUBT, INVTAX, INVSHIP, and INVTOTAL. The last two columns in the report contain data drawn from columns in the CUST table, FNAME, and LNAME.

INV table

INVCUST	INVNO	INVDATE	INVSUBT	INVSHIP	INVTAX	INVTOTAL	INVPROM
400012	062308	1990-12-22	200.00	4.45	.00	204.45	PCQ3
400011	062309	1990-12-22	15.00	.00	.00	15.00	PCQ3
400011	602310	1990-02-22	140.00	7.50	.00	147.50	PCQ3
400014	602311	1990-02-22	178.23	3.19	.00	181.42	PCQ3
400002	602312	1991-02-22	162.00	11.07	.00	173.07	PCQ3
400011	602313	1991-03-14	22.00	.50	.00	22.50	RXTY
400003	602314	1991-03-14	140.00	.00	9.80	149.80	RXTY
400004	602315	1991-03-14	178.23	3.19	.00	181.42	RXTY
400010	602316	1991-03-14	140.00	7.50	.00	147.50	RXTY
400011	062317	1991-03-17	289.00	9.00	.00	298.00	RXTY
400012	062318	1991-03-17	199.99	.00	.00	199.99	PCQ3
400015	062319	1991-03-17	178.23	3.19	.00	181.42	RXTY
400015	062320	1991-03-17	3245.00	160.00	.00	3405.00	RXTY
400001	062321	1991-04-03	200.00	5.60	.00	205.60	PCQ4
400014	062322	1991-04-03	15.00	.00	.00	15.00	PCQ4
400011	062323	1991-04-11	925.00	24.00	.00	949.00	PCQ4
400014	062324	1991-04-14	178.23	3.19	.00	181.42	PCQ4
400002	062325	1991-04-17	140.00	7.50	.00	147.50	PCQ3
400011	062326	1991-04-20	178.23	3.19	.00	181.42	PCQ4
400003	062327	1991-04-23	200.00	7.50	14.00	221.50	PCQ4
400004	062328	1991-04-24	178.23	3.19	.00	181.42	PCQ4
400010	062329	1991-04-29	140.00	7.50	.00	147.50	PCQ4
400011	062330	1991-04-30	2295.00	14.00	.00	2309.00	PCQ4
400012	062331	1991-05-07	178.23	.00	.00	178.23	PCQ4
400013	062332	1991-05-09	178.23	.00	.00	178.23	PCQ4
400015	062333	1991-05-17	178.23	.00	.00	178.23	PCQ4

CUST table

CUSTNO	FNAME	LNAME	ADDR	CITY	STATE	ZIPCODE
400001	KEITH	MCDONALD	4501 W MOCKINGBIRD	DALLAS	TX	75209
400002	ARREN	ANELLI	40 FORD RD	DENVILLE	NJ	07834
400003	SUSAN	HOWARD	1107 SECOND AVE #312	REDWOOD CITY	CA	94063
400004	CAROL ANN	EVANS	74 SUTTON CT	GREAT LAKES	IL	60088
400005	ELAINE	ROBERTS	12914 BRACKNELL	CERRITOS	CA	90701
400006	PAT	HONG	73 HIGH ST	SAN FRANCISCO	CA	94114
400007	PHIL	ROACH	25680 ORCHARD	DEARBORN HTS	MI	48125
400008	TIM	JOHNSON	145 W 27TH ST	SO CHICAGO HTS	IL	60411
400009	MARIANNE	BUSBEE	3920 BERWYN DR S #199	MOBILE	AL	36608
400010	ENRIQUE	OTHON	BOX 26729	RICHMOND	VA	23261
400011	WILLIAM C	FERGUSON	BOX 1283	MIAMI	FL	34002-1283
400012	S D	HOEHN	PO BOX 27	RIDDLE	OR	97469
400013	DAVID R	KEITH	BOX 1266	MAGNOLIA	AR	71757-1266
400014	R	BINDER	3425 WALDEN AVE	DEPEW	NY	14043
400015	VIVIAN	GEORGE	229 S 18TH ST	PHILADELPHIA	PA	19103
400016	J	NOETHLICH	11 KINGSTON CT	MERRIMACK	NH	03054

Figure 7-15   The contents of the INV and CUST tables

```
INVOICE REGISTER - 06/27/91                                             PAGE:    1

INVOICE     SUBTOTAL        TAX     SHIPPING        TOTAL   CUSTOMER
062308       200.00        0.00        4.45       204.45   400012   S D          HOEHN
062309        15.00        0.00        0.00        15.00   400011   WILLIAM C    FERGUSON
062310       140.00        0.00        7.50       147.50   400011   WILLIAM C    FERGUSON
062311       178.23        0.00        3.19       181.42   400014   R            BINDER
062312       162.00        0.00       11.07       173.07   400002   ARREN        ANELLI
062313        22.00        0.00        0.50        22.50   400011   WILLIAM C    FERGUSON
062314       140.00        9.80        0.00       149.80   400003   SUSAN        HOWARD
062315       178.23        0.00        3.19       181.42   400004   CAROL ANN    EVANS
062316       140.00        0.00        7.50       147.50   400010   ENRIQUE      OTHON
062317       289.00        0.00        9.00       298.00   400011   WILLIAM C    FERGUSON
062318       199.99        0.00        0.00       199.99   400012   S D          HOEHN
062319       178.23        0.00        3.19       181.42   400015   VIVIAN       GEORGE
062320      3245.00        0.00      160.00      3405.00   400015   VIVIAN       GEORGE
062321       200.00        0.00        5.60       205.60   400001   KEITH        MCDONALD
062322        15.00        0.00        0.00        15.00   400014   R            BINDER
062323       925.00        0.00       24.00       949.00   400011   WILLIAM C    FERGUSON
062324       178.23        0.00        3.19       181.42   400014   R            BINDER
062325       140.00        0.00        7.50       147.50   400002   ARREN        ANELLI
062326       178.23        0.00        3.19       181.42   400011   WILLIAM C    FERGUSON
062327       200.00       14.00        7.50       221.50   400003   SUSAN        HOWARD
062328       178.23        0.00        3.19       181.42   400004   CAROL ANN    EVANS
062329       140.00        0.00        7.50       147.50   400010   ENRIQUE      OTHON
062330      2295.00        0.00       14.00      2309.00   400011   WILLIAM C    FERGUSON
062331       178.23        0.00        0.00       178.23   400012   S D          HOEHN
062332       178.23        0.00        0.00       178.23   400013   DAVID R      KEITH
062333       178.23        0.00        0.00       178.23   400015   VIVIAN       GEORGE

TOTALS:    10072.06       23.80      285.26     10381.12          26 INVOICES ISSUED
```

Figure 7-16   Output of the INVREG program

The sixth column in the report in figure 7-16 contains data drawn from *both* tables (the INVCUST column in INV and the CUSTNO column in CUST). I've shaded this column in figure 7-16. Data from rows in the two tables are joined when the values in these two columns are the same. So, for the first invoice in the table in figure 7-15, DB2 used the value in the INVCUST column (400012) to identify the matching row in the CUST table, and from there, it retrieved the customer's name (S D HOEHN).

The design for the INVREG program   Figure 7-17 presents the structure chart for INVREG. The top-level module, 000-PREPARE-INVOICE-REGISTER, has four subordinates. The first, 100-OPEN-INVOICE-CURSOR, issues the SQL statement that directs DB2 to create the cursor-controlled results table this program uses. If module 100 is successful, module 000 invokes 200-PRINT-INVOICE-LINE repeatedly to retrieve rows from the results table (by performing 210-FETCH-INVOICE-ROW) and to print the data they contain (by performing 220-PRINT-REPORT-LINE).

As part of printing an invoice line, module 220 must determine whether it needs to start a new page and print a heading. If it does, it performs

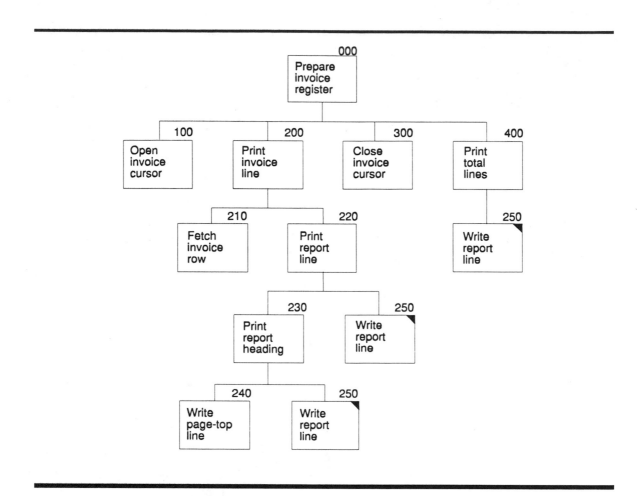

Figure 7-17   Structure chart for the INVREG program

module 230-PRINT-REPORT-HEADING. Module 230 has two subordinates: 240 and 250. The first, 240-WRITE-PAGE-TOP-LINE, issues a WRITE statement after advancing the listing to the next page, while the other, 250-WRITE-REPORT-LINE, issues a WRITE after advancing the listing the number of lines specified in a program variable. As you can see in the chart, module 250 is also called by modules 220 and 400.

When module 210 reaches the end of the results table, it sets a switch so module 200 won't invoke module 220 and so module 000 will stop performing module 200. Then, module 000 continues by invoking 300-CLOSE-INVOICE-CURSOR to release the cursor-controlled results table. Finally, module 000 performs 400-PRINT-TOTAL-LINES to print the line with the

```
*************************************************************
* DCLGEN TABLE(MMADBV.CUST)                                *
*         LIBRARY(MMA002.DCLGENS.COBOL(CUST))              *
*         ACTION(REPLACE)                                  *
*         STRUCTURE(CUSTOMER-ROW)                          *
*         APOST                                            *
* ... IS THE DCLGEN COMMAND THAT MADE THE FOLLOWING STATEMENTS *
*************************************************************
      EXEC SQL DECLARE MMADBV.CUST TABLE
      ( CUSTNO                        CHAR(6) NOT NULL,
        FNAME                         CHAR(20) NOT NULL,
        LNAME                         CHAR(30) NOT NULL,
        ADDR                          CHAR(30) NOT NULL,
        CITY                          CHAR(20) NOT NULL,
        STATE                         CHAR(2) NOT NULL,
        ZIPCODE                       CHAR(10) NOT NULL
      ) END-EXEC.
*************************************************************
* COBOL DECLARATION FOR TABLE MMADBV.CUST                  *
*************************************************************
  01  CUSTOMER-ROW.
      10 CUSTNO              PIC X(6).
      10 FNAME               PIC X(20).
      10 LNAME               PIC X(30).
      10 ADDR                PIC X(30).
      10 CITY                PIC X(20).
      10 STATE               PIC X(2).
      1U ZIPCODE             PIC X(10).
*************************************************************
* THE NUMBER OF COLUMNS DESCRIBED BY THIS DECLARATION IS 7 *
*************************************************************
```

Figure 7-18   DCLGEN output for the CUST table

total dollar amount and a count of the invoices listed. You can see the total line for this example at the bottom of the register in figure 7-16.

The source code for the INVREG program   Figures 7-18 and 7-19 present the DCLGEN output for the CUST and INV tables that the INVREG program uses, and figure 7-20 presents the program itself. Although this is a longer program than the other programs I've shown, it's no harder to understand. That's because most of the program is related to report preparation tasks, not to DB2 operations. For example, you can see the COBOL SELECT statement for the PRTOUT print file in the Environment Division and the file description (FD) for it in the File Section of the Data Division.

The Working-Storage Section includes two switches followed by groups of work fields for manipulating the date that will appear on the report (DATE-FIELDS), for accumulating running totals for the invoices it

```
*****************************************************************
* DCLGEN TABLE(MMADBV.INV)                                      *
*        LIBRARY(MMA002.DCLGENS.COBOL(INV))                     *
*        ACTION(REPLACE)                                        *
*        STRUCTURE(INVOICE-ROW)                                 *
*        APOST                                                  *
* ... IS THE DCLGEN COMMAND THAT MADE THE FOLLOWING STATEMENTS  *
*****************************************************************
      EXEC SQL DECLARE MMADBV.INV TABLE
      ( INVCUST                      CHAR(6) NOT NULL,
        INVNO                        CHAR(6) NOT NULL,
        INVDATE                      DATE NOT NULL,
        INVSUBT                 ,    DECIMAL(9, 2) NOT NULL,
        INVSHIP                      DECIMAL(7, 2) NOT NULL,
        INVTAX                       DECIMAL(7, 2) NOT NULL,
        INVTOTAL                     DECIMAL(9, 2) NOT NULL,
        INVPROM                      CHAR(10) NOT NULL
      ) END-EXEC.
*****************************************************************
* COBOL DECLARATION FOR TABLE MMADBV.INV                        *
*****************************************************************
 01   INVOICE-ROW.
      10 INVCUST            PIC X(6).
      10 INVNO              PIC X(6).
      10 INVDATE            PIC X(10).
      10 INVSUBT            PIC S9999999V99 USAGE COMP-3.
      10 INVSHIP            PIC S99999V99 USAGE COMP-3.
      10 INVTAX             PIC S99999V99 USAGE COMP-3.
      10 INVTOTAL           PIC S9999999V99 USAGE COMP-3.
      10 INVPROM            PIC X(10).
*****************************************************************
* THE NUMBER OF COLUMNS DESCRIBED BY THIS DECLARATION IS 8      *
*****************************************************************
```

Figure 7-19   DCLGEN output for the INV table

processes (INVOICE-TOTAL-FIELDS), and for managing report paging (PRINT-FIELDS). The next items in the Working-Storage Section are four group items for the lines the report contains: two kinds of headings, the report detail line, and the total line.

After the definitions of the report lines, I coded the four non-procedural SQL statements this program needs. The first two are INCLUDE statements for the CUST and INV tables' DCLGEN output. The third is an INCLUDE statement for the SQL communication area. And the last is a DECLARE CURSOR statement that describes the results table the program will use to produce its report.

```
000100 IDENTIFICATION DIVISION.
000200*
000300 PROGRAM-ID.         INVREG.
000400*
000500 ENVIRONMENT DIVISION.
000600*
000700 INPUT-OUTPUT SECTION.
000800*
000900 FILE-CONTROL.
001000*
001100     SELECT PRTOUT ASSIGN TO UT-S-PRTOUT.
001200*
001300 DATA DIVISION.
001400*
001500 FILE SECTION.
001600*
001700 FD  PRTOUT
001800     LABEL RECORDS ARE STANDARD
001900     BLOCK CONTAINS 0 RECORDS
002000     RECORD CONTAINS 132 CHARACTERS.
002100*
002200 01  PRTOUT-RECORD                    PIC X(132).
002300*
002400 WORKING-STORAGE SECTION.
002500*
002600 01  SWITCHES.
002700*
002800     05   VALID-CURSOR SW      PIC X        VALUE "Y".
002900          88   VALID-CURSOR                 VALUE "Y".
003000     05   END-OF-INVOICES-SW   PIC X        VALUE "N".
003100          88   END-OF-INVOICES              VALUE "Y".
003200*
003300 01  DATE-FIELDS.
003400*
003500     05   PRESENT-DATE        PIC 9(6).
003600     05   PRESENT-DATE-X      REDEFINES PRESENT-DATE.
003700          10   PRESENT-YEAR   PIC 99.
003800          10   PRESENT-MONTH  PIC 99.
003900          10   PRESENT-DAY    PIC 99.
004000*
004100 01  INVOICE-TOTAL-FIELDS     COMP-3.
004200*
004300     05   INVOICES-COUNT      PIC S9(9)    VALUE ZERO.
004400     05   INVOICES-SUBTOTAL   PIC S9(9)V99 VALUE ZERO.
004500     05   INVOICES-TAX        PIC S9(7)V99 VALUE ZERO.
004600     05   INVOICES-SHIPPING   PIC S9(7)V99 VALUE ZERO
004700     05   INVOICES-TOTAL      PIC S9(9)V99 VALUE ZERO.
004800*
004900 01  PRINT-FIELDS             COMP-3.
005000*
005100     05   PAGE-COUNT          PIC S9(5)    VALUE ZERO.
005200     05   LINE-COUNT          PIC S9(3)    VALUE +999.
005300     05   LINES-ON-PAGE       PIC S9(3)    VALUE +50.
005400     05   SPACE-CONTROL       PIC S9(3)    VALUE +1.
005500*
```

Figure 7-20   COBOL source code for the INVREG program (part 1 of 5)

```
005600 01   HEADING-LINE-1.
005700*
005800      05   FILLER       PIC X(19)      VALUE "INVOICE REGISTER - ".
005900      05   HL1-MONTH    PIC XX.
006000      05   FILLER       PIC X          VALUE "/".
006100      05   HL1-DAY      PIC XX.
006200      05   FILLER       PIC X          VALUE "/".
006300      05   HL1-YEAR     PIC XX.
006400      05   FILLER       PIC X(89)      VALUE SPACE.
006500      05   FILLER       PIC X(6)       VALUE "PAGE: ".
006600      05   HL1-PAGE     PIC Z(4)9.
006700      05   FILLER       PIC X(5)       VALUE SPACE.
006800*
006900 01   HEADING-LINE-2.
007000*
007100      05   FILLER       PIC X(20)      VALUE "INVOICE        SUBTOTAL".
007200      05   FILLER       PIC X(20)      VALUE "            TAX    SHIP".
007300      05   FILLER       PIC X(20)      VALUE "PING           TOTAL   ".
007400      05   FILLER       PIC X(20)      VALUE "CUSTOMER               ".
007500      05   FILLER       PIC X(20)      VALUE "                       ".
007600      05   FILLER       PIC X(20)      VALUE "                       ".
007700      05   FILLER       PIC X(12)      VALUE "                       ".
007800*
007900 01   REPORT-LINE.
008000*
008100      05   RL-INVNO     PIC X(6).
008200      05   FILLER       PIC XX         VALUE SPACE.
008300      05   RL-SUBTOTAL  PIC Z(8)9.99.
008400      05   FILLER       PIC XX         VALUE SPACE.
008500      05   RL-TAX       PIC Z(6)9.99.
008600      05   FILLER       PIC XX         VALUE SPACE.
008700      05   RL-SHIPPING  PIC Z(6)9.99.
008800      05   FILLER       PIC XX         VALUE SPACE.
008900      05   RL-TOTAL     PIC Z(8)9.99.
009000      05   FILLER       PIC XX         VALUE SPACE.
009100      05   RL-CUSTNO    PIC X(6).
009200      05   FILLER       PIC XX         VALUE SPACE.
009300      05   RL-FNAME     PIC X(20).
009400      05   FILLER       PIC XX         VALUE SPACE.
009500      05   RL-LNAME     PIC X(30).
009600      05   FILLER       PIC X(12)      VALUE SPACE.
009700*
009800 01   TOTAL-LINE.
009900*
010000      05   FILLER       PIC X(8)       VALUE "TOTALS: ".
010100      05   TL-SUBTOTAL  PIC Z(8)9.99.
010200      05   FILLER       PIC XX         VALUE SPACE.
010300      05   TL-TAX       PIC Z(6)9.99.
010400      05   FILLER       PIC XX         VALUE SPACE.
010500      05   TL-SHIPPING  PIC Z(6)9.99.
010600      05   FILLER       PIC XX         VALUE SPACE.
010700      05   TL-TOTAL     PIC Z(8)9.99.
010800      05   FILLER       PIC XX         VALUE SPACE.
010900      05   TL-COUNT     PIC Z(8)9.
011000      05   FILLER       PIC X(16)      VALUE " INVOICES ISSUED".
011100      05   FILLER       PIC X(47)      VALUE SPACE.
```

Figure 7-20   COBOL source code for the INVREG program (part 2 of 5)

```
011200*
011300      EXEC SQL
011400          INCLUDE CUST
011500      END-EXEC.
011600*
011700      EXEC SQL
011800          INCLUDE INV
011900      END-EXEC.
012000*
012100      EXEC SQL
012200          INCLUDE SQLCA
012300      END-EXEC.
012400*
012500      EXEC SQL
012600          DECLARE INVCURS CURSOR FOR
012700              SELECT    INVNO,    INVSUBT, INVTAX,  INVSHIP
012800                        INVTOTAL, CUSTNO,  FNAME,   LNAME
012900                  FROM  MMADBV.INV, MMADBV.CUST
013000                  WHERE INVCUST = CUSTNO
013100                  ORDER BY INVNO
013200      END-EXEC.
013300*
013400 PROCEDURE DIVISION.
013500*
013600 000-PREPARE-INVOICE-REGISTER.
013700*
013800      OPEN OUTPUT PRTOUT.
013900      ACCEPT PRESENT-DATE FROM DATE.
014000      MOVE PRESENT-MONTH TO HL1-MONTH.
014100      MOVE PRESENT-DAY   TO HL1-DAY.
014200      MOVE PRESENT-YEAR  TO HL1-YEAR.
014300      PERFORM 100-OPEN-INVOICE-CURSOR.
014400      IF VALID-CURSOR
014500          PERFORM 200-PRINT-INVOICE-LINE
014600              UNTIL END-OF-INVOICES
014700          PERFORM 300-CLOSE-INVOICE-CURSOR.
014800      PERFORM 400-PRINT-TOTAL-LINES.
014900      CLOSE PRTOUT.
015000      STOP RUN.
015100*
015200 100-OPEN-INVOICE-CURSOR.
015300*
015400      EXEC SQL
015500          OPEN INVCURS
015600      END-EXEC.
015700      IF SQLCODE NOT = 0
015800          MOVE "N" TO VALID-CURSOR-SW.
015900*
```

Figure 7-20   COBOL source code for the INVREG program (part 3 of 5)

```
016000 200-PRINT-INVOICE-LINE.
016100*
016200        PERFORM 210-FETCH-INVOICE-ROW.
016300        IF NOT END-OF-INVOICES
016400            IF VALID-CURSOR
016500                ADD 1          TO INVOICES-COUNT
016600                ADD INVSUBT    TO INVOICES-SUBTOTAL
016700                ADD INVTAX     TO INVOICES-TAX
016800                ADD INVSHIP    TO INVOICES-SHIPPING
016900                ADD INVTOTAL   TO INVOICES-TOTAL
017000                MOVE INVNO     TO RL-INVNO
017100                MOVE INVSUBT   TO RL-SUBTOTAL
017200                MOVE INVTAX    TO RL-TAX
017300                MOVE INVSHIP   TO RL-SHIPPING
017400                MOVE INVTOTAL  TO RL-TOTAL
017500                MOVE CUSTNO    TO RL-CUSTNO
017600                MOVE FNAME     TO RL-FNAME
017700                MOVE LNAME     TO RL-LNAME
017800                PERFORM 220-PRINT-REPORT-LINE.
017900*
018000 210-FETCH-INVOICE-ROW.
018100*
018200        EXEC SQL
018300            FETCH INVCURS
018400                INTO :INVNO,      :INVSUBT,   :INVTAX,    :INVSHIP,
018500                     :INVTOTAL,   :CUSTNO,    :FNAME,     :LNAME
018600        END-EXEC.
018700        IF SQLCODE NOT = 0
018800            MOVE "Y" TO END-OF-INVOICES-SW
018900            IF SQLCODE NOT = 100
019000                MOVE "N" TO VALID-CURSOR-SW.
019100*
019200 220-PRINT-REPORT-LINE.
019300*
019400        IF LINE-COUNT > LINES-ON-PAGE
019500            PERFORM 230-PRINT-REPORT-HEADING
019600            MOVE 1 TO LINE-COUNT.
019700        MOVE REPORT-LINE TO PRTOUT-RECORD.
019800        PERFORM 250-WRITE-REPORT-LINE.
019900        ADD 1 TO LINE-COUNT.
020000        MOVE 1 TO SPACE-CONTROL.
020100*
020200 230-PRINT-REPORT-HEADING.
020300*
020400        ADD 1 TO PAGE-COUNT.
020500        MOVE PAGE-COUNT TO HL1-PAGE.
020600        MOVE HEADING-LINE-1 TO PRTOUT-RECORD.
020700        PERFORM 240-WRITE-PAGE-TOP-LINE.
020800        MOVE 2 TO SPACE-CONTROL.
020900        MOVE HEADING-LINE-2 TO PRTOUT-RECORD.
021000        PERFORM 250-WRITE-REPORT-LINE.
021100*
```

Figure 7-20   COBOL source code for the INVREG program (part 4 of 5)

```
021200 240-WRITE-PAGE-TOP-LINE.
021300*
021400      WRITE PRTOUT-RECORD
021500          AFTER ADVANCING PAGE.
021600*
021700 250-WRITE-REPORT-LINE.
021800*
021900      WRITE PRTOUT-RECORD
022000          AFTER SPACE-CONTROL LINES.
022100*
022200 300-CLOSE-INVOICE-CURSOR.
022300*
022400      EXEC SQL
022500          CLOSE INVCURS
022600      END-EXEC.
022700      IF SQLCODE NOT = 0
022800          MOVE "N" TO VALID-CURSOR-SW.
022900*
023000 400-PRINT-TOTAL-LINES.
023100*
023200      IF VALID-CURSOR
023300          MOVE INVOICES-SUBTOTAL TO TL-SUBTOTAL
023400          MOVE INVOICES-TAX      TO TL-TAX
023500          MOVE INVOICES-SHIPPING TO TL-SHIPPING
023600          MOVE INVOICES-TOTAL    TO TL-TOTAL
023700          MOVE INVOICES-COUNT    TO TL-COUNT
023800          MOVE TOTAL-LINE        TO PRTOUT-RECORD
023900      ELSE
024000          MOVE "****  DB2 ERROR   --  INCOMPLETE REPORT  ****"
024100                                 TO PRTOUT-RECORD.
024200      MOVE 2 TO SPACE-CONTROL.
024300      PERFORM 250-WRITE-REPORT-LINE.
024400*
```

Figure 7-20   COBOL source code for the INVREG program (part 5 of 5)

Take a close look at the DECLARE CURSOR statement:

```
EXEC SQL
    DECLARE INVCURS CURSOR FOR
        SELECT    INVNO,    INVSUBT, INVTAX, INVSHIP,
                  INVTOTAL, CUSTNO,  FNAME,  LNAME
            FROM  MMADBV.INV, MMADBV.CUST
            WHERE INVCUST = CUSTNO
            ORDER BY INVNO
END-EXEC.
```

As you can see, the SELECT component names eight columns, five from the INV table and three from the CUST table. The WHERE clause specifies the join condition: DB2 will join data from rows in the two tables only when the contents of their customer number columns (INVCUST in the INV table and CUSTNO in the CUST table) are the same.

Because this SELECT will return a multi-row results table, I had to code it within a DECLARE CURSOR statement. However, you should realize that you can use joins in stand-alone SELECTs too. For example, if you were writing an inquiry program to display information for a single invoice, you could join the invoice data with the data for that invoices's customer in a stand-alone SELECT. That's because there is a one-to-one relationship between customers and invoices, and you'd be sure to get a single-row results table.

The Procedure Division code that opens and closes the cursor is what you'd expect. Module 100 creates the program's results table by issuing an OPEN statement for the INVCURS cursor. Then, module 200 is executed over and over as the program works through the cursor-controlled results table. Each time it runs, module 200 invokes module 210 to retrieve the next invoice row. Module 210 does that with this FETCH statement:

```
EXEC SQL
    FETCH INVCURS
        INTO :INVNO,      :INVSUBT, :INVTAX, :INVSHIP,
             :INVTOTAL, :CUSTNO,  :FNAME,  :LNAME
END-EXEC.
```

Notice that the INTO clause names host variables in the DCLGEN output for both the INV and CUST tables.

If the FETCH statement retrieves a row successfully, module 200 increments the counter fields, formats the report detail line, and invokes module 220 to print the line. Module 220, in turn, determines whether or not a page break needs to occur. If so, it prints a report heading by performing module 230. Whether a page break occurs or not, module 220 moves the detail line that was formatted in module 200 into the report output area (PRTOUT-RECORD). Then, it performs module 250 to write the line to the report.

When module 210 tries to FETCH a row after it has already retrieved the last one, it sets END-OF-INVOICES-SW to Y. Then, module 200 doesn't do anything else. When control passes back to module 000, it invokes module 300 to close the invoice cursor.

If everything to this point has been normal, the value of VALID-CURSOR-SW is Y, and module 400 moves the total values that were accumulated by module 200 into the total line fields. Then, it moves the entire total line to the report output area and invokes module 250 to write the report line. On the other hand, if any of the SQL statements in the program returned an unusual value in the SQLCODE field, the value of VALID-CURSOR-SW will be N. If that's the case, module 400 doesn't print the normal total line, but prints an error message instead.

Observations about the INVREG program   Of course, this program is just a simple example of how you can use joins to solve application problems. In a production environment, you're not likely to write an invoice register program that lists all of the invoices a firm has issued. However, it's a simple matter to adjust this program so it lists a more realistic subset of all invoices, such as those issued on a specific day. All you'd have to do is add an appropriate WHERE clause to the SELECT component of the DECLARE CURSOR statement.

You should realize that for this program to work, every customer number that occurs in a row in the INV table must match the customer number in one and only one row in the CUST table. As you may recall from chapter 4, this is called referential integrity. The DBA can insure that there are no duplicate customer numbers in the CUST table by defining a unique index over the customer number column. Then, DB2 won't allow any row that contains a customer number that already exists to be inserted in the CUST table, and it won't allow updates that would result in a duplicate customer number to be made. Also, application programs that insert rows into the invoice table would need to use a valid customer number from the CUST table for each new invoice.

I'm sure you'll agree that joins can save you a substantial amount of programming work. Think for a moment about how you'd have to write a program like the one I just showed you if you were using standard files. The program would read through the invoice file, and, for each invoice record, do a random read to retrieve the corresponding record from the customer file. Although it's possible to use this technique with DB2, it's much easier and more efficient to let DB2 take care of joining invoices and customers than doing it yourself.

But when you code SELECT statements to perform join operations, you need to be sure that you thoroughly understand the logic behind the organization of the data in the tables you use. Because DB2 can combine just about any column from any table with any other, it's up to you to be sure that a join makes sense. You should be able to depend on the system designer who plans your applications and decides how DB2 table data should be manipulated. If you're responsible for these tasks, take the time to gain a complete understanding of the data. If necessary, talk with the DBA responsible for the tables you need to access. DBAs are especially sensitive to issues that surround table design and data integrity, so you should get good, accurate advice.

Terms

union
join
Cartesian product
cross product
join predicate
join condition
qualified name
synonym
alias
correlation name

Objectives

1. Given specifications for a program that requires combining rows from similar results tables, code appropriate SELECT statements with the UNION keyword.

2. Given specifications for a program that requires joining columns from two or more tables, code appropriate SELECT statements.

3. Describe the result of not coding a WHERE clause on a SELECT statement that does a join.

4. Code a SELECT statement that assigns temporary synonyms to table names and uses those synonyms in qualified column names.

Chapter 8

How to use subqueries

A *subquery*, also called a *subselect*, is a SELECT that's nested inside another SQL statement. You're likely to use a subquery when one SQL statement depends on the results of another. To understand how this works, you can imagine that DB2 uses the subquery to create an intermediate results table that it makes available to the outer statement.

Quite frankly, subqueries can be confusing. If you find the material in this chapter challenging, you won't be alone. To help you learn subqueries, I'll present several examples that use the invoice and customer tables you've already seen. Figure 8-1 presents the versions of those tables I'll use in this chapter.

A simple subquery example

Think about how you'd solve this problem: Given the invoice table in figure 8-1, code the SQL statements a program needs to retrieve the invoice number, customer number, and invoice total from all the rows where the invoice total is greater than the *average* of all of the invoice totals. Because the invoice average is sure to vary each time an invoice is added to the INV table,

INV table

INVCUST	INVNO	INVDATE	INVSUBT	INVSHIP	INVTAX	INVTOTAL	INVPROM
400012	062308	1990-12-22	200.00	4.45	.00	204.45	PCQ3
400011	062309	1990-12-22	15.00	.00	.00	15.00	PCQ3
400011	602310	1990-02-22	140.00	7.50	.00	147.50	PCQ3
400014	602311	1990-02-22	178.23	3.19	.00	181.42	PCQ3
400002	602312	1991-02-22	162.00	11.07	.00	173.07	PCQ3
400011	602313	1991-03-14	22.00	.50	.00	22.50	RXTY
400003	602314	1991-03-14	140.00	.00	9.80	149.80	RXTY
400004	602315	1991-03-14	178.23	3.19	.00	181.42	RXTY
400010	602316	1991-03-14	140.00	7.50	.00	147.50	RXTY
400011	062317	1991-03-17	289.00	9.00	.00	298.00	RXTY
400012	062318	1991-03-17	199.99	.00	.00	199.99	PCQ3
400015	062319	1991-03-17	178.23	3.19	.00	181.42	RXTY
400015	062320	1991-03-17	3245.00	160.00	.00	3405.00	RXTY
400001	062321	1991-04-03	200.00	5.60	.00	205.60	PCQ4
400014	062322	1991-04-03	15.00	.00	.00	15.00	PCQ4
400011	062323	1991-04-11	925.00	24.00	.00	949.00	PCQ4
400014	062324	1991-04-14	178.23	3.19	.00	181.42	PCQ4
400002	062325	1991-04-17	140.00	7.50	.00	147.50	PCQ3
400011	062326	1991-04-20	178.23	3.19	.00	181.42	PCQ4
400003	062327	1991-04-23	200.00	7.50	14.00	221.50	PCQ4
400004	062328	1991-04-24	178.23	3.19	.00	181.42	PCQ4
400010	062329	1991-04-29	140.00	7.50	.00	147.50	PCQ4
400011	062330	1991-04-30	2295.00	14.00	.00	2309.00	PCQ4
400012	062331	1991-05-07	178.23	.00	.00	178.23	PCQ4
400013	062332	1991-05-09	178.23	.00	.00	178.23	PCQ4
400015	062333	1991-05-17	178.23	.00	.00	178.23	PCQ4

CUST table

CUSTNO	FNAME	LNAME	ADDR	CITY	STATE	ZIPCODE
400001	KEITH	MCDONALD	4501 W MOCKINGBIRD	DALLAS	TX	75209
400002	ARREN	ANELLI	40 FORD RD	DENVILLE	NJ	07834
400003	SUSAN	HOWARD	1107 SECOND AVE #312	REDWOOD CITY	CA	94063
400004	CAROL ANN	EVANS	74 SUTTON CT	GREAT LAKES	IL	60088
400005	ELAINE	ROBERTS	12914 BRACKNELL	CERRITOS	CA	90701
400006	PAT	HONG	73 HIGH ST	SAN FRANCISCO	CA	94114
400007	PHIL	ROACH	25680 ORCHARD	DEARBORN HTS	MI	48125
400008	TIM	JOHNSON	145 W 27TH ST	SO CHICAGO HTS	IL	60411
400009	MARIANNE	BUSBEE	3920 BERWYN DR S #199	MOBILE	AL	36608
400010	ENRIQUE	OTHON	BOX 26729	RICHMOND	VA	23261
400011	WILLIAM C	FERGUSON	BOX 1283	MIAMI	FL	34002-1283
400012	S D	HOEHN	PO BOX 27	RIDDLE	OR	97469
400013	DAVID R	KEITH	BOX 1266	MAGNOLIA	AR	71757-1266
400014	R	BINDER	3425 WALDEN AVE	DEPEW	NY	14043
400015	VIVIAN	GEORGE	229 S 18TH ST	PHILADELPHIA	PA	19103
400016	J	NOETHLICH	11 KINGSTON CT	MERRIMACK	NH	03054

Figure 8-1   Contents of the INV and CUST tables

you can't use a literal value in this kind of selection condition. Instead, you need to calculate the current average each time you do the inquiry.

Example 1
SQL statements without a subquery

```
EXEC SQL
     DECLARE INVCURS CURSOR FOR
          SELECT      INVNO,
                      INVCUST,
                      INVTOTAL
           FROM   MMADBV.INV
          WHERE INVTOTAL >
                 :COMPUTED-AVERAGE
END-EXEC.
     .
     .
     .
     .
     .
EXEC SQL
     SELECT AVG(INVTOTAL)
          FROM MMADBV.INV
          INTO :COMPUTED-AVERAGE
END-EXEC.
EXEC SQL
     OPEN INVCURS
END-EXEC.
```

Example 2
SQL statements with a subquery

```
EXEC SQL
     DECLARE INVCURS CURSOR FOR
          SELECT      INVNO
                      INVCUST,
                      INVTOTAL
           FROM   MMADBV.INV
          WHERE INVTOTAL >
                 (SELECT AVG(INVTOTAL)
                      FROM MMADBV.INV)
END-EXEC.
     .
     .
     .
     .
     .
     .
     .
     .
EXEC SQL
     OPEN INVCURS
END-EXEC.
```

Results table from both examples

INVCUST	INVNO	INVTOTAL
400015	062320	3405.00
400011	062323	949.00
400011	062330	2309.00

Figure 8-2   SQL statements with and without a subquery that retrieve rows from the INV table that have INVTOTAL column values greater than the average total

Figure 8-2 presents two solutions to this problem. Example 1 shows how you can solve this problem with the SQL features you already know. Here, the first SQL statement is a DECLARE CURSOR statement that would appear in the program's Data Division. As you can see, this statement's WHERE clause specifies that the rows that are selected for the cursor-controlled results table should be those where the INVTOTAL column's value is greater than the value of a program host variable called COMPUTED-AVERAGE.

Remember that a cursor-controlled results table isn't created until the cursor is opened. So before the OPEN statement is issued for this cursor, the program issues a SELECT with a column function to determine the current average of the INVTOTAL column's values. Even if you haven't read the chapter on column functions, you shouldn't have any problem understanding this if you know that

```
SELECT AVG(INVTOTAL)
```

returns a single-row results table with one column, and its value is the average of the values in the base table's INVTOTAL column. As a result, this SELECT statement stores the average invoice total in the program host variable COMPUTED-AVERAGE.

Then, the program issues the OPEN statement for the INVCURS cursor. When SQL processes that statement, DB2 uses the SELECT component of the DECLARE CURSOR statement to create the results table. The results table drawn from the base INV table in figure 8-1 is shown at the bottom of figure 8-2. From this point, the program can work through the results table with the FETCH statement, as in the program examples you've already seen.

The sequence of code in example 2 generates the same results table. However, it uses a subquery nested within the SELECT component of its DECLARE CURSOR statement. As you can see, the WHERE clause of the SELECT doesn't name a program host variable as the comparison value, like the WHERE clause in example 1 does. Rather, it refers to another SELECT statement. When DB2 generates the results table for this DECLARE CURSOR statement, it first processes the inner SELECT to calculate the average. Then, it uses that value to retrieve just the rows from the INV table that meet the selection condition in the outer SELECT.

How to code subqueries and the predicates that contain them

Example 2 in figure 8-2 illustrates just one of four ways you can use a subquery in a SELECT statement's WHERE clause. Figure 8-3 shows the syntax for all four. You might be surprised that figure 8-3 emphasizes the syntax of the WHERE clause that contains the subquery instead of the syntax of the subquery itself. In fact, you can use most of the features of SELECT in a subquery. There are just three rules that you need to keep in mind when you code a nested SELECT. They're presented at the top of figure 8-3. First, and most significant, is that the results table a subquery creates can contain only one column. Second, you can't code ORDER BY in a subquery, although you can use GROUP BY and HAVING.

The third rule has to do with the levels of nesting you can have with subqueries. DB2 lets you nest subqueries within subqueries, and there's no theoretical upper limit. However, in practical terms, you need to keep the number reasonable. For every additional level of subquery you use, you're imposing an additional processing load on DB2. Moreover, you're imposing

Rules that apply to nested SELECTS

- Results tables produced by subqueries must contain exactly one column.

- Nested SELECTs may not specify ORDER BY.

- Levels of nested SELECTs should be minimized for performance reasons.

Four ways to code predicates that contain subqueries

Simple comparison predicate

```
           (:host-variable,)  ( =  )
           | literal        |  | ¬= |
           | column-name    |  | >  |
WHERE      | function       |  | ¬> |  (subquery)
           | calculated-value| | <  |
           ( USER           )  | ¬< |
                               | <> |
                               | >= |
                               ( <= )
```

Predicate using the IN keyword

```
           (:host-variable )
           | literal        |
WHERE      | column-name    |  [NOT]  IN  (subquery)
           | function       |
           | calculated-value|
           ( USER           )
```

Comparison predicate using the ANY, SOME or ALL keyword

```
           (:host-variable )  ( =  )
           | literal        |  | ¬= |
           | column-name    |  | >  |   (ANY )
WHERE      | function       |  | ¬> |   |SOME| (subquery)
           | calculated-value| | <  |   (ALL )
           ( USER           )  | ¬< |
                               | <> |
                               | >= |
                               ( <= )
```

Predicate using the EXISTS keyword

```
WHERE [NOT] EXISTS (subquery)
```

Figure 8-3 How to code predicates that use subqueries

a processing load on yourself, because nesting subqueries within subqueries can soon become hard to follow.

Subqueries that are simple comparisons   In example 2 in figure 8-2, I coded the subquery right after the operator (>) in the outer SELECT's WHERE clause. When you use this technique, the subquery must return a very simple table: one row and one column. DB2 replaces the subquery with that value.

With the INV table data in figure 8-1, the result of the subquery in figure 8-2 is 399.27. So, for this particular execution of the statement, the WHERE clause in the outer SELECT effectively becomes:

```
WHERE INVTOTAL > 399.27
```

If you specify the result of a column function, like AVG, in the subquery, you can be sure that you'll get a one-column, one-row results table.

Subqueries with the IN keyword and with the ANY, SOME, or ALL keyword   The second way to code a subquery figure 8-3 presents is with the IN keyword. When you use IN, your subquery can return more than one row, although it's still restricted to one column. If you read chapter 5, you'll recall that when you use the IN keyword in the WHERE clause, you code a list of specific comparison values. One of the values in this list must match the value of the first expression in the clause for the condition to be met. Coding a subquery with IN is essentially the same, except you don't have to list the selection values explicitly. Instead, DB2 constructs the list of selection values for you according to your specifications on the inner SELECT statement. I'll show you an example of a subquery with the IN keyword in a moment.

The third way figure 8-3 shows to code a subquery is with the ANY, SOME, or ALL keyword. When you use one of these keywords, you also need to code an operator. This operator specifies what relationship the value you're comparing must have to any, some, or all of the values in the results table the subquery produces. You can use the ANY and SOME keywords interchangeably. They both specify that the comparison value must have the relationship the operator indicates to at least one of the values in the intermediate results table. In contrast, the ALL operator means the comparison value must have the relationship the operator specifies to every value in the intermediate results table.

Figure 8-4 shows three sample SELECT statements that all accomplish the same task: they create a results table that lists the names of customers who have invoices in the INV table with totals of $1000 or more. The first uses a subquery with IN, the second uses a subquery with ANY, and the

Example 1   SELECT that uses a subquery with IN

```
SELECT     FNAME, LNAME
    FROM   MMADBV.CUST
    WHERE CUSTNO IN
        (SELECT     INVCUST
            FROM   MMADBV.INV
            WHERE INVTOTAL >= 1000)
```

Example 2   SELECT that uses a subquery with ANY

```
SELECT     FNAME, LNAME
    FROM   MMADBV.CUST
    WHERE CUSTNO = ANY
        (SELECT     INVCUST
            FROM   MMADBV.INV
            WHERE INVTOTAL >= 1000)
```

Example 3   SELECT that uses a join to avoid a subquery

```
SELECT     FNAME, LNAME
    FROM   MMADBV.CUST, MMADBV,INV
    WHERE CUSTNO = INVCUST AND
          INVTOTAL >= 1000
```

Results table from all three examples

FNAME	LNAME
WILLIAM C	FERGUSON
VIVIAN	GEORGE

Figure 8-4   Equivalent SELECT statements that retrieve the names of customers with individual purchases of $1000 or more

third uses a join. If you look back to figure 8-1 you'll see that only two rows in the INV table have INVTOTAL values of $1000 or more. Those two rows correspond to customers 400011 and 400015 in the CUST table.

When DB2 processes the statement in the first example in figure 8-4, the subquery generates a two-row, one-column intermediate results table. The value in one row is 400011, and the value in the other is 400015. You can imagine that DB2 modifies the outer statement by substituting these values after IN, so its WHERE clause effectively becomes

```
WHERE CUSTNO IN ('400011','400015')
```

The final results table contains the two names you can see in the bottom of figure 8-4.

The second SELECT in figure 8-4 uses the ANY keyword with the equal sign operator. This is the same as coding the subquery with IN. It specifies that the values of the FNAME and LNAME columns in a row of the CUST table should be included in the final results table if the value of the CUSTNO column in that row is the same as any of the values in the intermediate results table the subquery creates. Of course, the outer statement would produce a different results table if I had coded an operator other than an equal sign with the ANY keyword.

If you read chapter 7, you may be wondering why you can't simply use a join to accomplish this task. As the third example in figure 8-4 shows, you can. In fact, it's likely to be more efficient to use a join than a subquery in a situation like this. That's because when you do a join, DB2 makes better use of any indexes that may be available than when you use a subquery. Therefore, you should use a join instead of a subquery when you can.

Unfortunately, though, you can't always use a join instead of a subquery. If you need to update or delete the data you retrieve, you can't use a join; you must use a subquery. That's because a join produces a read-only results table.

Subqueries with the EXISTS keyword   The fourth way you can code a subquery is with the EXISTS keyword. This approach differs from the first three because it doesn't create an intermediate results table that it makes available to the outer SELECT. Instead, it simply tests to determine whether any rows would be present if it did create an intermediate results table. If any would be, a predicate that specifies EXISTS would be satisfied; if not, a NOT EXISTS predicate would be satisfied.

Frankly, EXISTS is confusing. But it's even harder to grasp because it's most often used with a class of subqueries that I think are the single most difficult thing to understand about SQL: correlated subqueries.

Correlated subqueries

Correlated subqueries will be easier to grasp if you contrast them with basic subqueries, like the ones I've shown you so far in this chapter. You can think of a basic subquery as operating independently of the SELECT that contains it. DB2 processes a basic subquery before it processes the outer SELECT, and it makes the subquery's results table available to the outer SELECT. After the basic subquery has created its results table, it's finished, and its contents are fixed for the duration of the outer statement.

```
SELECT     FNAME, LNAME
    FROM   MMADBV.CUST CUSTTABL
    WHERE NOT EXISTS
        (SELECT *
            FROM   MMADBV.INV
            WHERE INVCUST = CUSTTABL.CUSTNO)
```

Results table

FNAME	LNAME
ELAINE	ROBERTS
PAT	HONG
PHIL	ROACH
TIM	JOHNSON
MARIANNE	BUSBEE
J	NOETHLICH

Figure 8-5   A SELECT statement that uses the EXISTS keyword with a correlated subquery

In contrast, a *correlated subquery* doesn't work independently of the outer SELECT. As its name suggests, it's correlated with it. Instead of being performed just once, a correlated subquery is performed once for *each row* the outer select processes. And each time a correlated subquery runs, it can produce a different results table. That's because it can use different selection criteria, drawn from the row the outer statement is currently evaluating. Let me show you an example and describe how it works.

A simple correlated subquery   Figure 8-5 shows a SELECT that uses a correlated subquery with the EXISTS keyword. The function of this statement is to produce a results table that contains the names of all customers who don't have any invoices. (You might use a statement like this to construct a list of inactive customers.)

To process this statement, DB2 works through the CUST table row by row and, for each, checks the INV table to see if there are any invoices for that customer. If there aren't, the FNAME and LNAME values from the CUST table row currently being evaluated are added to the results table the outer SELECT is constructing. Because the customer number value changes as the outer select moves from row to row, the inner select needs to be done over and over.

I want you to notice two things about this statement. First, the subselect doesn't explicitly name any columns. Because no data is transferred when you use the EXISTS keyword, it doesn't matter what you code for the column specification on the subselect. As a result, it has become almost a standard to code the easiest, most general thing: an asterisk.

The second point I want to discuss is that for this statement to work, some mechanism must be in place that lets the inner SELECT refer to a column in a table that it doesn't name in its own FROM clause. You might expect a simpler statement, like this:

```
SELECT     FNAME,LNAME
    FROM  MMADBV.CUST
    WHERE NOT EXISTS
        (SELECT *
            FROM MMADBV.INV
            WHERE INVCUST = CUSTNO)
```

to work. However, this statement will fail and return a negative SQLCODE value because DB2 isn't able to make sense of the column name CUSTNO in the subquery. That's true even though the statement seems perfectly clear and unambiguous.

To avoid this problem, you need to define a synonym for the table in the outer SELECT and use it as a qualifier in the inner select. (I introduced synonyms in chapter 7.) When you use a synonym in this context, it's called a *correlation name*, and the connection it makes is called *correlated reference*.

The synonym in the example in figure 8-5 is CUSTTABL. I created the synonym simply by providing a name for it after the name of the CUST table in the outer SELECT's FROM clause. Then, I used the synonym by combining it with the column name CUSTNO in the WHERE clause of the inner SELECT.

Although correlated and non-correlated subqueries work in different ways, the syntactical difference between them is subtle. DB2 performs a correlated subquery when you use a correlation name in a subselect. Although it seems like you'd code a more explicit clause to specify a correlated subquery, you don't.

Because correlated subqueries can require substantial system resources, you should consider alternative approaches when you can. For example, you can code a SELECT that uses a basic subquery to accomplish what the one in figure 8-5 does:

```
SELECT     FNAME,LNAME
    FROM  MMADBV.CUST
    WHERE CUSTNO NOT IN
        (SELECT INVCUST
            FROM MMADBV.INV)
```

This statement builds an intermediate results table that contains all of the customer numbers in the invoice table, then adds the FNAME and LNAME column values to the final results table only when the customer number for them isn't in the intermediate results table.

Often, you can use a join instead of a correlated subquery. When that's possible, you should. Joins are almost sure to be more efficient than correlated subqueries. Unfortunately, you can't always avoid correlated subqueries, as the next example illustrates.

A more complex correlated subquery   Think back to the example I showed you at the start of this chapter that retrieves data from rows in the INV table that have INVTOTAL column values greater than the average invoice total. That application lent itself well to a simple subquery that determines the current average value. Now, suppose that the application requirement was slightly different: Retrieve data from rows in the INV table that have INVTOTAL column values greater than the average invoice total for the customer associated with them, not the average invoice total for all customers.

This complicates the problem because it requires a correlated subquery. What makes this problem interesting is that both the outer SELECT and the subquery process the same table.

Figure 8-6 shows a SELECT that accomplishes this task. It creates a results table that contains the INVNO, INVCUST, and INVTOTAL column values for all the INV table rows whose INVTOTAL column's value is greater than the average amount calculated by the subquery. Because this statement requires a correlated subquery, I needed to add a correlation name for the INV table in the outer SELECT. To make the statement easier to understand, I selected a name that has some meaning: OUTERINV.

The subquery in figure 8-6 uses the AVG column function to compute the average of the values in the INVTOTAL column. It too needs a synonym, so I specified INNERINV. And I included a WHERE clause to restrict the rows used in the computation to just those associated with the current customer.

The current customer is the one whose number is in the INVCUST column in the row the outer SELECT is positioned on when it invokes the subquery. I referred to it in the inner SELECT with the fully qualified name OUTERINV.INVCUST. For each separate execution of the subquery, you can think of this as a constant value. For each subquery, DB2 evaluates all of the rows in the table to find those where the value of the INVCUST column, identified in the inner SELECT with the fully qualified name INNERINV.INVCUST, matches the value in OUTERINV.INVCUST. It uses the values from the INVTOTAL column from only those rows to calculate the average for the customer.

```
SELECT     INVNO, INVCUST, INVTOTAL
    FROM   MMADBV.INV OUTERINV
    WHERE INVTOTAL >
        (SELECT AVG(INVTOTAL)
            FROM   MMADBV.INV INNERINV
            WHERE INNERINV.INVCUST =
                    OUTERINV.INVCUST)
    ORDER BY 2
```

Results table

INVNO	INVCUST	INVTOTAL
062312	400002	173.07
062327	400003	221.50
062330	400011	2309.00
062323	400011	949.00
062318	400012	199.99
062308	400012	204.45
062311	400014	181.42
062324	400014	181.42
062320	400015	3405.00

Figure 8-6 A SELECT statement that uses a correlated subquery to retrieve rows from the INV table that have totals greater than the customer's average total

After the inner SELECT has determined the average invoice total for the current customer, DB2 substitutes the average in the WHERE clause of the outer SELECT. Then, if the invoice row the outer SELECT is evaluating has an INVTOTAL value greater than the calculated average, DB2 includes it in the final results table. Finally, DB2 moves on to the next INV table row, the value of OUTERINV.CUST changes to represent the number of the new current customer, and the process repeats.

How to use subqueries with INSERT, DELETE, and UPDATE statements

You're not restricted to using subqueries in SELECT statements. You can also code them in INSERT, UPDATE, and DELETE statements. When I introduced the INSERT statement in chapter 4, I showed you how to code a subselect in its WHERE clause to do a mass insert. You can't base a subquery on the same table you're modifying with the INSERT, UPDATE, or DELETE statement. Other than that, you use subqueries with INSERT, UPDATE, and DELETE the way you would expect to.

```
EXEC SQL
    INSERT INTO MMADBV.OLDCUST
         (SELECT    *
            FROM   MMADBV.CUST
            WHERE CUSTNO < '300000')
END-EXEC.
```

Figure 8-7   An INSERT statement that does a mass insert

How to use subqueries with the INSERT statement   In chapter 4, I used
the INSERT statement in figure 8-7 to illustrate a mass insert. This statement directs DB2 to create a results table that contains all the rows from
the CUST table with CUSTNO column values less than 300000 and add
them to a table named OLDCUST. Because the two tables this statement
accesses have identical structures, I didn't need to specify the columns
involved in the operation. As a result, the statement is simple.

You can code more complex mass insert statements as well. Figure 8-8,
for example, presents two INSERT statements you could code to copy rows
from the CUST table into an inactive customer table named INACTCST. In
this example, a CUST table row should be added to the INACTCST table if
there are no invoices for that customer in the INV table. To accomplish this
task, I coded two levels of subselects on both of these INSERT statements.
The outer subselect in both examples specifies the results table that will be
inserted into INACTCST. In both examples, I coded * in the SELECT clause
to retrieve all the columns in the order they're defined to DB2.

In example 1, I used the IN clause with the inner subselect. To satisfy
this statement, you can imagine that DB2 first builds a results table with
the INVCUST column values associated with all of the invoices in the INV
table. Then, it builds the results table it will insert into the INACTCST table
by selecting rows from the CUST table whose CUSTNO value is *not* in the
one-column table the innermost subselect generated. To process this statement, DB2 has to generate the inner table once. Then, it evaluates each
CUSTNO column value in the CUST table to determine if it has at least one
matching invoice. If it doesn't, that CUST row is added to the results table
for the outermost subselect. Finally, the INSERT adds all of the rows in that
results table to the INACTCST table.

Example 2 in figure 8-8 uses a correlated subselect with the EXISTS
keyword. For each row DB2 evaluates for the outer SELECT (which, in this
case, is all of the rows in the CUST table), it performs the inner SELECT.
The function of the inner SELECT is to determine whether or not a row

---

Example 1   An INSERT statement that uses a subquery with IN to do a mass insert

```
EXEC SQL
    INSERT INTO MMADBV.INACTCST
        SELECT *
            FROM MMADBV.CUST
            WHERE CUSTNO NOT IN
                (SELECT INVCUST
                    FROM MMADBV.INV)
    END-EXEC.
```

Example 2   An INSERT statement that uses a correlated subquery with EXISTS to do a mass insert

```
EXEC SQL
    INSERT INTO MMADBV.INACTCST
        SELECT *
            FROM MMADBV.CUST CUSTOMER
            WHERE NOT EXISTS
                (SELECT *
                    FROM MMADBV.INV
                    WHERE INVCUST = CUSTOMER.CUSTNO)
    END-EXEC.
```

Figure 8-8   Two INSERT statements that use subqueries to do mass inserts

meets the selection condition in the inner query. In this example, the inner query varies each time it executes, because the value in the CUSTNO column in the row being evaluated by the outer SELECT affects the inner SELECT. Because the inner and outer queries are related, I had to code a correlation name for the CUST table (CUSTOMER) that I could use to qualify the column name CUSTNO in the inner query.

Frankly, both of the statements in figure 8-8 are likely to be slow. As you may recall if you read chapter 5, any query that uses the IN keyword with NOT doesn't use available indexes, so performance could suffer in example 1 in figure 8-8. And because correlated subqueries by nature require lots of resources, example 2 is likely to have performance problems as well.

How to use subqueries with the UPDATE and DELETE statements
You can also code subqueries in the WHERE clauses of DELETE and UPDATE statements. With these statements, as with INSERT, the subquery can't name the table you want to modify. UPDATE and DELETE work in similar ways, so I'm only going to show you examples of DELETE with subqueries. That's because if you need to use a subquery with one of these

Example 1   A DELETE statement that uses a subquery with the NOT and IN keywords

```
EXEC SQL
    DELETE FROM MMADBV.CUST
        WHERE CUSTNO NOT IN
            (SELECT INVCUST
                FROM MMADBV.INV)
    END-EXEC.
```

Example 2   A DELETE statement that uses a correlated subquery with the NOT and EXISTS keywords

```
EXEC SQL
    DELETE FROM MMADBV.CUST CUSTOMER
        WHERE NOT EXISTS
            (SELECT *
                FROM MMADBV.INV
                WHERE INVCUST = CUSTOMER.CUSTNO)
    END-EXEC.
```

Example 3   A DELETE statement that uses a subquery with the IN keyword

```
EXEC SQL
    DELETE FROM MMADBV.CUST
        WHERE CUSTNO IN
            (SELECT CUSTNO
                FROM MMADBV.INACTCST)
    END-EXEC.
```

Figure 8-9   Three DELETE statements that use subqueries

statements, it's more likely to be DELETE than UPDATE. But in case you do need to code an UPDATE statement that changes a set of rows based on the results of a subquery, you should know that you can easily code the statement using these DELETE examples as models.

Figure 8-9 presents three DELETE statements that use subqueries to delete inactive rows from the CUST table. Any one of these statements could follow one of the mass insert statements in figure 8-8 to delete the CUST table rows that were added to the INACTCST table. The first two DELETE statements in the figure use the same subqueries that the INSERT statements in figure 8-8 did to identify rows in the CUST table for inactive customers. The first illustrates a subquery with NOT IN, and the second uses a correlated subquery with NOT EXISTS. As with the INSERT statements that use the same approaches, these statements are likely to perform slowly.

The third example in figure 8-9 will work more efficiently than the first two. This statement uses a subquery with IN to generate an intermediate table that contains the numbers of all of the customers that are in the INACTCST table. Then, the statement deletes the rows from the CUST table that have CUSTNO column values that are in that intermediate results table. Because DB2 is able to use available indexes to process this statement, it's more efficient than the first two examples.

A maintenance program that uses subqueries

Now that you understand how to use subqueries, I'll present two versions of a maintenance program that moves data from active tables to history tables. Although a firm might want to keep all of the data it has ever processed in the course of business available in one place, it's usually necessary to separate current and old data. How long information needs to remain active varies tremendously from site to site. So, I'm not going to suggest application design guidelines here. Instead, I'm going to offer a hypothetical situation and a program for it that illustrates the points I want to make. You can apply the principles the program illustrates in your own unique circumstances.

It's possible to take several approaches to coding the program I'll present here. So after I present the tables the program uses and the structure and source code for two versions of the program, I'll say a little more about still other approaches I could have taken.

The tables and the operation of the maintenance program   This maintenance program uses seven tables. Don't let that intimidate you; it's not as complicated as it might sound. And once you understand the tables and the relationships among them, the program will be easy to follow.

Figure 8-10 presents the CREATE TABLE statements for the seven tables the first version of the program uses. As you can see, I classified the tables in two ways. First, I grouped them by the kind of data they contain. The three tables in the first row of the figure contain invoice data, the two in the second row contain line item data, and the two in the last row contain financial transaction data. As you scan this figure, you'll see that the tables in each row have identical structures: the same number and type of columns with the same names. I've also grouped the tables in figure 8-10 in columns by their status. Three contain active data, three contain history (inactive) data, and one contains temporary work data. The purpose of the program is to move data from the active tables to the history tables.

You've already seen the INV table. Each row represents a single sales transaction. The INV table columns this program uses are INVNO and

Active tables

Invoice data

```
CREATE TABLE MMADBV.INV
  (INVCUST  CHAR(6)         NOT NULL,
   INVNO    CHAR(6)         NOT NULL,
   INVDATE  DATE            NOT NULL,
   INVSUBT  DECIMAL(9,2)    NOT NULL,
   INVSHIP  DECIMAL(7,2)    NOT NULL,
   INVTAX   DECIMAL(7,2)    NOT NULL,
   INVTOTAL DECIMAL(9,2)    NOT NULL,
   INVPROM  CHAR(10)        NOT NULL)
   IN DATABASE MMADB
```

Line item data

```
CREATE TABLE MMADBV.LITEM
  (LIINVNO  CHAR(6)         NOT NULL,
   LIPCODE  CHAR(10)        NOT NULL,
   LIQTY    DECIMAL(7)      NOT NULL,
   LIPRICE  DECIMAL(7,2)    NOT NULL,
   LIDISC   DECIMAL(7,2)    NOT NULL)
   IN DATABASE MMADB
```

Financial transaction data

```
CREATE TABLE MMADBV.FINTRAN
  (FTINVNO  CHAR(6)         NOT NULL,
   FTDATE   DATE            NOT NULL,
   FTAMT    DECIMAL(9,2)    NOT NULL,
   FTCHECK  CHAR(20),
   FTCCARD  CHAR(20),
   FTEXP    CHAR(5),
   FTNOTE   VARCHAR(254))
   IN DATABASE MMADB
```

History tables

```
CREATE TABLE MMADBV.INVHIST
  (INVCUST  CHAR(6)         NOT NULL,
   INVNO    CHAR(6)         NOT NULL,
   INVDATE  DATE            NOT NULL,
   INVSUBT  DECIMAL(9,2)    NOT NULL,
   INVSHIP  DECIMAL(7,2)    NOT NULL,
   INVTAX   DECIMAL(7,2)    NOT NULL,
   INVTOTAL DECIMAL(9,2)    NOT NULL,
   INVPROM  CHAR(10)        NOT NULL)
   IN DATABASE MMADB
```

```
CREATE TABLE MMADBV.LIHIST
  (LIINVNO  CHAR(6)         NOT NULL,
   LIPCODE  CHAR(10)        NOT NULL,
   LIQTY    DECIMAL(7)      NOT NULL,
   LIPRICE  DECIMAL(7,2)    NOT NULL,
   LIDISC   DECIMAL(7,2)    NOT NULL)
   IN DATABASE MMADB
```

```
CREATE TABLE MMADBV.FTHIST
  (FTINVNO  CHAR(6)         NOT NULL,
   FTDATE   DATE            NOT NULL,
   FTAMT    DECIMAL(9,2)    NOT NULL,
   FTCHECK  CHAR(20),
   FTCCARD  CHAR(20),
   FTEXP    CHAR(5),
   FTNOTE   VARCHAR(254))
   IN DATABASE MMADB
```

Work table

```
CREATE TABLE MMADBV.WORKTABLE
  (INVCUST  CHAR(6)         NOT NULL,
   INVNO    CHAR(6)         NOT NULL,
   INVDATE  DATE            NOT NULL,
   INVSUBT  DECIMAL(9,2)    NOT NULL,
   INVSHIP  DECIMAL(7,2)    NOT NULL,
   INVTAX   DECIMAL(7,2)    NOT NULL,
   INVTOTAL DECIMAL(9,2)    NOT NULL,
   INVPROM  CHAR(10)        NOT NULL)
   IN DATABASE MMADB
```

Figure 8-10   The CREATE TABLE statements for the seven tables processed by version 1 of the maintenance program

INVTOTAL. Although the INV table contains several other columns, none of them contains data for the specific items sold under the invoice or for financial transactions associated with the invoice, like payments and credits. That information is stored in the two other kinds of tables this program uses.

Line item information is stored in the LITEM table. Each product or service that's sold under a given invoice is represented by a different row in the LITEM table. For example, if a customer buys three different items on one invoice, one row in the INV table represents the overall transaction, and three rows in the LITEM table represent its details. The value in the LIINVNO column contains the invoice number, linking the row to the INV table row that "owns" it.

The financial transactions that take place after an invoice is issued are recorded in the FINTRAN table. A new row is added to this table for each financial transaction. Most invoices will have only one row in this table, the row that contains information for one complete payment. However, some customers may make partial payments and have credits or adjustments applied to an invoice. When that happens, each transaction is stored in a separate row. The two columns in this table that the program refers to are FTINVNO and FTAMT. The FTINVNO column links each transaction row with a row in the INV table, and the FTAMT column contains the dollar amount of the transaction.

When the values in the FTAMT column in all the rows in the FINTRAN table for a particular invoice add up to the amount in the INVTOTAL column in that invoice's INV table row, the invoice is paid. At that point, it can be moved from the current INV table to the history table INVHIST. At the same time, all of the rows in the LITEM and FINTRAN tables associated with that invoice should also be moved to their related history tables, LIHIST and FTHIST.

The seventh table in the figure, WORKTABLE, isn't an essential part of the system of tables for this application. In fact, its only purpose is to provide a temporary place to store data as the maintenance program moves rows from the active tables to the history tables. You'll see how it fits into the picture in a moment.

The design of the maintenance program   Figure 8-11 shows the structure chart for the first version of the maintenance program. First, it clears any data that may be in WORKTABLE (module 100). Then, it selects all of the invoices that should be moved from active to inactive status and inserts them into WORKTABLE (module 200). Last, it performs modules 300, 400, and 500 to move rows from the active to the inactive invoice, line item, and financial transaction tables.

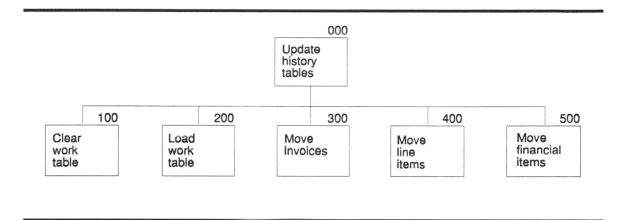

Figure 8-11   Structure chart for version 1 of the maintenance program

The source code for the maintenance program   Figure 8-12 presents the COBOL source code for the first version of the maintenance program. As with some of the other program examples I've shown you, I think you may be surprised that a program that does the sort of processing this one does is so short. In fact, a large proportion of the lines in this program take care of error handling. If I hadn't included that code, this program would be only about *half* as long as it is. That's a substantial testimonial to how much work DB2 can relieve you of.

One of the reasons this program is short is that I didn't code INCLUDE statements for the DCLGEN output for the seven tables the program processes. Admittedly, when you omit DCLGEN output, you lose some of the program-development support the DB2 precompiler offers. However, I wanted to illustrate just how removed a COBOL program can be from what DB2 does. This program issues SQL statements to do complicated processing. However, it doesn't retrieve any data from the tables it uses, nor does it add any data it supplies to those tables. So, none of the statements it issues need host variables. And because host variable definitions are what programs need DCLGEN output for, I was able to omit DCLGEN output here.

The high-level module in this program invokes each of its subordinates in sequence. However, after it has invoked module 100, it invokes the others only if the program hasn't detected any processing errors. All of the subordinate modules issue SQL statements, and all of them set the value of UPDATE-SUCCESSFUL-SW to N if they receive a negative return code. I checked for negative return codes in this program rather than non-zero return codes because I wanted to allow +100 as well as zero. Some of the

```
000100 IDENTIFICATION DIVISION.
000200*
000300 PROGRAM-ID.           UPDTHST1.
000400*
000500 ENVIRONMENT DIVISION.
000600*
000700 DATA DIVISION.
000800*
000900 WORKING-STORAGE SECTION.
001000*
001100 01  SWITCH.
001200*
001300     05  UPDATE-SUCCESSFUL-SW     PIC X     VALUE "Y".
001400         88  UPDATE-SUCCESSFUL              VALUE "Y".
001500*
001600     EXEC SQL
001700         INCLUDE SQLCA
001800     END-EXEC.
001900*
002000 PROCEDURE DIVISION.
002100*
002200 000-UPDATE-HISTORY-TABLES.
002300*
002400     PERFORM 100-CLEAR-WORK-TABLE.
002500     IF UPDATE-SUCCESSFUL
002600         PERFORM 200-LOAD-WORK-TABLE.
002700     IF UPDATE-SUCCESSFUL
002800         PERFORM 300-MOVE-INVOICES.
002900     IF UPDATE-SUCCESSFUL
003000         PERFORM 400-MOVE-LINE-ITEMS.
003100     IF UPDATE-SUCCESSFUL
003200         PERFORM 500-MOVE-FINANCIAL-ITEMS.
003300     IF UPDATE-SUCCESSFUL
003400         DISPLAY "UPDATE COMPLETED SUCCESSFULLY.".
003500     STOP RUN.
003600*
003700 100-CLEAR-WORK-TABLE.
003800*
003900     EXEC SQL
004000         DELETE FROM MMADBV.WORKTABLE
004100     END-EXEC.
004200     IF SQLCODE < 0
004300         DISPLAY "DELETE IN MODULE 100 FAILED."
004400         DISPLAY "SQLCODE = " SQLCODE
004500         MOVE "N" TO UPDATE-SUCCESSFUL-SW.
004600*
```

Figure 8-12   COBOL source code for version 1 of the maintenance program (part 1 of 3)

SQL statements in the program can return +100 if the table they reference has no rows, and that is a possibility.

The first subordinate module in this program, 100, issues a simple DELETE statement without a WHERE clause to delete all of the rows in

```
004700 200-LOAD-WORK-TABLE.
004800*
004900     EXEC SQL
005000         INSERT INTO MMADBV.WORKTABLE
005100             SELECT *
005200                 FROM   MMADBV.INV INVOICE
005300                 WHERE INVTOTAL =
005400                     (SELECT SUM(FTAMT)
005500                         FROM MMADBV.FINTRAN
005600                         WHERE FTINVNO = INVOICE.INVNO)
005700     END-EXEC.
005800     IF SQLCODE < 0
005900         DISPLAY "INSERT IN MODULE 200 FAILED."
006000         DISPLAY "SQLCODE = " SQLCODE
006100         MOVE "N" TO UPDATE-SUCCESSFUL-SW.
006200*
006300 300-MOVE-INVOICES.
006400*
006500     EXEC SQL
006600         INSERT INTO MMADBV.INVHIST
006700             SELECT *
006800                 FROM   MMADBV.WORKTABLE
006900     END-EXEC.
007000     IF SQLCODE < 0
007100         DISPLAY "INSERT IN MODULE 300 FAILED."
007200         DISPLAY "SQLCODE = " SQLCODE
007300         MOVE "N" TO UPDATE-SUCCESSFUL-SW
007400     ELSE
007500         EXEC SQL
007600             DELETE FROM MMADBV.INV
007700                 WHERE INVNO IN
007800                     (SELECT INVNO
007900                         FROM MMADBV.WORKTABLE)
008000         END-EXEC
008100         IF SQLCODE < 0
008200             DISPLAY "DELETE IN MODULE 300 FAILED."
008300             DISPLAY "SQLCODE = " SQLCODE
008400             MOVE "N" TO UPDATE-SUCCESSFUL-SW.
008500*
008600 400-MOVE-LINE-ITEMS.
008700*
008800     EXEC SQL
008900         INSERT INTO MMADBV.LIHIST
009000             SELECT *
009100                 FROM   MMADBV.LITEM
009200                 WHERE LIINVNO IN
009300                     (SELECT INVNO
009400                         FROM MMADBV.WORKTABLE)
009500     END-EXEC.
```

Figure 8-12   COBOL source code for version 1 of the maintenance program (part 2 of 3)

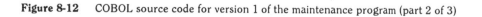

WORKTABLE. As you can see, immediately after the SQL statement, I
coded a condition that evaluates SQLCODE. If its value is less than zero,

```
009600        IF SQLCODE < 0
009700            DISPLAY "INSERT IN MODULE 400 FAILED."
009800            DISPLAY "SQLCODE = " SQLCODE
009900            MOVE "N" TO UPDATE-SUCCESSFUL-SW
010000        ELSE
010100            EXEC SQL
010200                DELETE FROM MMADBV.LITEM
010300                    WHERE LIINVNO IN
010400                        (SELECT INVNO
010500                            FROM MMADBV.WORKTABLE)
010600            END-EXEC
010700            IF SQLCODE < 0
010800                DISPLAY "DELETE IN MODULE 400 FAILED."
010900                DISPLAY "SQLCODE = " SQLCODE
011000                MOVE "N" TO UPDATE-SUCCESSFUL-SW.
011100*
011200 500-MOVE-FINANCIAL-ITEMS.
011300*
011400        EXEC SQL
011500            INSERT INTO MMADBV.FTHIST
011600                SELECT *
011700                    FROM  MMADBV.FINTRAN
011800                    WHERE FTINVNO IN
011900                        (SELECT INVNO
012000                            FROM MMADBV.WORKTABLE)
012100        END-EXEC.
012200        IF SQLCODE < 0
012300            DISPLAY "INSERT IN MODULE 500 FAILED."
012400            DISPLAY "SQLCODE = " SQLCODE
012500            MOVE "N" TO UPDATE-SUCCESSFUL-SW
012600        ELSE
012700            EXEC SQL
012800                DELETE FROM MMADBV.FINTRAN
012900                    WHERE FTINVNO IN
013000                        (SELECT INVNO
013100                            FROM MMADBV.WORKTABLE)
013200            END-EXEC
013300            IF SQLCODE < 0
013400                DISPLAY "DELETE IN MODULE 500 FAILED."
013500                DISPLAY "SQLCODE = " SQLCODE
013600                MOVE "N" TO UPDATE-SUCCESSFUL-SW.
013700*
```

Figure 8-12   COBOL source code for version 1 of the maintenance program (part 3 of 3)

the program displays a message to report which statement produced the
negative return code, then it displays the return code itself. The last statement in the condition sets the value of UPDATE-SUCCESSFUL-SW to N.
A four-line block of code like this follows all the other SQL statements in
the program.

If DB2 doesn't encounter any errors as it clears WORKTABLE, the program continues and invokes module 200. The purpose of module 200 is to identify all of the rows from the active invoice table that should be moved to the history table and insert them in WORKTABLE for use by the other statements in this program. The statement that does this task is the most complicated, and probably the most inefficient, in the program.

As you can see, the statement in module 200 is an INSERT that uses a subselect to generate an intermediate results table whose rows are added to the target table. The subselect is complex because it contains another subselect nested in its WHERE clause. I'd like you to take a close look at this statement.

First, the SELECT clause in the outer subselect specifies the asterisk. As a result, all of the columns from the source table will be included in the intermediate results table. The FROM clause of the outer subselect identifies the source table, MMADBV.INV, and supplies a correlation name for it, INVOICE. The WHERE clause specifies that rows should be included in the results table when the value in their INVTOTAL column is equal to the result of a calculation performed by the inner SELECT.

You should recall from this chapter that when you code a subquery immediately after a comparison operator, like this, it must return a simple results table: one column and one row. In this case, the inner SELECT specifies that the results table should contain the sum of all of the transaction amounts, SUM(FTAMT), associated with a specific invoice. To insure that the calculated value will be for one particular invoice rather than all invoices, I specified that a row in the FINTRAN table should be used in the sum calculation only when the value in its invoice number column (FTINVNO) is the same as the invoice number (INVNO) in the row in the INV table currently being evaluated by the outer SELECT.

Because the inner subselect is correlated with the outer subselect, it's processed once for each row DB2 considers in the outer subselect. As you can imagine, this could use a substantial amount of system resources. Part of my rationale for inserting the rows that meet this selection condition in a temporary work table is so I don't have to repeat this complicated subselect in other statements. After DB2 has finished processing the INSERT statement, WORKTABLE contains an image of all of the rows from the INV table that should be moved to the INVHIST table, and no others. As a result, the statements that follow can use simpler subselects based on the rows in WORKTABLE.

After module 200 has loaded copies of the selected invoice rows into WORKTABLE, module 300 actually moves them from the active table to the history table. First, it issues another SQL mass insert statement to move the appropriate rows into the INVHIST table. However, instead of selecting them directly from the INV table, it selects them from WORKTABLE. Because the mass insert in module 200 selected the right rows, the mass insert in module 300 can be less discriminating. It simply directs DB2 to add every row from WORKTABLE to the INVHIST table.

After the mass insert has finished, module 300 issues a DELETE statement to remove the affected rows from the INV table. This statement uses a subselect to identify those rows. This subselect generates an intermediate results table that contains the invoice numbers of all of the rows in WORKTABLE. Because I coded the subselect after the IN keyword, this statement removes all rows from the INV table with values in the INVNO column that appear in the intermediate results table the subselect generated.

The next two modules move rows from the LITEM and FINTRAN tables to their corresponding history tables if they're associated with any of the invoices represented in WORKTABLE. The SQL statements in these modules work in the same way, so I'll just describe those in module 400. First, module 400 does a mass insert to copy rows for affected invoices from the LITEM table to the LIHIST table. It retrieves all columns from the LITEM table rows whose invoice number column (LIINVNO) matches one of the numbers in the rows in WORKTABLE. This is the same approach I used in the subselect that I coded in the DELETE statement in module 300. I used the same subselect again in the DELETE statement that follows in module 400.

A version of the maintenance program that depends on DB2's referential integrity features   The version of the maintenance program I just presented works with tables that are logically related. However, when I created those tables, I didn't specify that they should depend on DB2's referential integrity support. If I had, the maintenance program would be even simpler. To understand how referential integrity can affect this program, I want to show you alternative versions of the tables, the structure chart, and the source code for this application.

Figure 8-13 shows the CREATE TABLE statements for the tables the second version of the maintenance program uses. They're the same as the tables the first version uses, except I coded PRIMARY KEY and FOREIGN KEY clauses to define the relationships among the active tables.

Only the statement for the INV table includes a PRIMARY KEY clause. It identifies INVNO as the primary key column. But the CREATE TABLE statements for all three of the active tables include the FOREIGN KEY clause. For both the LITEM and FINTRAN tables, the FOREIGN KEY clause specifies that they're dependent on the INV table. (The FOREIGN KEY clause in the CREATE TABLE statement for the INV table is irrelevant

Active tables

Invoice data

```
CREATE TABLE MMADBV.INV
  (INVCUST    CHAR(6)        NOT NULL,
   INVNO      CHAR(6)        NOT NULL,
   INVDATE    DATE           NOT NULL,
   INVSUBT    DECIMAL(9,2)   NOT NULL,
   INVSHIP    DECIMAL(7,2)   NOT NULL,
   INVTAX     DECIMAL(7,2)   NOT NULL,
   INVTOTAL   DECIMAL(9,2)   NOT NULL,
   INVPROM    CHAR(10)       NOT NULL,
   PRIMARY KEY (INVNO)
   FOREIGN KEY (INVCUST)
     REFERENCES MMADBV.CUST
       ON DELETE CASCADE)
   IN DATABASE MMADB
```

Line item data

```
CREATE TABLE MMADBV.LITEM
  (LIINVNO    CHAR(6)        NOT NULL,
   LIPCODE    CHAR(10)       NOT NULL,
   LIQTY      DECIMAL(7)     NOT NULL,
   LIPRICE    DECIMAL(7,2)   NOT NULL,
   LIDISC     DECIMAL(7,2)   NOT NULL)
   FOREIGN KEY (LI-INVNO)
     REFERENCES MMADBV.INV
       ON DELETE CASCADE)
   IN DATABASE MMADB
```

Financial transaction data

```
CREATE TABLE MMADBV.FINTRAN
  (FTINVNO    CHAR(6)        NOT NULL,
   FTDATE     DATE           NOT NULL,
   FTAMT      DECIMAL(9,2)   NOT NULL,
   FTCHECK    CHAR(20),
   FTCCARD    CHAR(20),
   FTEXP      CHAR(5),
   FTNOTE     VARCHAR(254),
   FOREIGN KEY (FTINVNO)
     REFERENCES MMADBV.INV
       ON DELETE CASCADE)
   IN DATABASE MMADB
```

History tables

```
CREATE TABLE MMADBV.INVHIST
  (INVCUST    CHAR(6)        NOT NULL,
   INVNO      CHAR(6)        NOT NULL,
   INVDATE    DATE           NOT NULL,
   INVSUBT    DECIMAL(9,2)   NOT NULL,
   INVSHIP    DECIMAL(7,2)   NOT NULL,
   INVTAX     DECIMAL(7,2)   NOT NULL,
   INVTOTAL   DECIMAL(9,2)   NOT NULL,
   INVPROM    CHAR(10)       NOT NULL)
   IN DATABASE MMADB
```

```
CREATE TABLE MMADBV.LIHIST
  (LIINVNO    CHAR(6)        NOT NULL,
   LIPCODE    CHAR(10)       NOT NULL,
   LIQTY      DECIMAL(7)     NOT NULL,
   LIPRICE    DECIMAL(7,2)   NOT NULL,
   LIDISC     DECIMAL(7,2)   NOT NULL)
   IN DATABASE MMADB
```

```
CREATE TABLE MMADBV.FTHIST
  (FTINVNO    CHAR(6)        NOT NULL,
   FTDATE     DATE           NOT NULL,
   FTAMT      DECIMAL(9,2)   NOT NULL,
   FTCHECK    CHAR(20),
   FTCCARD    CHAR(20),
   FTEXP      CHAR(5),
   FTNOTE     VARCHAR(254))
   IN DATABASE MMADB
```

Work table

```
CREATE TABLE MMADBV.WORKTABLE
  (INVCUST    CHAR(6)        NOT NULL,
   INVNO      CHAR(6)        NOT NULL,
   INVDATE    DATE           NOT NULL,
   INVSUBT    DECIMAL(9,2)   NOT NULL,
   INVSHIP    DECIMAL(7,2)   NOT NULL,
   INVTAX     DECIMAL(7,2)   NOT NULL,
   INVTOTAL   DECIMAL(9,2)   NOT NULL,
   INVPROM    CHAR(10)       NOT NULL)
   IN DATABASE MMADB
```

Figure 8-13   The CREATE TABLE statements for the seven tables processed by version 2 of the maintenance program

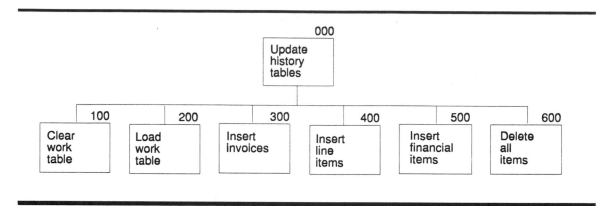

Figure 8-14   Structure chart for version 2 of the maintenance program

for this example because it specifies the relationship of invoice rows to *their* parent rows in the CUST table.)

I want to point out that the FOREIGN KEY clauses for the LITEM and FINTRAN tables both specify ON DELETE CASCADE. This directs DB2 to delete rows from these tables when it deletes their parent invoice rows. Because I coded ON DELETE CASCADE, I can simplify the maintenance program. When I issue a DELETE statement for the INV table, DB2 deletes not just the affected invoice rows, but also all of the LITEM and FINTRAN rows related to those invoices. As a result, I was able to leave the DELETE statements for the LITEM and FINTRAN tables out of the second version of the maintenance program.

Figure 8-14 presents the structure chart for this version of the maintenance program, and figure 8-15 presents the source code. If you look at the source code, you'll see that I moved the DELETE statement that dropped rows from the INV table out of module 300. If I had left it there, it would have removed rows from the LITEM and FINTRAN tables before modules 400 and 500 could insert them into their appropriate history tables. To solve this problem, I added another module, 600, that follows all of the other modules and that issues the DELETE statement. In the first version of the program, modules 300, 400, and 500 each contained a DELETE statement. In the second version, the one DELETE statement I coded in module 600 replaces them all.

You may wonder why I didn't define the history tables in figure 8-13 so they also take advantage of DB2's referential integrity support. Although referential integrity is a powerful feature, it isn't free. To enforce referential integrity, DB2 has to use a substantial amount of resources. Because it isn't likely that the history tables in this example are going to be subject to much

```
000100 IDENTIFICATION DIVISION.
000200*
000300 PROGRAM-ID.          UPDTHST2.
000400*
000500 ENVIRONMENT DIVISION.
000600*
000700 DATA DIVISION.
000800*
000900 WORKING-STORAGE SECTION.
001000*
001100 01  SWITCH.
001200*
001300     05  UPDATE-SUCCESSFUL-SW     PIC X     VALUE "Y".
001400         88  UPDATE-SUCCESSFUL               VALUE "Y".
001500*
001600     EXEC SQL
001700         INCLUDE SQLCA
001800     END-EXEC.
001900*
002000 PROCEDURE DIVISION.
002100*
002200 000-UPDATE-HISTORY-TABLES.
002300*
002400     PERFORM 100-CLEAR-WORK-TABLE.
002500     IF UPDATE-SUCCESSFUL
002600         PERFORM 200-LOAD-WORK-TABLE.
002700     IF UPDATE-SUCCESSFUL
002800         PERFORM 300-INSERT INVOICES.
002900     IF UPDATE-SUCCESSFUL
003000         PERFORM 400-INSERT-LINE-ITEMS.
003100     IF UPDATE-SUCCESSFUL
003200         PERFORM 500-INSERT-FINANCIAL-ITEMS.
003300     IF UPDATE-SUCCESSFUL
003400         PERFORM 600-DELETE-ALL-ITEMS.
003500     IF UPDATE-SUCCESSFUL
003600         DISPLAY "UPDATE COMPLETED SUCCESSFULLY.".
003700     STOP RUN.
003800*
```

Figure 8-15 COBOL source code for version 2 of the maintenance program (part 1 of 3)

update and delete activity, it would be a waste of system resources to define primary and foreign keys for them.

Other approaches to the maintenance program   As I mentioned when I started to describe the maintenance program, the approach I took is just one of several possibilities. One alternative is not to create a temporary work table at all. Instead, you could code the more complicated subselect I used in the INSERT statement in module 200 in the statements that actually add rows to the history tables. But as I mentioned, correlated

```
003900 100-CLEAR-WORK-TABLE.
004000*
004100      EXEC SQL
004200          DELETE FROM MMADBV.WORKTABLE
004300      END-EXEC.
004400      IF SQLCODE < 0
004500          DISPLAY "DELETE IN MODULE 100 FAILED."
004600          DISPLAY "SQLCODE = " SQLCODE
004700          MOVE "N" TO UPDATE-SUCCESSFUL-SW.
004800*
004900 200-LOAD-WORK-TABLE.
005000*
005100      EXEC SQL
005200          INSERT INTO MMADBV.WORKTABLE
005300              SELECT *
005400                  FROM   MMADBV.INV INVOICE
005500                  WHERE INVTOTAL =
005600                      (SELECT SUM(FTAMT)
005700                          FROM MMADBV.FINTRAN
005800                          WHERE FTINVNO = INVOICE.INVNO)
005900      END-EXEC.
006000      IF SQLCODE < 0
006100          DISPLAY "INSERT IN MODULE 200 FAILED."
006200          DISPLAY "SQLCODE = " SQLCODE
006300          MOVE "N" TO UPDATE-SUCCESSFUL-SW.
006400*
006500 300-INSERT-INVOICES.
006600*
006700      EXEC SQL
006800          INSERT INTO MMADBV.INVHIST
006900              SELECT *
007000                  FROM   MMADBV.WORKTABLE
007100      END-EXEC.
007200      IF SQLCODE < 0
007300          DISPLAY "INSERT IN MODULE 300 FAILED."
007400          DISPLAY "SQLCODE = " SQLCODE
007500          MOVE "N" TO UPDATE-SUCCESSFUL-SW.
007600*
007700 400-INSERT-LINE-ITEMS.
007800*
007900      EXEC SQL
008000          INSERT INTO MMADBV.LIHIST
008100              SELECT *
008200                  FROM   MMADBV.LITEM
008300                  WHERE LIINVNO IN
008400                      (SELECT INVNO
008500                          FROM MMADBV.WORKTABLE)
008600      END-EXEC.
008700      IF SQLCODE < 0
008800          DISPLAY "INSERT IN MODULE 400 FAILED."
008900          DISPLAY "SQLCODE = " SQLCODE
009000          MOVE "N" TO UPDATE-SUCCESSFUL-SW.
```

Figure 8-15   COBOL source code for version 2 of the maintenance program (part 2 of 3)

```
009100*
009200 500-INSERT-FINANCIAL-ITEMS.
009300*
009400       EXEC SQL
009500           INSERT INTO MMADBV.FTHIST
009600               SELECT *
009700                   FROM  MMADBV.FINTRAN
009800                   WHERE FTINVNO IN
009900                       (SELECT INVNO
010000                           FROM MMADBV.WORKTABLE)
010100       END-EXEC.
010200       IF SQLCODE < 0
010300           DISPLAY "INSERT IN MODULE 500 FAILED."
010400           DISPLAY "SQLCODE = " SQLCODE
010500           MOVE "N" TO UPDATE-SUCCESSFUL-SW.
010600*
010700 600-DELETE-ALL-ITEMS.
010800*
010900       EXEC SQL
011000           DELETE FROM MMADBV.INV
011100               WHERE INVNO IN
011200                   (SELECT INVNO
011300                       FROM MMADBV.WORKTABLE)
011400       END-EXEC
011500       IF SQLCODE < 0
011600           DISPLAY "DELETE IN MODULE 600 FAILED."
011700           DISPLAY "SQLCODE = " SQLCODE
011800           MOVE "N" TO UPDATE-SUCCESSFUL-SW.
011900*
```

Figure 8-15   COBOL source code for version 2 of the maintenance program (part 3 of 3)

subqueries are costly. So if you need to accomplish a task like this for a large table, you should minimize the number of correlated subqueries you use.

Another approach altogether is to adopt more of a record-at-a-time mind set. You could use a cursor-controlled results table to provide a list of invoices to be moved, and then work through it by fetching one invoice number after another. For each, your program would issue appropriate statements to INSERT and DELETE the related rows in the base tables. This approach offers the benefit of enabling you to do additional processing for each invoice, such as printing a line on a report to document its status change, or updating other DB2 data that requires information extracted from each invoice.

But with that benefit comes the additional cost of having to issue many separate SQL statements to take care of moving appropriate rows from the active tables to the history tables. For example, imagine the invoice table contains 1000 rows that need to be moved, each with 5 line items and an average of 2 financial transactions. Although the programs in figures 8-12 and 8-15 can take care of all of these rows by issuing only 9 and 7 SQL statements, a program that uses the cursor technique would have to issue thousands of SQL statements.

Obviously, the issues that surround DB2 performance for problems like these are complicated and vary from shop to shop and from application to application. So, when you need to develop a program that does processing like this, you should get the advice of your system designer or DBA.

Terms

subquery
subselect
correlated subquery
correlation name
correlated reference

Objectives

1. Code a SELECT within another SELECT as a subquery to meet a complex retrieval requirement.

2. Distinguish between how correlated and non-correlated subqueries work.

3. Code a SELECT within an INSERT statement to accomplish a mass insert operation.

4. Code a SELECT within an UPDATE or DELETE statement to modify table data based on the results of a subquery.

5. Given the specifications for a program that calls for SQL statements that use subqueries, design and code the program.

Chapter 9

How to use variable-length data and nulls

All of the examples I've shown you so far have used only a subset of the kinds of data DB2 can process. For instance, all of the columns that contain character data have had the CHAR (fixed-length) data type, and none of the columns have allowed null values. But in practice, the VARCHAR (variable-length) data type is widely used, and some columns do contain nulls. So to work at a professional level as a DB2 programmer, you need to understand and be able to work with both variable-length columns and nulls.

It may seem that variable-length columns and nulls don't belong together in the same chapter. However, they're related for three reasons. First, they both let you deal with situations where the amount of data for a column can vary, either in size or because the data may not be present at all. Second, they're both specified for individual columns by the DBA in the SQL CREATE TABLE statements that define tables. And third, they both require some additional programming work. In this chapter, I'll show you how to process both in COBOL programs.

```
****************************************************************
*  DCLGEN TABLE(MMADBV.CUST)                                   *
*          LIBRARY(MMA002.DCLGENS.COBOL(CUST))                 *
*          ACTION(REPLACE)                                     *
*          STRUCTURE(CUSTOMER-ROW)                             *
*          APOST                                               *
*  ... IS THE DCLGEN COMMAND THAT MADE THE FOLLOWING STATEMENTS *
****************************************************************
      EXEC SQL DECLARE MMADBV.CUST TABLE
      ( CUSTNO                      CHAR(6) NOT NULL,
        FNAME                       CHAR(20) NOT NULL,
        LNAME                       CHAR(30) NOT NULL,
        ADDR                        CHAR(30) NOT NULL,
        CITY                        CHAR(20) NOT NULL,
        STATE                       CHAR(2) NOT NULL,
        ZIPCODE                     CHAR(10) NOT NULL
      ) END-EXEC.
****************************************************************
*  COBOL DECLARATION FOR TABLE MMADBV.CUST                     *
****************************************************************
  01   CUSTOMER-ROW.
       10 CUSTNO            PIC X(6).
       10 FNAME             PIC X(20).
       10 LNAME             PIC X(30).
       10 ADDR              PIC X(30).
       10 CITY              PIC X(20).
       10 STATE             PIC X(2).
       10 ZIPCODE           PIC X(10).
****************************************************************
*  THE NUMBER OF COLUMNS DESCRIBED BY THIS DECLARATION IS 7    *
****************************************************************
```

Figure 9-1   DCLGEN output for the original version of the customer table (CUST)

An expanded version of the customer table

To help you understand how to use variable-length data and nulls in COBOL programs, I'm going to use an expanded version of the customer table you've seen in earlier chapters. Figure 9-1 shows the DCLGEN output for the original version of that table (CUST). This version has seven columns, all with the CHAR data type, and all defined with the NOT NULL attribute. So, each column is fixed-length, and must contain a value.

Now, consider the DCLGEN output for the expanded version of the customer table (VARCUST) in figure 9-2. I changed the data type of the FNAME, LNAME, ADDR, and CITY columns from CHAR to VARCHAR. Also, I added three new columns. Two of the new columns, HOMEPH and WORKPH, store customers' telephone numbers at home and at work. The third new column, NOTES, can be used to store special information about a customer.

```
*********************************************************************
* DCLGEN TABLE(MMADBV.VARCUST)                                     *
*        LIBRARY(MMA002.DCLGENS.COBOL(VARCUST))                    *
*        ACTION(REPLACE)                                           *
*        STRUCTURE(CUSTOMER-ROW)                                   *
*        APOST                                                     *
* ... IS THE DCLGEN COMMAND THAT MADE THE FOLLOWING STATEMENTS     *
*********************************************************************
      EXEC SQL DECLARE MMADBV.VARCUST TABLE
      ( CUSTNO                        CHAR(6) NOT NULL,
        FNAME                         VARCHAR(20) NOT NULL,
        LNAME                         VARCHAR(30) NOT NULL,
        ADDR                          VARCHAR(30) NOT NULL,
        CITY                          VARCHAR(20) NOT NULL,
        STATE                         CHAR(2) NOT NULL,
        ZIPCODE                       CHAR(10) NOT NULL,
        HOMEPH                        CHAR(16),
        WORKPH                        CHAR(16),
        NOTES                         VARCHAR(254)
      ) END-EXEC.
*********************************************************************
* COBOL DECLARATION FOR TABLE MMADBV.VARCUST                       *
*********************************************************************
  01  CUSTOMER-ROW.
      10 CUSTNO               PIC X(6).
      10 FNAME.
         49 FNAME-LEN         PIC S9(4) USAGE COMP.
         49 FNAME-TEXT        PIC X(20).
      10 LNAME.
         49 LNAME-LEN         PIC S9(4) USAGE COMP.
         49 LNAME-TEXT        PIC X(30).
      10 ADDR.
         49 ADDR-LEN          PIC S9(4) USAGE COMP.
         49 ADDR-TEXT         PIC X(30).
      10 CITY.
         49 CITY-LEN          PIC S9(4) USAGE COMP.
         49 CITY-TEXT         PIC X(20).
      10 STATE                PIC X(2).
      10 ZIPCODE              PIC X(10).
      10 HOMEPH               PIC X(16).
      10 WORKPH               PIC X(16).
      10 NOTES.
         49 NOTES-LEN         PIC S9(4) USAGE COMP.
         49 NOTES-TEXT        PIC X(254).
*********************************************************************
* THE NUMBER OF COLUMNS DESCRIBED BY THIS DECLARATION IS 10        *
*********************************************************************
```

Figure 9-2   DCLGEN output for the expanded version of the customer table that allows nulls and uses variable-length columns (VARCUST)

If you add the maximum column sizes in these two versions of the customer table, you'll see that the expanded version can use more than three times as much space as the original version, even though it doesn't contain much more data. Are these new columns worth the extra space?

System designers constantly face questions like this. They have to decide whether the value of particular data elements merits the costs of storing and processing them. For example, does the expanded customer table need a NOTES column? After all, most rows won't even have a NOTES value. And in those that do, the value in the column is likely to be much shorter than 254 characters, the maximum size allowed. So if NOTES data had to be stored in a fixed-length column, more than half of the space required for the entire table could be filled with spaces and, as a result, would be wasted.

I'd like you to notice the four different combinations of data type and "nullability" in figure 9-2: fixed-length and not nullable (CHAR NOT NULL), fixed-length and nullable (CHAR), variable-length and not nullable (VARCHAR NOT NULL), and variable-length and nullable (VARCHAR). As you can see, DB2's default is to allow nulls in a column unless the DBA explicitly specifies NOT NULL for it.

Column definitions in the first of the four groups (CHAR NOT NULL) have the same descriptions as the matching columns in the simpler version of the table in figure 9-1. The columns that have these characteristics are CUSTNO, STATE, and ZIPCODE. All three of these columns will have values in each row in the expanded customer table, and those values will always be six, two, and ten characters long. This combination of attributes is appropriate when a column must have a value, and when the size of that value is predictable. For example, the CUSTNO column must have a value in each row in the table, and its value will always be six characters long.

The second group of column definitions represents a new combination of attributes. I defined the two telephone number columns as fixed-length (CHAR), but without NOT NULL. When these columns contain a value, the value will be 16 characters long. But, if a telephone number is unavailable, null can be stored for the appropriate column. So, the amount of data stored in these columns will be either 16 characters or no characters.

Column definitions in the third group are for required data elements that can vary in length (FNAME, LNAME, ADDR, and CITY). Because these are required items, I coded NOT NULL in their definitions. Therefore, DB2 requires that a value be present in these columns in a new row, or it won't insert that row into the table.

Even though these columns must have values in every row, the sizes of those values can vary. Therefore, it can be wasteful to store them in fixed-length columns, like the ones the simpler version of the customer table in figure 9-1 uses. For example, if I had defined the CITY column with CHAR(20), a short name like DALLAS would be padded on the right with enough spaces to fill the column. In that case, more than two thirds of the data stored in the column would be spaces.

A solution to this type of problem is to use variable-length (VARCHAR) columns, as I did in the expanded version of the customer table in figure 9-2. But while variable-length columns can save storage space, they don't save it without a cost. First, each variable-length column requires a small amount of additional storage in each row for control information. Second, variable-length columns demand additional CPU resources when they're processed. And third, as you'll see in a moment, they complicate application programs.

The fourth category consists of optional columns that can vary in length. This column type has the VARCHAR data type and a definition that does not specify NOT NULL. NOTES is the only column in the expanded customer table in this category. Depending on what it contains, this kind of column can require you to apply the programming technique for either variable-length columns or for columns that may contain a null value.

By the way, I selected 254 as the size for the NOTES column because that's the maximum size DB2 allows for standard variable-length columns. DB2 *does* support longer variable-length columns, but it imposes some processing restrictions on them. Later in this chapter, I'll describe long character columns and the limitations on how you can use them.

How to work with variable-length columns

How much work variable-length columns cause for you as a programmer depends on how you need to process tables that contain them. If all you need to do is retrieve variable-length data, your programming tasks are simple. However, issuing INSERT or UPDATE statements that involve variable-length data is a different story.

Whenever you process data for a variable-length column in a program, you need to use a two-level data structure for its host variable. That's because your program has to process not just the data in the column, but also a number that represents its length. As you can see in figure 9-2, DCLGEN uses three data names in the host variable it creates for a VARCHAR column. For example,

```
10  CITY.
        49  CITY-LEN          PIC S9(4)    COMP.
        49  CITY-TEXT         PIC X(20).
```

is the host variable DCLGEN created for the CITY column. DCLGEN uses the name of the column for the group item (CITY). Then, it appends -LEN and -TEXT to the column name to form the names for the length and data components. The length component is a binary halfword, and the data component has the same COBOL PIC you'd expect if the column were fixed-length.

When you name a host variable for a variable-length column in an SQL statement, you specify the group item that contains the length and text components (CITY in this example). Then, when a SELECT or FETCH statement passes the contents of this column to a program, it returns the length of the column's value in the length field (CITY-LEN), and it stores exactly that number of characters in the text field (CITY-TEXT). And before you issue an INSERT or UPDATE statement, DB2 requires that you set the values of both of these components properly.

When you retrieve variable-length data, you need to realize that if the text component of the host variable contains a value that's longer than the item you are going to retrieve, the excess will remain in the text area. Figure 9-3 illustrates this. In the first example in the figure, I retrieved a city name that's 13 characters long (SAN FRANCISCO) into the CITY host variable. Then, I issued another SELECT to retrieve the city for another customer. DB2 returned this city name (DALLAS) in the text area and its length in the length area. Notice that the last seven characters of the previous city name (ANCISCO) remained in the text area.

I'm sure you realize that this is an easy problem to avoid. Just move space into the text area before you retrieve each row. That way, anything that was in the field from the previous SELECT will be removed. The second example in figure 9-3 illustrates this technique.

It's simple to avoid difficulties with variable-length columns when you retrieve data, but it's more of a challenge to work with variable-length data when you insert and update rows. Your program must move the proper value to the length field before it issues the INSERT or UPDATE statement. You're responsible for doing this. DB2 doesn't make any assumptions about the contents of host variable fields associated with variable-length columns, even the very reasonable assumption that trailing spaces should be excluded.

This is one situation where DB2 forces you to apply your COBOL skills more than you might have to in other situations. Although there are several ways to determine the length of the non-blank part of a text field, they're all clumsy. One technique that's relatively easy to understand involves a COBOL array. You can move the value into an array in working storage, then evaluate and count the characters in the string backwards from the end toward the beginning until you find a character that isn't a space. The maximum length of the column's text area minus the number of spaces you counted is the length of the value in the text area.

Example 1

COBOL statements	Host variable contents

```
MOVE SPACE TO CITY-TEXT.
.
.
EXEC SQL
    SELECT   CITY
        FROM   MMADBV.VARCUST
        INTO :CITY
        WHERE CUSTNO = '400007'
END-EXEC.
.
.
EXEC SQL
    SELECT   CITY
        FROM   MMADBV.VARCUST
        INTO :CITY
        WHERE CUSTNO = '400001'
END-EXEC.
.
.
```

CITY-LEN: `?`
CITY-TEXT:

CITY-LEN: `13`
CITY-TEXT: `SAN FRANCISCO`

CITY-LEN: `6`
CITY-TEXT: `DALLASANCISCO`

Example 2

COBOL statements	Host variable contents

```
MOVE SPACE TO CITY-TEXT.
.
.
EXEC SQL
    SELECT   CITY
        FROM   MMADBV.VARCUST
        INTO :CITY
        WHERE CUSTNO = '400007'
END-EXEC.
.
.
MOVE SPACE TO CITY-TEXT.
.
.
EXEC SQL
    SELECT   CITY
        FROM   MMADBV.VARCUST
        INTO :CITY
        WHERE CUSTNO = '400001'
END-EXEC.
.
.
```

CITY-LEN: `?`
CITY-TEXT:

CITY-LEN: `13`
CITY-TEXT: `SAN FRANCISCO`

CITY-LEN: `13`
CITY-TEXT:

CITY-LEN: `6`
CITY-TEXT: `DALLAS`

Figure 9-3 How variable length data is returned to your program

A subprogram that determines the length of a character string

If your shop uses variable-length columns extensively, the chances are it has a subroutine your programs can call to determine the length of the data in a field. Also, it's possible that your shop uses a customized DB2 exit routine to determine the sizes of variable-length data items in a way that's transparent to application programs. Check with your colleagues or your DBA to find out if either is the case. Both can save you a lot of trouble.

But if your shop *doesn't* have a standard subprogram or exit routine for determining the length of a string, you can use STRLEN, the subprogram I'll present here. In a moment, I'll show you the source code for STRLEN. But first, I'd like to describe what it does from the point of view of the calling program.

Figure 9-4 shows the COBOL I'd code to call STRLEN to set the length component for the FNAME column from the expanded customer table. As you can see, the code is simple. The CALL statement that invokes the subprogram passes it two arguments: a binary halfword (PIC S9(4) COMP) that contains the maximum length of the string, and a character field that actually contains the string. In the example in figure 9-4, I used the length and text components from the DCLGEN description of the FNAME host structure.

The longest text string the STRLEN subprogram can evaluate is 254 bytes long. However, because most values that the subprogram will examine will be shorter, the subprogram is written so it can evaluate any string up to the maximum. That means you have to tell STRLEN how long the string can be each time you call it.

One way to do that is to move a literal value to the first argument. For example, I could have coded

```
MOVE 20 TO FNAME-LEN
```

just before the subprogram call in figure 9-4. However, this technique would tie the program unnecessarily to the structure of the data it processes. If the structure of the table changes, program statements that contain literals, like this one, may have to be rewritten.

A more flexible approach is to use the COBOL special register LENGTH. For example,

```
MOVE LENGTH OF FNAME-TEXT TO FNAME-LEN
```

specifies that the actual length of the program host variable FNAME-TEXT should be moved to FNAME-LEN. So, after this statement is executed, the value of FNAME-LEN will be 20, regardless of the number of meaningful

```
MOVE LENGTH OF FNAME-TEXT TO FNAME-LEN.
CALL "STRLEN" USING FNAME-LEN
                    FNAME-TEXT.
```

Figure 9-4   Sample COBOL code for using the STRLEN subprogram

characters FNAME-TEXT contains. (You can think of LENGTH as returning the size of the container, not its contents.)

With this technique, a change to the table wouldn't have much of an effect on the source program. All you'd need to do is run it through the program preparation process (precompile, compile, bind, and link) so it uses data areas from the updated DCLGEN output for the table. You wouldn't need to change any Procedure Division statements.

When the subprogram is executed, it returns the actual number of characters in the text field up to the first trailing blank through the first argument. Because I used the length component of the host structure as the first argument in the CALL, the host structure will be properly formatted for use in an SQL statement that inserts or updates a table row after the subprogram runs.

Now that you have a clear idea of what the STRLEN subprogram does, you'll find it easier to understand how it does it. The source code for STRLEN is shown in figure 9-5. When the subprogram begins execution, the string is available in the array called WORK-TABLE. The subprogram first sets LENGTH-DETERMINED-SW to N. Then, it uses PERFORM UNTIL to invoke 100-EXAMINE-LAST-CHARACTER repeatedly as it works backward from the end of the string toward the beginning. The subprogram uses the TEXT-LENGTH field as a pointer that identifies the character in the string it's currently examining. Each time it executes, module 100 subtracts 1 from TEXT-LENGTH. When module 100 finds a non-blank character, it sets LENGTH-DETERMINED-SW to Y.

After the PERFORM UNTIL statement in module 000 is satisfied, control passes through the paragraph named 000-EXIT to the EXIT PROGRAM statement. This returns control to the calling program. The result is that when the subprogram ends, the value of the field the program names as the first argument on the call is the actual length of the data in the text field just examined, excluding trailing spaces.

Long variable-length columns

You'll seldom run into a column longer than the NOTES column in the expanded customer table. However, you should realize that DB2 does

```
000100 IDENTIFICATION DIVISION.
000200*
000300 PROGRAM-ID.           STRLEN.
000400*
000500 ENVIRONMENT DIVISION.
000600*
000700 DATA DIVISION.
000800*
000900 WORKING-STORAGE SECTION.
001000*
001100 01   SWITCH.
001200*
001300      05   LENGTH-DETERMINED-SW    PIC X   VALUE "N".
001400           88   LENGTH-DETERMINED          VALUE "Y".
001500*
001600 LINKAGE SECTION.
001700*
001800 01   TEXT-LENGTH                 PIC S9(4) COMP.
001900*
002000 01   WORK-TABLE.
002100*
002200      05   WT-CHARACTER              OCCURS 1 TO 254 TIMES
002300                                     DEPENDING ON TEXT-LENGTH
002400                                     PIC X.
002500*
002600 PROCEDURE DIVISION USING TEXT-LENGTH
002700                            WORK-TABLE.
002800*
002900 000-DETERMINE-STRING-LENGTH.
003000*
003100      MOVE "N" TO LENGTH-DETERMINED-SW.
003200      PERFORM 100-EXAMINE-LAST-CHARACTER
003300          UNTIL LENGTH-DETERMINED.
003400*
003500 000-EXIT.
003600*
003700      EXIT PROGRAM.
003800*
003900 100-EXAMINE-LAST-CHARACTER.
004000*
004100      IF WT-CHARACTER(TEXT-LENGTH) = SPACE
004200          SUBTRACT 1 FROM TEXT-LENGTH
004300      ELSE
004400          MOVE "Y" TO LENGTH-DETERMINED-SW.
004500      IF TEXT-LENGTH = 0
004600          MOVE "Y" TO LENGTH-DETERMINED-SW.
004700*
```

Figure 9-5   COBOL source code for the STRLEN subprogram

support longer columns. When a column is longer than 254 characters, it
must be variable length; 254 is the upper limit for a column with the CHAR
data type.

Long VARCHAR columns can't be used in

- a condition in a WHERE clause

- an ORDER BY clause

- a GROUP BY clause

- a function

- a subselect in an INSERT or DELETE statement

Figure 9-6   Processing restrictions on columns more than 254 characters long (long-string column)

Long columns won't present any unusual COBOL programming problems for you. You use the same techniques for them that you use for VARCHAR columns that contain 254 or fewer characters. (If you want to use the STRLEN program I just presented, you need to adjust the size of its array to match the longest string you need to evaluate.)

When a variable-length column can be longer than 254 characters, it's called a *long string column*. Although DB2 supports long string columns, it imposes some restrictions on the ways you can use them. Figure 9-6 lists them. These restrictions aren't likely to be problems for you because it's unusual to perform these functions on such a long column. Frankly, 254 characters is adequate for nearly all columns.

The maximum size a long string column can have depends on two factors: how much space other columns in the table require and the size of the storage pages used for the table. Page size is specified when a table space is created, and it can be 4K or 32K. A DBA can specify any size for a VARCHAR column, as long as it's within the limits these constraints impose.

Although a DBA can specify an exact size for this kind of column, it's also possible to let DB2 figure out the maximum size possible. If the DBA specifies LONG VARCHAR as the data type for a column, DB2 calculates its length based on the maximum page size in the table space and the amount of space the other columns require. Then, you can examine the table's DCLGEN output to determine how much space DB2 allotted to the column.

How to work with nulls

Like variable-length data, nulls also require you to do some additional programming work. When you name a host variable in an SQL statement for a column whose value may be null, you also need to name another variable that goes along with it called an *indicator variable*. You should provide a different indicator variable for each column your program accesses that may contain a null value.

SQL statements that retrieve data (SELECT and FETCH) set the indicator variable for a column to signal to your program whether its value is null. When you issue statements that change data (INSERT and UPDATE), DB2 determines whether it should set column values to null based on the indicator variable values you supply. You have to use this indirect mechanism in your programs because you can't "move null" into a field in COBOL. Remember, spaces are not null values.

To use indicator variables, you need to know four things: (1) how to code their definitions, (2) how to name them in your SQL statements, (3) how to interpret their values (for SELECT and FETCH statements), and (4) how to set their values (for INSERT and UPDATE statements).

Unfortunately, DCLGEN doesn't automatically define indicator variables for you. So you must define them yourself. Each indicator variable is a halfword binary item. You'd code an item like

```
05   IND-NOTES        PIC S9(4) COMP.
```

to define an indicator variable for the NOTES column in the expanded customer table.

To use a host variable for a column that may contain a null value in an SQL statement, you combine the host variable name with the corresponding indicator variable. For example, this SELECT statement retrieves the contents of the NOTES column from the expanded customer table:

```
SELECT     NOTES
    INTO  :NOTES:IND-NOTES
    FROM  MMADBV.VARCUST
    WHERE CUSTNO = :CUSTNO
```

The name of the indicator variable *immediately* follows the host variable name. You may not code a comma or space to separate them. And, as with other host variables you name in your SQL statements, you must precede the indicator variable name with a colon.

As you can see in figure 9-7, indicator variables complicate your SQL statements. This figure shows the complete set of indicator variables for the expanded customer table and a SELECT statement that uses them. Although indicator variables make your SQL statements more complex, you shouldn't omit them. If you don't supply an indicator variable for a column you name on an SQL statement, and the statement accesses a row with a

Indicator variables

```
*
  01  IND-VARIABLES.
*
      05  IND-HOMEPH              PIC  S9(4)  COMP.
      05  IND-WORKPH              PIC  S9(4)  COMP.
      05  IND-NOTES              PIC  S9(4)  COMP.
*
```

SELECT statement that uses indicator variables

```
EXEC SQL
    SELECT *
        INTO  :CUSTNO,
              :FNAME,
              :LNAME,
              :ADDR,
              :CITY,
              :STATE,
              :ZIPCODE,
              :HOMEPH:IND-HOMEPH,
              :WORKPH:IND-WORKPH,
              :NOTES:IND-NOTES
        FROM   MMADBV.VARCUST
        WHERE  CUSTNO = :CUSTNO
END-EXEC
```

Figure 9-7   Indicator variables for the expanded customer table and a SELECT statement that uses them

null value in that column, the statement will fail and return an SQLCODE value of −305.

After a program issues a SELECT or FETCH statement that uses indicator variables, it must evaluate those indicator variables. DB2 sets the value of an indicator variable to −1 after a SELECT or FETCH if the corresponding column's value is null. When that's the case, DB2 doesn't return anything into the primary host variable for the column, and you should disregard its contents. On the other hand, if the value in the column isn't null, DB2 does return its value in the primary host variable and reports the non-null state by setting the indicator variable to zero.

Although it's unusual, DB2 can also return values other then 0 and −1 in the indicator variable to report special conditions. If a value is null because of a conversion error, DB2 returns −2 in the indicator variable. If DB2 has to truncate the value it returns to fit it into the host variable, it reports the original length of the value in the indicator variable with a positive value. If you use properly defined host variables in your programs, this shouldn't occur.

Before you issue an INSERT or UPDATE statement that affects columns whose values may be null, you need to set the indicator variables for them appropriately. If the indicator variable for a column contains −1 when you issue either an INSERT or an UPDATE, then DB2 sets the value of that column to null, regardless of what's in the associated host variable. If you set the value of an indicator variable to 0 (or, for that matter, anything other than −1) before you issue the INSERT or UPDATE statement, DB2 stores the contents of the associated host variable in the table column.

Host structures and indicator structures

If you code SQL statements that specify host structures instead of individual host variables, and those host structures contain any elements that can be null, you must still provide indicator variables for them. To do that, you have to code an *indicator structure*. It's an array of halfwords, one for each column in the rows you access. The number of elements in the array, that is, the number of OCCURS items, must be the same as the number of columns that make up the host structure, even if some of those columns don't allow nulls. (DB2 returns zero in the indicator variable for a column whose value cannot be null).

If I wanted to use a host structure with an indicator structure to retrieve a row from the expanded customer table, I could code the items in figure 9-8. Here, the array of indicator variables includes 10 items, one for each column in the expanded customer table. The first item of the array corresponds to the first column in the host structure, and so on. For example, after this SELECT, IND-VARIABLE(8) will contain −1 if the value of the eighth column, HOMEPH, is null. To determine whether columns contain null values, the program must evaluate the appropriate items in the indicator array separately.

How nulls affect the operation of SQL statements

In some situations, nulls can have an impact on the way SQL statements work. If you work with tables that contain nulls, you should know what those effects are. Here, I'll describe three ways nulls can affect your SQL statements: in arithmetic operations, in operations that require sorting, and in selection conditions.

Nulls and arithmetic operations   DB2 can store null for a numeric column just as easily as it can for a string column. All that's necessary is for the DBA to define the column without NOT NULL. If you use a numeric

Indicator structure

```
*
 01   IND-STRUCTURE.
*
      05   IND-VARIABLE            PIC S9(4) COMP
                                   OCCURS 10 TIMES.
*
```

SELECT statement that uses an indicator structure

```
EXEC SQL
    SELECT *
        INTO :CUSTOMER-ROW:IND-STRUCTURE
        FROM  MMADBV.VARCUST
        WHERE CUSTNO = :CUSTNO
END-EXEC
```

Figure 9-8   Indicator structure for the expanded customer table and a SELECT statement that uses it

column that contains a null in an arithmetic expression in an SQL statement, DB2 returns null as the result of the expression. DBAs are well aware of this. For this reason (and others too) they're less likely to allow nulls for numeric columns than for string columns.

You might think that DB2 would automatically substitute zero as the value for the column that's null, but that's not the case. However, DB2 does provide a function that lets you supply an alternate value for a column when it's null: the VALUE scalar function. I'll have more to say about VALUE in *Part 2: An Advanced Course.*

Nulls also affect column functions like SUM and AVG. DB2 doesn't consider columns that contain nulls when it processes a column function. So, depending on your application requirements, you may get inaccurate results when you apply SUM or AVG to columns that contain nulls. In a moment, I'll show you an example that illustrates the effect this can have.

Nulls and operations that require sorting   Three of the DB2 features I've presented so far can cause DB2 to sort rows as it produces a results table: ORDER BY, GROUP BY, and DISTINCT. When you specify a column that contains nulls with any of these options, DB2 considers nulls to be equal, and it groups them together at the end of the collating sequence. You'll see an example of this in a moment, too.

Nulls in selection conditions and the IS NULL predicate   Because null isn't really a value of a column, you can't specify it directly in a condition. For example,

```
WHERE HOMEPH = NULL
```

is an invalid condition. However, DB2 does let you evaluate columns to determine if they contain null. You can code

```
WHERE HOMEPH IS NULL
```

instead of a condition with a comparison operator. This predicate identifies all of the rows in the expanded customer table where the HOMEPH column contains null. Also, you can use the NOT operator with the IS NULL predicate. So,

```
WHERE NOTES IS NOT NULL
```

specifies rows from the expanded customer table where the NOTES column contains some value. Any value, including one or more spaces, satisfies this condition.

When a basic predicate (that is, one that doesn't use NULL) directs DB2 to evaluate a column that contains null, DB2 doesn't resolve the condition to either true or false, as you'd expect. Instead, it's resolved to "unknown." Depending on what you need to accomplish, this may or may not be right for you. Let me show you an example to illustrate the effect of this "unknown" result, as well as other processing implications of nulls.

Three examples of how nulls affect the operation of SQL statements
To help you understand how nulls affect your SQL, I created a simple table (DEMO) that allows nulls in a numeric column, and I issued a few SELECT statements against it. Figure 9-9 shows those statements and the results tables they created.

The first example is a simple SELECT that retrieves all of the rows from the sample table. As you can see, the table has only two columns. The first, KEYCOL, contain values that identify each row. The second, NUMCOL, is a DECIMAL column that may contain nulls. As you can see in the results table example 1 produced, the table contains ten rows. One row contains a negative value in NUMCOL, three contain zero, four contain positive values, and two contain nulls. (I listed this table with SPUFI; it represents nulls with a series of hyphens.)

Notice the sequence of the rows in the results table in the first example. The numeric values are in ascending sequence, from smallest to largest.

Example 1   A SELECT statement that retrieves all the rows from the DEMO table

SQL statement

```
SELECT KEYCOL,NUMCOL
    FROM MMADBV.DEMO
    ORDER BY 2,1
```

Results table

KEYCOL	NUMCOL
07	-50.00
01	.00
03	.00
09	.00
04	100.00
02	150.00
05	150.00
06	200.00
08	....
10	....

Example 2   Three SELECT statements that use different selection conditions to retrieve specific rows from the DEMO table

SQL statement 1

```
SELECT KEYCOL,NUMCOL
    FROM MMADBV.DEMO
    WHERE NUMCOL = 0
    ORDER BY 2,1
```

Results table

KEYCOL	NUMCOL
01	.00
03	.00
09	.00

SQL statement 2

```
SELECT KEYCOL,NUMCOL
    FROM MMADBV.DEMO
    WHERE NUMCOL ¬= 0
    ORDER BY 2,1
```

Results table

KEYCOL	NUMCOL
07	-50.00
04	100.00
02	150.00
05	150.00
06	200.00

SQL statement 3

```
SELECT KEYCOL,NUMCOL
    FROM MMADBV.DEMO
    WHERE NUMCOL IS NULL
    ORDER BY 2,1
```

Results table

KEYCOL	NUMCOL
08	....
10	....

Example 3   A SELECT statement that uses column functions with the DEMO table

SQL statement

```
SELECT COUNT(*),
       SUM(NUMCOL),
       AVG(NUMCOL)
    FROM MMADBV.DEMO
```

Results table

1	2	3
10	550.00	68.7500

Figure 9-9   SELECT statements that illustrate the effects nulls can have on SQL operations

The two rows that contain nulls are at the end of the results table. Remember, nulls are at the end of the sort sequence DB2 uses. And for the purpose of sorting, nulls are considered equal to each other.

Now, take a look at example 2. Here, I've issued three SELECT statements that specify different selection conditions in their WHERE clauses. In the first, I requested data from rows in the DEMO table where the value of NUMCOL is 0. The results table contains just what you'd expect, the rows with key values 01, 03, and 09.

The result of the second SQL statement in example 2 may *not* be what you expect. Here, I requested data from rows where the value of NUMCOL is not 0. The results table includes the rows that contain positive and negative values, but not the ones that contain nulls. It seems logical that between the two conditions "equal to zero" and "not equal to zero," DB2 should return all of the rows in the table. But, it doesn't. Nulls are simply "unknown" and don't satisfy either selection condition. The only way to specify rows with null values in a selection condition is to use the IS NULL predicate. That's what I did in the third SQL statement in example 2.

Example 3 in figure 9-9 illustrates how nulls can affect the results of column functions. In this SQL statement, I coded three column functions: COUNT, SUM, and AVG. The first column in the results table this statement produced contains 10, the count of the rows in the DEMO table. The second column contains the total of the values in the NUMCOL column. The SUM function didn't include rows that contain nulls in its calculation. The AVG function works similarly. Because it disregarded rows that contain nulls in the NUMCOL column, the AVG function computed the average based on a set of eight rows, not ten. The result was 68.75 (550/8), not 55 (550/10), as you might expect.

An enhanced update program that handles variable-length data and nulls

Now, I'd like to show you a sample program that applies the features you learned in this chapter for processing variable-length columns and columns that contain nulls. It's a version of the update program I presented in chapter 4, upgraded to work with the enhanced customer table I've discussed throughout this chapter.

The operation of the update program

As you'll recall from chapter 4, the update program is not interactive. Instead, it works in a batch environment and takes its input from a standard VSAM entry-sequenced data set that contains transaction records. You can see the record layout for this program's transaction file in figure 9-10.

```
 01   CUSTOMER-TRANSACTION-RECORD.
 *
     05   CTR-TRANSACTION-CODE      PIC X.
     05   CTR-TRANSACTION-DATA.
          10   CTR-CUSTNO           PIC X(6).
          10   CTR-FNAME            PIC X(20).
          10   CTR-LNAME            PIC X(30).
          10   CTR-ADDR             PIC X(30).
          10   CTR-CITY             PIC X(20).
          10   CTR-STATE            PIC XX.
          10   CTR-ZIPCODE          PIC X(10).
          10   CTR-HOMEPH           PIC X(16).
          10   CTR-WORKPH           PIC X(16).
          10   CTR-NOTES            PIC X(254).
```

Figure 9-10   The record layout of the expanded customer transaction file

As in the original version of the update program, the first field in the record, CTR-TRANSACTION-CODE, can have one of three values: A, R, or D. A means the data that follows should be added to the customer table as a new row. R means the data that follows should replace an existing customer row. And D means the specified customer row should be deleted.

The second item in the transaction record description is a large group item (CTR-TRANSACTION-DATA) that contains a field for each column in the VARCUST table. In this version of the program, I described each field in the input transaction record separately. That's because I refer to them individually.

The program will have to evaluate the contents of most of the fields in the input record. If a field in a transaction record is blank, its corresponding column should be set to null if the column allows nulls. Also, the program needs to determine the number of meaningful characters in each field that corresponds to a VARCHAR column. It will use that number to set the length value for the column.

The design of the update program

Figure 9-11 presents the structure chart for the enhanced update program. The top-level module, 000-POST CUSTOMER-TRANSACTIONS, performs 100-POST-CUSTOMER-TRANSACTION repeatedly as it works through the transaction file. Each time it runs, module 100 performs 110-READ-TRANSACTION-RECORD to get the next record in the transaction file.

If module 110 successfully reads a new transaction record, module 100 proceeds. What it does depends on the value in the record's transaction-code field. It can add a new customer row (module 120), change an existing

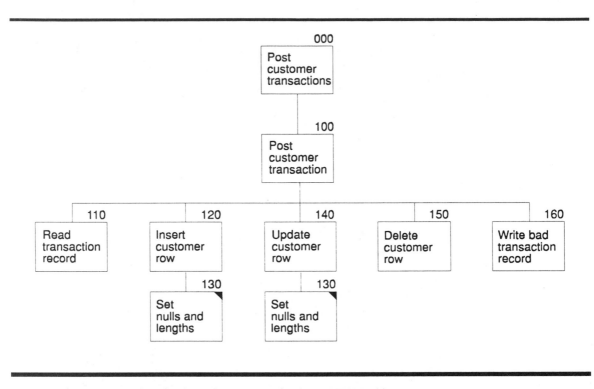

Figure 9-11   Structure chart for the update program for the VARCUST table

one (module 140), or delete one (module 150). Each of these modules issues the appropriate SQL statement. If the transaction code in the input record is something the program doesn't expect, or if one of the SQL statements fails, module 100 invokes module 160. Module 160 writes a record to a bad transaction file that another program can process later to produce an exception report. (I didn't include code for COMMIT and ROLLBACK processing in this program so you can concentrate on how it handles variable-length columns and nulls.)

If you recall the program in chapter 4, you'll remember that none of module 100's five subordinates had a subordinate module. In this version of the program, I added a module subordinate to the insert and update modules (120 and 140) that prepares the host variables for columns that have the VARCHAR data type or that may contain nulls. Module 130-SET-NULLS-AND-LENGTHS uses the techniques I described in this chapter to handle the different column types in the expanded customer table. When it needs to determine the number of characters in a variable-length string, module 130 uses the STRLEN subprogram I presented in figure 9-5.

The source code for the update program

The source code for the update program is presented in figure 9-12. The only thing you need to notice in the Working-Storage Section of this program is the set of indicator variables for the columns in the VARCUST table that can contain nulls. This group item is the same one I introduced in figure 9-7.

The first block of code I shaded in the Procedure Division is a series of ten MOVE statements that move values from the transaction record into host variables. In the original version of the update program, I was able to do this with a single statement that moved one group item from the input record into the host structure for the customer table. However, because the expanded version of the customer table uses variable-length columns, I couldn't use that technique. If I had, some data values from the transaction record would have been stored in the length components of the host variables for variable-length columns.

In the modules that issue INSERT and UPDATE statements, 120 and 140, I added one PERFORM statement to invoke module 130, the module that takes care of the tasks related to variable-length columns and nulls. Then, in the SQL statements in modules 120 and 140, I added the names of the new columns in the expanded customer table. And, for columns whose values can be null, I included indicator variables. I've shaded these elements too.

The SQL statement in the module that deletes a row, 150, is the same as in the original version of the program, except it names the VARCUST table instead of CUST. Also, the module that issues a COBOL WRITE statement for the bad transaction file, 160, is unaffected.

The biggest change to the program is in the new module that handles the tasks related to variable-length columns and nulls: 130. Module 130 has to handle values for variable-length columns that may not be null (FNAME, LNAME, ADDR, and CITY), the two fixed-length columns that may be null (HOMEPH and WORKPH), and the variable-length column that may be null (NOTES). Because the fixed-length columns that may not contain nulls (CUSTNO, STATE, and ZIPCODE) don't need any special processing, module 130 doesn't affect their host variables.

How the program processes data for variable-length columns that may not contain nulls   The first four groups of statements in module 130 prepare data for the FNAME, LNAME, ADDR, and CITY columns. The first shaded block of code in module 130 handles the FNAME column. This is the same code I showed you in figure 9-4 when I introduced the STRLEN subprogram. The subprogram evaluates the characters in the field named as the second argument (here, FNAME-TEXT) backwards starting at the charac-

```
000100 IDENTIFICATION DIVISION.
000200*
000300 PROGRAM-ID.          VNCUPDT.
000400*
000500 ENVIRONMENT DIVISION.
000600*
000700 INPUT-OUTPUT SECTION.
000800*
000900 FILE-CONTROL.
001000*
001100      SELECT CUSTTRAN ASSIGN TO AS-CUSTTRAN.
001200      SELECT BADTRAN  ASSIGN TO AS-BADTRAN.
001300*
001400 DATA DIVISION.
001500*
001600 FILE SECTION.
001700*
001800 FD  CUSTTRAN
001900      LABEL RECORDS ARE STANDARD
002000      RECORD CONTAINS 405 CHARACTERS.
002100*
002200 01  CUSTOMER-TRANSACTION-RECORD.
002300*
002400      05  CTR-TRANSACTION-CODE     PIC X.
002500      05  CTR-TRANSACTION-DATA.
002600          10   CTR-CUSTNO          PIC X(6).
002700          10   CTR-FNAME           PIC X(20).
002800          10   CTR-LNAME           PIC X(30).
002900          10   CTR-ADDR            PIC X(30).
003000          10   CTR-CITY            PIC X(20).
003100          10   CTR-STATE           PIC XX.
003200          10   CTR-ZIPCODE         PIC X(10).
003300          10   CTR-HOMEPH          PIC X(16).
003400          10   CTR-WORKPH          PIC X(16).
003500          10   CTR-NOTES           PIC X(254).
003600*
003700 FD  BADTRAN
003800      LABEL RECORDS ARE STANDARD
003900      RECORD CONTAINS 405 CHARACTERS.
004000*
004100 01  BAD-TRANSACTION-RECORD.
004200*
004300      05  BTR-TRANSACTION-CODE     PIC X.
004400      05  BTR-TRANSACTION-DATA     PIC X(404).
004500*
004600 WORKING-STORAGE SECTION.
004700*
004800 01  SWITCHES.
004900*
005000      05  END-OF-TRANSACTIONS-SW   PIC X     VALUE "N".
005100          88  END-OF-TRANSACTIONS            VALUE "Y".
005200      05  VALID-TRANSACTION-SW     PIC X     VALUE "Y".
005300          88  VALID-TRANSACTION              VALUE "Y".
005400*
```

Figure 9-12   COBOL source code for the update program for the VARCUST table (part 1 of 4)

```
005500 01  IND-VARIABLES.
005600*
005700      05   IND-HOMEPH              PIC S9(4) COMP.
005800      05   IND-WORKPH              PIC S9(4) COMP.
005900      05   IND-NOTES               PIC S9(4) COMP.
006000*
006100      EXEC SQL
006200          INCLUDE VARCUST
006300      END-EXEC.
006400*
006500      EXEC SQL
006600          INCLUDE SQLCA
006700      END-EXEC.
006800*
006900 PROCEDURE DIVISION.
007000*
007100 000-POST-CUST-TRANSACTIONS.
007200*
007300      OPEN INPUT  CUSTTRAN
007400           OUTPUT BADTRAN.
007500      PERFORM 100-POST-CUST-TRANSACTION
007600          UNTIL END-OF-TRANSACTIONS.
007700      CLOSE CUSTTRAN
007800            BADTRAN.
007900      STOP RUN.
008000*
008100 100-POST-CUST-TRANSACTION.
008200*
008300      MOVE "Y" TO VALID-TRANSACTION-SW.
008400      PERFORM 110-READ-TRANSACTION-RECORD.
008500      IF NOT END-OF-TRANSACTIONS
008600          MOVE CTR-CUSTNO   TO CUSTNO
008700          MOVE CTR-FNAME    TO FNAME-TEXT
008800          MOVE CTR-LNAME    TO LNAME-TEXT
008900          MOVE CTR-ADDR     TO ADDR-TEXT
009000          MOVE CTR-CITY     TO CITY-TEXT
009100          MOVE CTR-STATE    TO STATE
009200          MOVE CTR-ZIPCODE  TO ZIPCODE
009300          MOVE CTR-HOMEPH   TO HOMEPH
009400          MOVE CTR-WORKPH   TO WORKPH
009500          MOVE CTR-NOTES    TO NOTES-TEXT
009600          EVALUATE CTR-TRANSACTION-CODE
009700              WHEN "A"    PERFORM 120-INSERT-CUSTOMER-ROW
009800              WHEN "R"    PERFORM 140-UPDATE-CUSTOMER-ROW
009900              WHEN "D"    PERFORM 150-DELETE-CUSTOMER-ROW
010000              WHEN OTHER MOVE "N" TO VALID-TRANSACTION-SW
010100          END-EVALUATE
010200          IF NOT VALID-TRANSACTION
010300              PERFORM 160-WRITE-BAD-TRANSACTION.
010400*
010500 110-READ-TRANSACTION-RECORD.
010600*
010700      READ CUSTTRAN
010800          AT END
010900              MOVE "Y" TO END-OF-TRANSACTIONS-SW.
011000*
```

Figure 9-12   COBOL source code for the update program for the VARCUST table (part 2 of 4)

```
011100 120-INSERT-CUSTOMER-ROW.
011200*
011300      PERFORM 130-SET-NULLS-AND-LENGTHS.
011400      EXEC SQL
011500          INSERT INTO MMADBV.VARCUST
011600                  (  CUSTNO,               FNAME,
011700                     LNAME,                ADDR,
011800                     CITY,                 STATE,
011900                     ZIPCODE,              HOMEPH,
012000                     WORKPH,               NOTES)
012100          VALUES (:CUSTNO,               :FNAME,
012200                   :LNAME,               :ADDR,
012300                   :CITY,                :STATE,
012400                   :ZIPCODE,             :HOMEPH:IND-HOMEPH,
012500                   :WORKPH:IND-WORKPH,   :NOTES:IND-NOTES)
012600      END-EXEC.
012700      IF SQLCODE < 0
012800          MOVE "N" TO VALID-TRANSACTION-SW.
012900*
013000 130-SET-NULLS-AND-LENGTHS.
013100*
013200      MOVE LENGTH OF FNAME-TEXT TO FNAME-LEN.
013300      CALL "STRLEN" USING FNAME-LEN
013400                          FNAME-TEXT.
013500*
013600      MOVE LENGTH OF LNAME-TEXT TO LNAME-LEN.
013700      CALL "STRLEN" USING LNAME-LEN
013800                          LNAME-TEXT.
013900*
014000      MOVE LENGTH OF ADDR-TEXT TO ADDR-LEN.
014100      CALL "STRLEN" USING ADDR-LEN
014200                          ADDR-TEXT.
014300*
014400      MOVE LENGTH OF CITY-TEXT TO CITY-LEN.
014500      CALL "STRLEN" USING CITY-LEN
014600                          CITY-TEXT.
014700*
014800      IF HOMEPH = SPACE
014900          MOVE -1 TO IND-HOMEPH
015000      ELSE
015100          MOVE 0  TO IND-HOMEPH.
015200*
015300      IF WORKPH = SPACE
015400          MOVE -1 TO IND-WORKPH
015500      ELSE
015600          MOVE 0  TO IND-WORKPH.
015700*
015800      IF NOTES-TEXT = SPACE
015900          MOVE -1 TO IND-NOTES
016000      ELSE
016100          MOVE 0  TO IND-NOTES
016200          MOVE LENGTH OF NOTES-TEXT TO NOTES-LEN
016300          CALL "STRLEN" USING NOTES-LEN
016400                              NOTES-TEXT.
016500*
```

Figure 9-12   COBOL source code for the update program for the VARCUST table (part 3 of 4)

```
016600 140-UPDATE-CUSTOMER-ROW.
016700*
016800      PERFORM 130-SET-NULLS-AND-LENGTHS.
016900      EXEC SQL
017000          UPDATE MMADBV.VARCUST
017100              SET CUSTNO  = :CUSTNO,
017200                  FNAME   = :FNAME,
017300                  LNAME   = :LNAME,
017400                  ADDR    = :ADDR,
017500                  CITY    = :CITY,
017600                  STATE   = :STATE,
017700                  ZIPCODE = :ZIPCODE,
017800                  HOMEPH  = :HOMEPH:IND-HOMEPH,
017900                  WORKPH  = :WORKPH:IND-WORKPH,
018000                  NOTES   = :NOTES:IND-NOTES
018100          WHERE   CUSTNO  = :CUSTNO
018200      END-EXEC.
018300      IF     SQLCODE < 0
018400          OR SQLCODE = +100
018500              MOVE "N" TO VALID-TRANSACTION-SW.
018600*
018700 150-DELETE-CUSTOMER-ROW.
018800*
018900      EXEC SQL
019000          DELETE FROM MMADBV.VARCUST
019100              WHERE CUSTNO = :CUSTNO
019200      END-EXEC.
019300      IF     SQLCODE < 0
019400          OR SQLCODE = +100
019500              MOVE "N" TO VALID-TRANSACTION-SW.
019600*
019700 160-WRITE-BAD-TRANSACTION.
019800*
019900      WRITE BAD-TRANSACTION-RECORD
020000          FROM CUSTOMER-TRANSACTION-RECORD.
020100*
```

Figure 9-12   COBOL source code for the update program for the VARCUST table (part 4 of 4)

ter position identified by the value passed to it through the first argument
on the CALL statement. Then, it returns the actual number of meaningful
characters in the string to the calling program through the length field.

**How the program processes data for fixed-length columns that may
contain nulls**   The second kind of processing module 130 has to do is for
columns that aren't variable-length, but that may contain nulls. Only the
two telephone number columns, HOMEPH and WORKPH, fall into this category. The processing necessary for these columns is simple. All the program
has to do is move −1 to the indicator variable for one of these columns if its
host variable contains spaces, or 0 if it contains anything else. The second

shaded block of code in module 130 does this for the data in the HOMEPH
column.

**How the program processes data for variable-length columns that may
contain nulls**   The most complicated processing module 130 does is for
the NOTES column. That's because it's variable-length *and* can be null.
However, because you've seen how to handle both columns that can contain nulls and variable-length columns separately, I think you'll find the
code for the NOTES column easy to understand.

If the field in the transaction record for NOTES contains nothing but
spaces, the NOTES column should be set to null. So, the block of code that
handles the NOTES data begins by checking NOTES-TEXT to determine if
it's equal to space. If it is, the program moves −1 to the indicator variable
for NOTES, IND-NOTES. Then, when either an INSERT or UPDATE statement is executed, DB2 sets the value of the NOTES column to null in the affected row, regardless of what the NOTES-LEN and NOTES-TEXT fields contain.

If the value of the NOTES-TEXT field is not all spaces, the program
uses the same technique I described for the FNAME column to determine
the length of its contents. Although the NOTES column can contain more
than ten times as many characters as FNAME, I was able to use the same
coding technique for both because the STRLEN program adjusts its
operation to different string lengths based on the value it receives through
its first argument.

Discussion

Maybe I've been spoiled by how easy DB2 makes complicated tasks like
joins and subselects. That's my best explanation for why it bothers me that
it's necessary to code cumbersome COBOL to process data for variable-
length columns. To date, each major release of DB2 has included features
that make programming easier and more efficient. Perhaps a future release
will make it easier to handle a routine task like setting the length of
variable-length column values. Or, perhaps a future release of COBOL will
provide stronger string-handling features. Until then, if you have to develop
programs that process variable-length data, I hope the model programs in
this chapter will give you a good start.

Terms

long string column
indicator variable
indicator structure

Objectives

1. Explain why a DBA may define a string column as VARCHAR.

2. Explain why a DBA may define a column without the NOT NULL attribute.

3. Describe the COBOL programming requirements for working with DB2 variable-length data.

4. Describe the COBOL programming requirements for working with DB2 columns whose values may be null.

5. Describe the effect nulls can have on SQL statements involving arithmetic expressions, sorting, and condition-checking.

6. Given specifications for a program that will process data in a table that contains variable-length columns and/or columns whose values may be null, design and code the program.

Section

4

Program development

This section contains information you can use as you develop DB2 COBOL programs. Chapter 10 describes a TSO facility called DB2I that lets you perform a range of program development tasks interactively, and chapter 11 presents model JCL streams you can use to submit batch jobs for program development. To understand the information in chapter 11, you need to be familiar with the content of chapter 10, so you need to read chapter 10 first.

Even if you don't know the first thing about TSO, you'll be able to understand the procedures I present in this section. That's because I've used lots of illustrations with complete descriptions. This information will get you started using TSO, but before too long, you'll find you need to have an overview of TSO operations. Unfortunately, it's beyond the scope of this book to teach TSO. A first-rate resource for TSO users, new and experienced alike, is Doug Lowe's *MVS TSO, Part 1: Commands and ISPF.* If you'd like a copy, you can use the information at the end of this book to order one.

Chapter 10

How to use DB2I

In this chapter, I'll show you how to develop DB2 programs interactively through TSO. This chapter has five topics. The first introduces the DB2 Interactive (DB2I) environment. After you finish topic 1, you'll have the background you need in DB2I to use the information in the other four topics.

Topics 2 through 5 show you how to use the various services you can access through DB2I. Topic 2 presents SPUFI, a facility that lets you issue SQL statements interactively and see the results immediately at your terminal. Topic 3 shows you how to use the DCLGEN facility to create host variable definitions for tables. Topic 4 presents a set of panels you can use to prepare a program for execution by precompiling, binding, compiling, and link-editing it. And topic 5 shows you how to run a program that processes DB2 data online under TSO.

After you read topic 1, you can read topics 2 through 5 in any order you like. However, these topics follow a natural progression. So, unless you have an immediate need to learn about a subject I cover later, I recommend you read these topics in sequence.

An introduction to DB2I

The topics in this chapter present features you need to use for program development. You access all of the features I'll describe in this chapter through *DB2I*, which is short for *DB2 Interactive*. DB2I is a set of ISPF panels that let you perform DB2 program-development tasks in an online, interactive environment. This topic presents DB2I background that applies to all the features topics 2 through 5 cover.

How to access DB2I

DB2I is usually available as a choice on ISPF's Primary Option Menu. Figure 10-1 shows that menu on my system. Yours may be different, but DB2I will probably be there somewhere. If it isn't, check with a co-worker or your DBA to find out how to access it. You may need to have your TSO logon procedure adjusted so it displays an ISPF Primary Option Menu that includes DB2I.

To invoke DB2I from the screen in figure 10-1, I typed D in the *command area*, the second line of the screen. Then, when I pressed enter, the DB2I Primary Option Menu appeared. This menu is shown in figure 10-2. The four options I shaded in the figure are the four features I'll cover in the next four topics in this chapter. I'll cover SPUFI (option 1) in topic 2, DCLGEN (option 2) in topic 3, Program Preparation (option 3) in topic 4, and Run (option 6) in topic 5.

Even though I'm not covering Precompile and Bind (options 4 and 5) in separate topics, you'll still learn what you need to know about them in this chapter. That's because Program Preparation (option 3) includes both as substeps of a larger process that can also compile and link-edit a program. So, I'll present both the precompile and bind operations in topic 4.

Options 7 and 8 are for facilities that DBAs are more likely to use than programmers. I'll describe DB2I defaults (option D) in a moment. And the last option, X, is the option you select to leave DB2I.

To request any of the options on the DB2I Primary Option Menu, all you do is enter the appropriate option number or letter in the command area and press enter. In the next topics, I'll illustrate that for each option I shaded in figure 10-2. But now, I want to describe two general features of DB2I that apply regardless of the features you use: help and DB2I defaults.

```
----------------------- ISPF/PDF PRIMARY OPTION MENU ------------------------
OPTION  ===> D_
                                                       USERID   - MMA002
    0   ISPF PARMS  - Specify terminal and user parameters   TIME     - 21:47
    1   BROWSE      - Display source data or output listings  TERMINAL - 3278
    2   EDIT        - Create or change source data            PF KEYS  - 12
    3   UTILITIES   - Perform utility functions
    4   FOREGROUND  - Invoke language processors in foreground
    5   BATCH       - Submit job for language processing
    6   COMMAND     - Enter TSO command or CLIST
    7   DIALOG TEST - Perform dialog testing
    8   LM UTILITIES- Perform library administrator utility functions
    9   IBM PRODUCTS- Additional IBM program development products
   10   SCLM        - Software Configuration and Library Manager
    C   CHANGES     - Display summary of changes for this release
    D   DB2 V2      - Perform DATABASE 2 V2 interactive functions
    Q   QMF 2.4     - QMF  Version 2.4
    M   QMFMTOOL    - QMF  Message Tool
    S   SDSF        - Spool Display and Search Facility
    T   TUTORIAL    - Display information about ISPF/PDF
    X   EXIT        - Terminate ISPF using log and list defaults

  F1=HELP      F2=SPLIT      F3=END       F4=RETURN    F5=RFIND     F6=RCHANGE
  F7=UP        F8=DOWN       F9=SWAP      F10=LEFT     F11=RIGHT    F12=RETRIEVE
```

Figure 10-1   A choice for DB2I often appears on the ISPF Primary Option Menu. Here, it's D

```
                          DB2I PRIMARY OPTION MENU
  ===>  _

  Select one of the following DB2 functions and press ENTER.

    1   SPUFI                (Process SQL statements)
    2   DCLGEN               (Generate SQL and source language declarations)
    3   PROGRAM PREPARATION  (Prepare a DB2 application program to run)
    4   PRECOMPILE           (Invoke DB2 precompiler)
    5   BIND/REBIND/FREE     (BIND, REBIND, or FREE application plans)
    6   RUN                  (RUN an SQL program)
    7   DB2 COMMANDS         (Issue DB2 commands)
    8   UTILITIES            (Invoke DB2 utilities)
    D   DB2I DEFAULTS        (Set global parameters)
    X   EXIT                 (Leave DB2I)




  F1=HELP      F2=SPLIT      F3=END       F4=RETURN    F5=RFIND     F6=RCHANGE
  F7=UP        F8=DOWN       F9=SWAP      F10=LEFT     F11=RIGHT    F12=RETRIEVE
```

Figure 10-2   The DB2I Primary Option Menu

```
┌─────────────────────────────────────────────────────────────────────────┐
│                  HELP for DB2I PRIMARY OPTION MENU          Page 1 of 9   │
│  ===>  _                                                                  │
│                                                                           │
│                                                                           │
│   The DB2I (DB2 Interactive) task panels allow you to perform programmer, │
│   administrator, and operator tasks interactively by filling in fields    │
│   on task panels.                                                         │
│                                                                           │
│   This panel is an example of the HELP panels you can see if you press    │
│   the HELP PF key from a task panel.                                      │
│                                                                           │
│   Some HELP panels, like this one, show you a list of topics.  For information │
│   on any of the topics, type its letter on the command line and press ENTER.   │
│   To begin to see all topics in order, press ENTER only.                  │
│                                                                           │
│   Topics:                                                                 │
│       A  Using the HELP panels                                            │
│       B  Overview of DB2I                                                 │
│       C  Using PF keys with the task panels                               │
│       D  Default values on the task panels                               │
│                                                                           │
│                                                                           │
│    F1=HELP      F2=SPLIT     F3=END      F4=RETURN    F5=RFIND    F6=RCHANGE   │
│    F7=UP        F8=DOWN      F9=SWAP     F10=LEFT     F11=RIGHT   F12=RETRIEVE  │
│                                                                           │
└─────────────────────────────────────────────────────────────────────────┘
```

Figure 10-3   Pressing PF1 from a DB2I panel displays a Help panel for that task

How to get help in DB2I

Whenever you need to refresh your memory about a DB2I task, you can press the PF1 key to display one or more Help panels. For example, from the DB2I Primary Option Menu in figure 10-2, I pressed PF1, and the Help panel in figure 10-3 appeared.

Usually, the help information that's available for a task requires more than one panel. You can see how many panels (also called pages) there are for a task by looking in the upper right corner of any Help panel for that task. The panel in figure 10-3 is the first of nine.

As this screen shows, you press the enter key to move ahead to the next page. Some panels, like this one, include a menu that lets you jump directly to the page for a specific topic. To use the menu, key the character on the menu for the topic you want into the command area at the top of the screen before you press enter.

The information in the DB2I Help panels is brief. However, you'll find that it often contains just what you need to know, such as valid keywords and reminders about what infrequently used options do. So, if you have a question, take a second to try the Help panels before you turn to the

```
                        DB2I DEFAULTS
  ===>

  Change defaults as desired:

    1  DB2 NAME ............. ===> DSNB_     (Subsystem identifier)
    2  DB2 CONNECTION RETRIES ===> 0         (How many retries for DB2 connection)
    3  APPLICATION LANGUAGE   ===> COB2      (ASM, ASMH, C, COBOL, COB2, FORTRAN,
                                              PLI)
    4  LINES/PAGE OF LISTING  ===> 50        (A number from 5 to 999)
    5  MESSAGE LEVEL ........ ===> I         (Information, Warning, Error, Severe)
    6  COBOL STRING DELIMITER ===> DEFAULT   (DEFAULT, ' or ")
    7  SQL STRING DELIMITER   ===> DEFAULT   (DEFAULT, ' or ")
    8  DECIMAL POINT ........ ===> .         (. or ,)

    9  DB2I JOB STATEMENT:   (Optional if your site has a SUBMIT exit)
       ===>  //MMA00ZD JOB (....),'SECKOLS',CLASS=R,TIME=(1),MSGCLASS=R
       ===>
       ===>
       ===>


    F1=HELP      F2=SPLIT     F3=END      F4=RETURN    F5=RFIND     F6=RCHANGE
    F7=UP        F8=DOWN      F9=SWAP     F10=LEFT     F11=RIGHT    F12=RETRIEVE
```

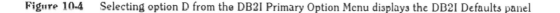

Figure 10-4 Selecting option D from the DB2I Primary Option Menu displays the DB2I Defaults panel

manuals. To leave a Help panel and return to your DB2I task panel, press the end key (PF3).

How to set DB2I defaults

When you use DB2I for the first time, you should check its defaults to make sure they're set properly for you. Once you set these values, they remain in effect until you change them to something else, so you won't return to this panel often. To display the current settings for defaults, I selected option D from the DB2I Primary Option Menu in figure 10-2. When I did, the DB2I Defaults panel in figure 10-4 appeared.

This example shows my processing defaults. The first eight items are all required. Appropriate values for the first two options (DB2 NAME and DB2 CONNECTION RETRIES) are installation-dependent. Check your shop's standards or ask a co-worker what values to use for these options.

The third option specifies the programming language you use. This value determines the format of the DCLGEN output DB2I will use and the compiler the Program Preparation panels will invoke. The IBM-supplied default is COBOL, which refers to VS COBOL. I've changed my default to

COB2 for VS COBOL II. Because you're a COBOL programmer, those are probably the only two application languages you'll need to use.

Even though COBOL is the IBM-supplied default, don't assume that the value on your system is still COBOL. Your shop may have replaced it with something else, such as ASM (Assembler F), ASMH (Assembler H), C (C/370 Language), FORTRAN (VS FORTRAN), or PLI (PL/I). So the first time you use DB2I, check the defaults and make sure the application language is set to the one you use.

Option 4 determines how many lines appear on a page of DB2I-generated output. This is relevant in SPUFI, which produces output that you may want to print. This also affects any printed output produced by language translators you use through the Program Preparation panel.

The MESSAGE LEVEL option specifies what kinds of messages should be displayed during BIND operations. If you specify I, you'll see all the messages. The other values cause only progressively more serious errors to be displayed. (W is for warning, error, and severe messages; E is for both error and severe messages; and S is for severe messages only.)

Options 6 and 7 let you specify the character you'll use as the delimiter for strings in COBOL statements and in SQL statements. You can explicitly specify an apostrophe (') or a quotation mark (") for either. Or, you can specify DEFAULT to make your shop's default your default. Option 8 lets you specify the character that will be used as a decimal point in numeric values. I use the period.

When you work with the Program Preparation panel, you can specify how a program should be compiled: under TSO or through a background job. If you use a background job, you can supply the JCL JOB statement for it in option 9. You can use up to four lines for the statement, if you need them. The JOB statement I use requires only one line.

Terms

DB2I
DB2 Interactive
command area

Objectives

1. Find and access DB2I on your TSO system.

2. Access help from a DB2I panel.

3. Set DB2I defaults.

Topic 2 How to use SPUFI

SPUFI (an acronym for *SQL Processor Using File Input*) lets you enter SQL statements at a TSO terminal for immediate processing, and then browse the results of the statements. You'll use SPUFI to experiment with SQL statements before you add them to a program, to prepare tables you'll use when you test a program, and to examine tables after a test run. In this topic, I'll give you an overview of SPUFI and show you a simple session with it. Then, I'll describe what you can and can't do with SPUFI and how to use its special-purpose panels. Finally, I'll offer some recommendations on how you can use different combinations of SPUFI's processing options for routine program-development tasks.

An overview of SPUFI

To access SPUFI, you need to invoke DB2I, as I described in the last topic. When you do, the panel in figure 10-5 appears. To start SPUFI, key in 1 in the command area and press enter.

After you invoke SPUFI, you see its main menu, shown in figure 10-6. The SPUFI main menu has just three groups of items. The first two specify the input and output data sets SPUFI will use, and the third specifies SPUFI processing options.

SPUFI requires that you specify both an input and an output data set. To understand why, take a look at figure 10-7. This figure presents an overview of how SPUFI works.

The input data set contains the SQL statements the user wants SPUFI to process. As the arrows in the figure indicate, the user works with ISPF EDIT to key in those SQL statements. At the end of the edit, the user can request that SPUFI execute the statements. Then, SPUFI reads the contents of the input data set and passes the statements in it to DB2. DB2 uses the appropriate tables to process those statements and returns the results to SPUFI. Next, SPUFI formats the results and stores them in the output data set. Finally, SPUFI lets the user examine the output data set with ISPF BROWSE.

If you've used other online data base facilities, this might seem clumsy to you. However, it can save you some time. For example, if you need to execute the same set of statements several times, such as when you're testing a program, you need to key them in only once. And after you browse the

```
                              DBZI PRIMARY OPTION MENU
  ===> 1_

  Select one of the following DBZ functions and press ENTER.

    1   SPUFI                 (Process SQL statements)
    Z   DCLGEN                (Generate SQL and source language declarations)
    3   PROGRAM PREPARATION   (Prepare a DBZ application program to run)
    4   PRECOMPILE            (Invoke DBZ precompiler)
    5   BIND/REBIND/FREE      (BIND, REBIND, or FREE application plans)
    6   RUN                   (RUN an SQL program)
    7   DBZ COMMANDS          (Issue DBZ commands)
    8   UTILITIES             (Invoke DBZ utilities)
    D   DBZI DEFAULTS         (Set global parameters)
    X   EXIT                  (Leave DBZI)




    F1=HELP       FZ=SPLIT     F3=END       F4=RETURN    F5=RFIND     F6=RCHANGE
    F7=UP         F8=DOWN      F9=SWAP      F10=LEFT     F11=RIGHT    F1Z=RETRIEVE
```

Figure 10-5   The DB2I Primary Option Menu choice for SPUFI is 1

```
                              SPUFI
  ===>

  Enter the input data set name:         (Can be sequential or partitioned)
    1   DATA SET NAME ... ===> SPUFI.INPUT(DEMO1)_
    Z   VOLUME SERIAL ... ===>            (Enter if not cataloged)
    3   DATA SET PASSWORD ===>            (Enter if password protected)

  Enter the output data set name:        (Must be a sequential data set)
    4   DATA SET NAME ... ===> DBZ.OUTPUT

  Specify processing options:
    5   CHANGE DEFAULTS   ===> NO         (Y/N - Display SPUFI defaults panel?)
    6   EDIT INPUT ...... ===> YES        (Y/N - Enter SQL statements?)
    7   EXECUTE ......... ===> YES        (Y/N - Execute SQL statements?)
    8   AUTOCOMMIT ...... ===> YES        (Y/N - Commit after successful run?)
    9   BROWSE OUTPUT ... ===> YES        (Y/N - Browse output data set?)




    F1=HELP       FZ=SPLIT     F3=END       F4=RETURN    F5=RFIND     F6=RCHANGE
    F7=UP         F8=DOWN      F9=SWAP      F10=LEFT     F11=RIGHT    F1Z=RETRIEVE
```

Figure 10-6   The SPUFI main menu

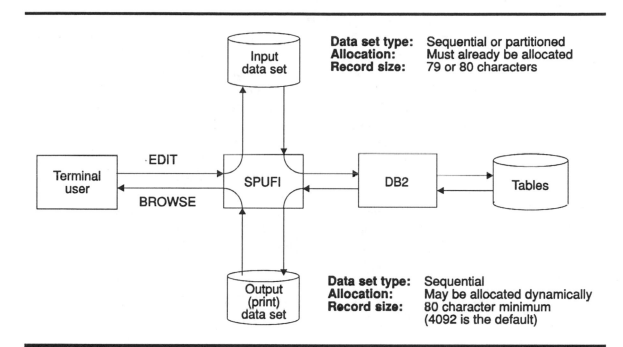

Data set type: Sequential or partitioned
Allocation: Must already be allocated
Record size: 79 or 80 characters

Data set type: Sequential
Allocation: May be allocated dynamically
Record size: 80 character minimum
(4092 is the default)

Figure 10-7 An overview of how SPUFI works

output data set SPUFI produces, you may want to save it and use it later. I think that's less likely, though.

The SPUFI input data set can be a member in a partitioned data set or a sequential file. In either case, you must have created and allocated the data set before you can use it in SPUFI. It should contain 80-character records, and its record format must be either F or FB. (Although SPUFI can also use an input data set that has 79-character records, I recommend that you use 80-character records.) In the example in figure 10-6, I specified the name of a partitioned data set (SPUFI.INPUT) and identified one of its members (DEMO1) as the input data set.

Unless you code a data set name between quotes, TSO adds your user-id to it as a high-level qualifier. So, because my TSO user-id is MMA002, the input data set SPUFI will use in the example in figure 10-6 is MMA002.SPUFI.INPUT(DEMO1).

If you need to access an input data set that isn't cataloged, or one that's password-protected, you must also supply the appropriate information for the VOLUME SERIAL and DATA SET PASSWORD fields. In this case, I didn't have to supply either, so I left these fields blank.

You name the output data set in item 4 on the SPUFI main menu. In figure 10-6, I used the name DB2.OUTPUT. Again, TSO will add my user-id to this name, so the full data set name will be MMA002.DB2.OUTPUT.

Unlike the input data set, DB2 can create the output data set dynamically. As a result, you don't have to allocate the output data set before you run SPUFI. If the output data set you specify already exists, SPUFI will replace the old data with the data from the current session.

You use the third group of items in the SPUFI main menu to control SPUFI's operations. Each time you use SPUFI to process the input data set, it can perform up to five steps. You can specify which ones it does by keying in YES or NO (or just Y or N) for the items in this group. In figure 10-6, I've set the processing options so SPUFI will do all but the first. Later in this topic, I'll say more about the CHANGE DEFAULTS option and about combinations of processing options that are appropriate for different program development tasks.

SPUFI "remembers" the values you key in on the main menu. In other words, each time you start a new SPUFI session, the settings on the main menu are the ones you used in your last session.

A simple SPUFI session

When you use SPUFI, it works through the steps you specified in the processing options group of the SPUFI main menu in the order they appear on the menu. In figure 10-6, I've enabled the EDIT INPUT, EXECUTE, AUTOCOMMIT, and BROWSE OUTPUT options.

When I pressed the enter key from the main menu, SPUFI started the processing for the first of the enabled options, EDIT INPUT. SPUFI uses the ISPF editor, so if you use ISPF regularly, you won't have to learn a new editing system. Part 1 of figure 10-8 shows the screen that appeared at the start of the edit step. Because I named a partitioned data set member that didn't exist for the input data set, EDIT presented a blank screen.

Part 2 shows the SQL statement I entered at this screen. You can include as many SQL statements as you need in a SPUFI input data set. In this case, I wanted to keep the example simple, so I used only one.

The SELECT I entered is like one you'd code in an application program, with three differences. First, I didn't bracket it with EXEC SQL and END-EXEC. Although you have to use those delimiters when you embed an SQL statement in a COBOL program, you don't use them in SPUFI.

Second, the statement doesn't include an INTO clause. You can't use INTO under SPUFI because no host variables are involved. (I realize that in an application program you wouldn't code an INTO clause on this SELECT either because it would have to be part of a DECLARE CURSOR statement;

however, you can't use INTO on SELECTs you issue through SPUFI at any time, even when you're sure they'll return single-row results tables.)

Third, I coded a single semicolon after the last line of the statement. When you code more than one SQL statement in a SPUFI input file, you must end each statement, except the last one, with a semicolon. Although the semicolon isn't required here because I only keyed in one statement, it's still OK to code it. And it's good to get into the habit of ending all SQL statements you issue through SPUFI with a semicolon, whether it's required or not.

By the way, although I think you're unlikely to do it, I want to point out that you can't code more than one SQL statement on a single line. SPUFI ignores anything on a line that follows a semicolon. So when you include multiple SQL statements in your input data set, code them on separate lines.

When I finished entering the SELECT statement in part 2 of figure 10-8, I pressed PF3 to end EDIT. Then, SPUFI displayed its main menu again. As part 3 of figure 10-8 shows, SPUFI indicated that it was in the middle of a session by displaying an asterisk after the EDIT INPUT processing option. The asterisk reports that the edit step is complete. When I pressed the enter key, the session continued with the next step, EXECUTE.

It can take some time for SPUFI to direct DB2 to execute the statements in the input data set, for DB2 to process them, and for SPUFI to format the output data set for display. Just how long depends on the complexity of the statements you issue, the sizes of the tables you access, and how busy your system is. If it takes so long that you can't wait for it, you can cancel the statements by pressing the PA1 key.

Usually, the statements you issue through SPUFI are processed quickly. In the session figure 10-8 illustrates, it took only a couple of seconds. Then, SPUFI automatically entered browse mode to display the result of the session, as shown in part 4 of figure 10-8.

In the output it displays, SPUFI includes the SQL statements it processed, the results tables they created, and status information about them. The output in part 4 of figure 10-8 shows the SELECT statement I entered and the first part of the results table it generated. SPUFI automatically shows table data in labeled columns that are appropriately sized. You can modify SPUFI's defaults to change these headings and column widths; I'll describe how in a moment.

Notice in part 4 of figure 10-8 that the results table contained more data than would fit on one screen. Two of the columns in the results table (ADDR and ZIPCODE) didn't fit, nor did rows for customers who live in states that fall near the end of the alphabet. To see other columns and rows,

Part 1

Because the CHANGE
DEFAULTS processing
option was set to NO for
this session, the first
step in the session is
EDIT. And because I
specified a new member
in the input partitioned
data set, EDIT begins
with a blank screen.

```
EDIT ---- MMA002.SPUFI.INPUT(DEMO1) ------------------------- COLUMNS 001 072
COMMAND ===>  _                                             SCROLL ===> PAGE
****** *********************************** TOP OF DATA *********************************
......
......
......
......
......
......
......
......
......
......
......
......
......
......
......
......
......
......

****** *********************************** BOTTOM OF DATA *********************************
   F1=HELP      F2=SPLIT      F3=END       F4=RETURN    F5=RFIND     F6=RCHANGE
   F7=UP        F8=DOWN       F9=SWAP      F10=LEFT     F11=RIGHT    F12=RETRIEVE
```

Part 2

I keyed in a SELECT
statement to retrieve all
seven columns from
every row of the CUST
table and to sequence
them by state.

```
EDIT ---- MMA002.SPUFI.INPUT(DEMO1) ------------------------- COLUMNS 001 072
COMMAND ===>                                               SCROLL ===> PAGE
****** *********************************** TOP OF DATA *********************************
......  SELECT CUSTNO,CITY,STATE,LNAME,FNAME,ADDR,ZIPCODE
......        FROM MMADBV.CUST
......        ORDER BY STATE; _
......
......
......
......
......
......
......
......
......
......
......
......
......
......
......

****** *********************************** BOTTOM OF DATA *********************************
   F1=HELP      F2=SPLIT      F3=END       F4=RETURN    F5=RFIND     F6=RCHANGE
   F7=UP        F8=DOWN       F9=SWAP      F10=LEFT     F11=RIGHT    F12=RETRIEVE
```

Figure 10-8   A simple SPUFI session

Part 3

When I pressed PF3 to end the EDIT step, the SPUFI main menu reappeared. SPUFI indicates the progress through the session by displaying an asterisk after the EDIT INPUT option. I pressed the enter key, and SPUFI began the EXECUTE step.

```
                                    SPUFI
===>
DSNE808A EDIT SESSION HAS COMPLETED. PRESS ENTER TO CONTINUE
Enter the input data set name:          (Can be sequential or partitioned)
 1  DATA SET NAME ... ===> SPUFI.INPUT(DEMO1)
 2  VOLUME SERIAL ... ===> _           (Enter if not cataloged)
 3  DATA SET PASSWORD ===>             (Enter if password protected)

Enter the output data set name:         (Must be a sequential data set)
 4  DATA SET NAME ... ===> DB2.OUTPUT

Specify processing options:
 5  CHANGE DEFAULTS   ===> NO          (Y/N - Display SPUFI defaults panel?)
 6  EDIT INPUT ...... ===> ▓           (Y/N - Enter SQL statements?)
 7  EXECUTE ......... ===> YES         (Y/N - Execute SQL statements?)
 8  AUTOCOMMIT ...... ===> YES         (Y/N - Commit after successful run?)
 9  BROWSE OUTPUT ... ===> YES         (Y/N - Browse output data set?)




 F1=HELP      F2=SPLIT     F3=END      F4=RETURN    F5=RFIND     F6=RCHANGE
 F7=UP        F8=DOWN      F9=SWAP     F10=LEFT     F11=RIGHT    F12=RETRIEVE
```

Part 4

After a moment, the first screen of the output appeared. In this case, it contained too many columns and too many rows to fit on one screen, so I pressed PF11 to scroll right to see the other columns in these rows.

```
 BROWSE -- MMA002.DB2.OUTPUT ------------------------- LINE 00000000 COL 001 080
 COMMAND ===> _                                        SCROLL ===> PAGE
 ****************************** TOP OF DATA ******************************
 ---------+---------+---------+---------+---------+---------+---------+---------+
 SELECT CUSTNO,CITY,STATE,LNAME,FNAME,ADDR,ZIPCODE                     00000100
    FROM MMADBV.CUST                                                   00000200
    ORDER BY STATE;                                                    00000300
 ---------+---------+---------+---------+---------+---------+---------+---------+
 CUSTNO  CITY                  STATE  LNAME                         FNAME
 ---------+---------+---------+---------+---------+---------+---------+---------+
 400009  MOBILE                AL     BUSBEE                        MARIANNE
 400013  MAGNOLIA              AR     KEITH                         DAVID R
 400006  SAN FRANCISCO         CA     HONG                          PAT
 400005  CERRITOS              CA     ROBERTS                       ELAINE
 400003  REDWOOD CITY          CA     HOWARD                        SUSAN
 400011  MIAMI                 FL     FERGUSON                      WILLIAM C
 400004  GREAT LAKES           IL     EVANS                         CAROL ANN
 400008  SO CHICAGO HTS        IL     JOHNSON                       TIM
 400007  DEARBORN HEIGHTS      MI     ROACH                         PHIL
 400016  MERRIMACK             NH     NOETHLICH                     J
 400002  DENVILLE              NJ     ANELLI                        ARREN
 400014  DEPEW                 NY     BINDER                        R
    F1=HELP      F2=SPLIT     F3=END      F4=RETURN    F5=RFIND     F6=RCHANGE
    F7=UP        F8=DOWN      F9=SWAP     F10=LEFT     F11=RIGHT    F12=RETRIEVE
```

Figure 10-8   A simple SPUFI session (continued)

Part 5

Scrolling right displayed
the next 80 characters.
To continue my browse, I
pressed PF10 to scroll
left (back to the screen
in part 4), then PF8 to
scroll down.

```
 BROWSE -- MMA002.DB2.OUTPUT ----------------------- LINE 00000000 COL 081 160
 COMMAND ===> _                                            SCROLL ===> PAGE
 ***************************** TOP OF DATA ******************************
 ---------+---------+---------+---------+---------+---------+---------+---------+


 ---------+---------+---------+---------+---------+---------+---------+---------+
          ADDR                      ZIPCODE
 ---------+---------+---------+---------+---------+---------+---------+---------+
          3920 BERWYN DR S #199     36608
          BOX 1266                  71757-1266
          73 HIGH ST                94114
          12914 BRACKNELL           90701
          1107 SECOND AVE. #213     94063
          BOX 1283                  34002-1283
          74 SUTTON CT              60088
          145 W 27TH ST             60411
          25680 ORCHARD             48125
          11 KINGSTON CT            03054
          40 FORD RD                07834
          3425 WALDEN AVE           14043
     F1=HELP      F2=SPLIT      F3=END     F4=RETURN   F5=RFIND    F6=RCHANGE
     F7=UP        F8=DOWN       F9=SWAP    F10=LEFT    F11=RIGHT   F12=RETRIEVE
```

Part 6

The output includes
status information for the
statement SPUFI
processed. SPUFI
automatically performed
a COMMIT after the
session because I
specified YES for the
AUTOCOMMIT
processing option on the
main menu (see part 3).

```
 BROWSE -- MMA002.DB2.OUTPUT ----------------------- LINE 00000020 COL 001 080
 COMMAND ===> _                                            SCROLL ===> PAGE
 400012  RIDDLE          OR    HOEHN               S D
 400015  PHILADELPHIA    PA    GEORGE              VIVIAN
 400001  DALLAS          TX    MCDONALD            KEITH
 400010  RICHMOND        VA    OTHON               ENRIQUE
 DSNE610I NUMBER OF ROWS DISPLAYED IS 16
 DSNE616I STATEMENT EXECUTION WAS SUCCESSFUL, SQLCODE IS 100
 ---------+---------+---------+---------+---------+---------+---------+---------+
 ---------+---------+---------+---------+---------+---------+---------+---------+
 DSNE617I COMMIT PERFORMED, SQLCODE IS 0
 DSNE616I STATEMENT EXECUTION WAS SUCCESSFUL, SQLCODE IS 0
 ---------+---------+---------+---------+---------+---------+---------+---------+
 DSNE601I SQL STATEMENTS ASSUMED TO BE BETWEEN COLUMNS 1 AND 72
 DSNE620I NUMBER OF SQL STATEMENTS PROCESSED IS 1
 DSNE621I NUMBER OF INPUT RECORDS READ IS 3
 DSNE622I NUMBER OF OUTPUT RECORDS WRITTEN IS 34
 ****************************** BOTTOM OF DATA ***************************



     F1=HELP      F2=SPLIT      F3=END     F4=RETURN   F5=RFIND    F6=RCHANGE
     F7=UP        F8=DOWN       F9=SWAP    F10=LEFT    F11=RIGHT   F12=RETRIEVE
```

Figure 10-8   A simple SPUFI session (continued)

Part 7

When I press PF3, the browse ends and the display returns to the SPUFI main menu. At this point, I can start another session or press PF3 again to end SPUFI.

```
                            SPUFI
  ===>

  Enter the input data set name:        (Can be sequential or partitioned)
   1  DATA SET NAME ... ===> SPUFI.INPUT(DEMO1)
   2  VOLUME SERIAL ... ===> _          (Enter if not cataloged)
   3  DATA SET PASSWORD ===>            (Enter if password protected)

  Enter the output data set name:       (Must be a sequential data set)
   4  DATA SET NAME ... ===> DD2.OUTPUT

  Specify processing options:
   5  CHANGE DEFAULTS   ===> NO         (Y/N - Display SPUFI defaults panel?)
   6  EDIT INPUT ...... ===> YES        (Y/N - Enter SQL statements?)
   7  EXECUTE ......... ===> YES        (Y/N - Execute SQL statements?)
   8  AUTOCOMMIT ...... ===> YES        (Y/N - Commit after successful run?)
   9  BROWSE OUTPUT ... ===> YES        (Y/N - Browse output data set?)



  F1=HELP      F2=SPLIT      F3=END      F4=RETURN    F5=RFIND     F6=RCHANGE
  F7-UP        F8-DOWN       F9-SWAP     F10=LEFT     F11=RIGHT    F12=RETRIEVE
```

Figure 10-8   A simple SPUFI session (continued)

you can use PF keys to scroll both horizontally and vertically when you browse SPUFI output.

Part 5 of figure 10-8 shows the screen after I pressed PF11 to scroll right. Here, you can see the contents of the two columns that weren't displayed on the screen in part 4, ADDR and ZIPCODE. Notice in the top line of the screen that the display is positioned not on the leftmost characters of the output data set, but on columns 81 through 160. (These are character columns in the output data set, not DB2 table columns.)

To continue to examine the output file, I pressed PF10 to scroll back to the screen in part 4 of the figure. Then, I pressed PF8 to scroll down to see the next rows in the results table. Part 6 of figure 10-8 shows them.

For each SQL statement that it processes, SPUFI displays the number of rows the statement affected and the SQLCODE it returned. As you can see in part 6 of figure 10-8, this SQL statement affected 16 rows, and returned 100 as the SQLCODE.

You may be surprised that the SQLCODE SPUFI returned was 100 instead of zero. In embedded SQL, 100 means that no rows could be found that meet a selection condition. But SPUFI returns 100 as the SQLCODE for a successful SELECT statement. Other statements, and SELECT in other situations, return the SQLCODE values I presented earlier in this book.

After it has processed all of the SQL statements in the input data set, SPUFI displays status lines for the entire session. Among them is an indication of whether or not SPUFI issued a COMMIT statement at the end of the session. In this case, because I specified YES for the AUTOCOMMIT processing option (in figure 10-6), SPUFI did perform a COMMIT. The COMMIT wasn't necessary here because the statement I processed didn't make any changes to the table. However, when you issue INSERT, UPDATE, and DELETE statements, COMMIT *can* matter. The other lines SPUFI includes at the end of its output file are statistics on the number of items processed during the session, both for input and output.

To end the browse step, and the session, I pressed PF3. Then, SPUFI returned to its main menu, shown in part 7 of figure 10-8. At this point, I can press PF3 again to end SPUFI. Or, I can start another SPUFI session, either with another input data set or with the same one. If I specify the same one, it's likely that I'd make adjustments to the SQL it contains (in the EDIT INPUT step) so it works differently.

SQL statements you can and cannot use through SPUFI

I don't want you to get the idea that all you can do with SPUFI is issue single, simple SELECT statements. You can issue complex SQL statements, groups of statements, and different kinds of statements. Here, I'll list the statements you can and cannot issue under SPUFI.

Statements you can use under SPUFI   Figure 10-9 lists the SQL statements you can issue through SPUFI that I think you are most likely to use. Most of the work you do through SPUFI will involve the basic SQL DML (Data Manipulation Language) statements you learned in this book, like SELECT and INSERT.

SPUFI also lets you issue DDL (Data Definition Language) statements. (SPUFI supports DDL statements in addition to those in figure 10-9, but you're unlikely to need them.) Even though DDL statements are usually issued by data base administrators, you may need to use them to create and modify test tables. To do that, you must have specific authorization (granted by your DBA), and you need to know how to code the statements. In *Part 2: An Advanced Course*, I'll show you how to code them.

Statements and features you cannot use under SPUFI   Although SPUFI lets you issue many SQL statements, it doesn't let you do everything. In

Data manipulation language (DML) statements	Data definition language (DDL) statements
COMMIT	ALTER INDEX
DELETE	ALTER TABLE
INSERT	CREATE INDEX
ROLLBACK	CREATE SYNONYM
SELECT	CREATE TABLE
UPDATE	CREATE VIEW
	DROP
	EXPLAIN

Figure 10-9   SQL statements you may need to use that SPUFI can process

particular, SQL commands and features that are peculiar to application programs can't be tested.

Those commands and features fall into the four groups figure 10-10 lists. The first group contains items that are related to cursor processing. You can't test any of the statements you use to work with a cursor-controlled results table (DECLARE CURSOR, OPEN, FETCH, or CLOSE). Also, you can't test UPDATE or DELETE statements that use the WHERE CURRENT OF clause to change or drop a row identified by a cursor. Although you can't test the cursor statements directly, you *can* test the SELECT that's a part of a DECLARE CURSOR statement.

The second group contains statements that let you use dynamic SQL from application programs. SPUFI can't process these statements because it doesn't support dynamic SQL. You'll learn about dynamic SQL in *Part 2: An Advanced Course*.

The statements in the third group are precompiler directives. SPUFI doesn't let you test DECLARE TABLE, INCLUDE or WHENEVER statements. I described the first two of these in chapter 2; I'll present WHENEVER in *Part 2: An Advanced Course*.

And finally, as I mentioned earlier in this chapter, you can't test any SQL statements that name program host variables. However, you can use those statements through SPUFI if you replace the host variables with literals. That's appropriate in WHERE clauses and in the VALUES and SET clauses of INSERT and UPDATE statements. To verify the operation of a SELECT statement that uses an INTO clause, simply omit the INTO clause. Then, check the results table the statement produces to make sure it

Cursor-related processing

DECLARE CURSOR statement
OPEN statement
FETCH statement
CLOSE statement
WHERE CURRENT OF clause with DELETE or UPDATE

Dynamic SQL

DESCRIBE statement
PREPARE statement
EXECUTE statement

Precompiler functions

DECLARE TABLE statement
INCLUDE statement
WHENEVER statement

Features related to program variables

Host variables (such as the INTO clause of SELECT)
Indicator variables

Figure 10-10   SQL statements and features SPUFI can't process

contains the correct row. (Remember, a SELECT statement that uses an
INTO clause can process only a single-row results table.)

Just as you can't name a host variable in a statement you test with
SPUFI, you can't name an indicator variable either. That's not a problem
because SPUFI automatically displays a series of hyphens in its output to
represent a null. To store a null in a table, use the NULL keyword of
INSERT's VALUES clause or UPDATE's SET clause.

How to use SPUFI's other panels

Depending on the processing options you specify, you may see one or two
other panels each time you run a SPUFI session. If you specify YES for the

```
                         CURRENT SPUFI DEFAULTS
       ===>

       Enter the following to control your SPUFI session:
         1  ISOLATION LEVEL   ===> RR        (RR=Repeatable Read, CS=Cursor Stability)
         2  MAX SELECT LINES  ===> 250       (Maximum number of lines to be
                                               returned from a SELECT)
       Output data set characteristics:
         3  RECORD LENGTH ... ===> 4092      (LRECL=Logical record length)
         4  BLOCK SIZE ...... ===> 4096      (Size of one block)
         5  RECORD FORMAT ... ===> VB        (RECFM=F, FB, FBA, V, VB, or VBA)
         6  DEVICE TYPE ..... ===> SYSDA     (Must be DASD unit name)

       Output format characteristics:
         7  MAX NUMERIC FIELD ===> 20        (Maximum width for numeric fields)
         8  MAX CHAR FIELD .. ===> 80        (Maximum width for character fields)
         9  COLUMN HEADING .. ===> NAMES     (NAMES, LABELS, ANY or BOTH)




         F1=HELP      F2=SPLIT      F3=END       F4=RETURN    F5=RFIND     F6=RCHANGE
         F7=UP        F8=DOWN       F9=SWAP      F10=LEFT     F11=RIGHT    F12=RETRIEVE
```

Figure 10-11   The Current SPUFI Defaults panel

CHANGE DEFAULTS processing option, SPUFI starts the session by displaying its Current SPUFI Defaults panel. And, if you specify NO for the AUTOCOMMIT processing option, DB2 doesn't automatically issue a COMMIT statement at the end of a successful session, as in figure 10-8. Instead, it displays the SPUFI Commit or Rollback panel to let you decide what to do on a case-by-case basis.

How to use SPUFI's Defaults panel   Figure 10-11 shows the SPUFI Defaults panel. It lets you set nine options. To change any of them, you just type a new value over the old one and press enter. If you press the end key (PF3) instead of enter, SPUFI will disregard your changes.

The first item, ISOLATION LEVEL, is a performance and data integrity option. I'll explain it in *Part 2: An Advanced Course*. Although the default value is RR, the other possibility, CS, will probably result in more efficient execution. However, because most SPUFI work involves small test tables you don't have to share with other users, it doesn't matter much which value you use.

MAX SELECT LINES, the second item, specifies how many rows SPUFI will include in its output data set when it processes a SELECT statement.

The default is 250. For most testing purposes, that's plenty. However, if you need to use a larger value, all you need to do is type it over 250.

The next four options let you change the attributes SPUFI uses when it creates an output data set. Unless you need to use SPUFI output for some purpose other than browsing in ISPF, you shouldn't change these values. However, if you have a use for the SPUFI data and it demands a different format, it's easy to modify. Just make sure the logical record length is at least 80, and the block size and record format specifications follow normal rules.

SPUFI formats the data in its output data set based on the total width of the columns it retrieves and on the value specified for the RECORD LENGTH option on the Defaults panel. SPUFI adds one record to the output data set for each row it receives from DB2 as a result of a SELECT statement. If a row contains more characters than will fit in a record in the output data set, SPUFI truncates it. That's improbable with the default record length (4092), but becomes more likely the smaller you make the output record length.

The last option in this group, DEVICE TYPE, lets you supply the unit name for the disk device where the output data set will be stored. The generic device type SYSDA lets MVS decide where to place the data set. Don't change this unless you need to store the output file on a specific volume.

The last three options on the Defaults panel let you change the characteristics of the output SPUFI creates. If you need to change any of the values on this panel, it's likely to be these.

SPUFI uses the widths of the table columns it retrieves to determine how wide to make the display columns in its output data set. If you look back to part 4 of figure 10-8, you'll see that SPUFI didn't provide as much space for the CUSTNO and STATE columns as it did for the CITY and LNAME columns. That's simply because CUSTNO and STATE are narrower than the other columns in the table.

Most of the time, the way SPUFI formats its output data set is acceptable. However, SPUFI won't automatically display all of the data in a very wide column. Its default maximum width for a character column in its display is 80 characters. If you SELECT a wider column, SPUFI truncates characters in positions 81 through the end of the column. You can override this by specifying a value larger than 80 for the MAX CHAR FIELD on the Defaults panel. You can also specify a different value for the maximum width of numeric columns after MAX NUMERIC FIELD. However, numeric columns are less likely to present a width problem for you than character columns.

Part 1

I reduced the default value for MAX CHAR FIELD from 80 to 10.

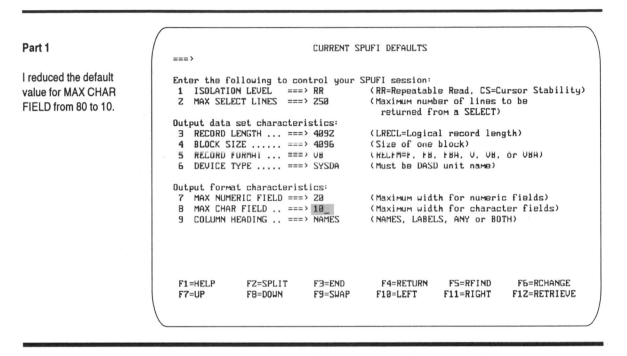

```
                          CURRENT SPUFI DEFAULTS
===>

Enter the following to control your SPUFI session:
  1  ISOLATION LEVEL   ===> RR      (RR=Repeatable Read, CS=Cursor Stability)
  2  MAX SELECT LINES  ===> 250     (Maximum number of lines to be
                                     returned from a SELECT)
Output data set characteristics:
  3  RECORD LENGTH ... ===> 4092    (LRECL=Logical record length)
  4  BLOCK SIZE ...... ===> 4096    (Size of one block)
  5  RECORD FORMAT ... ===> VB      (RECFM=F, FB, FBA, V, VB, or VBA)
  6  DEVICE TYPE ..... ===> SYSDA   (Must be DASD unit name)

Output format characteristics:
  7  MAX NUMERIC FIELD ===> 20      (Maximum width for numeric fields)
  8  MAX CHAR FIELD .. ===> 10_     (Maximum width for character fields)
  9  COLUMN HEADING .. ===> NAMES   (NAMES, LABELS, ANY or BOTH)




  F1=HELP      F2=SPLIT     F3=END      F4=RETURN   F5=RFIND    F6=RCHANGE
  F7=UP        F8=DOWN      F9=SWAP     F10=LEFT    F11=RIGHT   F12=RETRIEVE
```

Figure 10-12   How reducing the maximum column size default can affect SPUFI output

You can also specify a narrower maximum width. Figure 10-12 shows the effect of making the columns in a SPUFI output data set narrower. In the panel in part 1, I reduced the maximum length for character columns from 80 to 10 characters. This will make it possible to fit all of the columns in the customer table on the screen at the same time, but it will also cause some data to be truncated.

Parts 2 and 3 of the figure show the results. Notice in part 3 that SPUFI displayed warning messages for the columns where it had to truncate data. The three columns that weren't named in the messages, CUSTNO, STATE, and ZIPCODE, weren't large enough to be affected by the reduced column size.

If you get SPUFI messages like the ones I've shaded in part 3 of this figure, you don't need to worry. They mean data was truncated only in the SPUFI output. The data that's actually in the table you accessed is unchanged.

The last default in figure 10-11, COLUMN HEADING, lets you specify how SPUFI should identify the columns in its output. In the examples I've shown you in this topic, the default, NAMES, has been in effect. As a result,

Part 2

In this session, all of the columns from the customer table fit on the screen at one time. However, some data elements were truncated in the display.

```
 BROWSE -- MMA002.DB2.OUTPUT ----------------------- LINE 00000000 COL 001 080
 COMMAND ===>                                              SCROLL ===> PAGE
****************************** TOP OF DATA ****************************************
 ---------+---------+---------+---------+---------+---------+---------+---------+
 SELECT CUSTNO,CITY,STATE,LNAME,FNAME,ADDR,ZIPCODE                      00000100
    FROM MMADBV.CUST                                                    00000200
    ORDER BY STATE;                                                     00000300
 ---------+---------+---------+---------+---------+---------+---------+---------+
 CUSTNO  CITY         STATE  LNAME     FNAME      ADDR        ZIPCODE
 ---------+---------+---------+---------+---------+---------+---------+---------+

    400009  MOBILE       AL     BUSBEE    MARIANNE   3920 BERWY  36608
    400013  MAGNOLIA     AR     KEITH     DAVID R    BOX 1266    71757-1266
    400006  SAN FRANCI   CA     HONG      PAT        73 HIGH ST  94114
    400005  CERRITOS     CA     ROBERTS   ELAINE     12914 BRAC  90701
    400003  REDWOOD CI   CA     HOWARD    SUSAN      1107 SECON  94063
    400011  MIAMI        FL     FERGUSON  WILLIAM C  BOX 1283    34002-1283
    400004  GREAT LAKE   IL     EVANS     CAROL ANN  74 SUTTON   60088
    400008  SO CHICAGO   IL     JOHNSON   TIM        145 W 27TH  60411
    400007  DEARBORN H   MI     ROACH     PHIL       25680 ORCH  48125
    400016  MERRIMACK    NH     NOETHLICH J          11 KINGSTO  03054
    400002  DENVILLE     NJ     ANELLI    ARREN      40 FORD RD  07834
    400014  DEPEW        NY     BINDER    R          3425 WALDE  14043
     F1=HELP     F2=SPLIT     F3=END     F4=RETURN    F5=RFIND    F6=RCHANGE
     F7=UP       F8=DOWN      F9=SWAP    F10=LEFT     F11=RIGHT   F12=RETRIEVE
```

Part 3

The messages SPUFI displayed after it processed the SQL statement in the input data set include warnings that the data was truncated in four columns.

```
 BROWSE -- MMA002.DB2.OUTPUT ----------------------- LINE 00000020 COL 001 080
 COMMAND ===>                                              SCROLL ===> PAGE
    400012  RIDDLE       OR     HOEHN     S D        PO BOX 27   97469
    400015  PHILADELPH   PA     GEORGE    VIVIAN     229 S 1TH   19103
    400001  DALLAS       TX     MCDONALD  KEITH      4501 W MOC  75209
    400010  RICHMOND     VA     OTHON     ENRIQUE    BOX 29729   23261
 DSNE610I NUMBER OF ROWS DISPLAYED IS 16
 DSNE612I DATA FOR COLUMN HEADER CITY COLUMN NUMBER 2 WAS TRUNCATED
 DSNE612I DATA FOR COLUMN HEADER LNAME COLUMN NUMBER 4 WAS TRUNCATED
 DSNE612I DATA FOR COLUMN HEADER FNAME COLUMN NUMBER 5 WAS TRUNCATED
 DSNE612I DATA FOR COLUMN HEADER ADDR COLUMN NUMBER 6 WAS TRUNCATED
 DSNE616I STATEMENT EXECUTION WAS SUCCESSFUL, SQLCODE IS 100
 ---------+---------+---------+---------+---------+---------+---------+---------+
 ---------+---------+---------+---------+---------+---------+---------+---------+
 DSNE617I COMMIT PERFORMED, SQLCODE IS 0
 DSNE616I STATEMENT EXECUTION WAS SUCCESSFUL, SQLCODE IS 0
 ---------+---------+---------+---------+---------+---------+---------+---------+
 DSNE601I SQL STATEMENTS ASSUMED TO BE BETWEEN COLUMNS 1 AND 72
 DSNE620I NUMBER OF SQL STATEMENTS PROCESSED IS 1
 DSNE621I NUMBER OF INPUT RECORDS READ IS 3
 DSNE622I NUMBER OF OUTPUT RECORDS WRITTEN IS 38
 ********************** BOTTOM OF DATA *******************************************
     F1=HELP     F2=SPLIT     F3=END     F4=RETURN    F5=RFIND    F6=RCHANGE
     F7=UP       F8=DOWN      F9=SWAP    F10=LEFT     F11=RIGHT   F12=RETRIEVE
```

Figure 10-12   How reducing the maximum column size default can affect SPUFI output (continued)

SPUFI used the names of the columns as the headings for the data it displayed. In most circumstances, this will be the setting you'll use.

Instead of NAMES, you can code LABELS to direct SPUFI to use values specified by the DBA through the SQL LABELS ON statement. These values are simply literals a DBA can supply as additional documentation for a table. ANY specifies that any available labels should be used, but that column names should be used for columns that don't have labels. BOTH tells SPUFI to use both labels and column names for headings.

How to use SPUFI's Commit or Rollback panel   SPUFI treats each session as a single unit of work. When the session is over, the processing that was done can be committed or rolled back. You can control COMMIT and ROLLBACK processing, or leave it to SPUFI.

If you set the AUTOCOMMIT processing option to YES, SPUFI automatically issues a COMMIT statement after it has processed all of the statements in the input data set, if they all executed successfully. You'll remember from the simple example in figure 10-8 that SPUFI reported that it issued a COMMIT at the end of the session.

SPUFI operates differently when AUTOCOMMIT is YES and a statement in the input data set fails. Then, SPUFI stops processing the input data set at that point and issues a ROLLBACK statement to reverse what the preceding statements did.

To help you understand how SPUFI deals with SQL errors, I'd like to show you a simple SPUFI session that processes a statement that fails. Figure 10-13 shows a SPUFI input data set that contains two INSERT statements. DB2 will be able to process the first one successfully. However, the second one will fail because it will try to insert a row with a CUSTNO column value that already exists.

Figure 10-14 shows the output data set SPUFI produced when it processed the input data set in figure 10-13 with the AUTOCOMMIT option set to YES. As you can see in part 1 of figure 10-14, DB2 did process the first INSERT successfully, but the second failed with SQLCODE −803. In part 2, you can see that SPUFI automatically issued a ROLLBACK statement. So the effect of the first INSERT statement was reversed, and no changes were made to the table during the session.

Figure 10-15 shows another SPUFI session that also uses the input data set in figure 10-13. However, in this case, the AUTOCOMMIT option is set to NO. The first screen is the same as in figure 10-14; the first statement completed successfully, but the second one failed. Notice in part 2 of the figure that SPUFI did not automatically issue a ROLLBACK statement. Instead, it displayed the Commit or Rollback panel, as shown in part 3 of the figure.

```
EDIT ──── MMA002.SPUFI.INPUT(DEMO2) ──────────────────────── COLUMNS 001 072
COMMAND ===>                                                  SCROLL ===> PAGE
****** ***************************** TOP OF DATA ******************************
000100 INSERT INTO MMADBV.CUST
000200            (CUSTNO,FNAME,LNAME,ADDR,CITY,STATE,ZIPCODE)
000300     VALUES ('500001','SELMA','WEINGARD',
000400            '54 17 ST.','TALLAHASSEE','FL','32306');
000500 INSERT INTO MMADBV.CUST
000600            (CUSTNO,FNAME,LNAME,ADDR,CITY,STATE,ZIPCODE)
000700     VALUES ('400002','WILLIAM','KEPPEL',
000800            '4482 LAKE MURRAY BLVD','LA MESA','CA','92042');
****** ***************************** BOTTOM OF DATA ***************************




 F1=HELP      F2=SPLIT     F3=END       F4=RETURN    F5=RFIND     F6=RCHANGE
 F7=UP        F8=DOWN      F9=SWAP      F10=LEFT     F11=RIGHT    F12=RETRIEVE
```

Figure 10-13   A SPUFI input data set that contains two INSERT statements

This panel lets you decide what should happen at the end of a SPUFI session. Here, I keyed in ROLLBACK to reverse the changes SPUFI requested during the session. COMMIT, on the other hand, would cause SPUFI to commit all of the changes made up to the statement that failed. The third option, DEFER, tells SPUFI to hold the pending table changes until some additional processing is done. Because DEFER can monopolize system resources, you probably shouldn't use it.

I want to point out that although SPUFI treats a session as a single unit of work, you can intervene and divide it up yourself by explicitly including COMMIT and ROLLBACK statements in your input data sets. For example, if I had coded a COMMIT between the two INSERT statements in figure 10-13, the row inserted by the first statement would have been added to the table. That would be the case even if DB2 performed a ROLLBACK at the end of the session, either because AUTOCOMMIT was YES (as in figure 10-14) or because I specified ROLLBACK on the SPUFI Commit or Rollback panel (as in figure 10-15).

Part 1

An INSERT statement
that contains a value for
the CUSTNO column
that already exists can't
be processed.

```
 BROWSE -- MMA002.DB2.OUTPUT ----------------------- LINE 00000000 COL 001 080
 COMMAND ===>                                          SCROLL ===> PAGE
********************************* TOP OF DATA ********************************
---------+---------+---------+---------+---------+---------+---------+---------+
INSERT INTO MMADBU.CUST                                               00000100
        (CUSTNO,FNAME,LNAME,ADDR,CITY,STATE,ZIPCODE)                  00000200
    VALUES ('500001','SELMA','WEINGARD',                             00000300
            '54 17 ST.','TALLAHASSEE','FL','32306');                 00000400
---------+---------+---------+---------+---------+---------+---------+---------+
DSNE615I NUMBER OF ROWS AFFECTED IS 1
DSNE616I STATEMENT EXECUTION WAS SUCCESSFUL, SQLCODE IS 0
---------+---------+---------+---------+---------+---------+---------+---------+
INSERT INTO MMADBU.CUST                                               00000500
        (CUSTNO,FNAME,LNAME,ADDR,CITY,STATE,ZIPCODE)                  00000600
    VALUES ('400002','WILLIAM','KEPPEL',                             00000700
            '4482 LAKE MURRAY BLVD','LA MESA','CA','92042');         00000800
---------+---------+---------+---------+---------+---------+---------+---------+
DSNT408I SQLCODE = -803, ERROR:   AN INSERTED OR UPDATED VALUE IS INVALID
         BECAUSE THE INDEX CUSTX CONSTRAINS COLUMNS OF THE TABLE SUCH THAT NO
         TWO ROWS CAN CONTAIN DUPLICATE VALUES IN THOSE COLUMNS. RID OF
         EXISTING ROW IS X'0000021F'
DSNT415I SQLERRP = DSNXRUID SQL PROCEDURE DETECTING ERROR
    F1=HELP       F2=SPLIT      F3=END       F4=RETURN     F5=RFIND      F6=RCHANGE
    F7=UP         F8=DOWN       F9=SWAP      F10=LEFT      F11=RIGHT     F12=RETRIEVE
```

Part 2

Because the
AUTOCOMMIT option is
set to YES, SPUFI
issues a ROLLBACK
statement.

```
 BROWSE -- MMA002.DB2.OUTPUT ----------------------- LINE 00000020 COL 001 080
 COMMAND ===>                                          SCROLL ===> PAGE
DSNT416I SQLERRD = 110  13172739  0  13817814  1010237440  0 SQL DIAGNOSTIC
         INFORMATION
DSNT416I SQLERRD = X'FFFFFF92'  X'00C90003'  X'00000000'  X'00D2D7D6'
         X'C3C90000'  X'00000000' SQL DIAGNOSTIC INFORMATION
---------+---------+---------+---------+---------+---------+---------+---------+
DSNE618I ROLLBACK PERFORMED, SQLCODE IS 0
DSNE616I STATEMENT EXECUTION WAS SUCCESSFUL, SQLCODE IS 0
---------+---------+---------+---------+---------+---------+---------+---------+
DSNE601I SQL STATEMENTS ASSUMED TO BE BETWEEN COLUMNS 1 AND 72
DSNE620I NUMBER OF SQL STATEMENTS PROCESSED IS 2
DSNE621I NUMBER OF INPUT RECORDS READ IS 8
DSNE622I NUMBER OF OUTPUT RECORDS WRITTEN IS 31
******************************** BOTTOM OF DATA *****************************




    F1=HELP       F2=SPLIT      F3=END       F4=RETURN     F5=RFIND      F6=RCHANGE
    F7=UP         F8=DOWN       F9=SWAP      F10=LEFT      F11=RIGHT     F12=RETRIEVE
```

Figure 10-14 The SPUFI output produced by the input data set in figure 10-13 with the AUTOCOMMIT processing
option set to YES

Part 1

An INSERT statement
that contains a value for
the CUSTNO column
that already exists can't
be processed.

```
 BROWSE -- MMA002.DB2.OUTPUT ------------------------ LINE 00000000 COL 001 080
 COMMAND ===>                                              SCROLL ===> PAGE
 ********************************** TOP OF DATA **********************************
 ----------+---------+---------+---------+---------+---------+---------+---------+
 INSERT INTO MMADBV.CUST                                                00000100
         (CUSTNO,FNAME,LNAME,ADDR,CITY,STATE,ZIPCODE)                   00000200
     VALUES ('500001','SELMA','WEINGARD',                              00000300
            '54 17 ST.','TALLAHASSEE','FL','32306');                   00000400
 ----------+---------+---------+---------+---------+---------+---------+---------+
 DSNE615I NUMBER OF ROWS AFFECTED IS 1
 DSNE616I STATEMENT EXECUTION WAS SUCCESSFUL, SQLCODE IS 0
 ----------+---------+---------+---------+---------+---------+---------+---------+
 INSERT INTO MMADBV.CUST                                                00000500
         (CUSTNO,FNAME,LNAME,ADDR,CITY,STATE,ZIPCODE)                   00000600
     VALUES ('400002','WILLIAM','KEPPEL',                              00000700
            '4482 LAKE MURRAY BLVD','LA MESA','CA','92042');           00000800
 ----------+---------+---------+---------+---------+---------+---------+---------+
 DSNT408I SQLCODE = -803, ERROR:  AN INSERTED OR UPDATED VALUE IS INVALID
          BECAUSE THE INDEX CUSTX CONSTRAINS COLUMNS OF THE TABLE SUCH THAT NO
          TWO ROWS CAN CONTAIN DUPLICATE VALUES IN THOSE COLUMNS. RID OF
          EXISTING ROW IS X'0000021F'
 DSNT415I SQLERRP = DSNXRUID SQL PROCEDURE DETECTING ERROR
     F1=HELP      F2=SPLIT     F3=END      F4=RETURN   F5=RFIND    F6=RCHANGE
     F7=UP        F8=DOWN      F9=SWAP     F10=LEFT    F11=RIGHT   F12=RETRIEVE
```

Part 2

Because the
AUTOCOMMIT option
is set to NO, SPUFI
doesn't issue a
ROLLBACK statement.

```
 BROWSE -- MMA002.DB2.OUTPUT ------------------------ LINE 00000020 COL 001 080
 COMMAND ===>                                              SCROLL ===> PAGE
 DSNT416I SQLERRD = 110   13172739   0   13817814   1010237440   0 SQL DIAGNOSTIC
          INFORMATION
 DSNT416I SQLERRD = X'FFFFFF92'  X'00C90003'  X'00000000'  X'00D2D7D6'
          X'C3C90000'  X'00000000' SQL DIAGNOSTIC INFORMATION
 ----------+---------+---------+---------+---------+---------+---------+---------+
 DSNE614I AUTOCOMMIT IS NO; NO CHANGES COMMITTED
 ----------+---------+---------+---------+---------+---------+---------+---------+
 DSNE601I SQL STATEMENTS ASSUMED TO BE BETWEEN COLUMNS 1 AND 72
 DSNE620I NUMBER OF SQL STATEMENTS PROCESSED IS 2
 DSNE621I NUMBER OF INPUT RECORDS READ IS 8
 DSNE622I NUMBER OF OUTPUT RECORDS WRITTEN IS 30
 ********************************** BOTTOM OF DATA *******************************




     F1=HELP      F2=SPLIT     F3=END      F4=RETURN   F5=RFIND    F6=RCHANGE
     F7=UP        F8=DOWN      F9=SWAP     F10=LEFT    F11=RIGHT   F12=RETRIEVE
```

Figure 10-15   The SPUFI output produced by the input data set in figure 10-13 with the AUTOCOMMIT processing
option set to NO

Part 3

SPUFI displays the
Commit or Rollback
panel so you can decide
what action to take.

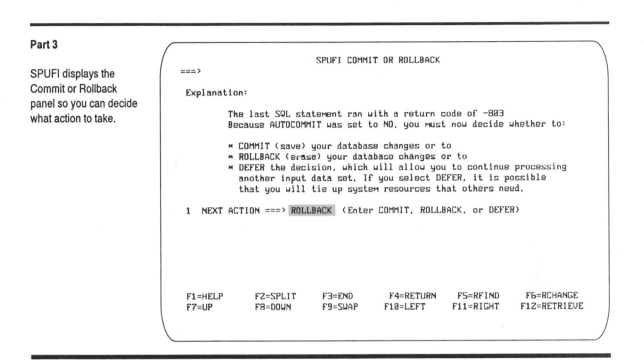

```
                        SPUFI COMMIT OR ROLLBACK
 ===>

   Explanation:

          The last SQL statement ran with a return code of -803
          Because AUTOCOMMIT was set to NO, you must now decide whether to:

          * COMMIT (save) your database changes or to
          * ROLLBACK (erase) your database changes or to
          * DEFER the decision, which will allow you to continue processing
            another input data set. If you select DEFER, it is possible
            that you will tie up system resources that others need.

   1   NEXT ACTION ===>  ROLLBACK   (Enter COMMIT, ROLLBACK, or DEFER)




        F1=HELP      F2=SPLIT     F3=END      F4=RETURN    F5=RFIND     F6=RCHANGE
        F7=UP        F8=DOWN      F9=SWAP     F10=LEFT     F11=RIGHT    F12=RETRIEVE
```

Figure 10-15   The SPUFI output produced by the input data set in figure 10-13 with the AUTOCOMMIT processing
option set to NO (continued)

Recommended processing option combinations

After you've used SPUFI for a little while, it will be natural for you to
request the right combination of processing options for a particular task.
However, until SPUFI becomes second nature to you, you might like to use
the recommendations in figure 10-16. These are the processing options I
suggest you use for routine, typical, program-development tasks.

Before I describe each combination, I want to point out that you'll
almost always specify NO for the CHANGE DEFAULTS option. Although
you'll sometimes need to change a default, most of the time you'll want to
leave them alone. After all, the point of having defaults is so you don't have
to deal with specifying the same things over and over.

The first column in figure 10-16 presents the option settings you
should use when you want to experiment with SELECT statements, or you
want to make a permanent change to a table, such as adding a few new
rows. As you can see, I suggest you specify YES for all the options except
CHANGE DEFAULTS. This is the same set of options I used in the first
example I showed you in this topic. With this combination of option settings, you can modify the SQL statements in the input data set, execute
them, have SPUFI automatically commit the changes if everything worked

SPUFI processing options	Test SELECT statements or Make permanent table changes	Test INSERT, UPDATE, and DELETE statements	Reset tables after testing a program	List and reset tables after testing a program
5 CHANGE DEFAULTS	NO	NO	NO	NO
6 EDIT INPUT	YES	YES	NO	NO
7 EXECUTE	YES	YES	YES	YES
8 AUTOCOMMIT	YES	NO	YES	YES
9 BROWSE OUTPUT	YES	YES	NO	YES

Figure 10-16   Recommended SPUFI options for routine program-development tasks

properly, and finally, review the output data set to see what happened. About 75 percent of the work I do with SPUFI is with this combination of processing options.

The second column in figure 10-16 lists the options I recommend when you're experimenting with statements that can modify tables (INSERT, UPDATE, and DELETE) and you want to be able to test them repeatedly without having to restore the table to its starting condition each time. I suggest you set the AUTOCOMMIT option to NO, so you can direct SPUFI to issue a ROLLBACK statement after it processes your input data set, even if all of the statements it contains executed successfully. This is a useful feature you can use to improve your productivity.

When you test an application program that modifies tables, the situation is more complicated. That's because when a program runs to completion, the table modifications it has requested are committed. So, you need to be able to restore your test table to its starting condition after one test to prepare for the next. That's easy to do if you keep a SPUFI input data set that contains the statements you need to reverse the changes your program made or to rebuild the test table from scratch.

The last two columns in figure 10-16 show the options you can use to do this most efficiently. One set lets you display the contents of the test tables, and the other doesn't. For both sets of recommendations, I've assumed that the statements in your input data set have already been tested. When that's the case, you don't have to edit them within SPUFI and you can specify NO for the EDIT INPUT option. When you use either of these combinations of options, SPUFI begins to execute your input data set immediately after you press enter from the SPUFI main menu. Because you will have already tested the SQL statements in the input data set and because you want the changes to be kept, you should specify YES for AUTOCOMMIT.

Because the last two sets of options don't involve editing the input data set and take advantage of AUTOCOMMIT, they can be quite efficient from your point of view. In fact, if you specify NO for BROWSE OUTPUT, using this approach to manage your test data is as simple as keying in the name of the proper input data set on the SPUFI main menu and pressing enter. (This is true, of course, only after you've already verified the operation of the statements in the input data set.)

Discussion

SPUFI is a valuable tool that you'll use often as you develop application programs that process DB2 data. Although you can argue that its interface could be more elegant, it's a practical product that you'll get used to quickly and come to depend on.

However, SPUFI is limited in the ways it can format and present output. As a result, you may want to use another IBM product to display the contents of your test tables: Query Management Facility. With QMF, you can easily produce formatted reports with control breaks. That can make it even easier for you to identify and extract the information you need as you test your programs. In *Part 2: An Advanced Course*, I'll show you how to use QMF.

Terms

SPUFI
SQL Processor Using File Input

Objectives

1. Access SPUFI from the DB2I Primary Options Menu.

2. Use SPUFI to key in, execute, and evaluate SQL statements.

3. Use appropriate combinations of SPUFI processing options for different program development tasks.

Throughout this book, I've used the SQL INCLUDE statement to copy library members that contain host variable definitions created by DCLGEN into my programs. In many shops, data base administration personnel are responsible for creating DCLGEN output. If that's the case, you don't need to learn how to do it. But if you do have to create DCLGEN output, don't worry; it's easy. In this topic, I'll show you how by presenting the DB2I panel you can use to work with DCLGEN and examples of DCLGEN output.

An overview of DCLGEN

DCLGEN can improve your productivity for two reasons. First, it can save you coding time. When you include DCLGEN output in your program, you don't have to code host variables for the DB2 data your program will process. And second, because DCLGEN extracts the information it needs to create host variable definitions directly from the DB2 catalog, you can be sure those definitions will be accurate.

DCLGEN can create host variable definitions for COBOL, COBOL II, PL/I, and C/370. The value you specified on the DB2I Defaults panel determines which language DCLGEN uses. (If you don't remember the Defaults panel, you can look back to figure 10-4 to refresh your memory.) Because I used COBOL II as the default language, DCLGEN will automatically create COBOL host variable definitions when I use it.

How to specify DCLGEN options

Figure 10-17 shows how to access DCLGEN: Select option 2 from the DB2I Primary Option Menu. When you do, the DCLGEN panel, shown in part 1 of figure 10-18, appears. As you can see, you supply three kinds of information through the DCLGEN panel. First, you identify the table that you want to create host variables for (options 1 and 2). Second, you name the data set that will contain the declarations DCLGEN will create (options 3 and 4). And third, you specify processing options for the DCLGEN run (options 5 through 8).

DCLGEN can create declarations for tables and views. You identify both in the same way. In part 1 of figure 10-18, I've specified the customer table. The name includes both my DB2 identifier (MMADBV) and the name of the table itself (CUST). The second item on the panel, AT LOCATION, lets you

```
                            DBZI PRIMARY OPTION MENU
  ===> 2_

  Select one of the following DB2 functions and press ENTER.

     1   SPUFI                    (Process SQL statements)
     2   DCLGEN                   (Generate SQL and source language declarations)
     3   PROGRAM PREPARATION      (Prepare a DB2 application program to run)
     4   PRECOMPILE               (Invoke DB2 precompiler)
     5   BIND/REBIND/FREE         (BIND, REBIND, or FREE application plans)
     6   RUN                      (RUN an SQL program)
     7   DB2 COMMANDS             (Issue DB2 commands)
     8   UTILITIES                (Invoke DB2 utilities)
     D   DBZI DEFAULTS            (Set global parameters)
     X   EXIT                     (Leave DB2I)




     F1=HELP       F2=SPLIT      F3=END       F4=RETURN    F5=RFIND     F6=RCHANGE
     F7=UP         F8=DOWN       F9=SWAP      F10=LEFT     F11=RIGHT    F12=RETRIEVE
```

Figure 10-17   The DB2I Primary Option Menu choice for DCLGEN is 2

specify a DB2 subsystem (other than your default subsystem) where the table resides. Usually, you'll leave this item blank.

The output DCLGEN creates may be a sequential data set or, more likely, a member in a partitioned data set. In the example in part 1 of figure 10-18, I specified that the output should be stored in a member named CUST in a partitioned data set named DCLGENS.COBOL. Unless you code quotes around it, TSO combines your user-id with the data set name you specify. So, because my TSO user-id is MMA002, the output data set DCLGEN will use is MMA002.DCLGENS.COBOL. If the data set has a password, you must supply it on item 4.

Any sequential data set you name should have 80-character records, and it must exist before you run DCLGEN. You can create a new partitioned data set member with DCLGEN, as long as the library that will contain it has already been allocated.

The first DCLGEN option, ACTION, lets you specify what DCLGEN should do if it tries to create a library member with a name that's already in use. If you specify ADD, DCLGEN only lets you add a new member to the destination data set. On the other hand, if you specify REPLACE, DCLGEN

Part 1

To use DCLGEN, you specify the name of the table you want to access, the data set where DCLGEN will store the output it produces, and the processing options you want to use.

```
                             DCLGEN
===>

Enter table name for which declarations are required:
 1  SOURCE TABLE NAME ===> MMADBU.CUST
 2  AT LOCATION ..... ===>                              (Optional)

Enter destination data set:          (Can be sequential or partitioned)
 3  DATA SET NAME ... ===> DCLGENS.COBOL(CUST)
 4  DATA SET PASSWORD ===>           (If password protected)

Enter options as desired:
 5  ACTION .......... ===> REPLACE   (ADD new or REPLACE old declaration)
 6  COLUMN LABEL .... ===> NO        (Enter YES for column label)
 7  STRUCTURE NAME .. ===> CUSTOMER-ROW_                (Optional)
 8  FIELD NAME PREFIX ===>                              (Optional)




 F1=HELP      FZ=SPLIT     F3=END      F4=RETURN    F5=RFIND     F6=RCHANGE
 F7=UP        F8=DOWN      F9=SWAP     F10=LEFT     F11=RIGHT    F1Z=RETRIEVE
```

Part 2

It only takes DCLGEN a moment to produce its output. When it's complete, it displays a status message. Then, you press enter to go back to the DCLGEN panel.

```
DSNE905I EXECUTION COMPLETE, MEMBER CUST ADDED
***
```

Figure 10-18   Creating DCLGEN output

```
********************************************************************
*  DCLGEN  TABLE(MMADBV.CUST)                                      *
*          LIBRARY(MMA002.DCLGENS.COBOL(CUST))                     *
*          ACTION(REPLACE)                                         *
*          STRUCTURE(CUSTOMER-ROW)                                 *
*          APOST                                                   *
********************************************************************
      EXEC SQL DECLARE MMADBV.CUST TABLE
      ( CUSTNO                          CHAR(6) NOT NULL,
        FNAME                           CHAR(20) NOT NULL,
        LNAME                           CHAR(30) NOT NULL,
        ADDR                            CHAR(30) NOT NULL,
        CITY                            CHAR(20) NOT NULL,
        STATE                           CHAR(2) NOT NULL,
        ZIPCODE                         CHAR(10) NOT NULL
      ) END-EXEC.
********************************************************************
*  COBOL DECLARATION FOR TABLE MMADBV.CUST                         *
********************************************************************
01  CUSTOMER-ROW.
    10  CUSTNO            PIC X(6).
    10  FNAME             PIC X(20).
    10  LNAME             PIC X(30).
    10  ADDR              PIC X(30).
    10  CITY              PIC X(20).
    10  STATE             PIC X(2).
    10  ZIPCODE           PIC X(10).
********************************************************************
*  THE NUMBER OF COLUMNS DESCRIBED BY THIS DECLARATION IS 7        *
********************************************************************
```

Figure 10-19   Typical DCLGEN output

will delete the old library member if one already exists with the name you specified for the new member. Usually, you'll use REPLACE.

The last three options let you control the format of the host variable definitions DCLGEN creates. The defaults for these items are NO for COLUMN LABEL and blank for both STRUCTURE NAME and FIELD NAME PREFIX. If you don't supply a value for STRUCTURE NAME, DCLGEN appends the name of the table to the characters DCL. (For example, the default name for the DCLGEN output for the CUST table would be DCLCUST). In part 1 of figure 10-18, I've keyed in another value, CUSTOMER-ROW, for STRUCTURE-NAME.

When I pressed the enter key from the panel in part 1 of figure 10-18, DCLGEN was invoked. After just a couple of seconds, it displayed the message in part 2 of the figure. As you can see, this run was successful.

Figure 10-19 shows the output it created. You've seen this DCLGEN output throughout this book, so it won't seem new to you now. DCLGEN

```
                              DCLGEN
    ===>

    Enter table name for which declarations are required:
    1   SOURCE TABLE NAME ===> MMADBV.CUST
    2   AT LOCATION ..... ===>                              (Optional)

    Enter destination data set:          (Can be sequential or partitioned)
    3   DATA SET NAME ... ===> DCLGENS.COBOL(CUST1)
    4   DATA SET PASSWORD ===>            (If password protected)

    Enter options as desired:
    5   ACTION .......... ===> REPLACE    (ADD new or REPLACE old declaration)
    6   COLUMN LABEL .... ===> NO         (Enter YES for column label)
    7   STRUCTURE NAME .. ===> CUSTOMER-ROW                 (Optional)
    8   FIELD NAME PREFIX ===> CR-                          (Optional)




    F1=HELP      F2=SPLIT     F3=END       F4=RETURN    F5=RFIND     F6=RCHANGE
    F7=UP        F8=DOWN      F9=SWAP      F10=LEFT     F11=RIGHT    F12=RETRIEVE
```

Figure 10-20   Creating DCLGEN output with a field-name prefix

used the names of the columns in the table as the names for the host variable definitions it created. Also, it used the STRUCTURE NAME value I specified (CUSTOMER-ROW) as the name of the group item for these fields.

You're less likely to use the other two options that affect the format of DCLGEN's output. COLUMN LABEL causes DCLGEN to include values the DBA coded with SQL LABELS ON statements. (LABELS ON lets the DBA add a short comment, 30 characters or less, to the catalog entry for a column). Although the COLUMN LABEL option changes the way DCLGEN's output looks, it doesn't affect the host variables it contains. That's because it adds labels as comments. I don't recommend this option because it produces more cluttered output and doesn't improve the usability of the output.

Unlike the COLUMN LABEL option, the FIELD-NAME-PREFIX *does* affect the way DCLGEN creates host variables. However, it's not very useful. Figures 10-20 and 10-21 show a DCLGEN panel that specifies this option and the output that results.

You can specify a string up to 28 characters long for the FIELD-NAME-PREFIX option. In figure 10-20, I keyed in CR-. Then, instead of using column names as host variable names, DCLGEN simply appended a

```
*********************************************************************
* DCLGEN TABLE(MMADBV.CUST)                                        *
*        LIBRARY(MMA002.DCLGENS.COBOL(CUST1))                      *
*        ACTION(REPLACE)                                           *
*        NAMES(CR-)                                                *
*        STRUCTURE(CUSTOMER-ROW)                                   *
*        APOST                                                     *
* ... IS THE DCLGEN COMMAND THAT MADE THE FOLLOWING STATEMENTS     *
*********************************************************************
      EXEC SQL DECLARE MMADBV.CUST TABLE
      ( CUSTNO                          CHAR(6) NOT NULL,
        FNAME                           CHAR(20) NOT NULL,
        LNAME                           CHAR(30) NOT NULL,
        ADDR                            CHAR(30) NOT NULL,
        CITY                            CHAR(20) NOT NULL,
        STATE                           CHAR(2) NOT NULL,
        ZIPCODE                         CHAR(10) NOT NULL
      ) END-EXEC.
*********************************************************************
* COBOL DECLARATION FOR TABLE MMADBV.CUST                          *
*********************************************************************
 01   CUSTOMER-ROW.
 *                          CUSTNO
      10 CR-1                   PIC X(6).
 *                          FNAME
      10 CR-2                   PIC X(20).
 *                          LNAME
      10 CR-3                   PIC X(30).
 *                          ADDR
      10 CR-4                   PIC X(30).
 *                          CITY
      10 CR-5                   PIC X(20).
 *                          STATE
      10 CR-6                   PIC X(2).
 *                          ZIPCODE
      10 CR-7                   PIC X(10).
*********************************************************************
* THE NUMBER OF COLUMNS DESCRIBED BY THIS DECLARATION IS 7         *
*********************************************************************
```

Figure 10-21   DCLGEN output with field-name prefixes

different number for each column to the prefix. The names of the columns associated with each host variable are included in the DCLGEN output, but as comments.

The names DCLGEN creates when you supply a value for FIELD-NAME-PREFIX aren't meaningful. Therefore, I don't recommend that you use this option. Even worse, if the structure of the table changes, new DCLGEN output could change host-variable names you use in your programs. Then, program statements that refer to the old names would have to be modified. This is error-prone and unnecessary work.

Discussion

If you need to change the contents of the output file DCLGEN creates, you can use the ISPF editor. For example, you might want to let DCLGEN create a starting member that contains proper host variable field definitions (PICTURE and USAGE clauses.) Then, you can edit the member so the names it uses follow your shop's programming standards. Also, you might want to add a block of comments to a DCLGEN item to provide in-line documentation.

Objectives

1. Access DCLGEN from the DB2I Primary Option Menu.

2. Use DCLGEN to create library members with host variable definitions for the tables you process in your programs.

After you've coded a COBOL program that will process DB2 data, you need to go through several steps to get it ready for testing. You can use DB2I's Program Preparation panel, and the panels subordinate to it, to control the whole process. To describe *all* of the details about the processing features you can manage with these panels would take an entire book. As a result, I'm going to focus only on the items that you're likely to need to modify on these panels. For more in-depth information about the facilities this topic introduces, refer to IBM's DB2 manuals or your shop experts.

How to access the Program Preparation panel

To access the Program Preparation panel, you need to invoke DB2I, as I described in topic 1. Then, select option 3, as figure 10-22 illustrates. When you do, you'll see the panel in figure 10-23. This is the main menu for the complete program development process.

On this panel, you specify options that apply to all program development steps, and you request just the steps you want to perform. In figure 10-23, I've shaded the steps I'll cover in this topic: PRECOMPILE, BIND, COMPILE OR ASSEMBLE, and LINK. Two of the other four are covered elsewhere in this chapter (CHANGE DEFAULTS in topic 1 and RUN in topic 5). The other two are for program development in languages other than COBOL. (PL/I MACRO PHASE, obviously, is for PL/I program development, and PRELINK is for C program development.)

Program preparation options

The first six items on the Program Preparation panel let you set options for the session that apply to all of the steps you request. As with the other DB2I panels, when you make an entry for one of these items, it's maintained, even if you log off. So, once you make a setting, it remains in effect until you change it to something else.

The first option, INPUT DATA SET NAME, specifies the data set that contains the source code for the program you want to prepare for execution. The data set can be sequential or partitioned. Most likely, you'll want to access a member of a partitioned data set. In the example in figure 10-23, I specified the member CUSTINQ in the data set DB2PROG.COBOL. Unless you code the data set name between quotes, TSO combines your user-id

```
                              DBZI PRIMARY OPTION MENU
      ===> 3_

      Select one of the following DBZ functions and press ENTER.

          1   SPUFI                    (Process SQL statements)
          Z   DCLGEN                   (Generate SQL and source language declarations)
          3   PROGRAM PREPARATION      (Prepare a DBZ application program to run)
          4   PRECOMPILE               (Invoke DBZ precompiler)
          5   BIND/REBIND/FREE         (BIND, REBIND, or FREE application plans)
          6   RUN                      (RUN an SQL program)
          7   DBZ COMMANDS             (Issue DBZ commands)
          8   UTILITIES                (Invoke DBZ utilities)
          D   DBZI DEFAULTS            (Set global parameters)
          X   EXIT                     (Leave DBZI)




          F1=HELP       FZ=SPLIT      F3=END       F4=RETURN    F5=RFIND     F6=RCHANGE
          F7=UP         F8=DOWN       F9=SWAP      F10=LEFT     F11=RIGHT    F1Z=RETRIEVE
```

Figure 10-22   The DB2I Primary Option Menu choice for Program Preparation is 3

with it. So, DB2I will use MMA002.DB2PROG.COBOL(CUSTINQ) in this
example.

The second option, DATA SET NAME QUALIFIER, provides a value
that's used as a qualifier in the names of any work data sets the steps of the
program preparation process create. The default is TEMP, so you'll see
names like TEMP.DBRM and TEMP.COBOL in the messages that appear as
you prepare a program through DB2I. In each session, the data in these
data sets is replaced with current data. So unless you need to keep the data
sets produced during program development, there's no reason to supply a
value other than TEMP. But if you do supply another value, it can't be
more than eight characters long.

PREPARATION ENVIRONMENT, the third option, lets you control
whether the program is submitted for preparation as a batch job or prepared in the TSO foreground. TSO foreground preparation is likely to be
faster than background preparation. However, it's a costly process. Some
shops prohibit programmers from developing programs in the foreground
and insist that they use background jobs. So, although FOREGROUND is
the default, you may need to override it with either BACKGROUND or
EDITJCL.

```
                        DBZ PROGRAM PREPARATION
  ===>

  Enter the following:
  1   INPUT DATA SET NAME .... ===> DBZPROG.COBOL(CUSTINQ)
  Z   DATA SET NAME QUALIFIER  ===> TEMP       (For building data set names)
  3   PREPARATION ENVIRONMENT  ===> FOREGROUND (FOREGROUND, BACKGROUND, EDITJCL)
  4   RUN TIME ENVIRONMENT ... ===> TSO        (TSO, CICS, IMS)
  5   STOP IF RETURN CODE >=   ===> 8          (Lowest terminating return code)
  6   OTHER OPTIONS ===>

  Select functions:          Display panel?      Perform function?
  7   CHANGE DEFAULTS ........ ===> N  (Y/N)      .............
  B   PL/I MACRO PHASE ....... ===> N  (Y/N)      ===> N  (Y/N)
  9   PRECOMPILE ............. ===> Y  (Y/N)      ===> Y  (Y/N)
  10  CICS COMMAND TRANSLATION ....  .....        ===> N  (Y/N)
  11  BIND ................... ===> Y  (Y/N)      ===> Y  (Y/N)
  12  COMPILE OR ASSEMBLE .... ===> Y  (Y/N)      ===> Y  (Y/N)
  13  PRELINK ................ ===> N  (Y/N)      ===> N  (Y/N)
  14  LINK ................... ===> Y  (Y/N)      ===> Y  (Y/N)
  15  RUN .................... ===> N  (Y/N)      ===> N  (Y/N)

  F1=HELP      FZ=SPLIT     F3=END      F4=RETURN   F5=RFIND    F6=RCHANGE
  F7=UP        F8=DOWN      F9=SWAP     F10=LEFT    F11=RIGHT   F1Z=RETRIEVE
```

Figure 10-23   The DB2I Program Preparation menu

If you choose BACKGROUND or EDITJCL, a batch job is prepared for submission. BACKGROUND causes the JOB statement you coded on the DB2I Defaults panel (presented in topic 1) to be used, and a job is constructed and submitted immediately. EDITJCL, on the other hand, lets you use ISPF EDIT to change the job, then explicitly issues a SUBMIT command for it.

The fourth option, RUN TIME ENVIRONMENT lets you specify whether your program will run under TSO, CICS, or IMS. In this topic, I'll just cover programs that will run under TSO. This setting applies to batch programs invoked via JCL as well as to interactive programs that will run under TSO, because batch programs are processed through a TSO interface.

Each of the program development steps you request depends on the success of the ones that precede it. If a step early in the process fails, the ones that follow are sure to fail too, and it doesn't make sense to invoke them. So the fifth item in the panel in figure 10-23, STOP IF RETURN CODE, lets you specify a return code value at or above which DB2I should automatically stop the program development process. The value I specified, 8, is right for most circumstances, and I recommend it for you.

The last item in this group, OTHER OPTIONS, lets you specify options for the DSNH CLIST. DB2I invokes DSNH to perform its program preparation functions. You can usually leave this item blank.

Program preparation functions

The Program Preparation panel also lets you select the panels DB2I will display and the program development functions it will perform during your session. For each of the steps of the program preparation process, DB2I lets you specify in the "Display panel?" column whether you want to adjust processing options for the step, and it lets you specify in the "Perform function?" column whether you actually want to perform the step.

This approach can save you time. After you've set the options for each step properly, you don't need to deal with them again unless you want to change them. Because the values you supply on the Program Preparation panel are automatically carried through the subordinate panels for each step, you can often simply name your source code file in this panel and disable all of the other panel displays.

When you press the enter key from the Program Preparation panel in figure 10-23, DB2I proceeds by displaying the screens you requested in the "Display panel?" column. After it has worked through each of those, it begins to execute the steps you requested in the "Perform function?" column. If you want to cancel the process, you can press the PA1 key. Of course, if one of the steps produces a return code greater than or equal to the value you specified for the STOP IF RETURN CODE field, DB2I stops the process automatically.

Precompile   Figure 10-24 shows the first panel you'd see after pressing enter from the Program Preparation panel in figure 10-23: the Precompile panel. The precompiler adds code you specify in INCLUDE statements (like the SQLCA and DCLGEN output) to your program, verifies and translates SQL statements into COBOL (which has to be compiled in a subsequent step), and builds a *data base request module* (*DBRM*) that the bind process uses.

The panel in figure 10-24 is the same one you see if you select option 4 from the DB2I Primary Option Menu to access the precompiler directly. However, when you access the panel through Program Preparation, some of the items on it are automatically set to agree with values you specified on the Program Preparation panel. INPUT DATA SET (the file that contains your original COBOL source code), DSNAME QUALIFIER (the qualifier added to the name of temporary data sets), and WHERE TO COMPILE all fall into this category. If you specified values for these items on the

```
                              PRECOMPILE
 ===>

 Enter precompiler data sets:
  1  INPUT DATA SET .... ===> DB2PROG.COBOL(CUSTINQ)
  2  INCLUDE LIBRARY ... ===> DCLGENS.COBOL

  3  DSNAME QUALIFIER .. ===> TEMP        (For building data set names)
  4  DBRM DATA SET ..... ===>

 Enter processing options as desired:
  5  WHERE TO PRECOMPILE ===> FOREGROUND  (FOREGROUND, BACKGROUND, or EDITJCL)
  6  OTHER OPTIONS ..... ===>




     F1=HELP       F2=SPLIT      F3=END       F4=RETURN    F5=RFIND      F6=RCHANGE
     F7=UP         F8=DOWN       F9=SWAP      F10=LEFT     F11=RIGHT     F12=RETRIEVE
```

Figure 10-24   The Precompile panel

Program Preparation panel, you can't change them here. You have to return to the Program Preparation panel to change them. An advantage of accessing the precompiler and the other functions you need through the Program Preparation panel is that you can specify global options once, at the
start of a session, rather than repeatedly, once for each function.

A value you are likely to change on the Precompile panel is the
INCLUDE LIBRARY value. It names the partitioned data set that contains
the DCLGEN output your program requests with INCLUDE statements. I
entered DCLGENS.COBOL to direct the precompiler to access
MMA002.DCLGENS.COBOL. Remember, if you don't code a data set name
between quotes, TSO combines your user-id with the name.

The fourth item, DBRM DATA SET, names the library that will hold the
DBRM the precompiler produces. The DBRM is used as input to the bind
step, which constructs an application plan for your program from the
DBRM. For simple applications, there's a one-to-one relationship between
programs and plans. When that's the case, there's no need to keep the
DBRM after the bind is complete, so you can use the name DB2I supplies
for it.

However, in some situations, you'll need to keep the DBRM. In a moment, when I describe the bind process, I'll explain why. If you're working in an environment where DBRMs need to be retained, you should supply a name for this data set. If this is necessary, get the right data set name from your DBA or supervisor. (If you must create a new DBRM library, you need to know that it should contain 80-character records, and those records may be blocked or unblocked.)

The last item on the Precompile panel lets you specify processing options. These are similar to the kinds of options you can supply for the COBOL compiler. For example, you can specify options to indicate whether you use a single or double quote as a delimiter character, or whether the precompiler should produce a source listing. For most applications, the defaults are satisfactory, and you won't need to change them. If you do, just code the proper option value for item 6. Refer to the *IBM DATABASE 2 Command and Utility Reference* manual for more information.

The precompiler generates and displays diagnostic messages at your terminal if it finds any invalid SQL statements in your source program. The messages it displays are usually sufficient to let you find and correct mistakes. If they're not, you can enable the SOURCE option to generate a complete listing for the precompilation. (You'll see an example of a precompiler diagnostic message later in this topic.)

Bind   The bind function builds an *application plan* that specifies how DB2 will access data to process the program's SQL statements. Also, it verifies the SQL statements in your program against the DB2 catalog. As a result, you can receive DB2 errors in the bind process just as you can in the precompile and compile phases.

The data base request module created in the precompile step is a coded representation of the SQL statements in your program. Each program you run must have its own DBRM, and you must bind it into an application plan.

Usually, there's a one-to-one relationship between programs and application plans. When a program is part of a multi-program application, each program still requires a different DBRM, but all of the DBRMs can be combined into a single application plan that describes them all. This can improve overall performance, and it's common for interactive applications. Also, if your program calls a subprogram that issues SQL statements, both need to be precompiled and compiled separately, but their DBRMs need to be combined into a single application plan.

When you run a program, DB2 compares timestamps that are a part of both the application plan and the program load module. If they don't agree, DB2 won't execute your program. Instead, it will return −818 as the SQLCODE.

```
                            BIND
===>

Enter DBRM data set name(s):
  1   LIBRARY(s)   ===> TEMP.DBRM
  2   MEMBER(s)    ===> CUSTINQ
  3   PASSWORD(s) ===>

  4   MORE DBRMS? ===> NO                        (YES to list more DBRMs)

Enter options as desired:
  5   PLAN NAME ............... ===> CUSTINQ    (Required to create a plan)
  6   ACTION ON PLAN .......... ===> REPLACE    (REPLACE or ADD)
  7   RETAIN EXECUTION AUTHORITY ===> YES       (YES to retain user list)
  8   ISOLATION LEVEL ......... ===> CS         (RR or CS)
  9   PLAN VALIDATION TIME ..... ===> BIND       (RUN or BIND)
 10   RESOURCE ACQUISITION TIME  ===> ALLOCATE  (USE or ALLOCATE)
 11   RESOURCE RELEASE TIME .... ===> DEALLOCATE (COMMIT or DEALLOCATE)
 12   EXPLAIN PATH SELECTION ... ===> NO        (NO or YES)
 13   OWNER OF PLAN (AUTHID).... ===> MMA002     (Leave blank for your primary ID)
 14   DEFER PREPARE ........... ===> NO         (NO or YES)


    F1=HELP      F2=SPLIT     F3=END      F4=RETURN    F5=RFIND     F6=RCHANGE
    F7=UP        F8=DOWN      F9=SWAP     F10=LEFT     F11=RIGHT    F12=RETRIEVE
```

Figure 10-25   The Bind panel

Some of the values on the Bind panel, shown in figure 10-25, are based on entries you made on earlier panels. For instance, the name for item 1, LIBRARY, is formed from the data set name qualifier you specified on the Program Preparation panel. You can't change it here. Similarly, the MEMBER (item 2) and PLAN NAME (item 5) values are based on earlier processing, and they can't be changed either.

Most of the items on the Bind panel let you control advanced features. For example, option 12 (EXPLAIN PATH SELECTION) has to do with the SQL EXPLAIN statement, a feature that lets you analyze the performance of a program. Option 14 (DEFER PREPARE) is meaningful only when a program uses dynamic SQL. And options 8, 10, and 11 (ISOLATION LEVEL, RESOURCE ACQUISITION TIME, and RESOURCE RELEASE TIME) are related to concurrency and locking issues. I'll describe what these options do and why you may select different values for them in *Part 2: An Advanced Course.* For now, I suggest you specify the values I've entered in the shaded parts of figure 10-25.

Compile and link   The next steps the Program Preparation panel lets you perform are compile and link. You use the one panel shown in figure

```
╭─────────────────────────────────────────────────────────────────╮
│             PROGRAM PREPARATION: COMPILE, PRELINK, LINK, AND RUN  │
│    ===>                                                           │
│                                                                  │
│    Enter compiler or assembler options:                          │
│    1   INCLUDE LIBRARY ===>                                      │
│    2   INCLUDE LIBRARY ===>                                      │
│    3   OPTIONS ....... ===>                                      │
│                                                                  │
│    Enter prelink and linkage editor options:                     │
│    4   INCLUDE LIBRARY ===>                                      │
│    5   INCLUDE LIBRARY ===>                                      │
│    6   INCLUDE LIBRARY ===>                                      │
│    7   LOAD LIBRARY .. ===> DB2PROG.LOAD                          │
│    8   PRELINK OPTIONS ===>                                      │
│    9   LINK OPTIONS .. ===>                                      │
│                                                                  │
│    Enter run options:                                            │
│    10  PARAMETERS .... ===>                                      │
│    11  SYSIN DATA SET  ===> TERM                                 │
│    12  SYSPRINT DS ... ===> TERM                                 │
│                                                                  │
│                                                                  │
│    F1=HELP      F2=SPLIT     F3=END      F4=RETURN   F5=RFIND    F6=RCHANGE │
│    F7=UP        F8=DOWN      F9=SWAP     F10=LEFT    F11=RIGHT   F12=RETRIEVE │
│                                                                  │
╰─────────────────────────────────────────────────────────────────╯
```

Figure 10-26   The Compile, Prelink, Link, and Run panel

10-26 to specify options for both. As you can see, this panel also lets you specify options for executing your program. However, because I discuss execution separately in the next topic, I'm going to describe only the items for compile and link here.

The first three items on this panel let you control execution of the COBOL compiler. The first two, both labeled INCLUDE LIBRARY, let you name one or two libraries that contain COPY members to be included by the compiler, such as record descriptions for standard files. Because the CUSTINQ program doesn't use any COPY members, I've left these options blank.

The third item, OPTIONS, lets you enter a list of options for the COBOL compiler. You separate the items in the list with spaces or commas. I didn't specify any options in the example in figure 10-26.

The second group of items on this panel is for the linkage editor. You can use the first three items here to name libraries that contain members you want the linkage editor to include as it creates the load module for your program. If your program calls any subprograms, you should name the libraries that contain them here. But, because the CUSTINQ program doesn't require any additional modules, I left items 4, 5, and 6 blank.

The seventh item on this panel names the library where the linkage editor will store the load module it creates. In figure 10-26, I specified DB2PROG.LOAD as the load library. As with the other examples you've seen, TSO will add my user-id to this data set name because I didn't code it between quotes.

The eighth and ninth items let you specify link-edit options. Because prelink applies only to C program development, you should leave the eighth item blank. If you want to specify link options, use item 9, separating the options with spaces or commas.

Both the compiler and the linkage editor produce print data sets. Unless you specified another qualifier for temporary data set names on the Program Preparation panel, DB2 uses the names TEMP.LIST and TEMP.LINKLIST for these data sets. Both will have your TSO user-id as their high level qualifier.

Terminal output from the program preparation process

After you've worked through all of the optional panels you requested on the Program Preparation panel, DB2I performs the steps you specified. As DB2I does this, it displays messages on your terminal to report its progress.

Figure 10-27 shows the terminal output that resulted from the settings I made on the panels in figures 10-23 through 10-26. The first messages were displayed by the precompiler. They include statistics for the precompile step and report the return code it produced. Here, the precompile step generated a zero return code (RC = 0). Notice that the messages report that the print output for the precompiler was stored in TEMP.PCLIST. The precompiler also created a new COBOL source file, TEMP.COBOL, but the messages on the screen in figure 10-27 don't tell you that. (Both data set names begin with the high-level qualifier MMA002.)

Because the precompile step's return code was less than 8, the value I specified for the STOP IF RETURN CODE option on the Program Preparation panel in figure 10-23, the process continued with the bind step. It too displayed status messages and was successful (RC=0).

After the bind step, the COBOL II compiler was invoked to process TEMP.COBOL, the modified source program the precompiler created. In this example, the compile step was successful too, as the zero return code indicates. The message for this step reports that the compiler listing was stored in the data set TEMP.LIST. Because these messages filled the screen, TSO displayed three asterisks to direct me to press enter to continue to review the output. When I did, the screen in part 2 of figure 10-27 appeared.

The screen in part 2 shows a control statement that was passed to the linkage editor, and a line that reports that the linkage editor executed

Part 1

The messages displayed
for the precompile, bind,
and compile steps.

```
SOURCE STATISTICS
   SOURCE LINES READ: 118
   NUMBER OF SYMBOLS: 28
   SYMBOL TABLE BYTES EXCLUDING ATTRIBUTES: 2216
THERE WERE 0 MESSAGES FOR THIS PROGRAM.
THERE WERE 0 MESSAGES SUPPRESSED BY THE FLAG OPTION.
110744 BYTES OF STORAGE WERE USED BY THE PRECOMPILER.
RETURN CODE IS 0
DSNH740I ======= PRECOMPILER FINISHED, RC =  0 ======= LISTING IN TEMP.PCLIST =
==============================
DSNT252I <  BIND OPTIONS FOR PLAN CUSTINQ
                  ACTION    REPLACE RETAIN
                  OWNER     MMA002
                  VALIDATE  BIND
                  ISOLATION CS
                  ACQUIRE   ALLOCATE
                  RELEASE   DEALLOCATE
                  EXPLAIN   NO
DSNT253I <  BIND OPTIONS FOR PLAN CUSTINQ
                  NODEFER           PREPARE
DSNT200I <   BIND FOR PLAN CUSTINQ  SUCCESSFUL
DSNH740I ======= BIND FINISHED, RC =  0 ==============================
DSNH740I ======= COB2 FINISHED, RC =  0 ======= LISTING IN TEMP.LIST ==========
***
```

Part 2

After I pressed the enter
key, a message reported
that the link-edit step
was successful.

```
===================
IEW0000     INCLUDE DSNHOBJ

DSNH740I ======= LINK FINISHED, RC =  0 ======= LISTING IN TEMP.LINKLIST ======
==========================
***
```

Figure 10-27   Message output produced during program preparation

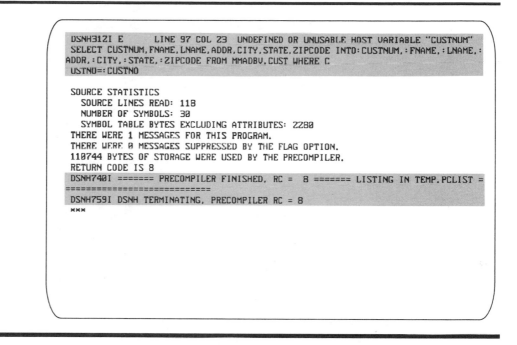

```
DSNH312I E       LINE 97 COL 23  UNDEFINED OR UNUSABLE HOST VARIABLE "CUSTNUM"
SELECT CUSTNUM,FNAME,LNAME,ADDR,CITY,STATE,ZIPCODE INTO:CUSTNUM,:FNAME,:LNAME,:
ADDR,:CITY,:STATE,:ZIPCODE FROM MMADBV.CUST WHERE C
USTNO=:CUSTNO

SOURCE STATISTICS
  SOURCE LINES READ: 118
  NUMBER OF SYMBOLS: 30
  SYMBOL TABLE BYTES EXCLUDING ATTRIBUTES: 2280
THERE WERE 1 MESSAGES FOR THIS PROGRAM.
THERE WERE 0 MESSAGES SUPPRESSED BY THE FLAG OPTION.
110744 BYTES OF STORAGE WERE USED BY THE PRECOMPILER.
RETURN CODE IS 8
DSNH740I ======= PRECOMPILER FINISHED, RC =  8 ======= LISTING IN TEMP.PCLIST =
============================
DSNH759I DSNH TERMINATING, PRECOMPILER RC = 8
***
```

Figure 10-28   A program-preparation session that ended with errors during the precompile step

successfully. Its print output was stored in the data set TEMP.LINKLIST. When I press enter from the screen in part 2 of the figure, the Program Preparation panel appears again, and I can start another session, request another DB2I function, or leave DB2I altogether.

Figure 10-27 illustrated a completely successful program preparation session. When a steps fails, what you see differs. For example, figure 10-28 shows the display that would result if the source program contained an SQL statement with an error the precompiler could detect. In this example, I changed the name of the column CUSTNO to CUSTNUM. (That's the sort of mistake that's easy to make if you're not completely familiar with the column names in the tables your program processes.)

The precompiler detected this error because the DCLGEN output it included for the CUST table contained the correct names of the table's columns. The message the precompiler displayed shows the faulty statement and the line number in the source program where it appears. Although this error message isn't formatted in an elegant way, it's informative enough to let you find the error in your source code and correct it.

Because this is a serious error, the precompiler's return code wasn't 0, but 8. As a result, DB2I skipped the remaining steps in the program

development session. The same thing can happen in the bind, compile, or
link-edit step if a serious processing error occurs.

Submitting a background job through the Program Preparation panel

Many shops don't let programmers do foreground program development
work, because it's more efficient to prepare and submit jobs for execution
in the background. You can direct DB2I to prepare a batch job if you specify either BACKGROUND or EDITJCL for the third option on the Program
Preparation panel. In either case, DB2I uses your specifications to construct a job that will perform the tasks you requested. As I mentioned earlier in this topic, they differ in that BACKGROUND automatically submits
the job, while EDITJCL invokes ISPF EDIT to let you review and modify the
job stream before you submit it.

Figure 10-29 show three screens from a session where I used this
facility. As you can see in part 1 of the figure, I specified EDITJCL and
turned off all of the "Display panel?" options. When I pressed enter, DB2I
built the job stream in a data set named MMA002.TEMP.CNTL and entered
ISPF EDIT.

Part 2 of the figure shows the EDIT screen and the first part of the job.
You might be surprised to discover that the job stream doesn't invoke programs like the precompiler and the linkage editor as separate job steps. Instead, a single job step invokes the TSO *Terminal Monitor Program* (*TMP*),
named IKJEFT01. The in-line data supplied for the SYSTSIN data set contains values you could enter through line-mode TSO to perform these tasks.
The job invokes a TSO CLIST called DSNH to perform the program development functions I requested. You can change any of the many options of
DSNH at this point, but you probably won't need to if you specified the
proper options on the Program Preparation panels.

I reviewed the options on the screens in parts 2 and 3 of the figure.
Then, from the screen in part 3, I keyed in the SUBMIT command to EDIT
to submit the job for processing. The message at the bottom of the screen
in part 3 acknowledges that the job was submitted and shows the job number assigned to it. To monitor the job's progress and review its print output,
I'd use the TSO OUTLIST facility.

Discussion

Although the interactive facilities of DB2 let you perform program development tasks easily, you may not always be allowed to use them. As I mentioned, foreground program development work may be prohibited in your
shop some or all of the time. As a result, you may need to know how to use

Part 1

Program Preparation
panel options for a
background job.

```
                          DB2 PROGRAM PREPARATION
 ===>

 Enter the following:
 1   INPUT DATA SET NAME .... ===> DB2PROG.COBOL(CUSTINQ)
 2   DATA SET NAME QUALIFIER  ===> TEMP        (For building data set names)
 3   PREPARATION ENVIRONMENT  ===> EDITJCL     (FOREGROUND, BACKGROUND, EDITJCL)
 4   RUN TIME ENVIRONMENT ... ===> TSO         (TSO, CICS, IMS)
 5   STOP IF RETURN CODE >=   ===> 8           (Lowest terminating return code)
 6   OTHER OPTIONS ===>

 Select functions:          Display panel?        Perform function?
 7   CHANGE DEFAULTS ........ ===> N  (Y/N)        .............
 8   PL/I MACRO PHASE ....... ===> N  (Y/N)      ===> N  (Y/N)
 9   PRECOMPILE ............. ===> N  (Y/N)      ===> Y  (Y/N)
 10  CICS COMMAND TRANSLATION ....  .  .....     ===> N  (Y/N)
 11  BIND ................... ===> N  (Y/N)      ===> Y  (Y/N)
 12  COMPILE OR ASSEMBLE .... ===> N  (Y/N)      ===> Y  (Y/N)
 13  PRELINK ................ ===> N  (Y/N)      ===> N  (Y/N)
 14  LINK ................... ===> N  (Y/N)·     ===> Y  (Y/N)
 15  RUN .................... ===> N  (Y/N)      ===> N  (Y/N)

 F1=HELP       F2=SPLIT      F3=END       F4=RETURN    F5=RFIND     F6=RCHANGE
 F7=UP         F8=DOWN       F9=SWAP      F10=LEFT     F11=RIGHT    F12=RETRIEVE
```

Part 2

After you press enter, you
modify the job with ISPF
EDIT.

```
 EDIT ---- MMA002.TEMP.CNTL ------------------------------------- COLUMNS 001 072
 COMMAND ===>                                                   SCROLL ===> PAGE
 ****** ***************************** TOP OF DATA ******************************
 000001 //MMA002D JOB ...
 000002 //TMP      EXEC PGM=IKJEFT01,DYNAMNBR=20
 000003 //SYSTSPRT DD SYSOUT=*
 000004 //SYSPRINT DD SYSOUT=*
 000005 //SYSTSIN  DD *
 000006 PROFILE    PREFIX(MMA002)
 000007 ALLOC      DD(SYSPROC) DSN('SYS4.DB2.PROD.VB.DSNCLIST') SHR
 000008 %DSNH BIND(YES) ACQUIRE(USE) ACTION(REPLACE)-
 000009  EXPLAIN(NO) -
 000010   NODEFER(PREPARE)-
 000011  CICSXLAT(NO)-
 000012  COMPILE(YES) -
 000013  DECIMAL(PERIOD) DELIMIT(DEFAULT) FLAG(I)-
 000014  HOST(COB2) ISOLATION(RR)-
 000015  INPUT(DB2PROG.COBOL(CUSTINQ))-
 000016  LINECOUNT(50) LINK(YES)-
 000017  LOAD(DB2PROG.LOAD)-
 000018  MACRO(NO) OUTNAME(TEMP)-
 000019  PRELINK(NO) -
 F1=HELP       F2=SPLIT      F3=END       F4=RETURN    F5=RFIND     F6=RCHANGE
 F7=UP         F8=DOWN       F9=SWAP      F10=LEFT     F11=RIGHT    F12=RETRIEVE
```

Figure 10-29   Using a background program-preparation job

Part 3

When you're done, key
in SUBMIT in the
command area and
press enter.

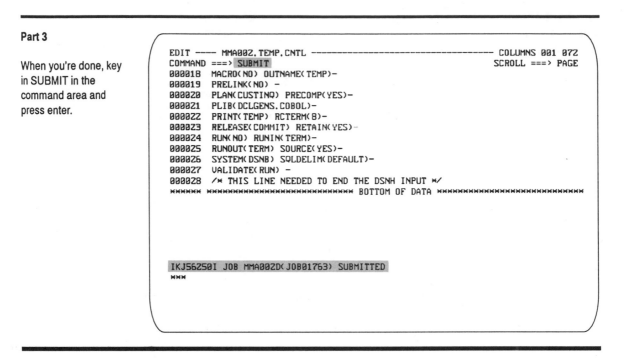

```
EDIT ---- MMA002.TEMP.CNTL ------------------------------- COLUMNS 001 072
COMMAND ===> SUBMIT                                       SCROLL ===> PAGE
000018  MACRO(NO) OUTNAME(TEMP)-
000019  PRELINK(NO) -
000020  PLAN(CUSTINQ) PRECOMP(YES)-
000021  PLIB(DCLGENS.COBOL)-
000022  PRINT(TEMP) RCTERM(8)-
000023  RELEASE(COMMIT) RETAIN(YES)-
000024  RUN(NO) RUNIN(TERM)-
000025  RUNOUT(TERM) SOURCE(YES)-
000026  SYSTEM(DSNB) SQLDELIM(DEFAULT)-
000027  VALIDATE(RUN) -
000028  /* THIS LINE NEEDED TO END THE DSNH INPUT */
****** *************************** BOTTOM OF DATA ***********************************




IKJ56250I JOB MMA002D(JOB01763) SUBMITTED
***
```

Figure 10-29   Using a background program-preparation job (continued)

batch facilities. The BACKGROUND and EDITJCL options of the Program
Preparation panel provide just one way to do program development in
batch. In the next chapter, I'll show you how to code your own job streams
for basic program development tasks.

Terms

data base request module
DBRM
application plan
Terminal Monitor Program
TMP

Objectives

1. Use the Program Preparation panel to specify the options for, and per-
    form the steps necessary to precompile, bind, compile, and link-edit a
    DB2 application program in the TSO foreground.

2. Use the Program Preparation panel to specify the options for a background job that will precompile, bind, compile, and link-edit a DB2 application program.

How to run a program under DB2I

After you've worked through the Program Preparation panels I presented in the last topic, you're ready to test your program. In this topic, I'll show you how to do that using DB2I.

DB2I provides two ways to run a program. One is as the last step of the Program Preparation process. I don't recommend this approach. It's usually easier to set up the Program Preparation environment for the steps I described in the last topic and to handle testing separately. So, in this topic, I'll show you how to use the second way: DB2I's Run panel.

How to access the Run panel

To access the Run panel, you need to invoke DB2I, as I described in topic 1. Then, select option 6, as figure 10-30 illustrates. When you press enter, the Run panel, shown in figure 10-31, appears.

The Run panel has two sets of options. You use the first set to identify the program you want to run. In the example in figure 10-31, I specified the program I used to illustrate program preparation in the last topic, the CUSTINQ member in the MMA002.DB2PROG.LOAD data set. (Remember, TSO adds your user-id to the beginning of a data set name if you don't code the data set name between quotes.) The second item, PASSWORD, is necessary only if your program is password protected. In this example, a password wasn't necessary.

The second group of options on the Run panel has three items. The first, PARAMETERS, lets you enter data that is passed to your program at execution time. The second, PLAN NAME, identifies the application plan created for the program during the bind process. In the example in figure 10-31, I supplied the application plan name. However, I didn't have to because its name is the same as the program name.

The last option lets you control where the program executes. I specified FOREGROUND in figure 10-31, so the program will execute under TSO. The other options for this item, BACKGROUND and EDITJCL, both cause DB2I to construct a batch job that will execute your program. These options work the same way here that they do on the Program Preparation panel I presented in the last topic: BACKGROUND causes the job to be submitted immediately, while EDITJCL lets you review and change it with ISPF EDIT before you submit it.

```
                              DB2I PRIMARY OPTION MENU
    ===> 6_

    Select one of the following DB2 functions and press ENTER.

    1   SPUFI                     (Process SQL statements)
    2   DCLGEN                    (Generate SQL and source language declarations)
    3   PROGRAM PREPARATION       (Prepare a DB2 application program to run)
    4   PRECOMPILE                (Invoke DB2 precompiler)
    5   BIND/REBIND/FREE          (BIND, REBIND, or FREE application plans)
    6   RUN                       (RUN an SQL program)
    7   DB2 COMMANDS              (Issue DB2 commands)
    8   UTILITIES                 (Invoke DB2 utilities)
    D   DB2I DEFAULTS             (Set global parameters)
    X   EXIT                      (Leave DB2I)




    F1=HELP       F2=SPLIT      F3=END        F4=RETURN     F5=RFIND      F6=RCHANGE
    F7=UP         F8=DOWN       F9=SWAP       F10=LEFT      F11=RIGHT     F12=RETRIEVE
```

Figure 10-30   The DB2I Primary Option Menu choice for running a program is 6

Allocating data sets

You don't have to do anything special to allocate the data sets that contain the DB2 tables you want to access, because they're managed by DB2. However, if your program uses any standard data sets, such as VSAM files, you need to allocate them before you execute the program. To do that, you use the TSO ALLOCATE command. When you issue an ALLOCATE command, you have to specify at least two things: the name your program uses to refer to the data set (for the DDNAME option) and the name MVS uses to refer to it (for the DSNAME option).

For example, the update programs I presented in chapters 4 and 9 used a VSAM input file that contained transaction records and created a VSAM output file that contained invalid transaction records. To run these programs, I had to allocate those data sets. The programs used the name BADTRAN to refer to the output data set. I used four different output data sets as I tested these programs, named MMA002.BADTRAN1, MMA002.BADTRAN2, MMA002.BADTRAN3, and MMA002.BADTRAN4. To use the first of these files in a test run, I issued the TSO command

```
ALLOC DDNAME(BADTRAN) DSNAME(BADTRAN1)
```

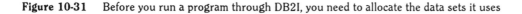

```
                                    RUN
===> TSO ALLOC DDNAME(SYSOUT) DSNAME(*);TSO ALLOC DDNAME(SYSIN) DSNAME(*)_

Enter the name of the program you want to run:
 1  DATA SET NAME ===> DBZPROG.LOAD(CUSTINQ)
 2  PASSWORD .... ===>              (Required if data set is password protected)

Enter the following as desired:
 3  PARAMETERS .. ===>
 4  PLAN NAME ... ===> CUSTINQ   (Required if different from program name)
 5  WHERE TO RUN  ===> FOREGROUND (FOREGROUND, BACKGROUND, or EDITJCL)








NOTE : Information for running command processors is on the HELP panel.
 F1=HELP      F2=SPLIT      F3=END       F4=RETURN    F5=RFIND     F6=RCHANGE
 F7=UP        F8=DOWN       F9=SWAP      F10=LEFT     F11=RIGHT    F12=RETRIEVE
```

Figure 10-31   Before you run a program through DB2I, you need to allocate the data sets it uses

Notice that I didn't code the high-level qualifier for the data set name.
That's because TSO automatically adds your user-id to a data set name if
the name isn't in quotes. The update programs also required a similar
allocation for the input transaction data set.

Some DB2 programs, such as the CUSTINQ program I used in figure
10-31, don't need to access standard data sets at all. However, the
CUSTINQ program does issue COBOL ACCEPT and DISPLAY statements,
and they require allocations: SYSIN for ACCEPT and SYSOUT for
DISPLAY. Because I wanted to use my TSO terminal for ACCEPT and
DISPLAY input and output, I issued two ALLOCATE commands with an
asterisk as the value for the DSNAME option for each. The command line
in figure 10-31 shows how I allocated those data sets.

The example in figure 10-31 illustrates not just the syntax of
ALLOCATE, but two other points you need to know. First, you issue a
native TSO command through ISPF by entering *TSO* before it. Second, you
can enter more than one TSO command at a time, if there's room in the
command line. Just separate the commands with a semicolon.

When you enter a TSO command in the ISPF command area, it's processed instead of the panel itself. So, when I press enter on the panel in

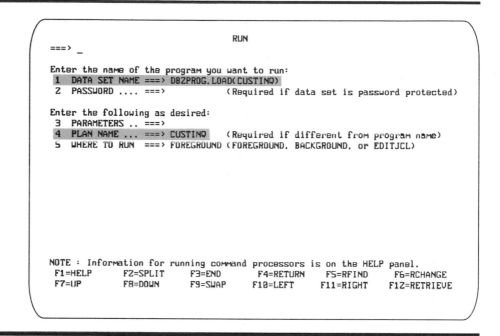

Figure 10-32 Press enter after you have allocated data sets and specified the proper data set name and application plan name

figure 10-31, the allocations are performed, but the program isn't invoked yet. Instead, the Run panel appears again, as shown in figure 10-32. If I needed to enter more allocations, I could key them in here.

Allocation can be more complicated if you're creating a new data set. Then, you have to supply the same sort of values that would be necessary on the JCL DD statement for a new file. I'm not going to cover those items here. For more information, you can refer to Doug Lowe's *MVS TSO, Part 2: Commands and Procedures.*

Running a program

After you've allocated your data sets and made sure that the Run panel options are correct, you can press enter. When I pressed enter on the panel in figure 10-32, my application program was loaded and executed. Figure 10-33 shows a sample of my interactions with it.

When a program you invoke from the Run panel ends, control returns to DB2I, and a message appears on the Run panel that reports the final status code for the execution. Although the message isn't particularly useful when you run a simple interactive program like CUSTINQ, it's more

```
 ------------------------------------------------
 KEY IN THE NEXT CUSTOMER NUMBER AND PRESS ENTER,
 OR KEY IN 999999 AND PRESS ENTER TO QUIT.
 400010
 ------------------------------------------------
    CUSTOMER 400010
    NAME      ENRIQUE              OTHON
    ADDRESS   BOX 29729
              RICHMOND             VA 23261
 ------------------------------------------------
 KEY IN THE NEXT CUSTOMER NUMBER AND PRESS ENTER,
 OR KEY IN 999999 AND PRESS ENTER TO QUIT.
 400020
 ------------------------------------------------
    CUSTOMER NUMBER 400020 NOT FOUND.
 ------------------------------------------------
 KEY IN THE NEXT CUSTOMER NUMBER AND PRESS ENTER,
 OR KEY IN 999999 AND PRESS ENTER TO QUIT.
 999999_
```

Figure 10-33   If you allocate SYSIN and SYSOUT data sets to your terminal, you can run simple interactive programs through DB2I

important when you execute a more complicated program that doesn't do any screen input or output. When that's the case, the operation of the program is behind the scenes, and the only feedback you get at your terminal is that message.

Discussion

I think it may be anticlimactic for you to see how little there is to executing a program, because you have to go through a lot of steps to get to that point. However, take my word...when you've successfully executed your first program, it will feel like a real accomplishment.

Although you may be able to use DB2I to test your programs, the chances are just as good that your shop standards will require you to do program tests through batch jobs. If you wish, you can use DB2I's Run panel to generate the background JCL. However, because you'll need to add DD statements to allocate the data sets your program will use, you'll probably want to create the JCL yourself. So, in the next chapter, I'll describe how to code and submit the JCL necessary to run a DB2 program in the background.

Objectives

1. Issue TSO ALLOCATE commands to allocate existing data sets an application program uses.

2. Use the Run panel to execute a DB2 program in the TSO foreground.

Chapter 11

How to do program development work outside DB2I

Even though DB2I provides a convenient way for you to do program-development work, some shops restrict its use for performance reasons. In this chapter, I'll show you how to code batch jobs to precompile, compile, link, bind, and execute COBOL programs that process DB2 data. Also, I'll show you a TSO alternative to using DB2I to bind and execute programs.

Although this chapter presents model CLISTs and job streams that you can use on your system, it doesn't present all you need to know about TSO and MVS job control language. For more information, you can refer to two of Doug Lowe's books: *MVS TSO, Part 2: Commands and Procedures* and *MVS JCL*.

How to use the DB2 cataloged procedures for program development

DB2 provides two cataloged procedures you can use to precompile, compile, and link COBOL programs: DSNHCOB (for VS COBOL programs) and

DSNHCOB2 (for VS COBOL II programs). Figures 11-1 and 11-2 present these procedures. The two procedures are similar, and because both procedures use the same ddnames for the data sets they process, the jobs you code to invoke them are nearly identical.

Figure 11-3 summarizes the processing done by both procedures. Each step of these procedures requires several data sets. Most are standard system data sets, and if the procedures are set up properly in your shop, you won't need to worry about most of them. However, you may need to provide DD statements for the data sets I've included in figure 11-3.

For the precompile step, PC, you must provide a DD statement for SYSIN, and you may need to provide them for SYSLIB and DBRMLIB as well. The SYSIN data set contains your original COBOL source code and is the primary input to the precompiler. This will probably be a member of a partitioned data set.

The precompiler looks in the data set you associate with the ddname SYSLIB for members your program requests with SQL INCLUDE statements. So, you should name the library that contains the DCLGEN output your program uses on the SYSLIB DD statement. Finally, the precompiler stores the *DBRM* (*data base request module*) it creates in the data set you specify on the DD statement for DBRMLIB.

The second step, COB, invokes the COBOL compiler. You probably don't need to supply any overriding DD statements for this step.

The last step, LKED, link-edits your program. You may need to provide DD statements for the LKED step for the SYSLMOD and SYSIN data sets. SYSLMOD identifies the load library where the linkage editor will store the load module it creates for your program. The SYSIN data set in the LKED step contains linkage editor control statements. For a DB2 program you plan to run in batch or directly under TSO, you must provide an INCLUDE statement for an interface module called DSNELI.

Figure 11-4 shows sample jobs to invoke the procedures in figures 11-1 and 11-2. The first invokes the VS COBOL procedure (DSNHCOB) and the second invokes the VS COBOL II procedure (DSNHCOB2). Except for the names of the procedures in the EXEC statements, the two jobs in figure 11-4 are identical.

Each EXEC statement not only invokes the procedure, but also supplies values for two symbolic parameters: MEM and USER. The procedures use these values to construct data set names. MEM supplies the name of the partitioned data set members the procedure will process, and USER provides the high-level qualifier for the names of those data sets. In the examples in figure 11-4, I specified my program name (CUSTINQ) for MEM and my TSO user-id (MMA002) for USER. Figure 11-5 shows the data set names that resulted.

```
//************************************************************************
//*         DSNHCOB - COMPILE AND LINKEDIT A COBOL PROGRAM
//*
//DSNHCOB PROC WSPC=500,MEM=TEMPNAME,USER=USER
//*
//*              PRECOMPILE THE COBOL PROGRAM
//************************************************************************
//PC        EXEC PGM=DSNHPC,PARM='HOST(COBOL)',REGION=4096K
//DBRMLIB   DD   DISP=OLD,DSN=&USER..DBRMLIB.DATA(&MEM)
//STEPLIB   DD   DISP=SHR,DSN=DSN220.DSNEXIT
//          DD   DISP=SHR,DSN=DSN220.DSNLOAD
//SYSCIN    DD   DSN=&&DSNHOUT,DISP=(MOD,PASS),UNIT=SYSDA,
//               SPACE=(800,(&WSPC,&WSPC))
//SYSLIB    DD   DISP=SHR,DSN=&USER..SRCLIB.DATA
//SYSPRINT  DD   SYSOUT=*
//SYSTERM   DD   SYSOUT=*
//SYSUDUMP  DD   SYSOUT=*
//SYSUT1    DD   SPACE=(800,(&WSPC,&WSPC),,,ROUND),UNIT=SYSDA
//SYSUT2    DD   SPACE=(800,(&WSPC,&WSPC),,,ROUND),UNIT=SYSDA
//*
//*              COMPILE THE COBOL PROGRAM IF THE PRECOMPILE
//*              RETURN CODE IS 4 OR LESS
//*
//COB       EXEC PGM=IKFCBL00,COND=(4,LT,PC)
//SYSIN     DD   DSN=&&DSNHOUT,DISP=(OLD,DELETE)
//*SYSLIB   DD   DSN=CICS170.COBLIB,DISP=SHR
//SYSLIN    DD   DSN=&&LOADSET,DISP=(MOD,PASS),UNIT=SYSDA,
//               SPACE=(800,(&WSPC,&WSPC))
//SYSPRINT  DD   SYSOUT=*
//SYSUDUMP  DD   SYSOUT=*
//SYSUT1    DD   SPACE=(800,(&WSPC,&WSPC),,,ROUND),UNIT=SYSDA
//SYSUT2    DD   SPACE=(800,(&WSPC,&WSPC),,,ROUND),UNIT=SYSDA
//SYSUT3    DD   SPACE=(800,(&WSPC,&WSPC),,,ROUND),UNIT=SYSDA
//SYSUT4    DD   SPACE=(800,(&WSPC,&WSPC),,,ROUND),UNIT=SYSDA
//*
//*              LINKEDIT IF THE PRECOMPILE AND COMPILE
//*              RETURN CODES ARE 4 OR LESS
//*
//LKED      EXEC PGM=IEWL,PARM='XREF',
//               COND=((4,LT,COB),(4,LT,PC))
//SYSLIB    DD   DSN=SYS1.COBLIB,DISP=SHR
//          DD   DISP=SHR,
//               DSN=DSN220.DSNLOAD
//*         DD   DISP=SHR,DSN=IMSVS.RESLIB
//*         DD   DISP=SHR,DSN=CICS170.LOADLIB
//*         DD   DISP=SHR,DSN=ISP.V2R3M0.ISPLOAD CAF SAMPLE NEEDS ISPLINK
//SYSLIN    DD   DSN=&&LOADSET,DISP=(OLD,DELETE)
//          DD   DDNAME=SYSIN
//SYSLMOD   DD   DISP=OLD,DSN=&USER..RUNLIB.LOAD(&MEM)
//SYSPRINT  DD   SYSOUT=*
//SYSUDUMP  DD   SYSOUT=*
//SYSUT1    DD   SPACE=(1024,(50,50)),UNIT=SYSDA
//*DSNHCOB PEND               REMOVE * FOR USE AS INSTREAM PROCEDURE
```

Figure 11-1   The DSNHCOB cataloged procedure (for VS COBOL)

```
//*******************************************************************************
//*         DSNHCOB2 - COMPILE AND LINKEDIT A COBOL PROGRAM
//*
//DSNHCOB2 PROC WSPC=500,MEM=TEMPNAME,USER=USER
//*
//*                PRECOMPILE THE COBOL PROGRAM
//*******************************************************************************
//PC       EXEC PGM=DSNHPC,PARM='HOST(COB2)',REGION=4096K
//DBRMLIB  DD   DISP=OLD,DSN=&USER..DBRMLIB.DATA(&MEM)
//STEPLIB  DD   DISP=SHR,DSN=DSN220.DSNEXIT
//         DD   DISP=SHR,DSN=DSN220.DSNLOAD
//SYSCIN   DD   DSN=&&DSNHOUT,DISP=(MOD,PASS),UNIT=SYSDA,
//              SPACE=(800,(&WSPC,&WSPC))
//SYSLIB   DD   DISP=SHR,DSN=&USER..SRCLIB.DATA
//SYSPRINT DD   SYSOUT=*
//SYSTERM  DD   SYSOUT=*
//SYSUDUMP DD   SYSOUT=*
//SYSUT1   DD   SPACE=(800,(&WSPC,&WSPC),,,ROUND),UNIT=SYSDA
//SYSUT2   DD   SPACE=(800,(&WSPC,&WSPC),,,ROUND),UNIT=SYSDA
//*
//*              COMPILE THE COBOL PROGRAM IF THE PRECOMPILE
//*              RETURN CODE IS 4 OR LESS
//*
//COB      EXEC PGM=IGYCRCTL,COND=(4,LT,PC)
//SYSIN    DD   DSN=&&DSNHOUT,DISP=(OLD,DELETE)
//STEPLIB  DD   DSN=SYS1.V1R3.COB2COMP,DISP=SHR
//*SYSLIB  DD   DSN=CICS170.COBLIB,DISP=SHR
//SYSLIN   DD   DSN=&&LOADSET,DISP=(MOD,PASS),UNIT=SYSDA,
//              SPACE=(800,(&WSPC,&WSPC))
//SYSPRINT DD   SYSOUT=*
//SYSUDUMP DD   SYSOUT=*
//SYSUT1   DD   SPACE=(800,(&WSPC,&WSPC),,,ROUND),UNIT=SYSDA
//SYSUT2   DD   SPACE=(800,(&WSPC,&WSPC),,,ROUND),UNIT=SYSDA
//SYSUT3   DD   SPACE=(800,(&WSPC,&WSPC),,,ROUND),UNIT=SYSDA
//SYSUT4   DD   SPACE=(800,(&WSPC,&WSPC),,,ROUND),UNIT=SYSDA
//SYSUT5   DD   SPACE=(800,(&WSPC,&WSPC),,,ROUND),UNIT=SYSDA
//SYSUT6   DD   SPACE=(800,(&WSPC,&WSPC),,,ROUND),UNIT=SYSDA
//SYSUT7   DD   SPACE=(800,(&WSPC,&WSPC),,,ROUND),UNIT=SYSDA
//*
//*              LINKEDIT IF THE PRECOMPILE AND COMPILE
//*              RETURN CODES ARE 4 OR LESS
//*
//LKED     EXEC PGM=IEWL,PARM='XREF',
//              COND=((4,LT,COB),(4,LT,PC))
//SYSLIB   DD   DSN=SYS1.V1R3.COB2LIB,DISP=SHR
//         DD   DISP=SHR,
//              DSN=DSN220.DSNLOAD
//*        DD   DISP=SHR,DSN=IMSVS.RESLIB
//*        DD   DISP=SHR,DSN=CICS170.LOADLIB
//*        DD   DISP=SHR,DSN=ISP.V2R3M0.ISPLOAD CAF SAMPLE NEEDS ISPLINK
//SYSLIN   DD   DSN=&&LOADSET,DISP=(OLD,DELETE)
//         DD   DDNAME=SYSIN
//SYSLMOD  DD   DISP=OLD,DSN=&USER..RUNLIB.LOAD(&MEM)
//SYSPRINT DD   SYSOUT=*
//SYSUDUMP DD   SYSOUT=*
//SYSUT1   DD   SPACE=(1024,(50,50)),UNIT=SYSDA
//*DSNHCOB2 PEND            REMOVE * FOR USE AS INSTREAM PROCEDURE
```

Figure 11-2   The DSNHCOB2 cataloged procedure (for VS COBOL II)

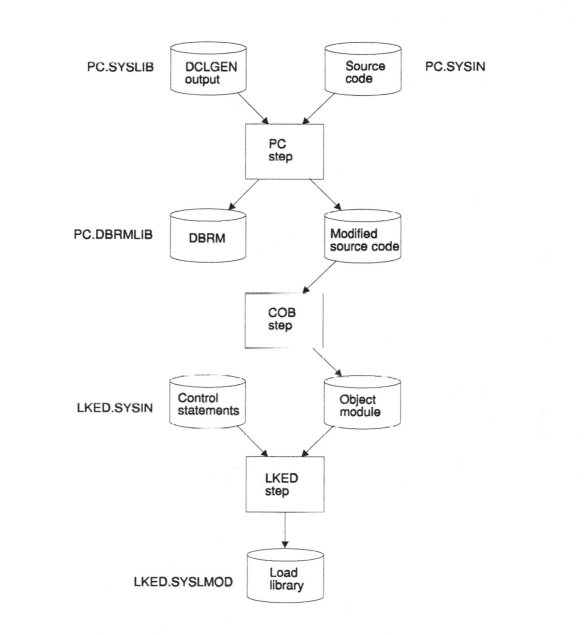

PC.SYSLIB — DCLGEN output

Source code — PC.SYSIN

PC step

PC.DBRMLIB — DBRM

Modified source code

COB step

LKED.SYSIN — Control statements

Object module

LKED step

LKED.SYSLMOD — Load library

Figure 11-3   The ddnames from the DSNHCOB and DSNHCOB2 cataloged procedures you need to know

JCL to invoke the DSNHCOB cataloged procedure (VS COBOL)

```
//MMA002X  JOB  (xxxx),'SECKOLS',CLASS=R,TIME=(1),MSGCLASS=R
//PCCL      EXEC  DSNHCOB,
//              MEM=CUSTINQ,
//              USER=MMA002,
//              PARM.PC='HOST(COBOL),QUOTE,SOURCE,XREF',
//              PARM.COB  'QUOTE,SOURCE,SXREF,NODYNAM',
//              PARM.LKED='LIST,XREF'
//PC.DBRMLIB    DD  DSNAME=MMA002.DB2PROG.DBRMS(CUSTINQ),DISP=SHR
//PC.SYSLIB     DD  DSNAME=MMA002.DCLGENS.COBOL,DISP=SHR
//PC.SYSIN      DD  DSNAME=MMA002.DB2PROG.COBOL(CUSTINQ),DISP=SHR
//LKED.SYSLMOD  DD  DSNAME=MMA002.DB2PROG.LOAD(CUSTINQ),DISP=SHR
//LKED.SYSIN    DD  *
      INCLUDE  SYSLIB(DSNELI)
/*
```

JCL to invoke the DSNHCOB2 cataloged procedure (VS COBOL II)

```
//MMA002X  JOB  (xxxx),'SECKOLS',CLASS=R,TIME=(1),MSGCLASS=R
//PCCL      EXEC  DSNHCOB2,
//              MEM=CUSTINQ,
//              USER=MMA002,
//              PARM.PC='HOST(COBOL),QUOTE,SOURCE,XREF',
//              PARM.COB='QUOTE,SOURCE,SXREF,NODYNAM',
//              PARM.LKED='LIST,XREF'
//PC.DBRMLIB    DD  DSNAME=MMA002.DB2PROG.DBRMS(CUSTINQ),DISP=SHR
//PC.SYSLIB     DD  DSNAME=MMA002.DCLGENS.COBOL,DISP=SHR
//PC.SYSIN      DD  DSNAME=MMA002.DB2PROG.COBOL(CUSTINQ),DISP=SHR
//LKED.SYSLMOD  DD  DSNAME=MMA002.DB2PROG.LOAD(CUSTINQ),DISP=SHR
//LKED.SYSIN    DD  *
      INCLUDE  SYSLIB(DSNELI)
/*
```

Figure 11-4   Sample JCL to invoke the DSNHCOB and DSNHCOB2 cataloged procedures

The EXEC statements in both jobs in figure 11-4 also supply parameters for each job step. The specific PARM values you code determine how the program that will be executed in each job step works. When a string of parameters includes special characters, you need to bracket the whole list with quotes, as I did in the examples in figure 11-4. You can use the specific parameter values in figure 11-4 as a starting point for the jobs you code. Then, you can refer to the IBM documentation for information about other values you can use for different purposes.

After the EXEC statement in each job in figure 11-4, I coded the overriding DD statements to replace the default data set names the procedures use. (If my program-development libraries followed the naming conventions used by the cataloged procedures, these DD statement overrides wouldn't

Data set	Specification in procedure	As constructed with USER=MMA002 and MEM=CUSTINQ
Precompiler DBRM output	`&USER..DBRMLIB.DATA(&MEM)`	`MMA002.DBRMLIB.DATA(CUSTINQ)`
Source library for precompiler INCLUDEs	`&USER..SRCLIB.DATA`	`MMA002.SRCLIB.DATA`
Load library for linkage editor output	`&USER..RUNLIB.LOAD(&MEM)`	`MMA002.RUNLIB.LOAD(CUSTINQ)`

Figure 11-5   Data set names constructed by the DSNHCOB and DSNHCOB2 cataloged procedures with values from symbolic parameters

be necessary.) Notice for each overriding DD statement, I coded a ddname that has the job step name as a qualifier.

The first three DD statements in the jobs in figure 11-4 are for the precompile step. The last two of the overriding DD statements are for the LKED (link-edit) step. Again, be sure you code a DD statement in the link-edit step for SYSIN. The SYSIN data set must contain an INCLUDE linkage editor statement that specifies the right interface module. For the TSO environment, the name of the module is DSNELI.

How to bind a program

To bind a program, you use the DB2 command DSN and request its BIND subcommand. When you bind a program through DB2I, it constructs control statements for DSN (based on values you entered on the Bind panel) and automatically invokes the command. When you work outside DB2I, you have to supply the control statements and invoke the command yourself.

Figure 11-6 shows a TSO CLIST that does a bind outside DB2I; its name is BINDPROC. The first line in the CLIST is a PROC statement. It defines MEM, the one symbolic variable the procedure uses. The second line invokes the DSN command and names the DB2 subsystem that will be used for the run: DSNB. After you invoke the command, you request the subcommands you want to execute. In figure 11-6, I've requested only one subcommand, BIND, but it's complicated. That's because I've specified a dozen options for it.

```
PROC 1 MEM
DSN SYSTEM(DSNB)
BIND MEMBER      (&MEM) -
     PLAN        (&MEM) -
     LIBRARY     (DB2PROG.DBRMS) -
     ACTION      (REPLACE) -
     RETAIN -
     ISOLATION (CS) -
     VALIDATE    (BIND) -
     ACQUIRE     (USE) -
     RELEASE     (COMMIT) -
     EXPLAIN     (NO) -
     OWNER       (MMA002) -
     NODEFER
END
```

Figure 11-6   Sample TSO CLIST for binding a program

I suggest you use the option values in figure 11-6 as a starting point when you code your own BIND subcommands. That means you can copy the CLIST code in figure 11-6 and use it pretty much as it is. However, you'll want to change the values for the LIBRARY and OWNER options so they're correct for you.

Because I used a symbolic variable for the MEMBER and PLAN options, I was able to generalize the CLIST. When I invoke the CLIST, I specify the name of my COBOL program on the command line. So, to invoke this CLIST to bind the CUSTINQ program, I'd issue the command

```
TSO EXEC DB2PROG(BINDPROC) 'CUSTINQ'
```

or, if my CLIST library is allocated properly, simply

```
BINDPROC CUSTINQ
```

Then, TSO substitutes the first parameter from the command line for the symbolic variable. As a result, the CLIST lines

```
BIND MEMBER      (&MEM) -
     PLAN        (&MEM) -
```

are processed as

```
BIND MEMBER      (CUSTINQ) -
     PLAN        (CUSTINQ) -
```

You may want to customize some of the other values, either with different literals in the CLIST or with symbolic variables. You can look back to chapter 10 for a brief discussion of the BIND options, or you can refer to the *IBM Database 2 Reference* manual for all the details if you need them.

Notice that each line of the BIND subcommand except the last ends with the DSN continuation character, a hyphen. You can also code several options on each line. For example,

```
DSN SYSTEM(DSNB)
BIND MEMBER(&MEM) PLAN(&MEM) LIBRARY(DB2PROG.DBRMS) -
     ACTION(REPLACE) RETAIN ISOLATION(CS) -
     VALIDATE(BIND) ACQUIRE(USE) RELEASE(COMMIT) -
     EXPLAIN(NO) OWNER(MMA002) NODEFER
END
```

works just as well as the example in figure 11-6. However, I think you'll agree that it's much less readable.

You can also bind a program in a batch job, but you still need to do it through the TSO DSN command. To issue a TSO command from a batch job, you have to run the TSO *Terminal Monitor Program* (*TMP*).

Figure 11-7 shows a batch job that performs the same bind operation as the CLIST in figure 11-6. In fact, the DSN command and the BIND subcommand options are the same in the two figures. The program name you specify on an EXEC statement to run the TMP is IKJEFT01. You need to provide several DD statements to use the TMP, but you can use the ones in figure 11-7 as a model.

For STEPLIB, you name the DB2 program load library DSNLOAD. The exact data set name you'll use depends on how your shop names DB2 data sets. The name IBM supplies is DSN220.DSNLOAD. (DSN is IBM's identifier for DB2 objects, and 220 refers to the version of DB2: version 2, release 2, modification 0). For DBRMLIB, you specify the data set where the precompiler stored the DBRM for your program. And for SYSTSIN, specify DD *. SYSTSIN is the data set that contains the DSN command and the BIND subcommand with its options. In figure 11-7, it's an in-stream data set.

You may want to combine a job like the one in figure 11-7 with JCL that invokes the DSNHCOB or DSNHCOB2 procedure. At the end of this chapter, I'll show you a job stream that combines not only the precompile, compile, and link functions with bind, but also with execute.

How to execute a program

To run a DB2 program outside DB2I, you use the DSN command and request its RUN subcommand. As when you use DSN to perform a bind, you can issue the command directly within TSO, or you can invoke it through the TMP in batch.

```
//MMA002X   JOB (xxxx),'SECKOLS',CLASS=R,TIME=(1),MSGCLASS=R
//BIND      EXEC PGM=IKJEFT01,DYNAMNBR=20
//STEPLIB   DD   DSNAME=DSN220.DSNLOAD,DISP=SHR
//SYSTSPRT  DD   SYSOUT=*
//SYSPRINT  DD   SYSOUT=*
//SYSUDUMP  DD   SYSOUT=*
//SYSOUT    DD   SYSOUT=*
//DBRMLIB   DD   DSN=MMA002.DB2PROG.DBRMS(CUSTINQ),DISP=SHR
//SYSTSIN   DD   *
DSN SYSTEM(DSNB)
BIND MEMBER    (CUSTINQ) -
     PLAN      (CUSTINQ) -
     LIBRARY   (DB2PROG.DBRMS) -
     ACTION    (REPLACE) -
     RETAIN -
     ISOLATION (CS) -
     VALIDATE  (BIND) -
     ACQUIRE   (USE) -
     RELEASE   (COMMIT) -
     EXPLAIN   (NO) -
     OWNER     (MMA002) -
     NODEFER
END
/*
```

Figure 11-7   Sample JCL for binding a program

Figure 11-8 shows two TSO CLISTs that execute DB2 programs. One runs the CUSTINQ program, and the other runs the UPDTROLL program I introduced in chapter 4. You need to provide three options for the RUN subcommand. The first option is the name of the program itself, and you use the PROGRAM keyword to specify it. In the first example in figure 11-8, the line

```
RUN PROGRAM(CUSTINQ) -
```

directs DSN to run the program named CUSTINQ. The second option you specify is the application plan for the program you created during the bind process. The line

```
PLAN(CUSTINQ) -
```

in the first example names the application plan CUSTINQ. And finally, you need to identify the library that contains the program load module the linkage editor created. The line

```
LIBRARY(DB2PROG.LOAD)
```

does this in the first example. As with other data set names you specify within TSO, if you don't surround the name with quotes, TSO adds your

CLIST to execute the CUSTINQ program

```
ALLOC DD(SYSOUT) DSN(*)
ALLOC DD(SYSIN) DSN(*)
DSN SYSTEM(DSNB)
  RUN PROGRAM(CUSTINQ) -
      PLAN(CUSTINQ)     -
      LIBRARY(DB2PROG.LOAD)
  END
FREE DD(SYSOUT)
FREE DD(SYSIN)
```

CLIST to execute the UPDTROLL program

```
ALLOC DD(CUSTTRAN) DSN(CT1)
ALLOC DD(BADTRAN) DSN(BADTRAN1)
ALLOC DD(SYSOUT) DSN(*)
DSN SYSTEM(DSNB)
  RUN PROGRAM(UPDTROLL) -
      PLAN(UPDTROLL)     -
      LIBRARY(DB2PROG.LOAD)
  END
FREE DD(CUSTTRAN)
FREE DD(BADTRAN)
FREE DD(SYSOUT)
```

Figure 11-8   Sample TSO CLISTs for executing programs

user-id to it as a qualifier. So, in the first example, DSN will retrieve and run the load module MMA002.DB2PROG.LOAD(CUSTINQ).

In addition to the lines the DSN command requires, I also included TSO ALLOCATE and FREE commands for the data sets the CUSTINQ and UPDTROLL programs need. The CUSTINQ program uses the terminal to interact with the user through ACCEPT and DISPLAY statements. For this to work, I allocated the ddnames SYSIN (for ACCEPT) and SYSOUT (for DISPLAY) to the terminal in the first example in figure 11-8. For example, in

```
ALLOC DD(SYSIN) DSN(*)
```

DSN(*) specifies that the terminal should be used for SYSIN operations.

The UPDTROLL program uses DISPLAY statements, so I included an ALLOCATE command for SYSOUT in the second example in figure 11-8. In addition, this program requires two VSAM data sets. The program uses the ddnames CUSTTRAN and BADTRAN for them, and the names of the data sets are MMA002.CT1 and MMA002.BADTRAN1. The two ALLOCATE commands

```
ALLOC DD(CUSTTRAN) DSN(CT1)
ALLOC DD(BADTRAN) DSN(BADTRAN1)
```

associate the ddnames and the data set names. Again, because I didn't enclose the data set names between quotes, TSO adds my user-id to them as a high-level qualifier to form the complete data set names.

Both CLISTs in figure 11-8 end with TSO FREE commands to release the data sets the programs used. You can identify the allocations you want to release by specifying either the DD option, as I did in the FREE command in the examples in figure 11-8, or by specifying the DSN option.

Figure 11-9 shows batch jobs that run the CUSTINQ and UPDTROLL programs. The JCL required to run a program is even simpler than that required to bind one. As with BIND, you have to supply a STEPLIB DD statement. SYSTSIN provides the control statements for the program run. You need to include DD statements for any data sets, other than tables, your program uses. The DD statements serve the same functions as the ALLOCATE commands in the CLIST examples in figure 11-8.

Frankly, it's unlikely that you'd want to run an interactive program like CUSTINQ in batch. But, if you did, all you would have to do is supply appropriate DD statements for SYSIN and SYSOUT. In the first job in figure 11-9, you can see that I coded the SYSIN data that otherwise would be entered in through the terminal keyboard as in-stream data, defined by

```
//SYSIN DD *
```

The statement

```
//SYSOUT DD SYSOUT=*
```

routes the output that would appear on the terminal screen to the job's print output.

The second example in figure 11-9 runs the batch update program UPDTROLL. It's a model for the kinds of batch jobs you're more likely to code. Because this program uses DISPLAY statements to provide messages, I had to code a DD statement for its SYSOUT output, just as I did for the CUSTINQ program. However, it doesn't use the ACCEPT statement for input, so I didn't need a DD statement for SYSIN. DD statements for the CUSTTRAN and BADTRAN data sets were required. For their DSN parameters, I coded the fully-qualified names for the data sets the program will access. That's because the DD statements in a batch job are evaluated outside TSO and, as a result, qualifiers won't automatically be appended to data set names.

JCL to execute the CUSTINQ program

```
//MMAO02X   JOB (xxxx),'SECKOLS',CLASS=R,TIME=(1),MSGCLASS=R
//RUNPROG   EXEC PGM=IKJEFTO1,DYNAMNBR=20
//STEPLIB   DD   DSNAME=DSN220.DSNLOAD,DISP=SHR
//SYSTSPRT  DD   SYSOUT=*
//SYSTSIN   DD   *
DSN SYSTEM(DSNB)
   RUN PROGRAM(CUSTINQ) -
       PLAN(CUSTINQ)     -
       LIBRARY(DB2PROG.LOAD)
   END
/*
//SYSIN     DD   *
400010
400020
999999
/*
//SYSOUT    DD   SYSOUT=*
```

JCL to execute the UPDTROLL program

```
//MMAO02X   JOB (xxxx),'SECKOLS',CLASS=R,TIME=(1),MSGCLASS=R
//RUNPROG   EXEC PGM=IKJEFTO1,DYNAMNBR=20
//STEPLIB   DD   DSNAME=DSN220.DSNLOAD,DISP=SHR
//SYSTSPRT  DD   SYSOUT=*
//SYSTSIN   DD   *
DSN SYSTEM(DSNB)
   RUN PROGRAM(UPDTROLL) -
       PLAN(UPDTROLL)    -
       LIBRARY(DB2PROG.LOAD)
   END
/*
//CUSTTRAN  DD   DSN=MMAO02.CT1,DISP=SHR
//BADTRAN   DD   DSN=MMAO02.BADTRAN1,DISP=SHR
//SYSOUT    DD   SYSOUT=*
```

Figure 11-9   Sample JCL for executing programs

Combining batch program-development functions into a single job

If you want to combine the precompile, compile, link, bind, and execute steps in one job, all you need to do is put together elements from the model jobs I've shown you in this chapter. Figure 11-10 presents a sample job that does just that.

To create this job, I used code from the job streams that run the DSNHCOB2 procedure (from figure 11-4), that bind a program (figure 11-7), and that execute a program (figure 11-9). You shouldn't have any trouble following how I put these elements together.

I first want you to notice the way I handled the bind and execute functions. Because both use the DSN command, I combined the control statements for them in one execution of the TSO Terminal Monitor Program instead of two. It's unlikely that the bind step would fail, so there's no compelling reason to code the execute function in a separate job step.

However, I didn't want the bind/execute step to be executed if the precompile/compile/link step was unsuccessful. So, I coded

```
COND=(4,LT)
```

on the JOB statement. It specifies that if any step in the job yields a return code greater than 4 (that is, a value that 4 is less than, or LT), then all subsequent steps should be skipped.

If you create a basic job like this, you can use it as a template. Each time you want to prepare a program, all you have to do is modify it so it specifies a different program name. Then, you can submit it for batch execution and review its contents online.

Terms

DBRM
data base request module
Terminal Monitor Program
TMP

Objectives

1. Code and submit a job stream that invokes the DSNHCOB or DSNHCOB2 procedure to precompile, compile, and link a DB2 COBOL program.

2. Use the DSN command through TSO to bind a program.

3. Code and submit a job stream that invokes the terminal monitor program to bind a program.

4. Use the DSN command through TSO to execute a program.

5. Code and submit a job stream that invokes the terminal monitor program to execute a program.

```
//MMA002X JOB (xxxx),'SECKOLS',CLASS=R,TIME=(1),MSGCLASS=R,COND=(4,LT)
//PCCL      EXEC   DSNHCOB,
//                 MEM=UPDTROLL,
//                 USER=MMA002,
//                 PARM.PC='HOST(COBOL),QUOTE,SOURCE,XREF',
//                 PARM.COB='QUOTE,SOURCE,SXREF,NODYNAM',
//                 PARM.LKED='LIST,XREF'
//PC.DBRMLIB   DD DSN=MMA002.DB2PROG.DBRMS(UPDTROLL),DISP=SHR
//PC.SYSLIB    DD DSN=MMA002.DCLGENS.COBOL,DISP=SHR
//PC.SYSIN     DD DSNAME=MMA002.DB2PROG.COBOL(UPDTROLL),DISP=SHR
//LKED.SYSLMOD DD DSNAME=MMA002.DB2PROG.LOAD(UPDTROLL),DISP=SHR
//LKED.SYSIN   DD *
     INCLUDE SYSLIB(DSNELI)
/*
//BINDEXEC    EXEC PGM=IKJEFT01,DYNAMNBR=20
//STEPLIB     DD   DSNAME=DSN220.DSNLOAD,DISP=SHR
//SYSTSPRT    DD   SYSOUT=*
//SYSPRINT    DD   SYSOUT=*
//SYSUDUMP    DD   SYSOUT=*
//SYSOUT      DD   SYSOUT=*
//DBRMLIB     DD   DSN=MMA002.DB2PROG.DBRMS(UPDTROLL),DISP=SHR
//BADTRAN     DD   DSN=MMA002.BADTRAN1,DISP=SHR
//CUSTTRAN    DD   DSN=MMA002.CT1,DISP=SHR
//SYSTSIN     DD   *
DSN SYSTEM(DSNB)
BIND MEMBER     (UPDTROLL)
     PLAN       (UPDTROLL) -
     LIBRARY    (DB2PROG.DBRMS) -
     ACTION     (REPLACE) -
     RETAIN -
     ISOLATION  (CS) -
     VALIDATE   (BIND) -
     ACQUIRE    (USE) -
     RELEASE    (COMMIT) -
     EXPLAIN    (NO) -
     OWNER      (MMA002) -
     NODEFER
RUN  PROGRAM    (UPDTROLL) -
     PLAN       (UPDTROLL) -
     LIBRARY    (DB2PROG.LOAD)
END
/*
```

Figure 11-10   Sample JCL to precompile, compile, link, bind, and execute the UPDTROLL program

Appendix A

SQL statements

This appendix presents the syntax for the SQL statements covered in this book. First, I'll list the statements alphabetically and provide references to the text sections that cover each. Next, I'll show the column specification options that you can use in stand-alone SELECT statements and in the SELECT component of DECLARE CURSOR statements. Then, I'll show the different ways you can code selection conditions in the WHERE clauses of SELECTs and in DELETE and UPDATE statements. And last, I'll show the syntax for specifying unions.

SQL statement syntax

CLOSE

```
EXEC SQL
    CLOSE cursor-name
END-EXEC.
```

> For more information, refer to figure 3-15 on page 71 and the associated text.

COMMIT

```
EXEC SQL
    COMMIT [WORK]
END-EXEC.
```

> For more information, refer to figure 4-17 on page 118 and the associated text.

DECLARE CURSOR

```
EXEC SQL
    DECLARE cursor-name CURSOR FOR
        SELECT [DISTINCT] column-specification[,column-specification...]
                FROM  table-name[ synonym][,table-name[ synonym] ...]
                [WHERE selection-condition]
              [ {FOR UPDATE OF update-column[,update-column...]    } ]
                {ORDER BY sort-column[ DESC][,sort-column[ DESC]...]}
                [GROUP BY column-name[,column-name...]
                [HAVING    selection-condition]]
END-EXEC.
```

> For more information about DECLARE CURSOR, refer to figure 3-12 on page 67 and the associated text.
>
> For more information about GROUP BY and HAVING, refer to figure 6-5 on page 159 and the associated text.
>
> For more information about column-specification, refer to the section on column specification options in this appendix.
>
> For more information about selection-condition, refer to the section on selection conditions in this appendix.
>
> For information about unions, refer to the section on the syntax of the UNION keyword in this appendix.

SQL statement syntax (continued)

DELETE

```
EXEC SQL
    DELETE FROM table-name
    [WHERE {selection-condition    } ]
           {CURRENT OF cursor-name}
END-EXEC.
```

> For more information about DELETE, refer to figure 4-3 on page 92 and the associated text.
>
> For more information about selection-condition, refer to the section on selection conditions in this appendix.

FETCH

```
EXEC SQL
    FETCH cursor-name
          INTO {:host-var[,:host-var...]}
               {:host-structure       }
END-EXEC.
```

> For more information, refer to figure 3-14 on page 70 and the associated text.

INCLUDE statement

```
EXEC SQL
    INCLUDE {member-name}
            {SQLCA      }
END-EXEC.
```

> For more information, refer to figure 2-8 on page 41 and the associated text.

INSERT

```
EXEC SQL
    INSERT INTO table-name [(column-name[,column-name...])]
    {VALUES ({:host-var}  [,{:host-var} ...])}
    {        {literal  }    {literal  }       }
    {        {NULL     }    {NULL     }       }
    {SELECT-statement                         }
END-EXEC.
```

> For more information, refer to figure 4-9 on page 100 and the associated text.
>
> For information about using a SELECT statement within an INSERT statement to do a mass insert, see chapter 4 and chapter 8.

SQL statement syntax (continued)

OPEN

```
EXEC SQL
    OPEN cursor-name
END-EXEC.
```

> For more information, refer to figure 3-13 on page 69 and the associated text.

ROLLBACK

```
EXEC SQL
    ROLLBACK [WORK]
END-EXEC.
```

> For more information, refer to figure 4-18 on page 119 and the associated text.

SELECT (stand-alone)

```
EXEC SQL
    SELECT          column-specification[,column-specification...]
        INTO        {:host-var[,:host-var...]}
                    {:host-structure         }
        FROM        table-name[ synonym][,table-name[ synonym] ...]
        [WHERE      selection-condition]
END-EXEC.
```

> For more information about stand-alone SELECT, refer to figure 3-1 on page 52 and the associated text.
>
> For information about other SELECT options you're not likely to use in stand-alone SELECTs, refer to the entry for DECLARE CURSOR in this appendix.
>
> For more information about column-specification, refer to the section on column specification options in this appendix.
>
> For more information about selection-condition, refer to the section on selection conditions in this appendix.

SQL statement syntax (continued)

UPDATE

```
EXEC SQL
    UPDATE table-name
                            (:host-var  )                    (:host-var  )
    SET     column-name={ literal    } [,column-name={ literal    } ...]
                         { expression }                 { expression }
                            ( NULL     )                    ( NULL     )
            (selection-condition      )
    [WHERE  {CURRENT OF cursor-name}]
END-EXEC.
```

> For more information about UPDATE, refer to figure 4-2 on page 91 and the associated text.
>
> For more information about selection-condition, refer to the section on selection conditions in this appendix.

Column specification options

```
column-name

*

{table-name}
{synonym  } .column-name

{table-name}
{synonym  } .*

:host-var

literal

USER

expression

function
```

> For more information, refer to figure 3-3 on page 54 and the associated text.

WHERE clause selection condition options

With a simple comparison

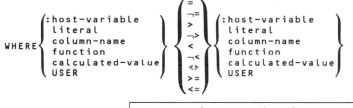

> For more information, refer to figure 3-8 on page 61 and the associated text.

With IN

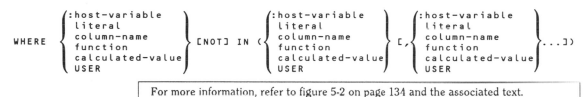

> For more information, refer to figure 5-2 on page 134 and the associated text.

With BETWEEN

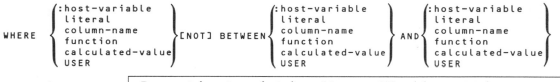

> For more information, refer to figure 5-3 on page 135 and the associated text.

With LIKE

```
WHERE column-name [NOT] LIKE {literal
                              :host-variable
                              USER}
```

> For more information, refer to figure 5-4 on page 136 and the associated text.

WHERE clause selection condition options (continued)

With AND, OR, and NOT

```
WHERE [NOT] selection-condition-1 {AND}  [NOT] selection-condition-2 ...
                                  {OR }
```

> For more information, refer to figure 5-6 on page 140 and the associated text.

With subqueries

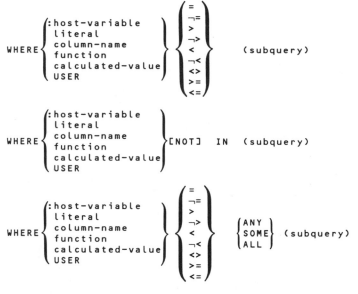

```
WHERE [NOT] EXISTS (subquery)
```

> For more information, refer to figure 8-3 on page 203 and the associated text.

The syntax of the UNION keyword

```
    SELECT-statement
UNION [ALL]
    SELECT-statement

[UNION [ALL]
    SELECT-statement...]

[ORDER BY sort-column[ DESC][,sort-column[ DESC]...]]
```

For more information, refer to figure 7-5 on page 175 and the associated text.

Appendix B

SQLCODE values

This appendix lists SQLCODE values you may encounter during routine program-development work. Many other SQLCODE values can appear in other situations. For other values, refer to the *IBM Database 2 Messages and Codes* manual.

+100   Row not found for FETCH, UPDATE or DELETE, or the result of a query is an empty table. (Under SPUFI, a successful SELECT returns +100.)

000   Successful execution.

−117   The number of INSERT values is not the same as the number of object columns.

−118   The object table or view of the INSERT, DELETE, or UPDATE statement is also identified in a FROM clause.

−119   A column identified in a HAVING clause is not included in the GROUP BY clause.

−121   The column *name* is identified more than once in the INSERT or UPDATE statement.

−122   A SELECT statement with no GROUP BY clause contains a column name and a SQL function in the SELECT clause or a column name is contained in the SELECT clause but not in the GROUP BY clause.

−125   An integer in the ORDER BY clause does not identify a column of the result.

−126   The SELECT statement contains both an UPDATE clause and an ORDER BY clause.

−127   DISTINCT is specified more than once in a subselect.

−128   Invalid use of NULL in a predicate.

−131   Statement with LIKE predicate has incompatible data types.

−132   A LIKE predicate is invalid because the first operand is not a column or the second operand is not a string.

−133   A SQL function in a HAVING clause is invalid because it applies an arithmetic operator to a correlated reference.

−134   Improper use of long string column *column-name* or a host variable of maximum length greater than 254.

−150   The object of the INSERT, DELETE, or UPDATE statement is a view for which the requested operation is not permitted.

−161   The INSERT or UPDATE is not allowed because a resulting row does not satisfy the view definition.

−198 The operand of the PREPARE or EXECUTE IMMEDIATE statement is blank or empty.

−203 A reference to column *column-name* is ambiguous.

−204 *name* is an undefined name.

−205 *column-name* is not a column of table *table-name*.

−206 *column-name* is not a column of an inserted table, updated table, or any table defined in a FROM clause.

−207 The ORDER BY clause is invalid because it includes a column name, but it applies to the result of a union.

−208 The ORDER BY clause is invalid because column *name* is not part of the results table.

−301 The value of a host variable cannot be used as specified because of its data type.

−302 The value of an input variable is too large for the target column.

−303 A value cannot be assigned to a host variable because the data types are not comparable.

−304 A value cannot be assigned to a host variable because the value is not within the range of the data type of the host variable.

−305 The NULL value cannot be assigned to a host variable because no indicator variable is specified.

−309 A predicate is invalid because a referenced host variable has the NULL value.

−312 Undefined or unusable host variable *variable-name*.

−313 The number of host variables specified is not equal to the number of parameter markers.

−401 The operands of an arithmetic or comparison operation are not comparable.

−402 An arithmetic function or operator *arith-item* is applied to character data.

−404 The UPDATE or INSERT statement specifies a string that is too long *column-name*.

−405 The numeric literal *literal* cannot be used as specified because it is out of range.

−406   A calculated or derived numeric value is not within the range of its object column.

−407   An UPDATE or INSERT value, or the value in a predicate is NULL, but the object column *column-name* cannot contain NULL values.

−408   An UPDATE or INSERT value is not comparable with the data type of its object column *column-name*.

−409   Invalid operand of a COUNT function.

−412   The SELECT clause of a subquery specifies multiple columns.

−414   The numeric column *column-name* is specified in a LIKE predicate.

−415   The corresponding columns, *column-number*, of the operands of a UNION do not have identical column descriptions.

−421   The operands of a UNION do not have the same number of columns.

−501   The cursor identified in a FETCH or CLOSE statement is not open.

−502   The cursor identified in an OPEN statement is already open.

−503   A column cannot be updated because it is not specified in the UPDATE clause of the SELECT statement of the cursor.

−504   The cursor name *cursor-name* is not defined.

−507   The cursor identified in the UPDATE or DELETE statement is not open.

−508   The cursor identified in the UPDATE or DELETE statement is not positioned on a row.

−510   The table designated by the cursor of the UPDATE or DELETE statement cannot be modified.

−511   The FOR UPDATE clause cannot be specified because the table designated by the cursor cannot be modified.

−517   Cursor *cursor-name* cannot be used because its statement name does not identify a prepared SELECT statement.

−518   The EXECUTE statement does not identify a valid prepared statement.

−519   The PREPARE statement identifies the SELECT statement of the opened cursor *cursor-name*.

−551   *auth-id* does not have the privilege to perform the operation *operation* on object *object-name*.

-552   *auth-id* does not have the privilege to perform the operation *operation*.

-802   Arithmetic overflow or division by zero has occurred.

-803   One or more INSERT or UPDATE values are invalid because the object columns are constrained such that no rows of the table can be duplicates with respect to the values of those columns.

-811   The result of an embedded SELECT statement is a table of more than one row, or the result of the subquery of a basic predicate is more than one value.

-815   A GROUP BY or HAVING clause is implicitly or explicitly specified in an embedded SELECT statement or a subquery of a basic predicate.

-818   The precompiler-generated timestamp x in the load module is different from the bind timestamp y built from the DBRM.

-901   Unsuccessful execution caused by a system error that does not preclude the successful execution of subsequent SQL statements.

-902   Unsuccessful execution caused by a system error that precludes the successful execution of subsequent SQL statements.

-904   Unsuccessful execution caused by an unavailable resource reason *reason-code*, type of resource *resource-type*, and resource name *resource-name*.

-911   The current unit of work has been rolled back due to deadlock or timeout. Reason *reason-code*, type of resource *resource-type*, and resource name *resource-name*.

-913   Unsuccessful execution caused by deadlock or timeout. Reason *reason-code*, type of resource *resource-type*, and resource name *resource-name*.

Appendix C

DB2 data types and equivalent COBOL field definitions

This appendix presents all of DB2's data types: numeric, character (string), and date and time. The date and time data types are DB2 defaults. They may have been modified at your installation.

Numeric data types

DB2 data type	Kind of data	Description
SMALLINT	Halfword integer data	A halfword integer may contain whole-number values between -32,768 and 32,767. It is always defined in COBOL with COMP usage and PIC S9(4). A typical COBOL definition is:

```
10   INVCOUNT   PIC  S9(4)  COMP.
```

| INTEGER | Fullword integer data | A fullword integer may contain whole-number values between -2,147,483,648 and 2,147,483,647. It is always defined in COBOL with COMP usage and PIC S9(9). A typical COBOL definition is: |

```
10   INVCOUNT   PIC  S9(9)  COMP.
```

| DECIMAL(p,s) | Packed decimal data | A decimal value contains an implicit decimal point. The value p (which cannot be greater than 15) specifies how many digits the number can contain, and the value s specifies how many of those digits are to the right of the implicit decimal point. The abbreviations p and s stand for precision and scale. A typical COBOL definition is: |

```
10   INVTOTAL   PIC  S9(7)V99  COMP-3.
```

This is an appropriate host variable definition for a column defined with DECIMAL(9,2).

| FLOAT(n) | Floating point data | A floating point number, either single-precision (if n is less than 21) or double-precision (if n is between 22 and 53). COBOL definitions do not include a PIC clause and are simply a field name followed by COMP-1 (for single-precision) or COMP-2 (for double-precision). Examples are: |

```
10   SINGLE-PRECISION-NUMBER   COMP-1.

10   DOUBLE-PRECISION-NUMBER   COMP-2.
```

String data types

DB2 data type	Kind of data	Description
CHAR	Fixed-length character (EBCDIC) data	Up to 254 bytes of alphanumeric data. Defined in COBOL as PIC X(n) where n is the number of characters the column contains. A typical example is:

```
01    CUSTNO            PIC X(6).
```

VARCHAR	Variable-length character (EBCDIC) data	A variable amount of alphanumeric data. The number of bytes in the data component is stored in a halfword. A typical COBOL example is:

```
01    NOTES.
      49    NOTES-LEN     PIC S9(4) COMP.
      49    NOTES-TEXT    PIC X(254).
```

The text component has a maximum length of 254 bytes in a "short" VARCHAR column. In a "long" VARCHAR column, which is subject to some processing restrictions, the text component's length can be over 32,000 bytes. The exact maximum length depends on the table's page size and the sizes of the other columns in the table.

GRAPHIC	Fixed-length DBCS data	Up to 127 characters of Double Byte Character Set (DBCS) data. Defined in COBOL with DISPLAY-1 usage and PIC G(n) where n is the number of characters the column contains. A typical example is:

```
01    DBCS-NAME         PIC G(20)
                        DISPLAY-1.
```

VARGRAPHIC	Variable-length DBCS data	A variable amount of DBCS data. The number of characters in the data component is stored in a halfword. A typical COBOL example is:

```
01    EXPL.
      49    EXPL-LEN      PIC S9(4) COMP.
      49    EXPL-TEXT     PIC G(127)
                         DISPLAY-1.
```

The text component has a maximum length of 127 characters in a "short" VARGRAPHIC column. As with VARCHAR, a "long" VARGRAPHIC column can be defined so it stores more characters, but it's subject to some processing restrictions. The exact maximum length depends on the table's page size and the sizes of the other columns in the table.

Date and time data type defaults

DB2 data type	Kind of data	Description
DATE	Date	A 10-byte string. A typical example is:

```
01    INVDATE            PIC X(10).
```

The internal structure of a date item is yyyy-mm-dd. To identify the parts of a DB2 date, you can move the value to a group item like

```
01    EDITED-DATE.
      05   ED-YEAR        PIC X(4).
      05   FILLER         PIC X.
      05   ED-MONTH       PIC XX.
      05   FILLER         PIC X.
      05   ED-DAY         PIC XX.
```

TIME	Time	An 8-byte string. A typical example is:

```
01    START-TIME         PIC X(8).
```

The internal structure of a time item is hh.mm.ss. To identify the parts of a DB2 time, you can move the value to a group item like

```
01    EDITED-TIME.
      05   ET-HOUR        PIC XX.
      05   FILLER         PIC X.
      05   ET-MINUTE      PIC XX.
      05   FILLER         PIC X.
      05   ET-SECOND      PIC XX.
```

TIMESTAMP	Date and time	A 26-byte string. A typical example is:

```
01 START-TIME     PIC X(26).
```

The internal structure of a timestamp item is yyyy-mm-dd-hh.mm.ss.mmmmmm. To identify the parts of a DB2 timestamp, you can move the value to a group item like

```
01    EDITED-TIMESTAMP.
      05   ETS-YEAR       PIC X(4).
      05   FILLER         PIC X.
      05   ETS-MONTH      PIC XX.
      05   FILLER         PIC X.
      05   ETS-DAY        PIC XX.
      05   FILLER         PIC X.
      05   ETS-HOUR       PIC XX.
      05   FILLER         PIC X.
      05   ETS-MINUTE     PIC XX.
      05   FILLER         PIC X.
      05   ETS-SECOND     PIC XX.
      05   FILLER         PIC X.
      05   ETS-MSECOND    PIC X(6).
```

Appendix D

Source code generated by the DB2 precompiler

This appendix presents the source code generated by the DB2 precompiler for the CUSTINQ program introduced in chapter 2.

```
000100 IDENTIFICATION DIVISION.
000200*
000300 PROGRAM-ID.            CUSTINQ.
000400*
000500 ENVIRONMENT DIVISION.
000600*
000700 INPUT-OUTPUT SECTION.
000800*
000900 FILE-CONTROL.
001000*
001100 DATA DIVISION.
001200*
001300 FILE SECTION.
001400*
001500 WORKING-STORAGE SECTION.
001600*
001700 01  SWITCHES.
001800*
001900     05  END-OF-INQUIRIES-SW      PIC X     VALUE "N".
002000         88  END-OF-INQUIRIES                VALUE "Y".
002100     05  CUSTOMER-FOUND-SW        PIC X     VALUE "Y".
002200         88  CUSTOMER-FOUND                 VALUE "Y".
002300*
002400*****EXEC SQL
002500*****    INCLUDE CUST
002600*****END-EXEC.
       ****************************************************************
       * DCLGEN TABLE(MMADBV.CUST)                                    *
       *        LIBRARY(MMA002.DCLGENS.COBOL(CUST))                   *
       *        ACTION(REPLACE)                                       *
       *        STRUCTURE(CUSTOMER-ROW)                               *
       *        APOST                                                 *
       * ... IS THE DCLGEN COMMAND THAT MADE THE FOLLOWING STATEMENTS *
       ****************************************************************
       *****EXEC SQL DECLARE MMADBV.CUST TABLE
       *****( CUSTNO                        CHAR(6) NOT NULL,
       *****  FNAME                         CHAR(20) NOT NULL,
       *****  LNAME                         CHAR(30) NOT NULL,
       *****  ADDR                          CHAR(30) NOT NULL,
       *****  CITY                          CHAR(20) NOT NULL,
       *****  STATE                         CHAR(2) NOT NULL,
       *****  ZIPCODE                       CHAR(10) NOT NULL
       *****) END-EXEC.
       ****************************************************************
       * COBOL DECLARATION FOR TABLE MMADBV.CUST                      *
       ****************************************************************
         01  CUSTOMER-ROW.
             10 CUSTNO             PIC X(6).
             10 FNAME              PIC X(20).
             10 LNAME              PIC X(30).
             10 ADDR               PIC X(30).
             10 CITY               PIC X(20).
             10 STATE              PIC X(2).
             10 ZIPCODE            PIC X(10).
       ****************************************************************
       * THE NUMBER OF COLUMNS DESCRIBED BY THIS DECLARATION IS 7     *
       ****************************************************************
```

```
002700*
002800*****EXEC SQL
002900*****      INCLUDE SQLCA
003000*****END-EXEC.
        01 SQLCA.
           05 SQLCAID      PIC X(8).
           05 SQLCABC      PIC S9(9) COMP-4.
           05 SQLCODE      PIC S9(9) COMP-4.
           05 SQLERRM.
              49 SQLERRML PIC S9(4) COMP-4.
              49 SQLERRMC PIC X(70).
           05 SQLERRP      PIC X(8).
           05 SQLERRD      OCCURS 6 TIMES
                          PIC S9(9) COMP-4.
           05 SQLWARN.
              10 SQLWARN0 PIC X.
              10 SQLWARN1 PIC X.
              10 SQLWARN2 PIC X.
              10 SQLWARN3 PIC X.
              10 SQLWARN4 PIC X.
              10 SQLWARN5 PIC X.
              10 SQLWARN6 PIC X.
              10 SQLWARN7 PIC X.
           05 SQLEXT       PIC X(8).
003100*
        77 SQL-NULL       PIC S9(9) COMP-4 VALUE +0.
        77 SQL-INIT-FLAG PIC S9(4) COMP-4 VALUE +0.
           88 SQL-INIT-DONE VALUE +1.
        01 SQL-PLIST2.
           05 SQL-PLIST-CON   PIC S9(9) COMP-4 VALUE +2656256.
           05 SQL-CALLTYPE    PIC S9(4) COMP-4 VALUE +30.
           05 SQL-PROG-NAME   PIC X(8)         VALUE "CUSTINQ ".
           05 SQL-TIMESTAMP-1 PIC S9(9) COMP-4 VALUE +344718938.
           05 SQL-TIMESTAMP-2 PIC S9(9) COMP-4 VALUE +502709272.
           05 SQL-SECTION     PIC S9(4) COMP-4 VALUE +1.
           05 SQL-CODEPTR     PIC S9(9) COMP-4.
           05 SQL-VPARMPTR    PIC S9(9) COMP-4 VALUE +0.
           05 SQL-APARMPTR    PIC S9(9) COMP-4 VALUE +0.
           05 SQL-STMT-NUM    PIC S9(4) COMP-4 VALUE +94.
           05 SQL-STMT-TYPE   PIC S9(4) COMP-4 VALUE +231.
           05 SQL-PVAR-LIST2.
              10 SQL-PVAR-SIZE  PIC S9(9) COMP-4 VALUE +16.
              10 SQL-PVAR-DESCS.
                 15 SQL-PVAR-TYPE1 PIC S9(4) COMP-4 VALUE +452.
                 15 SQL-PVAR-LEN1  PIC S9(4) COMP-4 VALUE +6.
              10 SQL-PVAR-ADDRS.
                 15 SQL-PVAR-ADDR1 PIC S9(9) COMP-4.
                 15 SQL-PVAR-IND1  PIC S9(9) COMP-4.
           05 SQL-AVAR-LIST2.
              10 SQL-AVAR-SIZE  PIC S9(9) COMP-4 VALUE +88.
              10 SQL-AVAR-DESCS.
                 15 SQL-AVAR-TYPE1 PIC S9(4) COMP-4 VALUE +452.
                 15 SQL-AVAR-LEN1  PIC S9(4) COMP-4 VALUE +6.
              10 SQL-AVAR-ADDRS.
                 15 SQL-AVAR-ADDR1 PIC S9(9) COMP-4.
                 15 SQL-AVAR-IND1  PIC S9(9) COMP-4.
                 15 SQL-AVAR-TYPE2 PIC S9(4) COMP-4 VALUE +452.
                 15 SQL-AVAR-LEN2  PIC S9(4) COMP-4 VALUE +20.
```

```
              15 SQL-AVAR-ADDR2 PIC S9(9) COMP-4.
              15 SQL-AVAR-IND2  PIC S9(9) COMP-4.
              15 SQL-AVAR-TYPE3 PIC S9(4) COMP-4 VALUE +452.
              15 SQL-AVAR-LEN3  PIC S9(4) COMP-4 VALUE +30.
              15 SQL-AVAR-ADDR3 PIC S9(9) COMP-4.
              15 SQL-AVAR-IND3  PIC S9(9) COMP-4.
              15 SQL-AVAR-TYPE4 PIC S9(4) COMP-4 VALUE +452.
              15 SQL-AVAR-LEN4  PIC S9(4) COMP-4 VALUE +30.
              15 SQL-AVAR-ADDR4 PIC S9(9) COMP-4.
              15 SQL-AVAR-IND4  PIC S9(9) COMP-4.
              15 SQL-AVAR-TYPE5 PIC S9(4) COMP-4 VALUE +452.
              15 SQL-AVAR-LEN5  PIC S9(4) COMP-4 VALUE +20.
              15 SQL-AVAR-ADDR5 PIC S9(9) COMP-4.
              15 SQL-AVAR-IND5  PIC S9(9) COMP-4.
              15 SQL-AVAR-TYPE6 PIC S9(4) COMP-4 VALUE +452.
              15 SQL-AVAR-LEN6  PIC S9(4) COMP-4 VALUE +2.
              15 SQL-AVAR-ADDR6 PIC S9(9) COMP-4.
              15 SQL-AVAR-IND6  PIC S9(9) COMP-4.
              15 SQL-AVAR-TYPE7 PIC S9(4) COMP-4 VALUE +452.
              15 SQL-AVAR-LEN7  PIC S9(4) COMP-4 VALUE +10.
              15 SQL-AVAR-ADDR7 PIC S9(9) COMP-4.
              15 SQL-AVAR-IND7  PIC S9(9) COMP-4.
003200 PROCEDURE DIVISION.
003300*
           SQL-SKIP.
               GO TO SQL-INIT-END.
           SQL-INITIAL.
               MOVE 1 TO SQL-INIT-FLAG.
               CALL "DSNHADDR" USING SQL-VPARMPTR OF SQL-PLIST2 SQL-PVAR-LIS
         -     T2.
               CALL "DSNHADDR" USING SQL-PVAR-ADDRS OF SQL-PLIST2 CUSTNO OF
               CUSTOMER-ROW SQL-NULL
               CALL "DSNHADDR" USING SQL-APARMPTR OF SQL-PLIST2 SQL-AVAR-LIS
         -     T2.
               CALL "DSNHADDR" USING SQL-AVAR-ADDRS OF SQL-PLIST2 CUSTNO OF
               CUSTOMER-ROW SQL-NULL FNAME OF CUSTOMER-ROW SQL-NULL LNAME OF
               CUSTOMER-ROW SQL-NULL ADDR OF CUSTOMER-ROW SQL-NULL CITY OF C
         -     USTOMER-ROW SQL-NULL STATE OF CUSTOMER-ROW SQL-NULL ZIPCODE O
         -     F CUSTOMER-ROW SQL-NULL.
               CALL "DSNHADDR" USING SQL-CODEPTR OF SQL-PLIST2 SQLCA.
           SQL-INIT-END.

003400 000-DISPLAY-CUSTOMER-ROWS.
003500*
003600     PERFORM 100-DISPLAY-CUSTOMER-ROW
003700         UNTIL END-OF-INQUIRIES.
003800     STOP RUN.
003900*
004000 100-DISPLAY-CUSTOMER-ROW.
004100*
004200     PERFORM 110-GET-CUSTOMER-NUMBER.
004300     IF NOT END-OF-INQUIRIES
004400         MOVE "Y" TO CUSTOMER-FOUND-SW
004500         PERFORM 120-GET-CUSTOMER-ROW
004600         IF CUSTOMER-FOUND
004700             PERFORM 130-DISPLAY-CUSTOMER-LINES
004800         ELSE
004900             PERFORM 140-DISPLAY-ERROR-LINES.
005000*
```

```
005100 110-GET-CUSTOMER-NUMBER.
005200*
005300     DISPLAY "----------------------------------------------".
005400     DISPLAY "KEY IN THE NEXT CUSTOMER NUMBER AND PRESS ENTER,".
005500     DISPLAY "OR KEY IN 999999 AND PRESS ENTER TO QUIT.".
005600     ACCEPT CUSTNO.
005700     IF CUSTNO = "999999"
005800         MOVE "Y" TO END-OF-INQUIRIES-SW.
005900*
006000 120-GET-CUSTOMER-ROW.
006100*
006200*****EXEC SQL
006300*****     SELECT CUSTNO,         FNAME,           LNAME,
006400*****            ADDR,           CITY,            STATE,
006500*****            ZIPCODE
006600*****     INTO   :CUSTNO,        :FNAME,          :LNAME,
006700*****            :ADDR,          :CITY,           :STATE,
006800*****            :ZIPCODE
006900*****     FROM   MMADBV.CUST
007000*****     WHERE  CUSTNO = :CUSTNO
007100*****END-EXEC.
           PERFORM SQL-INITIAL UNTIL SQL-INIT-DONE
           CALL "DSNHLI" USING SQL-PLIST2.
007200     IF SQLCODE NOT = 0
007300         MOVE "N" TO CUSTOMER-FOUND-SW.
007400*
007500 130-DISPLAY-CUSTOMER-LINES.
007600*
007700     DISPLAY "------------------------------------------------ ".
007800     DISPLAY "   CUSTOMER " CUSTNO.
007900     DISPLAY "   NAME      " FNAME " " LNAME.
008000     DISPLAY "   ADDRESS   " ADDR
008100     DISPLAY "             " CITY " " STATE " " ZIPCODE.
008200*
008300 140-DISPLAY-ERROR-LINES.
008400*
008500     DISPLAY "----------------------------------------------".
008600     DISPLAY "   CUSTOMER NUMBER " CUSTNO " NOT FOUND.".
008700*
```

Index

IMS for the COBOL Programmer

Part 1: DL/I Data Base Processing   Steve Eckols

This how-to book will have you writing batch DL/I programs in a minimum of time—whether you're working on a VSE or an MVS system. But it doesn't neglect the conceptual background you must have to create programs that work. So you'll learn:

- what a DL/I data base is and how its data elements are organized into a hierarchical structure

- the COBOL elements for creating, accessing, and updating DL/I data bases...including logical data bases and data bases with secondary indexing

- how to use DL/I recovery and restart features

- the basic DL/I considerations for coding interactive programs using IMS/DC or CICS

- how data bases with the 4 common types of DL/I data base organizations are stored (this material will help you program more logically and efficiently for the type of data base you're using)

- and more!

7 complete COBOL programs show you how to process DL/I data bases in various ways. Use them as models for production work in your shop, and you'll save hours of development time.

IMS, Part 1, 16 chapters, 333 pages, **$34.50**
ISBN 0-911625-29-1

IMS for the COBOL Programmer

Part 2: Data Communications and Message Format Service   Steve Eckols

The second part of *IMS for the COBOL Programmer* is for MVS programmers only. It teaches how to develop online programs that access IMS data bases and run under the data communications (DC) component of IMS. So you'll learn:

- why you code message processing programs (MPPs) the way you do (DC programs are called MPPs because they process messages sent from and to user terminals)

- what COBOL elements you use for MPPs

- how to use Message Format Service (MFS), a facility for formatting complex terminal displays so you can enhance the look and operation of your DC programs

- how to develop applications that use more than one screen format or that use physical and logical paging

- how to develop batch message processing (BMP) programs to update IMS data bases in batch even while they're being used by other programs

- how to use Batch Terminal Simulator (BTS) to test DC applications using IMS resources, but without disrupting the everyday IMS processing that's going on

- and more!

8 complete programs—including MFS format sets, program design, and COBOL code—show you how to handle various DC and MFS applications. Use them as models to save yourself hours of coding and debugging.

IMS, Part 2, 16 chapters, 398 pages, **$36.50**
ISBN 0-911625-30-5

  Call **toll-free**   1-800-221-5528   Weekdays, 8 a.m. to 5 p.m. Pac. Std. Time

COBOL books from Mike Murach & Associates, Inc.

Structured ANS COBOL

A 2-part course in 1974 and 1985 ANS COBOL   Mike Murach and Paul Noll

This 2-part course teaches how to use 1974 and 1985 standard COBOL the way the top professionals do. The two parts are independent: You can choose either or both, depending on your current level of COBOL skill (if you're learning on your own) or on what you want your programmers to learn (if you're a trainer or manager).

Part 1: A Course for Novices teaches people with no previous programming experience how to design and code COBOL programs that prepare reports. Because report programs often call subprograms, use COPY members, handle one-level tables, and read indexed files, it covers these subjects too. But frankly, this book emphasizes the structure and logic of report programs, instead of covering as many COBOL elements as other introductory texts do. That's because we've found most beginning programmers have more trouble with structure and logic than they do with COBOL itself.

Part 2: An Advanced Course also emphasizes program structure and logic, focusing on edit, update, and maintenance programs. But beyond that, it's a complete guide to the 1974 and 1985 elements that all COBOL programmers should know

how to use (though many don't). To be specific, it teaches how to:

- handle sequential, indexed, and relative files
- use alternate indexing and dynamic processing for indexed files
- code internal sorts and merges
- create and use COPY library members
- create and call subprograms
- handle single- and multi-level tables using indexes as well as subscripts
- use INSPECT, STRING, and UNSTRING for character manipulation
- code 1974 programs that will be easy to convert when you switch to a 1985 compiler

In fact, we recommend you get a copy of *Part 2* no matter how much COBOL experience you've had because it makes such a handy reference to all the COBOL elements you'll ever want to use.

COBOL, Part 1, 13 chapters, 438 pages, **$31.00**
ISBN 0-911625-37-2

COBOL, Part 2, 12 chapters, 498 pages, **$31.00**
ISBN 0-911625-38-0

VS COBOL II: A Guide for Programmers and Managers

Second Edition   Anne Prince

If you work in an MVS COBOL shop, sooner or later you're going to convert to VS COBOL II, IBM's 1985 COBOL compiler. Whether that day has arrived yet or not, this book will quickly teach you everything you need to know about the compiler:

- how to code the new language elements ...and what language elements you can't use any more
- CICS considerations
- how to use the new debugger
- how the compiler's features can make your programs compile and run more efficiently

- guidelines for converting to VS COBOL II (that includes coverage of the conversion aids IBM supplies)

So if you're in a shop that's already converted to VS COBOL II, you'll learn how to benefit from the new language elements and features the compiler has to offer. If you aren't yet working in VS COBOL II, you'll learn how to write programs now that will be easy to convert later on. And if you're a manager, you'll get some practical ideas on when to convert and how to do it as painlessly as possible.

This second edition covers Release 3 of the compiler, as well as Releases 1 and 2.

VS COBOL II, 7 chapters, 271 pages, **$27.50**
ISBN 0-911625-54-2

TSO books from Mike Murach & Associates, Inc.

MVS TSO

Part 1: Concepts and ISPF   Doug Lowe

See for yourself how quickly you can master ISPF/PDF (Versions 2 and 3) for everyday programming tasks in your MVS shop. This practical book will teach you how to:

- edit and browse data sets
- use the ISPF utilities to manage your data sets and libraries
- compile, link, and execute programs interactively
- use the OS COBOL or VS COBOL II interactive debugger
- process batch jobs in a background region

- manage your background jobs more easily using the Spool Display & Search Facility (SDSF)
- use member parts list to track the use of subprograms and COPY members within program libraries
- use two library management systems that support hierarchical libraries—the Library Management Facility (LMF) and the Software Configuration and Library Manager (SCLM)
- and more!

MVS TSO, Part 1, 8 chapters, 467 pages, **$31.00**
ISBN 0-911625-56-9

MVS TSO

Part 2: Commands and Procedures   Doug Lowe

If you're ready to expand your skills beyond ISPF and become a TSO user who can write complex CLIST and REXX procedures with ease, this is the book for you. It begins by teaching you how to use TSO commands for common programming tasks like managing data sets and libraries, running programs in foreground mode, and submitting jobs for background execution. Then, it shows you how to combine those commands into CLIST or REXX

procedures for the jobs you do most often...including procedures that you can use as edit macros under the ISPF editor and procedures that use ISPF dialog functions to display full-screen panels.

MVS TSO, Part 2, 10 chapters, 450 pages, **$31.00**
ISBN 0-911625-57-7

   Call **toll-free**   1-800-221-5528   Weekdays, 8 a.m. to 5 p.m. Pac. Std. Time

CICS for the COBOL Programmer

Second Edition   Doug Lowe

This 2-part course is designed to help COBOL programmers become outstanding CICS programmers.

Part 1: An Introductory Course covers the basic CICS elements you'll use in just about every program you write. So you'll learn about basic mapping support (BMS), pseudo-conversational programming, basic CICS commands, sensible program design, debugging using a transaction dump, and efficiency considerations.

Part 2: An Advanced Course covers CICS features you'll use regularly, though you won't need all of them for every program. That means you'll learn about browse commands, temporary storage, transient data, data tables (including the shared data table feature of CICS 3.3), DB2 and DL/I processing considerations, distributed

processing features, interval control commands, BMS page building, and more! In addition, *Part 2* teaches you which features do similar things and when to use each one. So you won't just learn how to code new functions...you'll also learn how to choose the best CICS solution for each programming problem you face.

Both books cover OS/VS COBOL as well as VS COBOL II. Both of them cover all versions of CICS up through 3.3. And all the program examples in both books conform to CUA's Entry Model for screen design.

CICS, Part 1, 12 chapters, 409 pages, **$31.00**
ISBN 0-911625-60-7

CICS, Part 2, 13 chapters, 375 pages
ISBN 0-911625-67-4; **Available October 1992**

The CICS Programmer's Desk Reference

Doug Lowe

Ever feel buried by IBM manuals?

It seems like you need stacks of them, close at hand, if you want to be an effective CICS programmer. Because frankly, there's just too much you have to know to do your job well; you can't keep it all in your head.

That's why Doug Lowe decided to write *The CICS Programmer's Desk Reference*. In it, he's collected all the information you need to have at your fingertips, and organized it into 12 sections that make it easy for you to find what you're looking for. So there are sections on:

- BMS macro instructions—their formats (with an explanation of each parameter) and coding examples

- CICS commands—their syntax (with an explanation of each parameter), coding examples, and suggestions on how and when to use each one most effectively

- MVS and DOS/VSE JCL for CICS applications

- AMS commands for handling VSAM files

- ISPF, ICCF, and VM/CMS editor commands

- complete model programs, including specs, design, and code

- a summary of CICS program design techniques that lead to simple, maintainable, and efficient programs

- guidelines for testing and debugging CICS applications

- and more!

So clear the IBM manuals off your terminal table. Let the *Desk Reference* be your everyday guide to CICS instead.

CICS Desk Reference, 12 sections, 489 pages, **$36.50**
ISBN 0-911625-43-7

Note: This book currently covers CICS elements and programming considerations through release 1.7. A second edition is planned for the fourth quarter of 1992.

Comment form

Your opinions count

If you have comments, criticisms, or suggestions, I'm eager to get them. Your opinions today will affect our products of tomorrow. And if you discover any errors in this book, typographical or otherwise, please point them out so we can make corrections when the book is reprinted.

Thanks for your help.

Mike Murach

Book title: DB2 for the COBOL Programmer, Part 1: An Introductory Course

_____

_____

_____

_____

_____

_____

_____

_____

_____

_____

_____

_____

_____

_____

_____

_____

_____

Name & Title _____

Company (if company address) _____

Address _____

City, State, Zip _____

Fold where indicated and tape shut.
No postage necessary if mailed in the U.S.

Order Form

Our Ironclad Guarantee

To our customers who order directly from us: You must be satisfied. Our books must work for you, or you can send them back for a full refund...no questions asked.

Name & Title _____

Company (if company address) _____

Street address _____

City, State, Zip _____

Phone number (including area code)_____

Qty	Product code and title	*Price
Data Base Processing		
____ DB21	DB2 for the COBOL Programmer Part 1: An Introductory Course	$32.50
____ DB22	DB2 for the COBOL Programmer Part 2: An Advanced Course	32.50
IMS1	IMS for the COBOL Programmer Part 1: DL/I Data Base Processing	34.50
____ IMS2	IMS for the COBOL Programmer Part 2: Data Communications and MFS	36.50
OS/MVS Subjects		
____ TSO1	MVS TSO, Part 1: Concepts and ISPF	$31.00
____ TSO2	MVS TSO, Part 2: Commands and Procedures	31.00
____ MJCL	MVS JCL	34.50
____ MBAL	MVS Assembler Language	36.50
____ OSUT	OS Utilities	17.50
DOS/VSE Subjects		
____ VJLR	DOS/VSE JCL (Second Edition)	$34.50
____ ICCF	DOS/VSE ICCF	31.00
____ VBAL	DOS/VSE Assembler Language	36.50

Qty	Product code and title	*Price
CICS		
____ CC1R	CICS for the COBOL Programmer Part 1 (Second Edition)	$31.00
____ CC2R	CICS for the COBOL Programmer Part 2 (Second Edition)	Available October 1992
____ CREF	The CICS Programmer's Desk Reference	36.50
COBOL Language Elements		
____ SC1R	Structured ANS COBOL, Part 1	$31.00
____ SC2R	Structured ANS COBOL, Part 2	31.00
____ RW	Report Writer	17.50
____ VC2R	VS COBOL II (Second Edition)	27.50
VSAM		
____ VSMX	VSAM: Access Method Services and Application Programming	$27.50
____ VSMR	VSAM for the COBOL Programmer (Second Edition)	17.50

☐ Bill the appropriate book prices plus UPS shipping and handling (and sales tax in California) to my ____VISA ____MasterCard:

    Card Number _____

    Valid thru (month/year) _____

    Cardowner's signature _____

☐ Bill me.

☐ Bill my company. P.O. #_____

☐ I want to **save** UPS shipping and handling charges. Here's my check or money order for $_____. California residents, please add sales tax to your total. (Offer valid in the U.S.)

To order more quickly,

Call **toll-free** 1-800-221-5528

(Weekdays, 8 to 5 Pacific Standard Time)

Fax: 1-209-275-9035

Mike Murach & Associates, Inc.

4697 West Jacquelyn Avenue
Fresno, California 93722-6427
(209) 275-3335

* Prices are subject to change. Please call for current prices.